Newly hatched chicks of Grey Plover (upper, left), Pacific Golden Plover (upper, right), Eurasian Golden Plover (lower, left) and American Golden Plover (lower, right).

TUNDRA PLOVERS:
THE EURASIAN, PACIFIC AND AMERICAN GOLDEN PLOVERS AND GREY PLOVER

TUNDRA PLOVERS:
THE EURASIAN, PACIFIC AND AMERICAN GOLDEN PLOVERS AND GREY PLOVER

by **Ingvar Byrkjedal** and
D.B.A. Thompson

Illustrations by
Ingvar Byrkjedal

Foreword by
Derek Ratcliffe

T & A D
POYSER

ISBN 0–85661–109–3

First published in 1998 by T & AD Poyser Ltd
24–28 Oval Road, London, NW1 7DX

Typeset by Phoenix Photosetting, Chatham, Kent
Printed and bound in Great Britain by
The Bath Press, Bath

A CIP record for this book is available from the British Library

For

DESMOND NETHERSOLE-THOMPSON

1908–1989

'In April, 1934, it was our happy lot for several days to watch Golden Plovers at the height of their courtship. So interesting did we find them that we vowed that future years would see us on the watch throughout their breeding cycle ... In the struggle for so-called "territory" three important principles are often involved, namely, sex, food and psychology. On these breeding-grounds we believe that the earlier fighting is largely prompted by sex but, as already explained, males in some cases also do battle for the possession of a possible display-centre prior to pairing ... The creation of a full breeding-biology about any one bird is a great task, but we are convinced that such is among the most vital needs of modern ornithology.'

Nethersole-Thompson & Nethersole-Thompson (1939)

'On warm spring days, after the winter snows, we remember mornings when the moors were alive with spring songs of golden plovers, and the becking of red grouse. And there was always the nostalgic scent of peat reek in the air.'

Nethersole-Thompson & Nethersole-Thompson (1961)

'The American and European golden plovers, *P. dominica* and *P. apricaria*, and the grey plover, *P. squatarola*, generally produce chicks which remain longer in the nest than those of almost any other waders.'

Nethersole-Thompson (1973)

'From the time that the first trips arrive on the fields until they flock in late summer these lovely waders never fail to fascinate ... No sound more piquantly symbolises the wild places than a solitary unseen golden plover piping mournfully in the dusk.'

Nethersole-Thompson & Nethersole-Thompson (1986)

Also by D.B.A. Thompson:

GULLS AND PLOVERS: THE ECOLOGY AND BEHAVIOUR OF MIXED SPECIES
FEEDING GROUPS
(with C.J. Barnard. Croom Helm, London, and Columbia University Press, Columbia 1985).

ECOLOGICAL CHANGE IN THE UPLANDS
(edited with M.B. Usher. Blackwell Scientific Publications, Oxford 1988).

HEATHS AND MOORLAND: CULTURAL LANDSCAPES
(edited with A.J. Hester and M.B. Usher. HMSO, Edinburgh 1995).

SCOTLAND – LAND OF MOUNTAINS
(with Colin Baxter. Colin Baxter Photography, Grantown-on-Spey, 2nd edn. 1998).

Contents

List of Plates

List of Figures

List of Tables

Foreword

by DR DEREK RATCLIFFE

Former Chief Scientist, Nature Conservancy Council,
Great Britain

AS a youngster, I was charmed by the Eurasian Golden Plover of our northern uplands, having encountered my first on a grouse moor in the foothills of the Lake District of northern England. It was a bird that I came to regard as the spirit of the moorlands in the spring, and I loved to hear its evocative territorial song as the plover floated with slow wingbeats high above its nesting grounds. I later read Henry Seebohm's books on the birds of Siberia, and was captivated by his descriptions of thrilling journeys to the arctic tundras around the Petchora and Yenesei Rivers – those vast solitudes that so far eclipse even the largest and loneliest of the boglands of Britain or Ireland. The accounts of the search for and finding of nests of Grey Plovers and Little Stints on their desolate barren grounds were enough to excite the sensibilities of anyone who enjoys tracking down the more difficult birds in their breeding haunts.

When I travelled among the British uplands more widely, the Eurasian Golden Plover seemed to have fair claim to be their most distinctive bird. Wherever the terrain was gentle, its plaintive voice was to be heard in the spring. Numbers were high on the grasslands, heather moors and blanket bogs of sheep walks and grouse moors in the Pennines, Cheviots and parts of the Southern Uplands. I found them in company with Eurasian Dotterel and Rock Ptarmigan on the arctic heaths of the windswept Grampian summits, and with Common Greenshanks and Red-throated Divers on the desolate wet flows almost down to sea-level in Sutherland and Caithness. At first their habitat seemed inviolate, but then some of their nesting grounds began to disappear, and on an ever-increasing scale, as coniferous afforestation advanced over many upland areas. In Fennoscandia, I was intrigued to find Eurasian Golden Plovers breeding on bogs within the great pine and spruce forests in the Boreal zone, and more constantly on lichen heaths amongst open birch scrub on the Lapland fells – nesting habitats they have lost or forsaken in Britain. Very widely they were birds of tundra and fell-field, from the high mountain barrens of the Jotunheim and Hardangervidda at 1500 m to sea level on the bleak Finnmark shore. And what handsome birds were most of these Fennoscandian goldies, compared with many of our paler birds at home.

The Eurasian Golden Plover long remained one of the least known of our upland birds, but such an attractive and widespread species could not escape attention for long. Over the last twenty years or so there has been growing interest in its natural history, and various studies have been reported. The former distinction between Southern and Northern subspecies has been removed in the light of modern knowledge. The other close relatives of the bird, in North America and Asia, are even less known, and have been subjected to still more recent taxonomic adjustments. The Grey Plover is a most striking cousin, widespread through much of the Arctic in summer, but known mainly by ornithologists in the UK as a winter visitor to our shores. All these birds belong to that class of waders which, in his book *The Borders and Beyond* (1924), Abel Chapman christened 'Globe-spanners', making twice-yearly migrations of great length between their northern breeding grounds and southern wintering places, often from one hemisphere far into the other. These plovers are true internationalists and, as such, have caught the attention of ornithologists in many different parts of the world.

How welcome, therefore, is the present work by two leading students of northern shorebirds, distilling all that is known about these plovers of the tundra and their movements across the globe. The authors have faced, and ably resolved, the difficult task of bringing together the contrasting material on the biology of breeding, migration and the non-breeding state. Their book is in the modern style, full of hard data and with numerous graphs and other figures to satisfy the specialist, but enlivened by good photographs and pleasing sketches, as well as by a continual sense of delight in these creatures of the wilderness. It is a work with something for all who are interested in birds, and an important addition to the literature of ornithology, as well as the Poyser series itself.

Students of evolution will be interested in the examination of relationships between these plovers. It is good to see full use being made of museum material, but much of the authors' understanding of the species' divergence comes from close attention to the living bird, and critical differences in behaviour and voice. Sonagrams become meaningful in the critical measurements of differences in calls. Not the least fascinating aspect of the shorebirds is the differing roles of the sexes within their remarkable variety of breeding systems. The tundra plovers are fairly orthodox in that male and female have a somewhat equal share of parental duties, though subtle differences in nest and chick defence behaviour have appeared between the four species. Within each species, males, females and juveniles have adopted slightly different migration schedules and wintering areas.

In presenting the picture of migration patterns and non-breeding distribution, the writers have necessarily drawn upon the large body of information from an impressively wide network of observers. The tundra is only the breeding ground, and a short-term one at that, for these birds mostly hasten to leave it again for warmer and more hospitable latitudes in which to pass the greater part of the year. Their striking black fronts of spring are acquired and then soon lost again in moults which are described in detail. The habitats of these plovers on passage and in winter are seen to be mostly very different from those in which they nest. In confirmation of their globe-spanner status, it is remarkable how many countries of the world find mention in this book.

In these days of depressingly numerous endangered species, it is encouraging to learn that the populations of these tundra plovers are mostly in good heart, with declines only local and some increases reported. The northern breeding haunts are still vast, almost beyond comprehension, and development or despoliation are still on an insignificant scale. Yet there is a worrying cloud on the horizon, in the prospect of global warming and all that this implies for the future of the arctic ecosystems and wildlife. And regardless of events in their breeding haunts, all migrants are highly vulnerable to happenings in their passage and wintering areas. This book is not only a fascinating account of the lives of wilderness birds, but contains a timely reminder of just how fragile that wilderness is, in an age when corrosive human influence reaches out to all corners of the Earth, however remote.

Derek Ratcliffe

Preface

Grey Plover chick in cotton-grass

I N Bergen on 4 May 1990, an unusually hot, dry day for that Norwegian city, we agreed to write this book. We first met in the autumn of 1981, and by the spring of the following year were regularly corresponding on golden plovers, Eurasian Dotterel and other shorebirds. The book's inception, however, was sparked by its dedicatee.

On Christmas Day 1984 in Culrain, Sutherland, the late Desmond Nethersole-Thompson was in sparkling form. He and Maimie had just completed *Waders: their breeding, haunts and watchers*, and their family was enjoying the banter around a roaring fire. They had devoured a huge turkey and trimmings, and Desmond was installed in his large armchair, cigar in hand, with two old dark green hard-backed school jotters on his lap. 'I've got something to show you!' he said, beaming, and then handed Des a beautifully inked manuscript titled *Some observations on the sexual life and breeding biology of the Southern Golden Plover* (Charadrius a. apricarius) *as observed in Inverness-shire*, completed on 19 June 1939. 'You and Patrick should write a book on golden plovers, and here's your head start' he announced! That night, Pat, then a PhD student working on the breeding biology of Common Redshanks, Des, a University Research Fellow at Liverpool, and Desmond poured over the 45 year old manuscript and drafted a synopsis for a book on the Eurasian Golden Plover. 'Don't worry' bellowed Desmond, by around midnight bubbling over with excitement, 'Trevor will take it!' And sure enough Trevor Poyser did indeed agree to publish the proposed book.

During the subsequent five years, Des and Ingvar met occasionally and the conversation tended to shift from Eurasian Golden Plovers to the Pacific and American golden plovers and the Grey Plover. Gradually we realized that a book was needed on all four species. Meanwhile, Pat asked us to press on without him, for he and Bill Hale had their sights on a monograph on the Common Redshank. Eventually, in Bergen, we shook hands on the book's beginning, and seven years later, in Ingvar's office at the Museum of Zoology, we completed the manuscript!

Our first memories of golden plovers are firmly imprinted. Des recalls two very early events, both at the Nethersole-Thompson field camp in NW Sutherland, Scotland. When nine years old one late evening in early May, he sat with his father waiting for a Common Greenshank to exchange with its mate on the nest. Desmond, in his huge camel duffel coat, sat motionless as the drizzle poured out of the grey skies and banks of cloud passed to reveal occasional glimpses of the mountain country. It cleared, and just before a watery sunset two male Eurasian Golden Plovers rose from a croft field to sing in the air, one pitted against the other, both gliding and then flapping their wings slowly. Their sounds, seeming like those of threnody, captured the antiquity and rawness of that land with its beacons of life. As the two males swished down to alight on the bounds of their territories, Desmond muttered 'cock goldies, look for the hens off the nest'. Alas, they were not seen! Later that month, Desmond and sons were heading for another Common Greenshank watch when a male goldie flew low off the ground. There was no sign of the nest, so they searched. 'No use' chastised Desmond, as he stuck his thumbstick in the shallow peat and shambled in growing circles away from the stick, shortly to shout 'got it!' And there, in a small broken hummock of woolly hair moss, were four creamy brown eggs in a deep scrape, superbly camouflaged and impossible to see at 3 m from the stick, with a small boy's footprint just centimetres away.

Later, there were numerous outings to look for goldies and to find out more about their nesting and chick-rearing behaviour. Derek Ratcliffe has been an intermittent companion of the Nethersole-Thompsons for over 30 years and his knack for finding goldies' nests is ever sharp. Desmond used to mutter disapprovingly into his straggling beard as Derek extolled the virtues of scanning continuously while walking in order to catch sight of the bird flicking from its nest. Not a great fan of cold searching, Desmond preferred to sit and watch, roundly condemning those of us who could not resist a wander in the hope of seeing a bird rise – and of course, to keep warm!

In autumn 1980, Des moved to Nottingham University to study the flocking behaviour of grassland plovers for a PhD under the supervision of Chris Barnard. Chris and Hilary Stephens were working on these birds close to Rempstone and had the relatively elevated farmland of Hill Farm as one of their study areas. Des has a crisp memory of his first visit there, with Dawn (his wife), in an old rusting blue 'Mini'. Here was farmland dominated by tall unkempt hedges and pastures that had not been ploughed in over a hundred years. Peering through a gap in one hedge Des saw the great spectacle of a huge flock of Eurasian Golden Plovers, which had just arrived from the north, feeding with Northern Lapwings. There were also a few

Black-headed Gulls which indulged in frenzied attacks at the plovers to steal their earthworm prey. It was great theatre, with the lapwings seeming to fare worse than the goldies against the gulls. Field after field had these flocks – many without goldies – and there were also Fieldfares and Redwings from the north. Sadly, most of these fields no longer have grassland plovers, and many of the old pastures – so important to these birds – have now been ploughed into arable land.

Ingvar remembers his first encounter with the Eurasian Golden Plover as a young schoolboy going on a bicycle ride with some friends one calm and hazy October afternoon at Jæren. He could see huge flocks of brown, pigeon-like birds in almost every field. Although these birds are commonly seen on agricultural land at Jæren during migration, Ingvar has never since seen them in such numbers. The boys, each with the beginnings of an interest in birds, felt more and more excited, especially as they could not quite figure out what the birds were. The sole Norwegian field guide to birds available at that time showed only illustrations of breeding plumages. Next day the boys eagerly browsed library books, and suspected golden plovers, finally confirmed in a visit to the exhibitions in Stavanger Museum. Ingvar learnt that most of these birds came from the desolate high mountains and vast, mysterious tundra up north, and were heading for their central southern European wintering grounds. But the books indicated that it was possible a few pairs might be found breeding in the heather moors at Jæren, not far from Ingvar's home.

In order to train as a bird ringer, Ingvar spent much time in 1964 with Erling Sømme, a close friend and a skilled ringer. Erling had a fast motorbike, which extended the action into outlying moorland regions, and here, on a dry and sunny June morning, whilst searching for Meadow Pipit nests, Ingvar and Erling found golden plovers. A pair gave alarm calls and behaved nervously. Erling soon concluded that they had chicks and suggested a watch from a distance. Despite this effort, nothing was found, but at least they knew that the species still bred at Jæren! During a visit to the same moor two days later they discovered five more pairs. This triggered a subsequent census of the breeding golden plovers at Jæren.

In the course of subsequent census work Ingvar more or less stumbled across a few golden plovers' nests. Yet, the one best remembered was found in 1972 at the very start of his studies of golden plover breeding biology on the moors of Jæren. A study of the breeding biology of these birds had been accepted as a topic for his *cand.real* thesis at the University of Bergen. It was one of the last days in April. Ingvar had just erected his tent and decided to take a short reconnaissance before turning in, the weather being unfavourable with a near gale-force wind and sleet sweeping across the moor. Walking against the wind was a struggle, whereas with the wind in the back one felt like dancing over the tussocks. There was something composed yet very wild about the whole setting. Suddenly a golden plover got up from almost under foot, wings flapping convulsively, and then it was gone. There, in a heathery tussock, lay the four eggs. What a contrast the bird made against the howling blizzard over the gloomy hills. Only a short gaze at the nest was allowed, and then away so as not to keep the bird off.

This was a very promising beginning to what was to become decades of golden plover watching! However, Bengt Berg, in his famous book published in 1917 about the Eurasion Dotterel, *Min vän fjällpiparen*, sympathizes with the sentiment of his

Lapland guide about the chances of finding Dotterel nests: 'There is no use searching – [the nest] lies there on the track before you, God willing, otherwise you don't find it at all.' In the days to come, Ingvar developed a strong suspicion that the same would apply to golden plover nests. How many of us have felt this way seeking out a nest, privately imploring our god to guide us to the spot where, for a short moment, time will stand still!

Having studied these Eurasian Golden Plovers for a number of years, Ingvar finally got an opportunity to fulfil a dream – to spend a summer with American Golden Plovers in the New World. One beautiful June evening he set out from Churchill Northern Studies Centre, close to Hudson Bay, Canada to find his first 'American'. Abounding White-crowned and American Tree sparrows, Bonaparte's Gulls, Hudsonian Godwits, and many other Nearctic novelties helped soothe the effects of badly felt jet lag. Then, without warning, there it was! An American Golden Plover male only 20 m away feeding on the tundra. What a sight! The clear contrasts of white, jet black, and golden made an overwhelming impression. And what a streamlined creature this was, compared with its thickset Eurasian cousin. The bird took flight and vanished over the tundra. The strains of jet lag went completely! A moment later, Ingvar met Bryan Sage and his companions who were in Churchill to photograph northern birds. They had just come across an American Golden Plover's nest and explained where it could be found. Having then found this in little time, and realizing that American Golden Plovers, quite unlike their Eurasian counterparts, readily returned to nests in full view of a human, Ingvar returned to the research station in a state of high glee!

Three years later, Ingvar was working again on tundra plovers abroad, this time at Yamal in northwest Siberia, where he was hoping to compare the anti-predator behaviour of Eurasian and Pacific golden plovers and Grey Plovers. Struggling for a few days with the familiar difficulties posed by the constantly alarm-calling Eurasian Golden Plovers, he found neither of the other two species in evidence. But then one day, as Ingvar took a break on the tundra to enjoy the sight of a distant Snowy Owl hunting, and listen to the grating displays of Pintail Snipes and a barking Arctic Fox, a slim medium-sized shorebird whizzed overhead and disappeared to the east towards some elevated tundra plain. It emitted a liquid, unmistakable golden plover call; this was the Pacific Golden Plover – at last!

Next day Ingvar hastened back to the plain in search of this enigmatic bird, and found it immediately. Several of the Pacifics held territories there, and the males were in frequent flight displays. Again, it was time to marvel over the beauty of this slender bird, with legs seeming far too long for a member of *Pluvialis*. Soon this was to become Ingvar's favourite of the three golden plovers. The song flight was an aerial ballet performance – dainty and elegant. The day passed only too quickly. Whether or not caused by that day's avian 'seduction', or the fact that he had left his map in camp, Ingvar found himself severely astray on his return to camp. After reaching an old Nenets' graveyard where he stumbled over bleached human skulls on the tundra, Ingvar hit the right direction to camp. There Nataliya Alekseeva and her team were about to launch a big signal rocket to indicate their base! In the following weeks, the plateau with its Pacific Golden Plovers pulled like a magnet, and even now the memories are vivid.

Ingvar met Grey Plovers farther north at Yamal. He reached the station Yaibari (the Nenets' name for Dunlin) by expedition helicopter, at the end of which his head was aching from the noise and vibration of the machine. After a pint of *kvas* and a splendid meal he was taken by the station leader, Vadim Ryabistev, onto the tundra plains where there were breeding Grey Plover. Vadim and his team had found a few Grey Plover nests, and Ingvar was taken on a round of these, though he still felt rough after the flight! Then he set out to find some birds for himself. Just imagine the thrill of acquainting yourself with the haunts and habits of a new bird! Ingvar knew the species well from its autumn migration in Norway, but this was his first encounter on the breeding grounds. And what a bird it was compared with the shy, timid, hunch-backed apparition seen along the European coasts on migration!

If the Pacific Golden Plover is the ballet dancer, then the Grey Plover is the macho *Pluvialis*! Ingvar and Vadim saw stunningly forceful and speedy chases between males, and when a male Grey Plover, with great determination, attacked a Rough-legged Buzzard flying along a tundra slope (having a go at its keel!), Ingvar was reminded of a MiG-29 fighter plane! The female landed beside its clutch. As Ingvar went to the nest both parents alarmed overhead – a climax to a terrific evening on the tundra. Were there mosquitoes? Oh, of course – billions, but who cares when a new experience is forming to last a lifetime!

Our times have heralded great advances in the study of ecology and behaviour. There have been important theoretical developments, and major, detailed studies of some species. New molecular techniques have revolutionized the prospects for studies of animals at individual and population levels. The sophistication of field equipment seems to be accelerating: sound recorders and video cameras, as well as radio telemetry equipment, are nowadays small and manageable, and have become relatively inexpensive. Computers of a power only dreamt of a few years ago are now standard tools for scientists. Such developments will undoubtedly speed up research and our understanding of plovers. However, there is still no real substitute for the notebook and pencil, with the keen eye feeding the brain. The birds themselves, of course, still guard their secrets jealously, and there are vast areas still to be visited!

Being dispersed and space demanding, the tundra plovers pose formidable challenges for conservation. Yet habitat conservation measures aimed at these birds could also benefit a number of other, less widely dispersed species of animals and plants. We have worked on this book in the belief that a sound knowledge of the birds should help raise their importance in the consciousness of humans, and should contribute to necessary conservation actions. This book draws together some 50 years' personal work on the tundra plovers, and substantial information from the literature and correspondence. We hope it will encourage people to press on with further studies, for much is still to be learnt.

Sadly, like many others, we have seen some of our study areas and other places of interest change for the worse over only a few years, with their birds declining or going completely. That this should be so for a group of birds intimately associated with the wilds of the far north, among some of our most natural yet freshly formed landscapes, has touched us deeply.

Ingvar Byrkjedal and Des Thompson
March 1998

Acknowledgements

A LARGE number of people and organizations have helped with this book, and we are greatly in debt to them all.

The late Desmond Nethersole-Thompson's seminal input is alluded to in the Preface, and in many ways he has been with us throughout our discussions and writing. His knowledge, experiences and insights were unique, and we have benefited particularly from his personal unpublished and published observations. Derek Ratcliffe has provided the Foreword; we thank him for this, for sharing his experiences of Eurasian Golden Plovers and their northern haunts, and for numerous comments.

Sven-Axel Bengtson deserves special mention for supervising and guiding Ingvar during his early research, and for first bringing us together. John Atle Kålås shared much of the research by Ingvar on the Hardangervidda, contributed many ideas, and has become a close friend to us both. Phil Whitfield has been a critical, encouraging and stimulating reader of drafts. Göran Högstedt has been a constant source of refreshing ideas and information, and has periodically reminded us that we really ought to finish the book! Chris Barnard will recognize Göran's last sentiment, for he had to put up with Des's endless draft PhD thesis chapters. Pat Thompson played an important role in planning the book; Terry Burke has helped in many ways during its production; David Stroud has helped us greatly through his editorial involvement in the excellent *Wader Study Group Bulletin* and *International Wader Studies,* and in many other ways Derek, Phil and David have commented on much of the book in draft, and some of their observations or comments appear as personal communications. Terry, Pat, Roddy Fairley, Colin Galbraith and Chris Thomas have criticized one or more of the chapters in draft.

It is a special pleasure to acknowledge the outstanding efforts and often direct help of researchers working on tundra plovers, notably Oscar W. Johnson, Peter Connors, Theunis Piersma, Joop Jukema, Peter Evans, Phil Hockey, Jane Turpie, Ray Parr, Derek Yalden, Dennis Paulson, Chris Thomas and Mark O'Connell. While writing, we have constantly referred to or discussed the work of Lew Oring, Derek Ratcliffe, Bill Hale, Aleksandr Ya. Kontrat'ev, Ted Miller, Dave Parmelee, Richard Holmes, Frank Pitelka, Guy Morrison, Pete Myers, Joanna Burger, Pavel Tomkovich, Phil Whitfield, Paul Jönsson, Mike Barter, Brett Lane, Bill Sutherland, John Goss-Custard and Bruno Ens. All of these people have helped us in more ways than they probably realize.

A number of researchers have generously shared with us their unpublished information on tundra plovers. For this, we would like to thank Vadim K. Ryabitsev and Tore Larsen for data on Grey Plover and Pacific Golden Plover, Brian J. McCaffery for breeding season information on Pacific and American golden plovers in Alaska, Pavel S. Tomkovich for his information on breeding distributions and numbers of tundra plovers in Russia, and Jorge Bruno Nacinovic for information about the non-breeding distribution of Grey Plover and American Golden Plover in Brazil. Several people have kindly allowed us to quote from their unpublished PhD theses, notably Mark Whittingham, Dave Parish, David Allen and John McLennan. We are grateful to Godtfred Anker Halvorsen for co-authoring Chapter 5, and to Rubin Sanson for helping us make preparations of salt glands.

Considerable information on alpine/sub alpine (montane) breeding of Eurasian Golden Plovers in Scotland has come from Scottish Natural Heritage's Montane Ecology Project, and we are grateful to Phil Whitfield, Sue Holt, Hector Galbraith, Rik Smith, Stuart Rae, Keith Duncan, Stuart Murray, Ian Owens, Alan Mee and Rebecca Denny for their work in sometimes treacherous conditions.

We are grateful to some organizations for specific help. In the British Trust for Ornithology (BTO), Rob Fuller, Jeremy Greenwood, Simon Gillings and Peter Lack have been helpful on distribution issues, not least in pooling together the observations of the remarkable band of members of the BTO. The Royal Society for the Protection of Birds (RSPB) and Birdlife International are thanked for involving us in their *Habitats for birds in Europe: a conservation strategy for the wider environment* project which developed a habitat conservation strategy for birds of moorland, mires and tundra. In addition to ourselves, this involved the following: Vladimir Galushin, Alexander Mischenko, Vladimir Morozov, I.P. Tatarinkova (Russia); Lennart Saari (Finland); John Atle Kålås, Karl-Birger Strann (Norway); Lennox Campbell, Mike Evans and Graham Tucker (UK).

We have had immense help from curators and their staff in museums throughout the world. They readily sent us print-outs or copies of specimen files and shipped specimens to us on loan. When we realized that a large amount of material was available in the museums, which was potentially of significant importance for our studies of differential migration of the sexes and age classes, we requested museums to make photocopies of specimens for us. Large numbers of photocopied specimens were then sent to us in order that we could make checks on their age in a simple and inexpensive way! Our work has benefited from the excellent service rendered by the following: J. Phillip Angle, Smithsonian Institution, Washington DC; Stephen F. Bailey, California Academy of Sciences, San Fransisco; Allan J. Baker and J.A. Dick, Royal Ontario Museum, Toronto; Robert Barrett, Tromsø Museum, Tromsø; George D. Baumgardener, Texas A & M University; Hans Martin Berg, Naturhistorisches Museum, Wien; D.A. Boag, University of Alberta, Department of Zoology, Edmonton; Mauro Bon, Museo Civico di Storia Naturale di Venezia; John M. Condit, Ohio State University; H.W.R. Copland, Manitoba Museum of Man & Nature; Tristan Davis, Museum of Natural History, Lawrence; Graham Cowles, British Museum (Natural History), Tring; D.L. Dartnall, City Museum and Art Gallery, Gloucester; James J. Dinsmore, Iowa State University, Ames; Pierre Drapeau, Université de Montréal; S. Eck, Staatlisches Museum für Tierkunde, Dresden; Maria Avelina Ferreira, Museu e Laboratório Zoológico, Coimbra; Clem Fisher, Liverpool Museum; Jon Fjeldså and Tove Hatting, Zoological Museum, Copenhagen; G. Frish, Naturhistoriska Riksmuseet, Stockholm; K.L. Garrett, Natural History Museum of Los Angeles County, Los Angeles; Alice Gartzke, Boston Museum of Science; Belinda Gilles, Museum of Victoria, Victoria, Australia; Mary Hennen, Chicago

Academy of Sciences, Chicago; Janet Hinshaw, Museum of Zoology, University of Michigan, Ann Arbor; Paul C. James, Museum of Natural History, Regina, Saskachewan; Ned K. Johnson, Museum of Vertebrate Zoology, Berkeley; Claus König, Staatliches Museum für Naturkunde in Stuttgart; Lloyd Kiff, Western Foundation of Vertebrate Zoology, Los Angeles; Nathan E. Kraukunas, Milwaukee Public Museum, Milwaukee; Vladimir Loskot, Zoological Institute, Academy of Sciences, St. Petersburg; James M. Loughlin, The Carnegie Museum of Natural History, Pittsburgh; G. Mauersberger, Museum für Naturkunde der Humboldt Universität zu Berlin; Nancy Clover McCartney, University of Arkansas, Fayetteville; Bob McGowan, National Museums of Scotland, Edinburgh; Jorge Bruno Nacinovic, Museu Nacional, Rio de Janeiro; Jorge R. Navas, Muso Argentino de Ciencias Naturales, Buenos Aires; Roxanna Normark and Kevin J. McGowan, Cornell University, Div. Biological Sciences, Ithaca; Henri Ouellet and Michel Gosselin, Canadian Museum of Nature, Ottawa; T. Parker, Liverpool Museum; Dennis R. Paulson and James R. Slater, Museum of Natural History, Tacoma; Richard S. Peigler, Denver Museum of Natural History, Colorado; M.G. Ramalhinho, Museu Bocage, Lisboa; Josef H. Reichhof, Zoologische Staatssammlung, Munchen; J.W. Remsen and Steven W. Cardiff, Museum of Zoology, Louisiana State University, Baton Rouge; Mark Robbins, The Academy of Natural Sciences, Philadelphia; Karl L. Schuchmann, Zoologisches Forschungsinstitut und Museum Alexander Koenig, Bonn; Kolbjørn Skipnes, Stavanger Museum, Stavanger; Tore Slagsvold and Jan Lifjeld, Zoological Museum, Oslo; Richard A. Sloss, American Museum of Natural History, New York; Richard Sutcliffe, Glasgow Museums & Art Galleries, Glasgow; Pavel S. Tomkovich, Zoological Museum, Moscow; Philip Unitt, San Diego Natural History Museum, San Diego; S. Unnithan, Bombay Natural History Society, Bombay; Risto A. Väisänen, Zoological Museum, University of Helsinki; J.F. Voisin, Muséum National d'Histoire Naturelle, Paris; and Chris Wood, The Burke Museum, Seattle.

As it turned out, some specimens of the museum collections of tundra plovers had recently been measured by other researchers. We are very grateful to Meinte Engelmoer for a summary of unpublished measurements of Grey Plover specimens from all parts of its breeding range. Peter G. Connors very kindly sent us all his measurements of specimens of American and Pacific golden plovers from Alaska, the background material for his publication in 1983 on golden plover taxonomy. Bill Hale gave us hundreds of sheets of measurements which he and students had made of museum specimens of all three species of golden plover (of which we made extensive use, in particular those of Eurasian Golden Plovers from Britain).

We obtained nest cards of tundra plovers from the Finnish Nest Record Scheme, North American Nest Record Card Program, Prairie Nest Record Cards and Ontario Nest Record Scheme. For this, we would like to thank Risto Väisänen, Pixie Senesac, H.W.R. Copland and Ross D. James.

A number of people have been helpful by sending us publications not readily obtainable, containing important information on tundra plovers. Help in obtaining Russian literature was especially welcome, and we are much obliged to Nataliya S. Alekseeva, Vadim K. Ryabitsev, Pavel S. Tomkovich, Aleksandr Ya. Kondratev, I.P. Tatarinkova and Vladimir Loskot. We would also like to give our special thanks to Lloyd Kiff, H.W.R. Copland and Tex A. Sordahl for copying some less accessible American publications for us.

Various people have helped us with queries relating to tundra plovers, provided information or discussed ideas and we thank them all here: David Atkinson, Ian Bainbridge, Chris Barnard, Leo Batten, Colin Baxter and family, Mike Begon, John Blackwood, George Boobyer, Alan Brown, Andy Brown, Chris Brown, Philip Burton, Roger Burton, Nigel Buxton, Arthur Cain, Ian Colquhoun, Andrew Coupar, John Craig, Dave Curtis, Colin Dallas, Nick Davidson, Andy Douse, Nick Dulvy, Keith Duncan, the late Nigel Easterbee, Svein Efteland, Roddy Fairley, Peter Ferns, Helen Forster, Colin Galbraith, Hector Galbraith, Joyce Garland, John Gittins, Rawdon Goodier, John Gordon, John Goss-Custard, Paul Haworth, Dave Horsfield, Pete Hudson, Ross Johnstone, Hans Källander, Terry Keatinge, Derek Langslow, Dennis Lendrem, Richard Lindsay, Ron MacDonald, Pete McGregor, John Mackay, Ed Mackey, Sandy MacLennan, Mike Matthew, Jill Matthews, Neil Metcalfe, John Miles, Greg Mudge, Martin Nugent, Geoff Parker, David Parkin, Sandy Payne, Ron Pearson, Barrie Pendlebury, Nick Picozzi, Mike Pienkowski, Dave Pons, Eugene Potapov, Stuart Rae, Steve Redpath, Tim Reed, Eliane Reid, Jim Reid, Pete Reynolds, Helen Riley, David Rohweder, Alex Scott, Maureen Scott, Phil Shaw, Kevin Shepherd, Mike Shepherd, John Smyth, Torstein Solhøy, Erling Sømme, Jonathan Stacey, Hilary Stead, Iain and Sarah Taylor, Dave Thompson, Peter Tilbrook, Dave Townshend, the late Colin Tubbs, Michael B. Usher, Dick Waite, Pat Yalden, Jeff Watson, the late William Wilkinson and Valerie Wilson.

The views expressed in this book are in a private capacity and are not to be taken as representing those of SNH or the University of Bergen.

We pay homage to the following people who have influenced our approach to research: Chris Barnard, Tim Birkhead, John and Hilary Birks, Dave Bryant, Terry Burke, Tim Clutton-Brock, John Coulson, Nick Davies, the late George Dunnet, Peter Evans, Göran Högstedt, John Krebs, Arne Lundberg, Robert Moss, Ian Newton, Lew Oring, Ian Patterson, Chris Perrins, Derek Ratcliffe, Bill Sutherland, Pavel Tomkovich, Staffan Ulfstrand, Adam Watson and Phil Whitfield.

We are most grateful to those who provided us with photographic material for the book: Nataliya S. Alekseeva, Nicola Crockford, Peter Evans, Robin Fisher, Ingvar Grastveit, Dennis Green, Richard Lindsay, Terje Lislevand, Jan Rabben, Stuart Rae, Derek Ratcliffe, Vadim K. Ryabitsev, Bryan Sage and Bill Sutherland.

For financial support of our work we acknowledge the Science and Engineering Research Council, University of Liverpool Research Fellowships Committee, British Ecological Society, Nature Conservancy Council, Scottish Natural Heritage, L. Meltzers Høyskolefond, and The Nansen Foundation. We thank the many private landowners and their staff in Britain and Norway for access to their land. We particularly wish to thank the late Marjorie Fergusson, Bob McLeod, the Allsopps, the Allinghams, and Duncan and Marlene Shaw. During field work in Canada and Russia, Ingvar enjoyed excellent support and hospitality at the field stations visited. Special thanks go to the staff at Churchill Northern Studies Centre, Manitoba, and to the field teams at the stations Hanovey and Yaibari at Yamal. Particular thanks go to Nataliya S. Alekseeva and Vadim K. Ryabitsev, who currently lead these two stations in a most efficient and pleasant way. Also, thanks to V.N. Bol'shakov, director of the Institute of Plant and Animal Ecology, Sverdlovsk (now Ekaterinburg), for providing Ingvar with a formal invitation to work on the two stations at Yamal.

Trevor Poyser was kind enough to accept the original synopsis for the book, and we thank him and Andy Richford for their encouragement. Andy has been a patient and considerate mentor. We also thank Sylvia Sullivan and Roopa Baliga for help in processing the manuscript and proofs.

Des thanks his mother, Maimie Nethersole-Thompson, for coaxing him to finish the book and for all her support, not least in caring for the 'Greenshank' family of eight in a tiny hut in NW Scotland. Father and brothers and sisters Patrick, Eamonn, Maimie, Katharine and the late Richard Thompson have all helped collect some of the Eurasian Golden Plover information given for north Scotland.

Finally, we warmly acknowledge our own families for giving us time and support to work on the book. Ingrid, Åse and Synnøve, and Dawn, John Matthew and James deserve more gratitude than we can give.

CHAPTER 1
The Tundra Plovers:
An Introduction

Eurasian Golden Plover

But to-day I felt more clearly the promise of the tundra – its huge fertility, its immensity, its strange, indefinable magic ... On every hillock stood a plover in gold-studded livery, playing on his wild pipe, or malingering piteously to lead one from his hidden nursery.

Maud Haviland describing the tundra at Gol'chikha in *A summer on the Yenisei* (1915).

THIS is a book about four species, known collectively as the **tundra plovers,** which belong to the genus *Pluvialis.* In one way this is a comparative study of the morphology, biogeography and behaviour of the Grey Plover and the three species of golden plovers. In another way it is a journey into the far north, in search of answers to questions about pairing, timing of breeding, habitat use, social behaviour and parental care. Most of all this is a book by and for people who love the birds and their haunts. You may have been on a large coastal mudflat, in the midst of an agricultural landscape, or even wandering across huge tundra plains close to the North Pole. It does not really matter, for so long as you have watched a tundra plover, and thought about its behaviour, ecology and appearance, you are with us.

TUNDRA PLOVERS: THE FOUR SPECIES

The genus *Pluvialis* belongs to the order Charadriiformes, known as waders in the Old World and **shorebirds** in the New World (we prefer to use the latter term for this order). The shorebirds consist of nine families, the Charadriidae (**Plovers**) being one. The **Grey Plover** (*Pluvialis squatarola*) is the largest of the four *Pluvialis* species. It has a circumpolar arctic breeding distribution, though it is absent from the Atlantic part of the Arctic. This striking bird lacks the golden dorsal 'spangling', so typical of the golden plovers, and also has a hind toe. The Grey Plover is almost exclusively confined to coastal beaches and mudflats outside the breeding grounds, where it is one of the most widespread of all shorebirds, being found in every continent except Antarctica.

The **Eurasian Golden Plover** (*P. apricaria*) breeds across northern Europe from the eastern tip of Greenland right over to the southernmost part of Taimyr Peninsula in Siberia. It is the most southerly of the three golden plovers, characteristic of sub-arctic upland heath and bog, and forest edge tundra.

The **Pacific Golden Plover** (*P. fulva*), formerly known as the Asiatic or Palearctic race of the **Lesser Golden Plover**, breeds in arctic and sub-arctic tundra from the Yamal Peninsula, across Siberia, into western Alaska. The **American Golden Plover** (*P. dominica*) breeds in the New World, from northern Alaska across the sub-arctic into Baffin Island and down the west coast of Hudson Bay. Until recently this was the Lesser Golden Plover, conspecific with what is now the Pacific Golden Plover. But as we shall see later, there is no evidence of inter-breeding where the two birds overlap in Alaska, and they are now regarded as separate species.

Collectively, the four species have many traits in common, and constitute a genus of birds derived, we will argue later, from a single ancestor. Traditionally, there has been no English name in common usage for the genus *Pluvialis*. Witherby *et al.* (1940) used the term 'golden plovers', appropriate in the 1940s because the genus did not include the Grey Plover. Johnsgard (1981) used 'great plovers' for the four species, whilst Cramp & Simmons (1983) referred to them as the 'tundra plovers'. We regard the **tundra plovers** as an appropriate term. Being widespread and often highly conspicuous these, more than any other plovers, constitute a distinctive component of the bird life on the arctic and sub-arctic plains and uplands. Even the Eurasian Golden Plover breeds in tundra, or in open moorland, mire and alpine (sometimes referred to as montane or high mountain) expanses which have affinities with the tundra landscapes of Europe. After all, the word 'tundra' originates from the Finnish word 'tunturi' – a region in northern Finland which is beyond the tree limit. There, in those parts where the surface permafrost layer becomes waterlogged during the summer thaw, the pool-vegetated ridge patterns resemble those of the blanket bog pool-hummock systems of northern and northwestern Britain and Fennoscandia occupied by Eurasian Golden Plovers.

SCOPE

While we concentrate a good deal on the Eurasian Golden Plover we draw equally heavily on published work and recent studies of the four *Pluvialis* species. Almost every aspect of their biology throws up questions. Even a cursory examination of basic breeding distribution maps prompts questions. Why is the Eurasian Golden Plover such a southern nester, and yet found over such a vast subarctic area? Why does the Pacific Golden Plover not occur on the tundra west of the Urals, and why does it occur so sparingly at the western tip of Alaska? Why does the American Golden Plover not breed in Asia, when its distribution reaches the western extremities of Alaska? Why does the Grey Plover breed across the arctic tundra, in both Siberia and North America, yet remain absent from northern Fennoscandia and Greenland? And why do the American and Pacific golden plovers avoid the blanket bog habitats of the southern coast of Alaska, preferring instead the drier tundra farther north, yet the Eurasian Golden Plover breeds in both water-logged blanket mire, and dry and wet types of tundra?

Chapter 2 introduces the plovers of the world. There are 67 species belonging to 10 genera of which *Vanellus*, *Charadrius* and *Pluvialis* are the most prominent. The chapter summarizes those features which set apart the tundra plovers from the others. Taxonomy, geographical variation, plumage and moults are treated in **Chapters 3** and **4**. We discuss the problems of taxonomic status. The latest evidence for specific status of the Pacific and American golden plovers is presented. Some researchers maintain that there are two distinct subspecies of *P. apricaria*, others that it is a monotypic species with polymorphic variation in the form of a cline. In the Grey Plover and Pacific Golden Plover there is an increase in body size towards the Bering Strait, both from the west and from the east. Eurasian Golden Plovers decrease in size eastwards. We present detailed illustrations and descriptions of the birds for different times of the year, and have outlined the field marks to aid identification.

This leads us to phylogeny and biogeography (**Chapter 5**). Based on external morphological characters of adult birds and downy patterns of chicks, a cladistic analysis (giving a phylogenetic 'tree') is presented, with the Common Ringed Plover group as an 'outgroup'. The phylogenetic results are discussed in relation to hypotheses about a common northern tundra ancestor, and subsequent occurrences of each species. Our findings are contentious and may well generate some debate!

Chapter 6 outlines the distribution, population trends and status of the four *Pluvialis* species. Here we address matters such as why there is an Atlantic hiatus in the breeding distribution of Grey Plovers, and why the status of Eurasian and American golden plovers has changed in such different ways. For the British Isles, Fennoscandia and the East Baltic states, population changes of Eurasian Golden Plover are examined in relation to variation in upland agricultural reclamation, grazing pressures, deforestation, afforestation and recreation.

The breeding cycle is considered in **Chapters 7** to **9**. The pre-laying period is covered first. Timing, numbers and sex ratio of birds arriving, pair formation, courtship, nest site selection, aggression and territorial behaviour are all discussed. For the first time, there is full comparative information on display flights of all four species. Relationships within the pair are discussed, and the following are detailed: timing of laying, laying intervals, clutch size, weights and measurements of eggs, incubation behaviour (pattern of nest attendance, sex differences, incubation period and hatching sequence), hatching success, development and care of chicks, and anti-predator behaviour. We provide a particularly detailed assessment of song flights/displays and alarm calls. As in most of the chapters, much of the information has not been published before.

Chapter 10 takes us into post-breeding movements and migration. Spending more than half the year away from its breeding grounds the Eurasian Golden Plover is a partial migrant in the British Isles, but wholly migratory elsewhere. The other three species migrate much farther south. The Pacific Golden Plover ranges from the Pacific Islands, through coastal Australasia and India, to northeast Africa, whereas the American Golden Plover is confined to central South America in winter. The Grey Plover has a world-wide wintering range, mainly in the Subtropics and Tropics though significant numbers are found also in the temperate zone.

On the non-breeding grounds (**Chapter 11**) we look briefly at the behaviour and ecology of the birds on territories, or in single- and mixed-species flocks. Common associates with Eurasian Golden Plovers in winter, Northern Lapwings and Black-headed Gulls, are introduced. We outline their effects on feeding site usage, time budgeting, energy intake and anti-predator behaviour. The costs and benefits of single-species versus mixed-species flocking are viewed within a highly dynamic association of these species. Although the Eurasian Golden Plover is evidently entirely non-territorial in winter, individuals of the other tundra plovers can be territorial (in some areas predominantly so). We offer some ideas on the extent of territorial behaviour on the non-breeding grounds.

Chapter 12 reviews food and feeding habits. Although worms, insects, and molluscs constitute the basic food of these plovers, consumption of large quantities of berries testifies to the importance of fruit and vegetable matter even for shorebirds. **Chapter 13** deals with relationships with other birds. Comparisons across the four species reveal fascinating differences in habitat use, competition and anti-predator behaviour. In areas where American Golden Plovers breed near Grey Plovers the two species show habitat segregation, with the former being the more aggressive of the two. Pacific Golden Plovers in Siberia breed on different habitats depending upon whether or not their close neighbours are Eurasian Golden Plovers or Grey Plovers. One curious feature is the tendency for some shorebirds (notably Dunlin) to form associations with the tundra plovers (and indeed other birds) on the breeding grounds, giving rise to the 'plover's page' relationship.

Finally, **Chapter 14** considers conservation issues. As with many shorebirds, conservation has to have a global outlook because of the myriad habitats and countries used. The decline, since the mid-19th century, of the Eurasian Golden Plover in western Europe provides us with a key to the changing fortunes of an animal subjected to environmental and human-related pressures. These issues are explored, ending with a short consideration of global warming, which may have a catastrophic impact on tundra plovers especially the Grey Plover. There were drastic declines in populations of American Golden Plovers caused by late 19th century market hunting; their subsequent rapid recovery following protection illustrates the potential impacts of persecution.

We should mention a few conventions used in the book. As mentioned above, we refer to waders as shorebirds. The English names of shorebirds seem to have been modified, so for consistency we have used the list provided by Piersma *et al.* (1997). Hence the Lapwing, Dotterel and Ringed Plover breeding in Europe are the Northern Lapwing, Eurasian Dotterel and Common Ringed Plover, respectively! Scientific names for birds and mammals are given in Appendix 1, but for other taxa are given in the text. Occasionally we refer to 'goldies'; this is a popular name for golden plovers, in particular the Eurasian Golden Plover. On the few occasions when we have needed to distinguish between our observations we have used our initials (IB or DBAT). We have tried not to cite other workers' unpublished work (after all, if it is not published it is not in the public domain), but have included reference to written or oral personal communications (pers. comm.).

STUDY AREAS AND EARLY STUDIES

Between us, we have spent over 50 years studying tundra plovers. IB has studied Eurasian Golden Plovers in Norway since 1967, American Golden Plovers in Canada in 1986, and Eurasian and Pacific golden plovers and Grey Plovers in Siberia in 1989. DBAT has studied upland/peatland birds, notably shorebirds, in northern Scotland (as part of the Nethersole-Thompson family) since 1964, and with the Nature Conservancy Council (now Scottish Natural Heritage) since 1986. He has researched Eurasian Golden Plovers in winter flocks in the Midlands of England during 1980–1984, making occasional visits to that area thereafter.

Essentially, our studies have encompassed four different habitats: open dwarf shrub-dominated heath and blanket bog (often termed moorland); alpine/montane (high mountain) plateaux; tundra; and lowland agricultural pastureland. The pictures and short descriptions below convey the diversity of these and other sites where tundra plovers have been studied. As we repeatedly refer to many of these areas, they are shown in Fig. 1.1.

Jæren and other West Norwegian heath sites

The region of Jæren is essentially a vast glacial deposit sloping slowly from about 400 m above sea level (asl), down to sea level. Although most of the lower parts have dense human populations and are intensively cultivated for agriculture, parts of the uplands there have remnants of heather moors, which were much more widespread only 70–80 years ago. These moors used to have high numbers of breeding Eurasian Golden Plovers. Considered the unofficial bird of the region under the local name 'heluna', the species was well known and appreciated by the local people. In the course of the 20th century, agriculture quickly overwhelmed the heather moors, and the habitat nowadays is found almost exclusively in the higher uplands of this southwest Norwegian region.

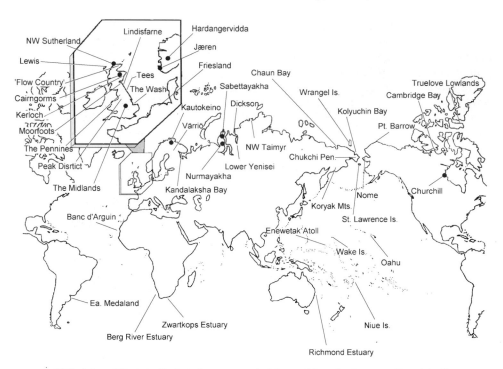

FIG. 1.1.   *The principal study areas worked by us (●) and others mentioned in the text.*

In 1968, IB started a census of the remaining Eurasian Golden Plovers breeding in the Jæren region. Over the next couple of years a total of 200–250 pairs were found (Byrkjedal 1974). Many of the birds showed very little plumage distinctness and the population was considered to be the last remnant of *P. a. apricaria* in Norway (Haftorn 1971; we discuss the sub-species issues in Chapter 3). IB began to study their breeding ecology and plumage variation in 1973, and carried on for two more seasons (and again in 1990), in an area covering 9 km², 200–360 m asl. In this area, almost daily field work was carried out from March/April to June. Here 24–26 pairs of golden plovers bred, a density of 2.7–2.9 pairs km⁻². The area is characterized by dry gravelly moraine ridges covered by Ling *Calluna vulgaris* (Plate 1). The ridges formed a mosaic with sedge-dominated bogs with dominant sedges *Carex* spp., cotton-grass *Eriophorum vaginatum*, heath rush *Juncus squarrosus* and cross-leaved heath *Erica tetralix*. A zone of Mat Grass *Nardus stricta* occurs on the transition between the *Calluna*-covered drier parts and the bogs, and Deer-sedge *Scirpus cespitosus* is widespread throughout the area.

The high plumage variability among golden plovers at Jæren (Fig. 1.2) prompted IB to undertake visits in 1974 to some other potential breeding sites along the western coast of Norway. He visited breeding grounds of golden plovers at Karmøy, an island north of Jæren, which also has typical heather moor habitat. The localities Bremangerlandet, Hareidlandet and Smøla were visited next. Although coastal, and within the moorland region, the vegetation on these sites is particularly short and

FIG. 1.2. *Examples of individual plumage variation in Pacific Golden Plover males (six upper left), Grey Plover females (three lower left) and Eurasian Golden Plover males (right). These are based on original sketches in the field by IB.*

has a strong component of Woolly Fringe Moss, *Racomitrium lanuginosum*, giving the heaths a grizzled look, somewhat resembling alpine/montane lichen heaths.

Northwest Sutherland and northern Scotland wet heaths and blanket bogs

During 1964–1998 DBAT and the rest of the Nethersole-Thompson family have studied Eurasian Golden Plovers and other shorebirds. Their NW Sutherland study

PLATE 1.   *Moorland on gravelly moraines at Synesvarden, Jæren, Norway, where IB studied the breeding of Eurasian Golden Plovers. (IB)*

is described by Nethersole-Thompson & Nethersole-Thompspon (1979, 1986), Thompson *et al.* (1986, 1988), Thompson (1990a) and Thompson & Thompson (1991). Plate 2 shows a view looking out of this treeless steep-sided glen, composed of Lewisian Gneiss bedrock, a small river and many large and small blanket bog pool complexes. The main plant constants are *Scirpus cespitosus, Eriophorum vaginatum,* and variable amounts of heather (*Calluna vulgaris* and *Erica tetralix*) with Purple Moor Grass *Molinia caerulea* interspersed with bog mosses *Sphagnum* spp. and *Racomitrium lanuginusum.* Only a few croft fields (around 5 ha) were present and used by feeding birds within the 16 km² area. Numbers of breeding golden plovers recorded there have varied between a maximum of 31+ pairs in 1976 and a minimum of 7 pairs in 1992. Generally, this has been regarded as a low density breeding population (*sensu* Ratcliffe 1976).

During 1994 and 1995 a detailed study of Eurasian Golden Plovers in NE Sutherland was made by a team from Durham University, funded and supported by Scottish Natural Heritage, SNH (O'Connell *et al.* 1996; Downie *et al.* 1996; Whitfield 1997a,b). This provided important information on habitat use by birds and relied heavily on radio telemetry. Again the blanket bog here was characterized by large pool complexes, though there were many more 'improved' and 'semi-improved' pastures around the edges of some of the bog systems, and there was some commercial forestry (Plate 3). There have also been many ornithological surveys of the northern peatlands of Scotland (e.g. Stroud *et al.*

PLATE 2. *Northwest Sutherland, Scotland, showing wet heath and blanket bog terrain dominated by Lewisian Gneiss, with low densities of breeding Eurasian Golden Plovers, where DBAT studied this and other shorebird species.*

1987; Thompson *et al.* 1988; Avery & Haines Young 1990; Brown & Shepherd 1993; Lavers & Haines-Young 1996). Ray Parr's (1993a) PhD study in NE Sutherland and Caithness is noteworthy, for with his dogs he managed to survey a large number of study plots using a variety of dawn and dusk census methods.

Open heath/blanket bog study areas in other parts of Britain

A few other detailed studies of Eurasian Golden Plover have been made. During 1972–1998 Derek Yalden and colleagues have researched these birds on the relatively eroded *Eriophorum vaginatum*-dominated blanket bogs of the Peak District (e.g. Yalden 1991; Yalden & Yalden 1989, 1990, 1991; Yalden & Pearce-Higgins 1997). North of here, Mark Whittingham carried out his PhD research on habitat use by goldies on complexes of blanket bog, wet heath and pastures in the North Pennines (Whittingham 1996a,b). Derek Ratcliffe made a detailed study in this area, on Alston Moor and Tailbridge, with contrasting limestone–influenced rough grassland with blanket bogs (Ratcliffe 1976), and this work was developed by Chris Thomas (1986), and more widely for other shorebirds by David Baines (1988).

In Galloway, S. Scotland, Phillip Edwards studied plumage variation in golden plovers in a mosaic of dry heather moorland and rough grassland (Edwards 1982). Derek Langslow studied golden plovers in the Moorfoots, with classic grouse moor country close to Edinburgh, where he found some of the highest breeding

PLATE 3.   *Blanket bog complex of Blar nam Faoileag, North Scotland, which has pasture fields nearby used by 'off-duty' Eurasian Golden Plovers during incubation period. (Richard Lindsay)*

densities recorded in Scotland (Langslow 1983). This study was begun by Derek Ratcliffe in 1963, who contracted Derek Langslow and Len Campbell to develop his study.

Farther north, Ray Parr made another important study on *Calluna*-dominated 'eastern' grouse moorland in NE Scotland (Parr 1980). There, between 1973 and 1989, he quantified the extent of 'sequential nesting' (early breeding season 'surplus' pairs bred only after others had failed, sometimes taking over the unsuccessful pair's territory within a few days of them having lost their eggs or chicks, Parr 1979). Sadly, Parr's Kerloch study population is now renowned for having plummeted from around 60 pairs in the late 1970s to only one pair in 1989 (Parr 1992, 1993a,b). Two of Parr's mentors, Desmond Nethersole-Thompson and Adam Watson, had earlier noted changes in golden plover populations in various parts of the Cairngorms (Nethersole-Thompson & Watson 1981; Thompson *et al.* 1996). Nethersole-Thompson made a particularly intimate study of goldies in the foothills of the Cairngorms (Nethersole-Thompson & Nethersole-Thompson 1939, 1961, 1986). Brown & Stillman (1993) reviewed golden plover-habitat associations in the eastern Highlands, reaching some conclusions at variance with a comparable study of birds in the southern Pennines (Haworth & Thompson 1990).

As we go to press, some remarkable findings are emerging from Phil Whitfield's research on the Lewis peatlands, at the western extremity of Britain (Plate 4). There, densities of breeding golden plovers (and other shorebirds, notably Dunlin)

PLATE 4. *Peatlands bordering crofting lands on Lewis, Western Isles, Scotland, close to Stornoway. (DBAT)*

are greater than recorded anywhere else on blanket bogs (Whitfield 1997a, pers. comm.).

Arctic-alpine/montane plateaux in Norway and Scotland

Situated within a mild oceanic climate the Norwegian moorlands have Eurasian Golden Plovers on an early breeding schedule. At the same latitude, but around a thousand metres higher up, large golden plover populations breed on open arctic-alpine habitats in a much more restricted summer season (resembling that of the Arctic) although they are only a few tens of kilometres from the coast. These habitats, above the natural tree-line, are termed 'alpine' or 'arctic-alpine' heaths (or 'montane' in some of the British literature, e.g. Ratcliffe 1976, 1990; Ratcliffe & Thompson 1988; Thompson & Brown 1992; Horsfield & Thompson 1997).

Starting in 1974, IB selected a 17 km² study site at Hardangervidda, over 1300 m asl, to compare the breeding ecology of golden plovers with those of the moorlands. Field work was done more or less continually from mid-May to late July, with briefer visits in August and September. Hardangervidda is a 10 000 km² large mountain plateau in central-south Norway, most of it over 1000 m asl, with a flora and fauna having clear arctic affinities. Whilst Norwegian moorland habitats are usually snowfree in March (when golden plovers arrive and disperse onto their territories) Hardangervidda has immense snow-cover until May (Plates 5 & 6). Prof Sven-Axel Bengtson advised IB to collect a number of golden plovers to study diets. The skins

PLATE 5.   *Snow cover at Hardangervidda, Norway, is substantial when Eurasian Golden Plovers arrive. Plovers nevertheless disperse to snow-free patches and start to defend their breeding territories. (IB)*

PLATE 6.   *Typical snow cover at Hardangervidda, Norway, around when Eurasian Golden Plovers lay their eggs. (IB)*

from the birds taken were used to extend IB's study of plumage variation. In particular, he could check whether or not females were consistently duller coloured than their mates, a supposition made in previous studies based on field observations of birds. The birds were duly taken on the hills adjacent to the study area, on similar habitat.

In 1977 the studies at Hardangervidda were extended to a 14 km² large area, Steinbuheii, at 1200–1350 m asl, situated a few kilometres north of the 1974 site. In a 6 km² accurately censused part of the study area the recorded number of golden plover territories varied between 20 and 25 per annum over six summers, a breeding density of 3.3–4.2 pairs km⁻². Eurasian Dotterel, as well as Dunlin and Purple Sandpiper, were included in the programme, which aimed to study habitat use, mating systems and anti-predator behaviour of these species.

The Hardangervidda plateau rests largely on granite. In sheltered places and along waterbodies and wet mires extensive willow *Salix* shrubs grow. The breeding grounds of golden plovers there are mainly found in the subalpine dwarf shrub zone and on drier alpine heaths above. The dwarf shrubs are composed of various Ericaceae on exposed ground, and dominated by prostrate Dwarf Birch *Betula nana* in more sheltered places. The study site at Steinbuheii (Plate 7) has at least eight structurally distinguishable plant communities (Byrkjedal 1989b): Least Willow *Salix herbacea* snowbeds, Mountain Sedge *Carex bigelowii* heaths, lichen, Three Pointed Rush *Cladonia-Juncus trifidus* heaths (Plate 8), Blaeberry *Vaccinium myrtillus* heaths, grass meadows, *Nardus stricta* snowbeds, *Carex-Eriophorum* bogs, and *Betula nana* fields (of which the first three make up about 20% of plant cover).

In 1987, in the Scottish Highlands, DBAT established a detailed study of habitat use and breeding biology of the Eurasian Dotterel and other montane/alpine birds (Plate 9). As part of this research, led first by Hector Galbraith and since 1990 by Phil Whitfield, we have collected information on Eurasian Golden Plovers. The four key study areas in the central and eastern Highlands range in altitude from 800–900 m to 1000–1200 m asl. Principal habitats are dominated by open, broken *Juncus trifidus* and *Racomitrium lanuginosum* heaths with extensive snowbed, spring and flush communities (in the highest sites), more continuous *Racomitrium-Carex bigelowii* moss heaths with limited snowbeds (and blanket bog in two of these sites), lichen-rich *Racomitrium* heaths adjoining a large, partially eroded blanket bog complex, *Nardus stricta* grasslands, and prostrate Blaeberry–Crowberry *Vaccinium myrtillus* – *Empetrum nigrum* and *Calluna* dwarf shrub heaths. Average densities ranged between 1.0 and 2.2 pairs km⁻² in occupied areas (much lower than on Hardangervidda but close to those on the moorland remnants of Jæren).

Open boreal forest

Raised bogs and other open spaces with short vegetation, situated in boreal pine *Pinus* spp. and spruce *Picea* spp. forests on both sides of the Baltic Sea, hold large numbers of breeding Eurasian Golden Plovers. Densities on such bogs were analysed by Alexandersson (1987) for a major part of southwestern Sweden. Studies of Eurasian Golden Plovers on raised bogs in Estonian forests were published by Aino Kumari in the 1950s. We have drawn particularly on her analysis of a large number of golden plover stomachs from these bogs.

PLATE 7. *Steinbuheii study area, Hardangervidda, Norway, about 1300 m above sea level, may look uniform, but consists of mosaics of several montane (alpine) plant communities. (IB)*

In Finnish Lapland, data on breeding Eurasian Golden Plovers have been collected over a period of 20 years as part of the ornithological activity of the Värriö Subarctic Research Station (Pulliainen & Saari 1993). This is an area primarily covered by forest composed of spruce, pine, and birch (*Picea abies, Pinus sylvestris* and *Betula* spp., respectively), with golden plovers breeding on open spaces of bogs and alpine fell summits.

Near Kautokeino, northern Norway, Tore Larsen, Jostein Moldsvor and IB collected breeding data on golden plovers while studying Bar-tailed Godwits and Spotted Redshanks for two summers, within a 14 km² area, about 400 m asl, in open,

PLATE 8 (opposite top). *Lichen heath with* Juncus trifidus, *frequently used as nest habitat by Eurasian Golden Plovers at Hardangervidda. The Gordon Setter is pointing at a nearby golden plover nest. (IB)*
PLATE 9 (opposite bottom). *Looking north-east across the A9 road at Drumochter, central Scottish Highlands, towards the arctic-alpine mountain breeding grounds of Eurasian Golden Plovers and Eurasian Dotterel. (DBAT)*

PLATE 8

PLATE 9

stunted birch forest on lichen-covered gravel ridges, alternating with sedge and palsa bogs (Plate 10). Palsa is peaty soil with large, permanent ice lenses, in parts forming large mounds and elevations of drier gound surrounded by wet boggy patches and 'strings'.

Eurasian tundra

Having studied anti-predator behaviour of breeding golden plovers in Europe and North America, and wondering whether 'clever' nest predators could impose constraints on the evolution of certain anti-predator behaviours, IB sought a site with breeding tundra plovers but no corvids. Flat arctic tundra well north of the forest line readily commended itself, and in order to include studies of Eurasian Golden Plover, this had to be in Russia! Having heard about the impressive activities at ornithological stations on the Yamal Peninsula in NW Siberia, IB got in touch with Vadim K. Ryabitsev at the Academy of Sciences in Sverdlovsk (now Ekaterinburg). This led to a stay at Yamal in the summer of 1989, at two stations in succession – 'Hanovey' at Nurmayakha River (mid-June–early July) and 'Yaibari' at Sabettayakha River (most of July). At Hanovey, IB had the opportunity to study Eurasian and Pacific golden plovers, and at Yaibari Grey Plovers and to some extent Pacific Golden Plovers.

Yamal, essentially a plain of fine grained clay deposits, has a very flat terrain, intersected by meandering streams. The tundra there thus has a plateau-like

PLATE 10.   *Breeding grounds of Eurasian Golden Plovers among stunted birch trees, Kautokeino, Finnmark, northern Norway. (IB)*

appearance, dominated by a windswept short growing moss-lichen vegetation – the 'plakors' according to the Russians. Streams cut their way rather steeply into the fine-grained ground, producing steep slopes ('ovrags'), often having a lush vegetation of willows (*Salix*) and tall herbs. Along the streams, which often meander strongly, there are entirely level floodplains ('poimas') with sedges and willow patches. It is frightening terrain, where you can easily become detached from your base-camp!

Of the two stations visited by IB, Hanovey was situated at 69°N on sub-arctic tundra (Plate 11). Here the poimas and ovrags, as well as depressions in the plakors, had a dense cover of prostrate *Betula nana*. At Yaibari, at about 71°30′N, a more typical arctic tundra was found, with no lush shrub vegetation (Plate 12). The wetter tundra at Yaibari, apart from the floodplains, was to a significant extent an ice wedge polygon tundra, vegetated with a thick carpet of mosses and sedges, creating a peaty, hummocky ground surface. Typical plakor tundra at Yaibari was very windswept and even had scattered patches of exposed sand with no vegetation. At both stations, Ericaceae such as *Empetrum* spp. and *Cassiope* spp. grew abundantly on the plakors. The studies in Russia involved following the fate of as many nests as possible, observing displays of the birds, recording their songs and other vocalizations, and studying their anti-predator behaviour.

The ornithological investigation of the Russian tundra has a long history (Il'ičev & Flint 1985), and much of the literature is not readily accessible.

PLATE 11. *At Nurmayakha, Yamal Peninsula, northwest Siberia, Pacific and Eurasian golden plovers nested on the flat, elevated plateaux but frequently fed on the wetter floodplains. (Natalya S. Alekseeva)*

PLATE 12.   *Grey Plover nesting grounds at Sabettayakha, Yamal Peninsula, northwest Siberia: high-polygon sedge-moss tundra in foreground and dry lichen tundra plateaux in background. (IB)*

Far from the main areas of habitation, investigations are based largely on summer expeditions. A number of early explorers brought back ornithological material from these areas. However, more recent expeditions have contributed to an upsurge in the study of the northern birds. Stations have been erected in many sites, at which research is being conducted over a number of successive summers. The more recent ornithological investigations of the tundra of the former Soviet Union appear to have been directed from three main centres. While Northwest Siberia has been investigated by the Academy of Sciences in Ekaterinburg, Moscow University has mainly been in charge of studies on the tundra from north-central Siberia and eastwards. However, from northeastern Siberia to the Chukchi Peninsula, a group from the Academy of Sciences has conducted significant field studies from Magadan. In addition, ornithologists from the Academy of Sciences – the Yakutian Group in Novosibirsk – has been active, especially in the lower regions of the Lena River.

A research station situated in the Kandalaksha Bay, White Sea, has been in operation for almost half a century. Belopol'skij *et al.* (1970) summarize the results from the station in the 1950s and 1960s, and present especially valuable information on the migration schedules of Grey Plover and Eurasian Golden Plover from this northern boreal site and adjacent subarctic tundra.

To a Western readership, the visit to the Bol'shezemelskaya tundra at the mouth of the Petchora River over 120 years ago by Henry Seebohm and J.A. Harvie-Brown, first published in 1880, and reprinted in 1901 and 1979, was for a long period a prime source of ornithological knowledge on the north Russian tundra. Their work essentially involved collecting birds, with the Grey Plover one of the target species. On hitting a good breeding site, they rendered excellent descriptions of 10 nest, with enough detail on the birds to be of interest – even today.

Moving east of the Urals, we reach the Yamal Peninsula. Research activity here carries on today, based at some of the numerous field stations organized by the Academy of Sciences in Ekaterinburg, including those on northern tundra. The Grey Plover is one of the target species for this research (V. Ryabitsev pers. comm.). In 1989, T.R. Andreeva published an analysis of the diet of a number of common shorebirds from plakor tundra in the catchment area of the Shchuch'ey River at southern Yamal. This analysis included details of a good number of stomach contents of Eurasian Golden Plover, collected in 1979–85.

Farther east, the moss-lichen tundra of the lower parts of Yenisei River was visited by Maud Doria Haviland in the summer of 1914, resulting in two papers on tundra plovers: a short note on Grey Plover and a more detailed article on Pacific Golden Plover, the latter remaining on important source of information in the western literature on the behaviour of this species on its Palearctic breeding grounds. The article contains remarkably good photographs, for its time, of a male Pacific Golden Plover.

On the east side of the Yenisei River mouth is the Taimyr peninsula – a legendary place in the minds of shorebird enthusiasts! Information on the breeding ecology of tundra plovers from this area comes principally from Pavel S. Tomkovich and N.V. Vronskij (who worked at Dickson in 1981–84 and on the barren tundra of northwestern Taimyr in 1983), and from a West European-Russian expedition to northeastern Taimyr in 1991 (Underhill *et al.* 1993). The main information on tundra plovers relates to phenology and habitat use. The known breeding range of Eurasian Golden Plover has been extended considerably following work by Tomkovich and Vronskij.

Moving on to northern Yakutia, where the open tundra runs in a fairly narrow zone along the Arctic Ocean, information on the breeding biology of Grey Plovers and Pacific Golden Plovers emerged from work done by Pavel Tomkovich in the Buor-Khaya Bay in the summer of 1977. South of the tundra zone, a team from Novosibirsk worked in the years 1973–1985 on the avifauna of subarctic and northern boreal wetlands along the lower part of Lena River, between 64° and 71°N. This is south of the breeding grounds for tundra plovers in Yakutia, but Grey Plovers, and in particular Pacific Golden Plover, stop-over on these areas during migration. In their ornithological book on this area, Yu.V. Labutin, N.I. Germogenov and V.I. Pozdnyakov (1988) presented a quantitative description of the diet of Pacific Golden Plovers on autumn migration based on many stomach samples obtained in 1975–85.

Much more information has been published in recent decades on the avifauna of northeastern Siberia and the Chukchi Peninsula (the 'Northern Far East' according to the Russians). Already, before World War II, Leonid Portenko led extensive ornithological work on the Chukchi Peninsula, continuing through the 1960s. This resulted in a two volume work, which has been translated into German as well as English. The information presented in the 1981 English translation provides a highly welcome insight into the life of northeastern Palearctic birds. Very useful data are given for breeding Grey Plovers and Pacific Golden Plovers.

In the more recent decades, the Northern Far East has been visited by a number of Russian ornithologists. From their field work at sites ranging from northeasternmost Chukchi Peninsula, down to the Anadyr region, Koryak Mountains, and even to Kamchatka, V.E. Flint, Pavel Tomkovich, A.A. Kistschinski and A.G. Sorokin have published information on the breeding biology of Grey Plovers and in particular Pacific Golden Plovers. The nesting habitats there include typical arctic tundra, and even more interestingly, montane heaths in the Koryak mountains. During his work on Kamchatka, Pavel Tomkovich reached the world's southernmost known breeding grounds of Pacific Golden Plovers. His contribution to ornithological knowledge of these parts has been truly monumental.

Special mention must be made of the studies by Aleksandr Ya. Kondrat'ev in the 1960s and 1970s. He worked on a number of study sites on the tundra bordering the Arctic Sea, from the Lower Kolyma and Chaun Bay to the Kolyuchin Bay on the north coast of the Chukchi Peninsula. He studied a broad spectrum of topics, such as incubation rhythm and sex roles, and dealt with nesting success. A great number of shorebirds were represented in his studies, including Grey Plover and Pacific Golden Plover. His results were published in a book in 1982 (*Biology of waders on the tundra of Northeastern Asia*, in Russian). This is an outstanding source book on the breeding biology of northeast palearctic shorebirds. In 1977 Kondrat'ev co-authored a German paper, with V.E. Flint, summarizing their notes on the breeding biology of Grey Plovers in the Northern Far East. Studies of the avifauna on the sites originally worked by Kondrat'ev have continued, and more recent results have been given in *Birds of northern plains* by Kretchmar *et al.* (1991, in Russian).

In the Northern Far East, Wrangel Island has been visited frequently by biologists. In spite of its isolation from the Chukchi Peninsula by the broad De Long Strait, the island holds a surprisingly rich terrestrial avifauna. Leonie Portenko stayed on the island to study birds in 1938–39, but more recent work (1970s and 1980s) has been reported by M.S. Stischov and his co-workers (1991), giving information on breeding Grey Plovers and Pacific Golden Plovers.

North American tundra

Having worked on various aspects of the ecology of Eurasian Golden Plovers, IB wanted to make comparisons with the closely related American Golden Plover, and so spent the summer of 1986 in Churchill, Manitoba (Plate 13). Churchill, situated on the low lying flat country west of Hudson Bay, is on the transition zone between tundra and boreal forest. The open space housing golden plovers is just a narrow strip of subarctic tundra along the coast, gradually turning into forest tundra or muskeg inland.

The tundra consists of sedge bogs, and dry eskers and gravel ridges covered profusely by lichens. Scattered pines (*Pinus glauca* and *P. mariana*) and tamarack (*Larix laricina*), with their growth forms characteristic of areas with snow and hard wind, grow on the tundra. The study area covered 3.75 km², and altogether 23 golden plover nests were found. The study focused on anti-predator behaviour and nesting success, but sound recordings were also made, as opportunities offered.

PLATE 13. *Lichen tundra with dwarf shrub of Ericaceae, including* Rhododendron lapponicum, *used as nesting grounds by American Golden Plover at Churchill, Manitoba, Canada. Stunted tamaracks* Larix laricina *in background. (IB)*

The Churchill area is perhaps more frequently visited by birders than any other northern Canadian site. The ornithology of the area is reviewed by Jehl & Smith (1970). Studies involving American Golden Plovers in the area were made by Baker (1977) on diet, but some important notes were published by Joseph A. Hagar (1966) in his treatise of the Hudsonian Godwit

Oil and gas exploitation during the last decades has opened up many parts of the North American arctic, in the course of which ornithological exploration has grown. Before then, the Canadians were active, going on ornithological expeditions, particularly in the 1950s and 1960s. These multi-purpose expeditions collected data on tundra plovers, and specimens for the Canadian scientific museums. We have made extensive use of information derived from these specimens, having extracted information on breeding from egg specimen labels, as well as on geographical variation from study skins. Among those who undertook these expeditions we should mention E. Otto Höhn, T.H. Manning, D.J.T. Hussel, G.L. Holroyd, W.E. Renaud, A.H. Macpherson, G.R. Parker, R.K. Ross and David F. Parmelee (a close friend of the Nethersole-Thompson family). Many of the sites visited by expeditions were very remote, yet some parts were thoroughly researched: from Southampton Island in the northern part of Hudson Bay to high arctic sites in the North West Territories, such as Victoria Island, Banks Island, Devon Island, Bathurst Island, Prince of Wales Island and parts of Baffin Island.

A few studies in the far north dealt with tundra plovers in particular. Drury (1961) compared nest protection behaviour and song and other displays of American Golden Plover and Grey Plover at Bylot Island, NE of Baffin Island. At Bathurst Island, Harold Mayfield (1973) made detailed studies of the behaviour of Grey Plovers at two nests during incubation and hatching, and David Hussell and Gary Page (1976) studied breeding Grey Plovers over five summers at Truelove Lowlands, an arctic oasis in the desert-like Devon Island. Hussel & Page's study contains the only detailed published description of chick development of any of the tundra plovers. During two summers of ornithological work at the Melville Peninsula, Robert Montgomerie and colleagues (1983) made detailed behavioural ecological studies of a number of birds. They gave interesting, though brief, reports on the relationship between breeding Grey Plovers and American Golden Plovers.

Some North American sites have been visited particularly frequently for scientific collecting. Churchill, Manitoba used to be one such site. Another is Point Barrow and its environs in northernmost Alaska. Collecting has been undertaken in many places in Alaska, particularly along the coast. One of the more famous enterprises was Herbert Brandt's visit to the Yukon River Delta in 1924, where he collected specimens and information on a number of birds, including Pacific Golden Plovers and Grey Plovers.

In Alaska, oil exploitation has prompted a number of biological investigations in many parts of the state. Alas, most of the reports on this sort of work belong to the 'grey literature' which is not circulated widely, to the extent that some are difficult to obtain. Two published books draw heavily on such material from Alaska: Johnson & Herter's (1989) *The birds of the Beaufort Sea*, and Kessel's (1989) *The birds of the Seward Peninsula*.

Studies dealing especially with tundra plovers in Alaska are those by Peter Connors and his co-workers, who compared habitats of co-occurring American and Pacific golden plovers. There are also the on-going studies by Oscar Johnson and his team on site fidelity of Pacific Golden Plovers. The latter track radio transmitter-marked birds, some of which have been followed from their Hawaiian wintering quarters to their breeding grounds in western Alaska. Franz Sauer (1962) made a classic study of Pacific Golden Plover at St Lawrence Island in the Bering Sea. In an effort to secure a few golden plover chicks for captive rearing as part of a migration and navigation experiment, Sauer collected very detailed information on many aspects of breeding biology.

Non-breeding grounds

In winter, the Grey Plover occupies estuaries and coastal mudflats and beaches. In NE England, Peter Evans and later Mike Pienkowski, Pat Dugan and Dave Townshend began a detailed study of feeding and social behaviour in 1975, comparing a population on the Tees Estuary with another at Lindisfarne farther north (where both intra-specific aggression and territorial behaviour are rare). The Tees (Plate 14) has large stretches of mudflats, with some gullies and creeks used by the birds, though substantial areas have been reclaimed for industrial purposes (e.g. Evans *et al.* 1979, 1984; Pienkowski 1982; Townshend 1985).

Philip Hockey and Jane Turpie have studied Grey Plovers on the Zwartkops

PLATE 14. *Creeks used by territorial Grey Plovers on the Tees Estuary, North England. (Peter Evans)*

Estuary, eastern Cape Province, South Africa, where they have concentrated on foraging energetics and night feeding (e.g. Turpie & Hockey 1993). More recently, they have extended their work to nine study areas in East Africa, South Africa and some islands in the western Indian Ocean (Turpie & Hockey 1997). Some of the most important, early work on this species was done by a Yale PhD student, Myron C. Baker (1973, 1974), on a small mudflat near City Point, New Haven, Connecticut. Other studies have been made on the Nakdong Estuary, South Korea (Piersma 1985), in Guinea-Bissau (Zwarts 1985) and in the Banc d'Arguin, Mauritania (e.g. Ens *et al.* 1990; Piersma 1982, Piersma *et al.* 1990a,b).

The Eurasian Golden Plover has been studied extensively on its wintering grounds in the British Isles, notably in Oxfordshire (Fuller & Youngman 1979), the English Midlands (e.g. Thompson 1984; Barnard & Thompson 1985), North Yorkshire (Gregory 1987) and NE Scotland (McLennan 1979). Comparisons of distribution and habitat use across the British Isles have been made by Fuller & Lloyd (1981), Fuller (1986), Kirby & Lack (1993) and Cranswick *et al.* (1996). Grasslands, particularly permanent pastures, are the preferred feeding habitat (Plate 15), and ploughed fields are the preferred roosting grounds in most parts. Land higher than 200 m asl tends to be avoided in winter, though there are some local exceptions. It is nonetheless striking how little we still know about the effects of different agricultural regimes on Eurasian Golden Plovers in winter (e.g. Tucker *et al.* 1994; Gillings & Fuller 1996). In the Netherlands and Germany, van Eerden & Keij (1979) compared the results of two large surveys of the birds on passage, where agricultural fields are important.

PLATE 15.   *Part of a permanent pastureland complex near Wysall in the English Midlands, used by grassland plovers. The fields had large flocks of Eurasian Golden Plovers, Northern Lapwings and Black-headed Gulls. (DBAT)*

Most of DBAT's work on wintering Eurasian Golden Plovers was done with Chris Barnard during October–early March in 1980–1984 in the English Midlands between Nottingham and Loughborough. The farmland there consisted of a mixture of arable, young pastures (<4 years since last ploughed) and old pastures (>25 years since last ploughed, often with pronounced ridge and furrow surface features of medieval origins) (Plate 16). Many of the fields had brown earth soils, though some had clay-loams. Pasture sizes ranged from 1.04–17.53 ha (most bordered by 1.5–3.0 m high mixed hedgerows), and several contained livestock (dairy cattle, and to a lesser extent horses and sheep). One winter range of golden plovers studied intensively (Hill Farm) had an estimated 800 goldies along with 1000 lapwings and around 50 Black-headed Gulls (Thompson 1983a,b, 1984, 1986; Barnard & Thompson 1985; Thompson & Barnard 1983, 1984; Thompson & Lendrem 1985). Sadly, visits to these areas in 1995 and 1996 have not produced plovers – fewer old pastures remain and the hedges have been cleared out or reduced in length and height (Chapter 14).

The winter range of Pacific Golden Plovers is very varied, taking in cultivated, coastal and even residential areas. The most detailed research has been carried out by Oscar Johnson and colleagues on the Hawaiian Islands (e.g. Johnson *et al.* 1981a,b, 1989; Johnson & Connors 1996). Their main study site was the Bellows Air Force Station, Oahu, where many of the birds were territorial, showing high rates of survival and site fidelity (they breed in Alaska). Some Pacific Golden Plovers there

PLATE 16. *Ridge-furrow, permanent pasture bordered by oak trees* (Quercus robur) *in English Midlands. This field had not been ploughed in more than 200 years.* *(DBAT)*

roost on flat roofs in urban areas (Johnson & Nakamura 1981), and forage in open stands of tall (≥20 m high) iron wood (*Casuarina* spp.) as well as on lawns and gardens in urban areas such as in 'down-town Honolulu' (Johnson & Connors 1996). Special studies of Pacific Golden Plovers have been made on other Pacific islands. Studies including moult and energetics were carried out at Enewetok Atoll in the Marshall Islands by Oscar Johnson and on Wake Island by David Johnston and Robert McFarlane (1967), while Kinsky & Yaldwyn (1981) recorded information on the Pacific Golden Plover at Niue Island, southeast of Samoa.

In northern New South Wales, Rohweder & Baverstock (1996) compared nocturnal and diurnal habitat use by Pacific Golden Plovers and a number of other shorebirds on the Richmond River Estuary. More extensive work by David Rohweder at the same estuary, using an image intensifier and a diffused infra-red spotlight, as well as radio telemetry, has revealed marked differences in habitat use, diet and feeding density between night and day (Rohweder 1996, unpubl.). Other more general studies have been made in India (Ripley 1982; Hussain 1987). Unlike the Eurasian Golven Plover, the Pacific Golden Plover can overwinter at high altitudes – up to at least 2500 m asl (O.W. Johnson, unpubl.). The American Golden Plover overwinters mainly around the Rio de la Plata grasslands of east Argentina and Uruguay (and parts of the southern reaches of Brazil, Johnson & Connors 1996). Little detailed research has been carried out there, though there are concerns about agricultural development, pollution and even the spread of human settlements affecting grasslands used by the birds (Myers 1984; Bucher & Nores 1988; Blanco *et al.* 1993; Gill *et al.* 1995; Johnson & Connors 1996). There are unofficial reports that extensive deforestation farther north, in Amazonia, may be creating new habitat for migrating and wintering American Golden Plovers (and other plovers).

TUNDRA PLOVERS IN THE FIELD: APPROACHES TO STUDYING THEM

Watching flocks

The sight of golden plovers on grasslands, be these pampas in Argentina or old hedge-bounded pastures in England, presents a daunting challenge for the observer keen to understand bird behaviour. We have three pieces of advice. First, watch the flocks with an open mind – do not take notes during the first few days, but instead just watch, listen and think about what is happening! Second, form clear questions that can be tested in the field, ideally experimentally. Do there appear to be aggressive or other sorts of interactions in the flock? Are some birds territorial? Is the flock randomly or non-randomly distributed? Is the flock moving around? Are birds coming into and leaving the flock periodically? Are there other species with the goldies? What are they feeding on? Are there any predators? From these simple questions you should be forming broad hypotheses about what appears to be influencing the size of the flock, the distances between individuals, and the social and other influences on energy intake. Our third suggestion is that you should be consistent in the way that you then make observations: do not adopt subtle changes in methods which might inadvertently bias the trends or patterns you are trying to measure.

Much can be gained from making regular circuits round your study site, noting and mapping the composition, size and distribution of flocks. You should distinguish between roosting, pre-foraging, foraging and post-foraging flocks or assemblies. By watching the birds carefully you should be able to determine what they are taking. If earthworms are being consumed, can you measure their lengths in relation to the bird's bill (DBAT has seen golden plovers grappling with 18 cm worms!)? Thompson (1983a) and Barnard & Thompson (1985) give details on estimating the energy value of earthworms taken. They recommended sampling the turf to a depth of 3.0 cm (the maximum to which Eurasian Golden Plovers probe) using 0.25 m-square quadrats, and then hand sorting the material to extract all potential prey (kept in a Biofix solution). Great care should be taken to sample prey where birds actually feed, and allowances should be made for the chances of observed birds taking some broken pieces of worms (which, length-for-length, are thicker and therefore more energy-rich, see Thompson 1983a; Barnard & Thompson 1985). Faeces should be collected to confirm the composition of diet, though there will be taxonomic biases (Chapter 12).

Technology is a great help to studies in the non-breeding season. We have used the following gadgets: tripod-mounted image-intensifier to provide virtual daylight conditions for night-time observations of birds; wide-angle lens telescopes to greatly ease close, 'focal' observations of individuals; and an optical range finder for giving distances between the observer and the study bird (and some models will also give azimuth and elevation angles to birds in flight) which is invaluable for precise mapping and sampling of where birds have been feeding or have taken off. Recently, Oscar Johnson and colleagues have used radio-tagging to track Pacific Golden Plovers from Hawaii to their Alaskan breeding grounds.

Whenever studying birds in the wild, one has to think of their anti-predator behaviour. The Norwegian zoologist Robert Collett commented on the difficulties of getting within range of Eurasian Golden Plover flocks. The best way, he claimed, is to '. . . . walk as though you intend to pass by; then it is possible to get close enough to send a shotgun load with some effect into the flock' (Collett 1921). No wonder they are shy! At the other extreme, the virtual absence of shyness to hunters in American Golden Plovers (e.g. Plate 17) led to a drastic population decline in their numbers.

Population estimates and nest finding

Among the four species of tundra plover, the Eurasian Golden Plover is, in most respects, the trickiest to observe particularly on the breeding grounds. Its cryptic behaviour during the incubation phase makes nest finding, and even censusing of territorial pairs, very time consuming. Approached by a human, an incubating bird tends to leave the nest stealthily at long distance and stay out of sight. Alternatively,

PLATE 17.   *American Golden Plovers sometimes allow close approaches by humans near their nest. (IB)*

it may squat on the nest and let you pass by at just a few metres distance. Moreover, its mate may be far beyond the territory, feeding. Before laying, and especially after hatching, the pair is much more conspicuous. The best time for accurately censusing breeding pairs is just before laying. At this time the pairs are scattered on their territories. Yet, exoduses by pairs undertaking extra-territorial feeding may cause an under-estimation of numbers, so repeated censuses are advisable. We have found mapping of singing males, rather like the standard method used for censusing passerine territories (Enemar 1959) to be a useful census technique. Repeated mapping of the same area is ideal. Best results are obtained in the pre-laying period, yet after laying there are often song flight activities before morning and after evening changeovers at the nest (though poor weather can restrict success). After hatching, Eurasian Golden Plovers are noisy and conspicuous, and usually both parents are present near the brood. Pairs tend to meet a human intruder, and in dense golden plover populations this can give rise to an overestimation of numbers (Kålås & Byrkjedal 1984)

Finding nests of Eurasian Golden Plovers is frequently something of a challenge. The most successful technique for most shorebirds (e.g. Northern Lapwing, Eurasian Curlew, Eurasian Oystercatcher, Stone Curlew), watching birds back to the nest, works with this species only when watching from several hundred metres distance (Ratcliffe 1976). Often the conditions are difficult for distant watching, not least where there are convex slopes and 'dead' ground. Watching from a parked car can be successful, as the birds tend not to bother much about vehicles (e.g. R. Parr pers. comm.). However, most places that have breeding golden plovers are not approachable by vehicle. We have found that where the terrain allows, co-operation between two persons can be quite successful – one flushing the bird while walking, with the other one watching at a distance from a concealed vantage point. Radio communication between the observers is very helpful, and the watcher needs a good telescope, not least if the walker directs the watcher's attention to golden plovers appearing on his/her way. Golden plovers that have risen from a nest often return quickly to sit if the walker keeps strolling away from the plover. So, having seen a flushed golden plover re-settle on a nest, the watcher can then direct the walker up to the nest while constantly keeping the telescope bearing on the nest site.

A lone observer, however, can spend much time watching off-duty birds, which may stay away from the nest for many hours while their mates are sitting! Many plover watchers have pitiful tales to relate – the wrong end of a line, including hours spent watching a bird which seemed just about ready to return to its nest! Watching from a vantage point at the time of morning and evening changeovers of incubation duties can sometimes be successful. Here, areas may be narrowed down to those where a closer look might be worthwhile.

Walking and scanning for birds flying off the nest at a distance may be a useful method. However, as Ratcliffe (1976) pointed out this is a '. . . special technique which has to be diligently cultivated; the impulse to look at the ground at one's feet has to be resisted, and the gaze concentrated as far ahead as possible, not in one place, but scanning continuously over a wide arc. . . . Ideally, one tries to pick up the first flick of movement as the bird raises its wings and exposes its light underparts. . . . A plover just off the nest has a distinctive flight, skimming low over the ground in an unhurried way as though trying to appear casual'. It should be added that once a bird is thus observed, the exact spot where it came from must be constantly kept in sight as one approaches – you can easily lose the spot merely by taking your eye off it to check on a footstep!

We strongly agree with Ratcliffe (1976) that cold searching for nests is usually a waste of time and effort. However, in dense populations with very regular spacing of nests Ratcliffe has had some success: once some nests have been found, other nests may become easier to locate as '. . . areas of "no man's land" become apparent'. In situations where the birds sit tightly, dragging a rope between two persons may put up golden plovers from the nest. But this is not an exercise to be recommended for people with a weak back, and on rough or rocky ground it can stretch a co-operative friendship to the limit!

With experience, one gets a certain feeling for what kind of ground will not have a golden plover's nest. For instance, as a rule, nests are not found in dense tall heather (>25 cm tall), or on ground that is soaked with water or flooded after heavy rain. In the early nesting season, those areas where there is remaining winter snow will not have nests.

During his field work IB has used 'pointing' dogs to find nests of Eurasian Golden Plover. This worked well with Brittany Spaniels, Pointers and Gordon Setters. An absolute prerequisite is, of course, a well trained dog (Plate 18). The best dogs are those not interested in foot scents of the birds but which instead search at moderate speeds, carrying their heads high. Having found a nest, the dog must remain staunchly 'on point', awaiting the approach of the human. For the bird's safety, the dog should be leashed before the bird is put off the nest.

Finding chicks is usually an even more difficult task than finding nests, although the parent birds are easily located and the presence of chicks is readily discerned from by the parents' behaviour. If you watch from a distance, and then rush forward when the chicks are being brooded, you may reach the brood in time. However, due to the long distances needed to watch the birds one often finds, upon reaching the brood site, that the chicks have dispersed from where they were brooded and are near-impossible to find. The chicks are not at all easily located by searching and listening for their contact calls. One has to be very careful because the chicks can be very well camouflaged against the ground/bog vegetation. Again, watching from a car may be a better solution, but this has its practical limitations. We should add here that for protected species any examination of nests or chicks for scientific or educational purposes requires a special licence in many countries, notably in the UK.

Tundra plovers are robust to nest inspections. We have no evidence of nest desertion as a result of our checking of nests. However, we suspect nest inspections can increase predation risk, as flying predators may watch birds being flushed from nests, and mammalian predators can follow human scent (also Parr 1993a,b; R. Parr pers. comm.). Nest inspections should, therefore, be kept to a minimum. No nest inspections should be made in the presence of potential predators. The relatively featureless ground on which tundra plovers breed usually makes it necessary to put up nest markers (e.g. sticks, stones) in order to re-find the nests. Such markers should be no more conspicuous or closer to nests than necessary, as predators such as corvids may associate conspicuous markers with food (Picozzi

PLATE 18.   *Trained pointing dogs can be a great help in finding nests of the elusive Eurasian Golden Plover. Absolute obedience is mandatory lest the dog becomes a nuisance! Having found a golden plover nest at Hardangervidda, Norway, this well trained Brittany Spaniel relaxes beside its 'quarry'. (IB)*

1975). A prismatic compass for precise bearings is a boon to re-finding nests on featureless ground.

The three other species of tundra plover are much more complying than Eurasian Golden Plovers. They are fairly easily censused throughout the whole breeding season. As with Eurasian Golden Plovers, extra-territorial feeding can take place during the incubation phase, but more frequently both birds are on territory at the same time – with the off-duty mate uttering warning calls. American and Pacific golden plovers leave the nest at much shorter distances than Eurasian Golden Plovers, usually behave conspicuously, and are fairly easily watched back to nest from a distance of around 100 m. At Churchill, Manitoba, IB sat in the open tundra and watched an American Golden Plover male back to its nest from about 60 m distance – when, simultaneously, another male appeared suddenly and settled on a nest only 5 m from him! Grey Plovers are less likely to settle at short distances, and usually leave their nests when the observer is 200–300 m away. However, they frequently meet the approaching observer noisily, and they return fairly quickly to the nest if the observer lies down to watch from a distance. The whitish dorsal pattern coloration of Grey Plovers make them very easy to see as they walk back to their nest, even at a long distance.

Trapping individuals

During our breeding season studies, we and others have made some use of individually marked birds. IB trapped a number of Eurasian Golden Plovers at Hardangervidda for colour- ringing and also a few for radio-tagging. He also colour-ringed some American Golden Plovers at Churchill, Manitoba. The colour rings have primarily been used to keep a track of individual birds feeding outside territories, and when recording time activity budgets. Mark Whittingham (1996a,b) and Mark O'Connell *et al.* (1996) have had particular success in radio-tracking adult as well as chick Eurasian Golden Plovers.

Trapping tundra plovers can be a straightforward business, yet trappability differs between species as well as individuals. Again, it is the Eurasian Golden Plover that causes the problems. A number of traps have been tested, most of them with moderate success. Mistnets are usually a waste of time! Used on territories in the pre-laying period, mistnets in combination with a decoy male golden plover (model or stuffed bird) may be successful. But trapping females just before or during laying must be avoided, as trapping and handling the birds may cause injuries to oviductal eggs and ultimately to the birds themselves.

Trapping on the nest is best, and walk-in traps and hoop traps are most often employed (e.g. Parr 1979, 1980, 1993a,b). A walk-in trap is, in principle, a meshed wire cage placed over the nest, with an entrance for the bird. A wide opening makes the birds hesitate less before entering the trap. A closing mechanism is necessary. We prefer a trap with a sliding door kept open by a clip tied to a string pulled through the trap mesh and stretched taut over the eggs. As the bird settles, the clip is pulled out and the door quickly slides down to close the trap.

Hoop traps consist of two metal hoops covered with a fairly baggy piece of net and joined by a springy joint. The hoops are folded over each other to form a crescent around the nest. A string releaser is pulled over the nest, so that the hoop snaps over the bird as it settles on the nest. The bird must be taken out of the trap immediately. This is mandatory for hoop traps, in which a struggling bird can damage itself and eggs. In cage traps, caught birds often continue to sit after the door has closed, as if nothing has happened. In our experience, American Golden Plovers are fairly readily caught on the nest, whereas Eurasian Golden Plovers may be much more difficult. With the Eurasian Golden Plover, once the trap is set the trapper has to depart from the nest site or else the birds will not even come near the nest. An eye must be kept on the trap but only from a very long distance, or from a blind (or a parked car). Annoyingly, the cage's door releaser may malfunction and the trapper has to reset the mechanism. After a few such malfunctions, the birds get shy and it is best to wait a couple of days before making another attempt. However, the releaser mechanism may be improved, e.g. by letting the string run to a mouse trap, placed on top of the cage, so that it triggers the door releaser! Even a light pull on the string releases this setup (but blue thumbnails are an almost unavoidable by-product of this method!). IB has used a manual release mechanism which involves tying the releaser string to a 'servo' radio control of the type used on model aircraft, and fixing the servo to the ground a couple of metres from the trap. The trigger string must run through a narrow tube on the ground, to prevent the bird from inadvertently releasing the trap by stepping on the string. This method seldom malfunctions, and the trap can be released from a distance of many hundred metres (often a necessity for Eurasian Golden Plovers).

Like many birds, Eurasian Golden Plovers (and probably also the other species of tundra plovers) may desert after being trapped on the nest. However, desertion is less likely to happen the closer to hatching the bird is trapped. Trapping on the nest can be considered safe in the last one and a half weeks before hatching.

Tundra plovers do not show any discomfort from wearing colour rings. Eurasian Golden Plovers also accepted radio transmitters without showing any observed changes in behaviour. The transmitters we used (TX142-1S, Televilt) were about 20 mm × 8 mm × 5 mm in size, weighted about 3–4 g and were equipped with a 15 cm long antenna. These were fixed to the mantle feathers with an adhesive, with the antenna lying mid-dorsally, pointing backwards (Plate 19). These transmitters came off with the moult, before the birds left the breeding grounds. O'Connell *et al.* (1996) used a Biotrack SS-2 radio-tag (4 g) glued to dorsal feathers. A TRX 1000s receiver supplied by Wildlife Materials Inc. was used in conjunction with a three-element yagi antenna to locate radio-tagged birds. Positions of birds were then plotted on 1:10 000 maps.

PLATE 19.   *Radio tagged Eurasian Golden Plover at Hardangervidda, Norway.*
(IB)

SUMMARY

1. The book is concerned with the Grey Plover and the Eurasian, Pacific and American golden plovers. It provides much new and previously unpublished information.

2. Our study areas, and those of other researchers, are described. We give detailed descriptions of work on moorland (including dwarf shrub heaths and blanket bogs) and arctic-alpine heaths of Britain and Norway, northern open Boreal forests, and Eurasian and American tundra, as well as the principal studies on the non-breeding grounds.

3. There is a noticeable gap in comprehensive information on over-wintering American Golden Plovers, and on Eurasian Golden Plovers outside the British Isles.

4. Background information is given on study techniques and methods employed by us and others.

CHAPTER 2

Tundra Plovers and their Allies

Northern Lapwing, Grey Plover and Common Ringed Plover

Although the family is commonly divided into two subfamilies, the lapwings (Vanellinae) and the true plovers (Charadriinae), the grey and golden plovers of the genus *Pluvialis* may be an outgroup of the other two, having derived from a common ancestor early on. Perhaps *Pluvialis* should not be included in the subfamily Charadriinae, but rather have a subfamily of its own.

Theunis Piersma, Popko Wiersma and Jan van Gils (1997)

THIS chapter provides a background account on the plovers as a whole in order to give a context to the biology, ecology and behaviour of the genus *Pluvialis*. In Chapter 3 we go on to detail the taxonomy of the tundra plovers. According to the classification of Wetmore (1960), largely adopted in check-lists and handbooks over recent decades, plovers are assigned to the order **Charadriiformes**. This is a large assemblage of non-passerines, comprising waders, gulls, terns, skuas and auks. Representing a wide range of adaptations, the order is not the easiest to define morphologically. However, a fairly consistent evolutionary history (phylogeny) has been confirmed by the DNA-hybridization technique (Sibley & Ahlquist 1990).

The suborder **Charadrii** (waders or shorebirds) contains the plovers, currently classified as follows:

Family: Charadriidae (67 species) – plovers
  Sub-family: Vanellinae (25 species) – lapwings
          Vanellus (24 species)
          Erythrogonys (1 species, Red-kneed Dotterel)
      Charadriinae (41 species) – 'true' plovers
          Pluvialis (4 species) – 'tundra plovers'
          Charadrius (32 species) – 'sand plovers', 'dotterels' in Australia
          Elseyornis (1 species, Black-fronted Dotterel)
          Peltohyas (1 species, Inland Dotterel)
          Anarhynchus (1 species, Wrybill)
          Phegornis (1 species, Diademed Plover)
          Oreopholus (1 species, Tawny-throated Dotterel)
      Pluvianellinae (1 species) – Magellanic Plover *Pluvianellus*

According to Sibley & Ahlquist (1990), plovers are phylogenetically closer to gulls, terns and auks (family: Laridae) than to snipes, woodcocks, sandpipers and curlews (family: Scolopacidae).

Collectively, the plovers are small to medium-sized birds, compactly built (15–40 cm long), with short bills, large eyes, thick necks and short–medium length legs. They tend to run in bursts, pausing to scan, and sometimes crouch before pecking. In flight plovers are fast, capable of exceptional speeds and distances. Yet the closer we look at the features of these birds – such as their morphology, behaviour, ecology and migration – the more complex is this remarkable family.

DISTRIBUTION AND HABITATS

The bulk of the species of **Charadriidae** are found in the tropical and subtropical regions. This is especially the case with lapwings, while true plovers show more of a tendency to extend into the temperate zone and even into northern mountain and arctic areas. Tundra plovers, as the name implies, are among the northernmost of the plovers, yet spend the non-breeding season in the temperate zone through to the tropics.

While breeding, plovers inhabit open expanses with short vegetation, such as grasslands, heaths, and arid flats with little vegetation, even though some of the lapwings nest in wetland habitats. Nearly all plover species are territorial during the breeding season. Most of the tropical and subtropical species of lapwings and true plovers are resident, whereas those breeding outside these regions make seasonal movements, and these movements are usually accompanied by a change from inland to coastal or freshwater habitats, such as mudflats and beaches.

Tundra plovers are among the plovers that undertake the longest migration movements, and one of them, the Grey Plover, moves almost entirely from inland tundra to coastline habitats, while the three species of golden plover do so to varying extents. As an aid to their long migration flights, true plovers, including the tundra plovers, have pointed wings which are suited for swift journeys. The resident tropical plovers have much less pointed wings, and most of the lapwings have fairly rounded wing-tips, a wing shape apparently more adapted to aerial manoeuvrability than to long-distance migration. Incidentally, it was a shooting party's argument about which was faster, a Eurasian Golden Plover or a Red Grouse, that led to the production of the *Guinness Book of Records* – one of the world's best selling books!

BEHAVIOUR

As Piersma *et al.* (1997) point out, we still know little about most of the lapwings; among the true plovers over half of the species are marginally or poorly understood. Yet, the plover family has been found to display a bewildering range of sex roles and mating systems. Although social monogamy and biparental care of offspring seems to be most common in plovers, as in birds in general, uniparental care as well as polygyny, polyandry, and double-clutching are all systems represented in the plover family.

When studied more thoroughly, a number of allegedly monogamous species are likely to turn out to be polygynous on a regular basis. Tundra plovers though are clearly monogamous, and as long as males and females share incubation equally and, as they do, in extremely long stints, it is highly unlikely that polygyny will be a successful option for these species.

The tundra plovers are territorial, as are the majority of lapwings and other 'true' plovers (with the exception of the Eurasian Dotterel). However, assumptions tend to be made about territorial habits, and some plover species may well be found to have more complex social systems (e.g. Brown-chested and White-tailed Lapwings and Red-kneed Dotterel are semi-colonial).

PLUMAGE AND APPEARANCE

The tundra plovers range in total length from about 23 to 30 cm and are thus more similar in size to the lapwings (*Vanellus*: 21–38 cm; but Red-kneed Dotterel: 17.5–19.5 cm) than to the rest of the true plovers, most of which are less than 20 cm (range 14–28 cm). Within the Charadriidae as a whole, sexual size dimorphism (i.e. the difference between male and female) is typically slight, although more prominent in the lapwings than in true plovers (male larger then female in 13 species of lapwing; in true plovers female is the larger in two species and male is larger in one). On the other hand, plumage dimorphism is more pronounced in true plovers than in lapwings. Males are brighter than females in 30 species, and the female is brighter than the male in only one species of the true plovers; while in lapwings clear plumage dimorphism is found in only two species (males being the brighter). Tundra plovers conform with the majority of the true plovers concerning sexual dimorphism.

Plumage patterns

Both lapwings and true plovers show bold plumage patterns, but these are more pronounced in lapwings. In lapwings, common characteristics include wings with black primaries contrasting with conspicuous white areas on the upperside and/or the underside of the wings, and white tail coverts. All species except one have head markings, and only two have no distinct breast markings. In lapwings the patterns are variable between species, while in the true plovers many species show variation over similar breast and facial patterns, such as transverse black breast bands, a black 'eye-patch', and white collar; some species have rufous chests and head markings. With their more or less black 'hourglass-shaped' ventral area, circumscribed to a varying degree by a white border, tundra plovers resemble the bold lapwing patterns rather than those of the majority of true plovers. This hourglass pattern is found in all four tundra plovers in breeding plumage, and testifies to their close relationship. The dorsal patterns are even more distinctive. Lapwings as well as true plovers, other than the tundra plovers, show near plain-coloured mantle, scapulars and wing coverts with narrow light fringes to the feathers at most. In the tundra plovers, however, dorsal feathers have prominent edge spots producing a highly spotted – almost chequered – pattern. A faint resemblance is found in the juvenile plumage of only four species of lapwing. Interestingly, the spangled pattern turns up to a varying extent in a number of species within the scolopacids, notably in the genera *Numenius, Limosa* and *Tringa*.

Although rich in contrasts, the plumage of plovers is not particularly rich in colours. Yet, sharp colours are displayed by the bare parts among a number of the lapwing species and some of the plovers. Legs, bill, irides and in some species bare skin around or in front of the eyes (wattles) may have a pure yellow or a pure red colour. Wattles are present in nine species of lapwing but in none of the plovers, yet nine species of true plovers possess bright yellow or red skin on the rim of their eyelids. In tundra plovers, legs, bills and eyes are dark without any conspicuous coloration. In lapwings, wattles vary in size between the species, and in five of the species they form lappets hanging down over the base of the bill. Three lapwing species have crests, which add to their striking appearance, and five species have well developed carpal spurs not found in other plovers.

Breeding compared with non-breeding seasons

Among most species of lapwings there are only minor changes in plumage patterns with season, yet the majority of true plovers change to a non-breeding plumage less marked than the breeding plumage (although essentially the same patterns are retained). The tundra plovers, unlike most other plovers, completely lose any sign of their bold frontal and ventral markings in favour of a pale greyish-whitish-yellowish coloration on these body parts during the non-breeding season. Interestingly, there seems to be a relationship between the degree of seasonal change of plumage patterns and migration tendency. In migratory lapwing species most have different breeding and non-breeding plumages; in sedentary species (with the possible exception of the Yellow-wattled Lapwing) there are no differences. In the *Charadrius* genus, all 15 migratory species have different breeding and non-breeding plumages; in the 17 sedentary species only seven have these differences.

LOCOMOTION

Many shorebirds feed among tall, wetland vegetation by wading. Typically, they walk by movement of both the tarsus and the tibia, while shifting the centre of gravity very little and giving the impression of deliberate strides (Klomp 1954). These shorebirds lift their legs high and fold their toes to reduce resistance in vegetation or water. This is aided by a long tibia and tarsus relative to the femur, and by a narrow pelvis. Plovers, as a whole, do not comply with this and instead move by running, using 'bursts' of rapid gaits, during which the body's centre of gravity is shifted forwards at each step. Their low foot trajectory and virtual absence of toe folding renders them poor movers in tall vegetation and in water. Instead, in plovers running puts much more of the leg movement on the femora, and indeed the plover's femur is proportionately longer than in most other shorebirds (Fig. 2.1). The tundra plovers have the longest femora relative to tarsus and tibia, and the Eurasian Golden Plover has the longest of all, presumably because it is the species most confined to non-aquatic habitats.

Plover chicks hatch at an advanced stage with respect to their leg development. Long-legged shorebirds, such as Black-tailed Godwit chicks, hatch with a tarsus length of only 41–46% of adults (godwit specimens at Museum of Zoology, University of Bergen). Tundra plover chicks have tarsi 18–30% shorter than those of adults. Shortly after hatching, plover broods often quit their relatively barren nesting sites to reach good feeding patches. The longer-legged chicks are probably more capable of following their parents' long journeys to the feeding grounds, and they may also be more efficient at catching prey *en route* and in habitats similar to those used by their parents. In Northern Lapwing, Galbraith (1988c) found a tendency for chicks with longer legs at hatching to survive better.

VISUAL HUNTING FOR ACTIVE PREY

Body movements

Unlike most other shorebirds, plovers feed in 'run-stop-peck' sequences. They stand for a moment watching for prey, make swift and forceful pecks at detected prey, then run a few steps, watch again, etc. (e.g. Burton 1974; Pienkowski 1981). Prey, such as quick-moving arthropods, are picked from the surface, while earthworms, bristle worms (polychaetes), and insect larvae, are extracted from the immediate sub-surface layer (Thompson 1983a). Plovers lack the sensory nerve-endings in the bill-tip found in many of the long-billed shorebirds, which detect sub-surface prey by touch (and perhaps taste) while their bill is inserted in the substrate. Instead, plovers' bills are equipped with a hard, horny tip which aids in grasping prey. Being short and straight, their bills can swiftly be brought to bear on the prey, important when prey such as moving insects or crustaceans are visible only briefly. A short bill closes with strong force, which is of considerable importance when extracting long invertebrates such as worms from their burrows. Interestingly, the golden plovers possess a relatively unspecialized jaw musculature, with fewer muscular reductions than in most shorebirds, adding to the force and range of movement of the jaw adductors involved in closing of the lower jaw (Burton 1974).

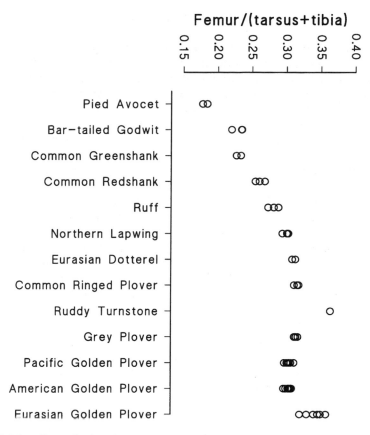

FIG 2.1. *Femur:leg length ratio in some shorebirds. The upper four species feed in taller marsh vegetation and in water, by a walking locomotion.*
Measurements were made from osteological material. Data on non-tundra plovers from Klomp (1954); tundra plovers from our own measurements. Each individual represented by ○.

Since plovers often swiftly change direction during feeding, sometimes even while running towards prey, their broad pelvis is probably of great importance in keeping them steady and in balance. A broad pelvis, with legs farther apart than in many other shorebirds, seems to facilitate rapid changes in direction according to where prey are located, enabling the bird to make quick sideways shifts to attack its prey (Klomp 1954). Tundra plovers share the rather plump appearance common to plovers as a whole and possess particularly well developed neck muscles. These seem to aid the bird in keeping its head erect during food searching, facilitating swift and powerful head and neck actions to capture and extract prey. Differences between the four species probably relate to their principal feeding habitats. The Eurasian

Golden Plover obtains most of its food from terrestrial habitats. It has the thickest neck, presumably to provide greater shock resistance against hard substrates, and to power the extraction of large earthworms from the ground. The other three are less stocky, and peck at surface items or feed more in softer mudflat and beach sediments, where prey are more easily extracted.

Although observations of captive Eurasian Golden Plovers suggest that they can detect moving earthworms by ear (Fallet 1962), tundra plovers usually hunt by sight (e.g. Thompson 1983a). Consequently, they possess large and well developed eyes. They are capable of feeding at night even outside their arctic and subarctic breeding grounds. Night-time feeding is carried out to a considerable extent, particularly during pre-migratory fattening periods in early spring (Burton 1974; Wood 1986; Zwarts *et al.* 1990b; Turpie & Hockey 1993).

The eyes

The visual cells in the retina show adaptations for high light sensitivity, as described for Grey Plover by Rojas de Azuaje *et al.* (1993). Compared with shorebirds that use tactile means to find their prey, Grey Plover retinae have a high rod:cone ratio. The 'rods' are the more light sensitive retinal visual receptors, found to be numerous in nocturnal vertebrates, whereas 'cones' are less light sensitive, but can discriminate colours. Rods with a particularly long outer segment are found in the eye of Grey Plovers, and are densely distributed in several areas of the retina, improving visual acuity in poor light (Rojas de Azuaje *et al.* 1993).

Adaptations to this visually based hunting technique in tundra plovers, as in other plovers, is evident from the embryonic stage. The detection of prey at a distance requires a well developed optic tectum of the brain, which is a more complex structure than the part of the brain controlling the motor responses of pecking and food begging behaviours (The Nucleus basalis, Nol 1986). The complex feeding technique of the plovers, first as chicks and later as adults, may require a better development of neurofunctions at hatching. From a comparative study, Nol (1986) concluded that the development of this particular part of the brain, after all the slowest growing organ in birds, may account for the long incubation time of plover eggs (when adjusted for egg mass) compared with other shorebirds.

ADAPTATIONS TO A SALTY ENVIRONMENT

Grey, and to a varying extent, golden plovers feed in coastal habitats outside the breeding season. Like other birds exposed to salty conditions, they possess supraorbital glands, which are extra-renal excretory organs used for achieving electrolyte homeostasis and water balance (e.g. Schmidt-Nielson *et al.* 1958; Holmes & Phillips 1985). These glands, which are flattened and crescentic, are situated in grooves on top of the skull, one on each side, above the eyes. They consist of a number of longitudinal lobes containing excretory tubules that drain into a central canal of each lobe, uniting into a duct. The duct from each of the two glands passes anteriorly into the beaks, and the fluid of salt excretion is discharged from the nasal cavity via the nostrils. Marine bird species possess large salt glands with many lobes (e.g. Staaland 1967 for shorebirds), yet birds confined to salt water habitats for only part of the year show atrophy of their salt glands during their non-marine period, suggesting an energetic cost in maintaining large, activated glands (Burger & Gochfeld 1984). However, each lobe remains intact throughout the year, and at least in shorebirds their number shows very little intra-specific variation (Staaland 1967).

Differences within tundra plovers

Within tundra plovers the number of longitudinal lobes differs, as does the size of the glands themselves. Examinations in a microscope of cross-sections of glands from Grey Plover (the most maritime of the four species) and Eurasian Golden Plover (the least maritime) shows six lobes in the former but only four in the latter (Fig. 2.2). Furthermore, Grey Plovers have relatively much larger glands than Eurasian Golden Plovers. In the Grey Plover, the skull depressions housing the glands meet centrally on the skull roof, and with the orbital rims only slightly ossified the gland ducts enter a wide groove behind the lacrymal bones, which jut

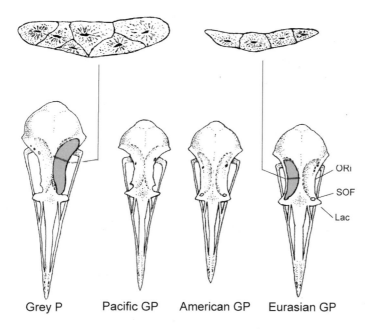

Grey P   Pacific GP   American GP   Eurasian GP

FIG. 2.2. *Skulls and salt glands of tundra plovers.*
One gland (shaded) is shown in position for Grey Plover and Eurasian Golden Plover. Enlarged cross sections show the longitudinal lobes, each with a central canal surrounded by excretory tubules in a radiation pattern. The skulls of Grey Plover, American and Eurasian golden plovers were drawn from specimens labelled as adults, whereas the Pacific Golden Plover specimens examined were judged to be adult from skull roof ossification. Juvenile golden plovers show orbital rim and lacrymal characteristics like those of adult (and juvenile) Grey Plover (Lowe 1922; Bock 1958). ORi = orbital rim, SOF = supraorbital foramen, Lac = lacrymal bone.

out and support a membrane which in turn supports part of the glands (see also Lowe 1922; Bock 1958). In the Eurasian Golden Plover, the gland grooves on the skull are separated centrally by a broader ridge 1.5–2 mm apart, the depressions are shallower, and the orbital rims are more fully ossified and merge with the lacrymal bones. Behind the latter, the ducts of the nasal glands enter a smaller foramen.

These contrasts reflect the differences in salt load the two species endure during their non-breeding season, with the largely terrestrial Eurasian Golden Plover having relatively smaller glands, fewer ducts, and less space for gland hypertrophy (Fig. 2.2). We have not studied glands of American and Pacific golden plovers under a microscope, but we have examined a number of skulls of these species. In agreement with Bock (1958), the skull of the American Golden Plover was found to possess essentially the same features as those of the Eurasian Golden Plover, but interestingly the Pacific Golden Plover has a skull more similar to that of the Grey Plover. This suggests that the Pacific Golden Plover is primarily a species adapted to a marine non-breeding environment. Its widespread use of terrestrial habitats during the winter, in parts of its range, may well be of more recent origin.

TUNDRA PLOVERS AS A SEPARATE GENUS

It is quite clear from comparisons with other plovers that the tundra plovers constitute a well defined, monophyletic group within the subfamily Charadriinae, justifying a separate genus, *Pluvialis*. Its members share a number of characters that separate them from other plover genera. One such trait is the spangled dorsal pattern in all plumages of tundra plovers. Barred tail feathers, pronounced golden yellow plumage colour (although in Grey Plover only displayed in fresh juvenile plumage), and the special ventral patterns formed by black and white are also typical for tundra plovers.

Downy chicks have a black spotted pattern resembling that of many other plovers, but the clear yellow ground colour of the dorsal side is unique to tundra plover chicks. These characteristics exclude the Red-breasted Plover, a species included in *Pluvialis* by Bock (1958) and Jehl (1968), but later shifted to the genus *Charadrius* on the basis of the behaviour and plumage of its downy chicks (Phillips 1980).

It is arguable that the genus *Pluvialis* should have a subfamily of its own (Piersma *et al.* 1996, 1997), not least because only this genus seems to have its origins in the northern hemisphere (Chapter 5). After all, Sibley & Ahlquist, and others (see Piersma *et al.* 1996), have found that the tundra plovers may be an 'outgroup' of the lapwings and the true plovers, having evolved from a common ancestor early on. If the plovers have originated in the southern hemisphere, at low altitude (where most species are found today), the northern distribution and arctic origins of the tundra plovers adds weight to their status as a subfamily rather than just a genus of the so-called 'true' plovers. These true plovers hold several species groups, and in many ways the loose grouping of these together is unsatisfactory. A phylogenetic analysis of this subfamily is needed using a methodology which would show much more clearly the genealogical relationships between genera and species. We shall return to this issue so far as tundra plovers are concerned in Chapter 5.

SUMMARY

1. The plover family, Charadriidae, has three subfamilies (lapwings, 'true' plovers and Magellanic Plover) with 67 species. Tundra plovers, *Pluvialis*, form one of 10 genera of the family.

2. Particular contrasts are drawn between the genera *Vanellus, Charadrius* and *Pluvialis*. The first exhibit sexual dimorphism in size, the other two in plumage patterns. Migratory species tend to have differing breeding and non-breeding plumages, whereas sedentary species tend not to.

3. Particular morphological features of the tundra plovers are highlighted, notably in relation to their style of movement while foraging. A high femur:tibia length ratio and a broad pelvis aid in swift attacks on agile ground-living prey. Eyes are well developed to detect prey even at night. The skull shows modifications to accommodate larger supraorbital glands in the more marine species.

4. Special features of tundra plovers include a dorsal spangled pattern, golden-yellow colours at least in the juvenile plumage, a barred tail, the yellow down colour of chicks, and a black and white frontal-ventral pattern in breeding plumage.

5. Given the northern origins of the tundra plovers they should perhaps be given subfamily status. A phylogenetic analysis of the 'true' plovers would be valuable.

CHAPTER 3

Taxonomy and Geographical Variation

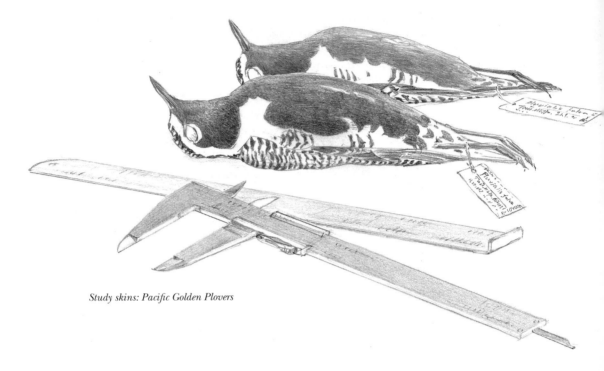

Study skins: Pacific Golden Plovers

Conversely, the absence of prominent morphological differences between sympatric forms assortatively mating is no reason to merge them, when the two forms themselves show such a reluctance to merge. We must not confuse our own ability to distinguish forms with the ability of the birds themselves.

Peter G. Connors (1983), writing on the taxonomy, distribution and evolution of Pacific and American golden plovers.

THE taxonomy and species composition of the genus *Pluvialis* has been hotly debated through the 20th century. We intend that this and the next two chapters should clarify the position of the genus so far as taxonomic, plumage and phylogenetic issues are concerned. At the end of this chapter we dwell on the nature and extent of geographical variations in size.

The genus contains the following species and subspecies:

Pluvialis squatarola (Linné 1758), Grey Plover
P. apricaria (Linné 1758), Eurasian Golden Plover
    P. a. apricaria (Linné), Southern Eurasian Golden Plover
    P. a. altifrons (Brehm 1831), Northern Eurasian Golden Plover
P. fulva (Gmelin 1789), Pacific Golden Plover
P. dominica (P.L.S. Müller 1776), American Golden Plover

On the basis of the presence of its rudimentary hind toe (hallux) and some skull traits the Grey Plover was for a time confined to a monotypic genus *Squatarola* (Lowe 1922, 1933). A closer examination has shown most of these traits to be common to golden and Grey plovers (Bock 1958), however, and one genus is now considered sufficient.

COMMON NAMES

While *P. squatarola* has been referred to as the Grey Plover in Britain and the Black-bellied Plover in America, English names in more or less common usage for the three species of golden plovers have varied and occasionally confused ornithologists. Often, the commonly occurring species in a particular geographical area has been referred to in the literature only as the Golden Plover (Golden-Plover in the recent American literature). This is still common practice in Europe for *P. apricaria*, has occurred frequently in America for *P. dominica*, and is occasional in the Australasian literature for *P. fulva*. The greatest confusion has arisen in the literature over *dominica* and *fulva* during the time they were considered subspecies of *P. dominica*, when either could be referred to as 'Golden Plover' or 'Lesser Golden Plover'. In those cases where a scientific trinomen was not given the identity of the golden plover in question is not always obvious.

Sometimes *P. dominica* has been referred to as the 'American Lesser Golden Plover', 'Common American Golden Plover', and even 'Atlantic American Golden Plover'. A large number of names have been used for *P. fulva*, such as 'Pacific Lesser Golden Plover', 'Pacific Golden Plover', 'Pacific Plover', 'Siberian (Lesser) Golden Plover', 'Least Golden Plover', 'Eastern Golden Plover', and 'Western American Golden Plover'!

The common names used by us are the ones suggested by Connors (1983) and Hayman *et al.* (1986), and which seem to have gained a foothold in the more recent literature. Despite some confusion, we have by and large been able to sort out which species are dealt with in the literature. Only occasionally have we been in doubt as to whether *P. dominica* or *P. fulva* is the species concerned, in which case we refer to the 'Lesser Golden Plover', a collective name for these two closely related species.

GREY PLOVER: TAXONOMY THROUGH TIME

Affinities with golden plovers

The Grey Plover was described under the name of *Tringa Squatarola* (sic) by Linné in his 10th edition of *Systema Naturae* (1758), based on the juvenile or non-breeding plumage. In the 12th edition of his tome, Linné described the breeding plumage of the Grey Plover as a different species under the name *T. Helveticus*. A number of synonyms from subsequent descriptions, by other authors, appear in more or less regular use in the older literature (we have counted at least 25 synonyms for Grey Plovers, eight for Eurasian, 11 for Pacific and eight for American golden plovers). The assignment of the species to a separate (monotypic) genus, *Squatarola*, by Cuvier in his *Règne Animale* (1817) gained fairly wide acceptance until just a few decades ago. The main reason for erecting that genus was, as already mentioned, the presence of a minute hind toe in the Grey Plover – meagre foundation indeed for an avian genus! Lowe (1922) presented eight skull characters which he considered to support the maintenance of *Squatarola* as a separate genus. However, from examination of a number of specimens, Bock (1958) found two of the characters to be linked to the development of the supraorbital glands related to feeding in salt water, and the other characters did not differ consistently from those of *Pluvialis*. Bock concluded that there were no reasons to maintain the genus *Squatarola*. As we shall see in the next chapter, plumage patterns of full-grown birds as well as the coloration of the downy chicks further support the inclusion of the Grey Plover in the genus *Pluvialis*.

Subspecies are abandoned

The subspecies concept is a difficult one! According to Mayr (1969) a subspecies is 'an aggregate of phenotypically similar populations of a species, inhabiting a geographic subdivision of the range of a species, and differing taxonomically from other such populations of the species.' We have two major problems with the application of the subspecies category. First, the degree of distinction required for subspecific recognition can be arbitrary. Second, there can be a tendency for different characters to show independent geographical trends. Both problems apply to Grey Plovers (Fig. 3.1).

Based on geographical variation in size, three subspecies (ssp.) of Grey Plover figured in the literature for some time: (a) the nominate form of western and central Palearctic, ssp. *squatarola*; (b) the eastern Palearctic, ssp. *hypomela*; based on Pallas's description of the Grey Plover (from Krasnoyarsk); and (c) the ssp. *cynosurae* from North America. The ssp. *hypomela* was suggested by Mathews (1913) on the basis of the larger size of eastern Palearctic birds and also from a supposedly paler winter plumage, whilst ssp. *cynosurae*, described by Thayer & Bangs (1914), was based on the smaller size of American birds. However, following a detailed examination of museum skins, Low (1938) dismissed both of these subspecies because measurements from various populations seemed to overlap, and he was unable to detect differences in winter plumage colours between eastern and western Palearctic birds. Our own measurement indicate that wing lengths of birds from northeastern Canada are on the small side, and those from northeast Asia (especially from Wrangel Island) are the largest (Fig. 3.1), forming a continuum of sizes. Furthermore, Portenko (1972) urged ornithologists not even to maintain a subspecific distinction for the Wrangel Island population – despite these birds having shorter bills and tarsi, as well as longer wings, compared with those from adjacent mainland populations.

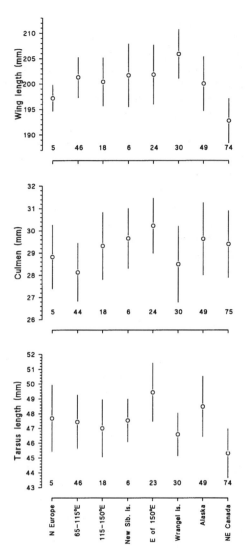

FIG. 3.1. *Geographical variation in body size of Grey Plovers, based on measurements of museum specimens.*

In recognizing subspecies the *degree* of difference between populations involved is crucial. A simple statistical procedure can help us estimate the degree of difference. We can calculate the coefficient of differences (CD) between populations, with differences between population means of, for example, body size measurements divided by their summed standard deviations giving the CDs. No statistical method, however, can tell us how much overlap is 'permissible' between two subspecies. A subspecies is often accepted where geographically adjacent populations have less than 90% 'joint non-overlap', i.e. 90% of population *A* differs from 90% of population *B* (Mayr 1969, pp 188–193). The corresponding CD value (derived from Mayr's tables) of ≥ 1.28 for a subspecies is not approached by Grey Plover biometrics available to us when adjacent geographical areas (Fig. 3.1) are compared, thus supporting the conclusions of Low (1938) and Portenko (1972) that no subspecific recognition is warranted in this species.

The subspecies concept may seem convenient for labelling populations which are not just a part of smooth clinal variation. Nevertheless, we are not enthusiastic about the subspecies concept as a whole. By assigning a taxonomic rank to populatons showing non-clinal variation in a set of characters, such populations tend to be regarded as 'definitive' units. One may then obscure, rather than clarify, interesting and important geographical variations in other morphological or behavioural features of the birds.

SUBSPECIES OF THE EURASIAN GOLDEN PLOVER: ARE THESE VALID?

History

In his 10th edition of *Systema Naturae* (1758) Linné described the Eurasian Golden Plover both as *Charadrius apricarius* and *Charadrius Pluvialis*, referring to birds in breeding plumage and juvenile plumage, respectively, which he thought represented different species. This was an error commonly made by the early taxonomists, at a time when moult and plumage changes were poorly understood. In his short species diagnosis, Linné (1758) referred to his work *Fauna Svecica*, which in turn referred to paintings meticulously made from fresh specimens by Linné's mentor Olof Rudbeck Jr. These paintings (Plates 20(a) and (b)) may serve, for practical purposes, as type specimens for the Eurasian Golden Plover. As the breeding plumage bird was described before the juvenile, the former gains status as the accepted species description, according to 'page priority' (*International Code of Zoological Nomenclature*, Article 24.A).

The English translation of the Latin word *apricarius* is 'living in sunny places' and of *pluvialis* is 'rain-maker'. The latter, referring to the juvenile plumage, was probably known to Linné chiefly from the wetter, autumn migration period. According to Linné's lecture notes the Eurasian Golden Plover was thought to congregate in flocks at the onset of rain (Löwendahl 1986). The name *pluvialis* was not, as commonly believed, a reference to the foot paddling or trembling also seen in the Northern Lapwing just before rainfall! In 1760, Brisson introduced the genus *Pluvialis* for golden plovers. The scientific name *Pluvialis* has no gender and can be considered masculine or feminine. Species names under this genus have varyingly been placed in masculine (ending in *-us*) and feminine (ending in *-a*) forms. However, as Brisson regarded generic *Pluvialis* as feminine, it is more correct to put the species name in the feminine gender, i.e. *apricaria* instead of *apricarius* (BOU 1933). This applies also to the other members of the genus.

During the early 20th century, ornithologists began to notice that golden plovers breeding in Britain were less distinctly coloured (notably paler) than those on the northern Scandinavian breeding grounds. Mrs A. C. Meinertzhagen (1921) gave

PLATE 20(a).   *Olof Rudbeck's plates referred to by Linné in his description of Eurasian Golden Plover. Breeding plumage shown above, juvenile plumage shown overleaf in Plate 20b. These were described by Linné as separate species (*Charadrius apricarius *and* Charadrius pluvialis*). Courtesy of Uppsala University Library, Uppsala, Sweden.*

the British population subspecific rank, under the name *Pluvialis apricarius oreophilus*. Subsequently, birds of similar appearance were found to inhabit the areas around the North Sea and Southern Baltic (e.g. Lönnberg 1923, 1924; Steiniger 1959; Lepiksaar & Zastrov 1963; Fabricius & Hald-Mortensen 1969). Birds from Iceland, most of Fennoscandia and northern Russia were, on the other hand, considered to be the nominate subspecies (i.e. *P. a. apricaria*), referring to Linné's description of the species. However, giving the Baltic island of Öland as type locality, Linné's description was considered by the BOU (1924, 1932) to pertain to the southern subspecies, even though Rudbeck's plates, referred to by Linné, were obviously based on birds from Lapland, an area inhabited by the 'northern'

PLATE 20(b).   *The juvenile plumage of Eurasian Golden Plover referred to in caption to Plate 20a. Courtesy of Uppsala University Library, Uppsala, Sweden.*

subspecies (Lönnberg 1923; Meinertzhagen 1950)! Hence, *apricaria* was adopted as the subspecific name for the 'southern' subspecies, and *altifrons* (Brehm 1831) for the 'northern' subspecies.

But zoologists and naturalists, principally in Britain, were not content with this. It was soon evident that the variation within populations of the 'southern' subspecies was substantial, and that an increasing amount of *altifrons*-like birds occurred in the north of the British Isles (e.g. Tucker 1949; Smith 1957; Nethersole-Thompson 1957). To add to this confusion, the type locality for Mrs Meinertzhagen's description was Orkney in northern Scotland, where both *apicaria*- and *altifrons*-like birds are found. Moreover, a number of *apricaria*-like birds seemed to breed even farther north, on the Faroes (Williamson 1948; Vaurie 1964), Brehm's type locality for *altifrons*. In 1957 the late Professor V. C. Wynne-Edwards published a classic short paper challenging the subspecies recognition of the Eurasian Golden Plover. He suggested that the variation was of intra-population origin – a form of polymorphism.

The alternative hypothesis held the plumage variation to be a result of geographical isolation, which was insufficient to give rise to separate species. The

PLATE 21. *Eurasian Golden Plover male showing pale ('southern') breeding plumage. Britain. (R.H. Fisher)*

isolation was thought to have occurred during the last glaciation (Lönnberg 1924; Larsson 1957) on two tundra refugia, one in France (giving rise to the southern subspecies), and the other in northern Russia (giving rise to the northern subspecies) (Hale 1980). According to Hale's hypothesis, variation in some populations and a mooted tendency for a north–south cline in Britain are results of secondary contact and hybridization between the two forms (Fabricius & Hald-Mortensen 1969; Byrkjedal 1978b; Hale 1980).

Our view

Plumage variation in Eurasian Golden Plovers breeding in parts of Norway, especially in the highly variable South Norwegian populations, have been

PLATE 22.   *Eurasian Golden Plover female in pale ('southern') breeding plumage. Britain. (Dennis Green)*

PLATE 23.   *Eurasian Golden Plover male in dark ('northern') breeding plumage. Smøla, Norway. (Jan Rabben)*

quantitatively recorded using a system which scores gradual steps – from winter plumage-like birds to maximum plumage contrast (Byrkjedal 1978b). A re-analysis of the S. Norway material (with subsequent enlargements) has shown two patterns. First, there is an abrupt change from pale *apricaria*-like plumages on the southwestern coast to darker *altifrons*-like plumages in neighbouring populations, both to the north along the coast and in the interior south Norwegian mountains – a change over only 200 km (Fig. 3.2, Appendix 2). Second, the CD for plumage gradings (*sensu* Mayr 1969) between southwestern (Jæren and Karmøy) and other populations, of 1.22 for males and 1.51 for females, represents 89% and 93% joint non-overlap, respectively. The lack of gradual clinal variation and the low morphological overlap in the Norwegian material suggests that the two forms are geographically and morphologically sufficiently well defined to be regarded as valid subspecies (if we recall that 90% is the CD threshold, Mayr 1969) – but only just.

In Britain, however, the gradual cline said to exist from diffusely coloured birds in the south to more distinctly coloured in the north, would call for a different conclusion. Furthermore, in areas such as the Cairngorms and Sutherland, Scotland, birds nesting at lower altitude seem to be paler than those at high altitudes (where they breed later), and towards the south of Britain these altitudinal differences in plumage may be even greater, for instance in the North Pennines. In other words, an altitudinal as well as a latitudinal cline in plumage distinctness may exist in Britain. On the East Baltic breeding grounds and in southern Sweden there may also be

PLATE 24. *Eurasian Golden Plover female in dark ('northern') breeding plumage. Smøla, Norway. (Jan Rabben)*

smooth clinal variation in plumage distinctness, with gradually darker birds towards the north (Lepiksaar & Zastrov 1963; Karvik 1964; Ahlén & Tjernberg 1992).

The plumage variation in Norway could be due to abrupt changes in environmental factors over short distances. Clearly, we need more data on Eurasian Golden Plover plumage variation in relation to both latitude and altitude. Such information is needed from all parts of its breeding range. Some workers have begun to look at this (D.P. Whitfield, C.J. Thomas, D.W. Yalden, G.W. Pearce-Higgins and A. Mee pers. comm.).

The validity of ssp. *apricaria* and *altifrons* remains to be resolved. However, we agree with the recent literature (e.g. Glutz von Blotzheim *et al.* 1975; Cramp & Simmons 1983) that workers should refrain from the trinominal designation of the Eurasian Golden Plover.

Variation in the body size measurements of the Eurasian Golden Plover (Fig. 3.3) seems to follow a cline from the south and west (long wings, small bills and tarsi) towards the north and east (short wings, long bills and tarsi). Measurements of Icelandic and Faroese birds ('*altifrons*') are more similar to those of Britain, southwestern Norway and southern Sweden ('*apricaria*', or '*apricaria*'/'*altifrons*'), rather than to the birds from northern Scandinavia and Russia. Furthermore, the clinal variation in size continues within the '*altifrons*' areas of Fennoscandia and Russia.

It is notable, therefore, that size variations do *not* follow the pattern of plumage variation on which the subspecies were based. This may, in time, prove crucial in strengthening the case that subspecies do not exist after all.

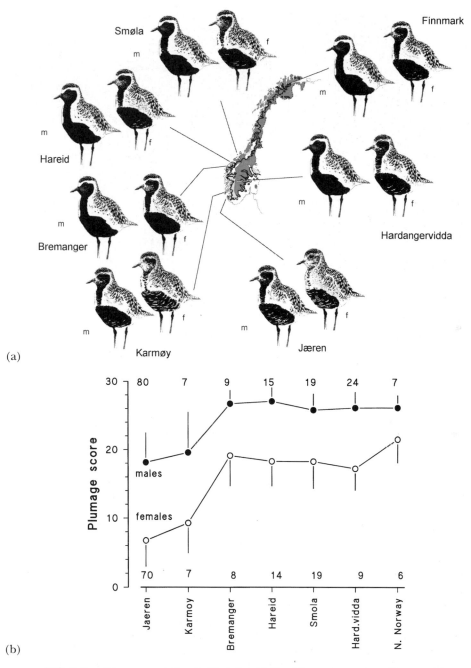

(a)

(b)

FIG. 3.2. *Plumage variation in Eurasian Golden Plovers in southern Norway. (a) shows average plumages for birds at each of seven locations (dark shading shows core breeding area; pale shading shows peripheral breeding areas; thick line shows the 1000 m contour); (b) gives means and standard deviations. For further details, see Appendix 2.*

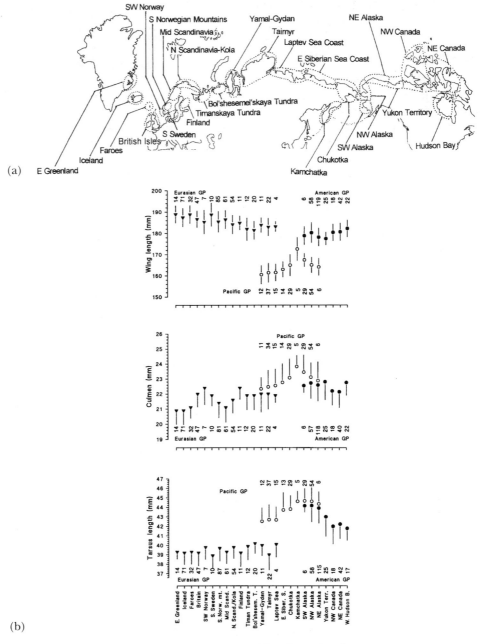

FIG. 3.3. *Geographical size variation in golden plovers, based on museum specimens. (a) indicates the areas from which the samples (shown in (b) were taken. Measurements of American and Pacific golden plovers from Alaska supplied by J. P. Connors; Eurasian Golden Plovers from Greenland, Iceland, Faroes, Britain, Finland, and partly north Norway-Kola, and northern Russia supplied by W. G. Hale; remainder measured by IB.*

Systematic Relationships between American and Pacific Golden Plovers

History

The imponderables described above are relatively minor compared with those associated with the systematic relationships between American and Pacific golden plovers! The original descriptions of both species were made on the basis of specimens taken outside the breeding ranges: the American Golden Plover in 1776 by P.L.S. Müller, from Santo Domingo, Hispaniola; and Pacific Golden Plover in 1788 by J.F. Gmelin, from Tahiti.

The discovery of the Pacific Golden Plover has a particularly distinguished history, dating from Captain James Cook's explorations of the Pacific, as outlined by Johnson (1993). Although the first specimens recorded were from Cook's first voyage, when four birds were shot on 8 October 1770 on an island off Java, it was not until Cook's second voyage that specimens of taxonomic significance were obtained, when a bird was taken in the afternoon of 26 August 1773. J.R. Forster, one of the naturalists on the expedition, rendered a description in his log. Later on, at other Pacific islands, more specimens were shot by the expedition. Forster made paintings of these specimens (see Johnson 1993), but the specimens themselves as well as the type specimen from Tahiti appear to have been subsequently lost.

While waiting for the publication of the biological results of Cook's expedition, which became much delayed, Forster appears in the meantime to have given J. Latham access to his notes and paintings, upon which Latham published a written description of the species in 1785 in his *General Synopsis of Birds*. However, being in English and not conforming to Linnean nomenclature, the description did not count as a valid scientific description of the species. It was J.F. Gmelin who, without even having seen an illustration, let alone a specimen, became the recognized authority of the species. He merely translated Latham's English name for the species, 'Fulvous Plover', for his 13th edition of *Systema naturae* (1788–89), into Latin to give the world *Charadrius fulvus*!

The general morphological similarities between American and Pacific golden plovers have led most authors, since the end of the 19th century, to consider them as one species. Two main factors account for this. First, the geographical variation in size indicates possible clinal variation from one form to the other across the Bering Strait (e.g. Seebohm 1888). Second, most of the earliest authors were familiar with the two forms only from museum specimens. But, as pointed out by Connors *et al.* (1993), Pacific and American golden plovers, even in their breeding plumages, look more different in the field than they do in museum trays.

Two species: a breakthrough for Peter Connors' group

Although Conover (1945) indicated that the two 'forms' appear to breed sympatrically in West Alaska, most authors seemed to have adhered to the view expressed by Bailey (1926), Gabrielson & Lincoln (1959) and Vaurie (1964) that they might interbreed in the area of overlap. The fact that the two forms meet in part of their breeding area is most fortunate, because the evidence for any lack of interbreeding in sympatry is the ultimate test of species status. Connors (1983) explored this possibility for American and Pacific golden plovers, using museum skins. Using Discriminant Function Analyses of measurements and scorings of plumage characters, Connors compared Siberian and Canadian-East Alaskan birds ('parent populations') with those from the overlap zone in West Alaska. In this material, parent population birds separated well, with only 4% overlap, and the method correctly identified 93% of the 369 specimens examined from west Alaska as either *P. dominica* or *P. fulva*. The observed frequencies of character overlap were actually very close to the expected no-hybridization frequencies, even when the analysis was performed separately for four different regions of western Alaska. This indicated such strong positive assortative mating patterns in these two forms that they should clearly be considered as separate species.

Connors' (1983) conclusions gained wide acceptance in the subsequent literature. However, the museum data he used could not definitely prove sympatric breeding. Vital data relating to mating behaviour, such as displays and vocalizations, as well as ecological aspects relevant for assortative mating, were not readily available. So, a follow-up field study was conducted by Connors and co-workers in western Alaska (Connors *et al.* 1993). From this important work it became evident that the two golden plover forms frequently bred on adjacent territories, yet preferred somewhat different habitats (American on drier tundra than Pacific golden plover). Their vocalizations, especially their flight songs, important in announcing un-mated status, were widely different. Furthermore, the field observations in areas of sympatry revealed no case of mixed pairs. Even preliminary molecular data supported the genetic distinctiveness of the two species. Thus, the conclusion about separate status was strongly supported. As Connors *et al.* (1993) stated rather bluntly: 'They have been considered subspecies only because their plumages are sufficiently similar that ornithologists had found them difficult to separate. It is now apparent that even this aspect of the two forms is more distinctive than previously appreciated'.

Nomenclature committees tend to show a certain (and often sound) conservatism. However, there are few other cases in ornithology where the species status of closely related forms has been so well documented as with American and Pacific golden plovers. Ironically, the major ornithological nomenclature authority (the AOU) in Connors' own home country seems to have been one of the last to adopt his well supported conclusions (AOU 1993). No matter, because some 220 years after J.R. Forster made his find, Peter G. Connors and colleagues proved conclusively what has long been evident to the birds themselves – American and Pacific golden plovers are two species, not one!

GEOGRAPHICAL VARIATION IN SIZE

Tundra plovers exhibit geographical variation in size, evident from the series of museum specimens examined by us. Measurements of 948 golden plover skins from the breeding season have been available to us. For Grey Plover our presentation rests entirely on material from 252 birds (averages, standard deviations and sample sizes from various populations; kindly supplied by Dr

Meinte Engelmoer, who had measured a large portion of the Grey Plover skins present in various museums around the world). For American and Pacific golden plovers, Dr Peter Connors sent us his measurements of Alaskan specimens, while Professor Bill Hale supplied measurements of Canadian and northeast Alaskan specimens of American Golden Plover. Bill also provided us with measurements of Eurasian Golden Plovers from Greenland, Iceland, Britain, Faroes, and northern Russia. Other specimens were measured by IB. Although the measurements were taken in the same manner, slight individual differences could introduce a bias that could influence the pattern of geographical variation. To reduce this problem we examined measurements of specimens by Connors, Hale and IB, and then adjusted measurements to make them comparable (Hale's adjusted by −1.2% in Wing, −4.2% in Bill, −4.1% in Tarsus). A grand total of exactly 1200 tundra plover skins forms the basis of our present study of geographical size variation.

Finding sexes to differ very little in size (Table 1), we pooled data for males and females. Geographical variation in wing length, bill length and tarsus length, the most commonly used bird body size measurements, are shown in Fig. 3.1 for Grey Plovers and in Fig. 3.3 for golden plovers. In the Pacific Golden Plover, and to some extent the Grey Plover, the variations in the three body dimensions show a similar geographical pattern, whereas in American and Eurasian golden plovers wing, bill, and tarsus vary differently.

In Grey Plovers, as well as Pacific Golden Plovers, body dimensions tend to increase towards the Bering Sea region from both east and west. Grey plovers at Wrangel Island are remarkably long-winged, short-billed, and short-legged, whereas in the Canadian Arctic they have particularly short wings. Pacific Golden Plovers breeding at Kamchatka seem to be at the larger extreme for the species (however, a larger sample size would have been desirable). American Golden Plovers decrease in wing length towards the Bering Sea but increase in tarsus length. Eurasian Golden Plovers decrease in wing length from the west towards Siberia, and they generally increase in bill length in that direction, although birds breeding in Britain, southern Scandinavia and Finland deviate by being particularly long-billed. In summary, most of the body size variation has a stronger east–west than north–south component.

SUMMARY

1. The tundra plovers comprise four species – Grey Plover (*Pluvialis squatarola*), Eurasian Golden Plover (*P. apricaria*), Pacific Golden Plover (*P. fulva*) and American Golden Plover (*P. dominica*).

2. The subspecies concept applied to tundra plovers is discussed. No subspecies of Grey Plover are nowadays accepted. Presently, there is little evidence for two subspecies of Eurasian Golden Plover. Nevertheless, there is marked plumage variability in the latter, which we illustrate.

3. The American and Pacific golden plovers are clearly two distinctive species, with sympatry but a lack of any inter-breeding and significant differences in plumage, vocalizations and behaviour.

4.   On their breeding grounds, Pacific Golden Plovers and Grey Plovers increase in size towards the Bering Strait. American Golden Plovers have shorter wings and longer legs towards the north and west, whereas Eurasian Golden Plovers have shorter wings and longer bills towards the north and east.

CHAPTER 4
Plumages and Moults

Shed feather of Eurasian
Golden Plover

But inevitably, a thing adapted perfectly to its surroundings – a snowflake or a sailing ship, a spoon – acquires a true beauty of refinement: the soft dove-brown of the buff-breasted sandpiper, the marsh gold of the golden plover, and the leaf tones of the woodcock are as lovely as the plumages of more flamboyant birds. Like essences of carth and grass, thcy carry with thcm the warm shades of sunlight, of cloud shadow and the swift seasons.

Peter Matthiesen writing about North American shorebirds, in Stout (1967)

SURELY no birdwatcher who has seen tundra plovers can fail to admire their spangled plumage. While our enthusiasm does not extend to that of Alaskan Inuits, who used dried skins of Grey Plovers as 'talismans to secure good luck in deer hunting' (Ray 1885), we have nevertheless had heated discussions over the plumage characteristics of the four species. Between us, we have handled hundreds of museum skins (some even taken and labelled by the Norwegian explorers Fridtjof Nansen and Roald Amundsen, and by the pioneer ornithologist Henry

Seebohm), looked carefully at hundreds of birds, and in IB's case sketched and painted scores.

We have made a particularly close study of the plumage characteristics. First, we outline their key features, then we describe variation in moults, before going on to discuss some possible explanations for the adaptive significance of different plumage patterns and size variations.

PLUMAGES

There are splendid 'feather-by-feather' descriptions of the various plumages of fully grown tundra plovers published in the most recent German and Western Palearctic handbooks (Glutz von Blotzheim 1975; Cramp & Simmons 1983). We summarize these, but also add our own observations, notably on the chicks. Figures A and B in Appendix 3 give the plumage topography of the tundra plover adult and chicks, respectively. Appendix 3C–J provides detailed descriptions. So far as chicks are concerned, good colour plates are found for three of the species in Fjeldså (1977), Glutz von Blotzheim *et al.* (1975), Johnsgard (1981) and Cramp & Simmons (1983). However, no detailed comparisons of downy plumages of all four species have been published before. Tables 2 & 3, Appendix 3B and Frontispiece provide our own comparisons of chicks (including body size measurements), based on museum material as well as photographs of live chicks.

Definitions of plumage sequences and moults

The plumage sequences of shorebirds are as follows (after Hayman *et al.* 1986): a) downy chick; b) juvenile plumage; c) first non-breeding plumage; d) first breeding plumage; e) second (adult) non-breeding plumage; and f) second (adult) breeding plumage (and so on until death). In our description of tundra plover plumages we use this terminology. In addition, there is a special plumage particular to tundra plovers and a few other birds, referred to as 'eclipse' plumage. This occurs between the breeding and non-breeding plumages. Several terms occur variously in the European and American literature for breeding and non-breeding plumages. In order to clarify the usage of our own terms, we offer the following matches: breeding plumage (summer plumage, nuptial plumage, alternate plumage); non-breeding plumage (winter plumage, basic plumage).

Similarly, moult sequences are: a) post-juvenile (juvenile to first non-breeding); b) first pre-breeding (first non-breeding to first breeding); c) first post-breeding (first breeding to second non-breeding); d) adult pre-breeding (non-breeding to breeding); and e) adult post-breeding (breeding to non-breeding). The eclipse moult occurs between d) and e). Again, a number of terms appear in the world literature: post-juvenile moult can be referred to as first pre-basic moult; pre-breeding moult as pre-nuptial or pre-alternate moult; and post-breeding moult as post-nuptial or pre-basic moult.

Downy chicks

The most prominent feature of tundra plover chicks is their plain yellow back and crown, both mottled with black flecks (Frontispiece). This yellow coloration is a characteristic of the tundra plovers and the yellow and black mottling also extends down the thigh and over the upper side of the wings. Undersides are greyish-white in all four species, with a greyish-yellowish tinge to cheek and sides of the breast.

The main differences between the species are found in their facial patterns of 'arcs' and stripes, coloration of nape, and the appearance of two parallel stripes along the back. All four possess a black loral stripe extending from near the eye towards the base of the bill, though in golden plovers this stripe takes one upward and one downward line, lacking in the Grey Plover. The colour of the down above the loral stripe, at the base of the bill, is yellow in Grey Plovers, whitish to white in American and Eurasian golden plovers, and pale yellow in the Pacific Golden Plover. This is also the case with the superciliary zone (not to be confused with the supraorbital zone, which is yellow in all four species). In the nape, there are also differences, being white and unpatterned in Grey Plover, white with a longitudinal spotted band in American Golden Plover, white with more dispersed grey spots in Eurasian Golden Plover, and weakly spotted on a faint yellowish background in Pacific Golden Plover. Even in the longitudinal dorsal stripes we see differences – whitish and prominent in American and Eurasian golden plovers, less prominent and pale yellow in Pacific Golden Plover, and absent in the Grey Plover.

Patterns are boldest in American and Eurasian golden plover chicks, less so in those of Pacific Golden Plover and Grey Plover. Intriguingly, the differences seem greatest between the two closely related American and Pacific golden plovers. Some of these contrasts were made by Conover (1945) and Gabrielson & Lincoln (1959).

Juvenile plumage

In general, juvenile plumages of all four species (Appendix 3C,E,G,I) possess dark brownish feathers dorsally, with yellow notches and spots along feather margins. Face and breast have yellowish feathers with brownish wedge-shaped tips, and flank feathers have a narrow dark terminal band. In the course of time the yellow colour fades, and especially in Grey Plovers and American Golden Plover soon turns off-white or white.

Non-breeding plumage

The non-breeding plumages (Appendix 3C,E,G,I) resemble the juvenile plumages, but in all four species dorsal winter plumage feathers have yellowish (golden plovers) or whitish (Grey Plover) edges or fringes. The tail feathers have complete transverse white or yellowish bands, and breast and upper flank feathers have a greyish or brownish central wedge, giving a scaled, rather than streaked appearance. As in juvenile plumage, the belly is white in all four species. The feather patterns differ in detail between the species (Appendix 3C,E,G,I). Grey Plovers and Pacific Golden Plovers have lighter dorsal feathers and well developed fringes, differing from the darker American, and in particular Eurasian, golden plovers, which give a more spangled or freckled impression.

According to Kozlova (1961), Johnston & McFarlane (1967) and Kinsky & Yaldwyn (1981) adult Pacific Golden Plovers in non-breeding plumage may be sexed fairly reliably from patterns of outer tail feathers, males having clear, evenly spaced, transverse blackish and white bars compared with the more diffuse brownish (broad) and whitish (narrow) bars of females (Fig. 4.1). We have found that this difference is also present in the breeding plumage, not only in Pacific, but also in American and Eurasian golden plovers. Whether or not it holds for the latter two in the non-breeding plumage deserves examination.

Breeding plumage

In breeding plumage, all four species are resplendent with a more or less black ventral area from face to belly, bordered by a broad almost clear white band, while dorsal feathers are black/dark brown with white (Grey Plover) or yellow (golden plovers) spots (Appendix 3D,F,H,J). Although we describe the moult later, we should mention here that the less complete moult of females gives them a less distinct appearance, and in southwestern parts of their range Eurasian Golden Plover males as well as females show a less complete moult, notably of the face, breast and belly. Retained non-breeding plumage feathers look faded, and the light feather spots are more or less abraded, giving the feathers a raggedness. A mixture of old and new feathers, also on the dorsal side, can be seen even in the field.

PLATE 25.   *Juvenile Eurasian Golden Plover, autumn. Norway. (Terje Lislevand)*

PLATE 26. *Juvenile Grey Plover, autumn. West coast of Norway. (Ingvar Grastveit)*

PLATE 27. *Pacific Golden Plover in non-breeding plumage. Hawaii. (Bryan Sage)*

Variations in these patterns are an invaluable aid during field studies, and have enabled us to recognize individual birds (Chapter 1). We have found this method to be most useful with Eurasian and Pacific golden plovers, and Grey Plovers, with the American Golden Plovers seeming to show less detectable individual variation. Individual marks are likely to appear on the dark facial-ventral area and the bordering white band in male and female Eurasian and female Pacific golden

male   female

FIG. 4.1. *Outermost tail feather of adult male and female Pacific Golden Plover in non-breeding plumage (redrawn from Kinsky & Yaldwin (1981) and study skins).*

plovers. Yet Pacific Golden Plovers tend to show individual patterns along the flanks, and Grey Plovers (females in particular) on the back (Fig 1.2).

In the Pacific Golden Plover, and especially the Grey Plover, one-year olds spending the summer on their non-breeding grounds retain a significant amount of non-breeding plumage feathers, and they can also be recognized as one-year old birds from their wing feathers being in active moult over the summer (Appendix 3D,H). Moreover, their outer tail feathers are particularly pale and patternless, unlike the more strongly barred winter tail feathers of adults (Kozlova 1961; Kinsky & Yaldwyn 1981). One-year old Eurasian Golden Plovers, which mostly appear on the breeding grounds, can be distinguished from older birds by their extremely worn wing-tips, and from all of their secondaries being worn equally (Jukema 1982).

Eclipse plumage

The 'eclipse plumage', described in detail by Jukema & Piersma (1987) for Eurasian Golden Plover, but occurring also in at least the two other golden plover species, involves the ventral side feathers, notably the breast. Scattered among the breeding plumage feathers, eclipse feathers are yellowish and have a varying degree of dark pigmentation at the tip (Appendix 3F). At the time Eurasian Golden Plovers begin their southbound migration, winter feathers start to replace breeding as well as eclipse plumage feathers. Hence, the eclipse plumage is chiefly held during the chick-rearing period (Jukema & Piersma 1987). According to Sauer (1962),

PLATE 28. *Grey Plover male in fresh breeding plumage shows much white dorsally.* *(IB)*

PLATE 29. *Grey Plover male on nest near Sabettayakha, Yamal Peninsula, northwest Siberia. (IB)*

PLATE 30. *Grey Plover female on nest, Sabettayakha, Yamal Peninsula, northwest Siberia. (IB)*

PLATE 31. *Pacific Golden Plover male in fresh breeding plumage. Nurmayakha, Yamal Peninsula, northwest Siberia. (IB)*

PLATE 32. *Pacific Golden Plover male in breeding plumage, having started to moult face and breast feathers. Note 'leggy' appearance. Yamal Peninsula, northwest Siberia. (Vadim K. Ryabitsev)*

PLATE 33.   *Pacific Golden Plover female in breeding plumage. Yamal Peninsula, northwest Siberia. (Vadim K. Ryabitsev)*

breeding Pacific Golden Plovers enter an 'eclipse' plumage from mid-July, and a similar change in American Golden Plovers has been observed at Churchill, Manitoba (by IB). Franz Sauer apparently thought that this was the start of the moult from summer to winter plumage. However, skins of Pacific Golden Plovers in the collection in Moscow and St Petersburg examined by IB showed pigmented (yellow/brown) feathers comparable with those of Eurasian Golden Plovers in eclipse plumage (as described by Jukema & Piersma 1987) (Appendix 3F,H). Surprisingly, only a few feathers of this pigmented type were found when examining late July skins of American Golden Plovers held by the Canadian Museum of Nature. As far as the Grey Plover in this plumage is concerned, we need more information!

In all plumages, except for downy chicks, wing undersides show the same patterns, being white with black axillaries in Grey Plover, brownish-grey (including axillaries) in American and Pacific golden plover, and whitish (including axillaries) in Eurasian Golden Plover.

Field identification

Many of the detailed plumage differences between the species given above and in Appendix 3 are of limited value in field identification. Pacific and American golden plovers in the field have received a great deal of attention because they have only recently been split into two species (e.g. Pym 1982; Hayman *et al.* 1986; Alström

PLATE 34. *American Golden Plover male in breeding plumage. Churchill, Manitoba, Canada. (William J. Sutherland and Nicola Crockford)*

PLATE 35. *American Golden Plover female in breeding plumage. Churchill, Manitoba, Canada. (IB)*

1990; Roselaar 1990; Golley & Stoddart 1991; Lewington *et al.* 1991; Gantlett & Millington 1992; Larsson 1992). Based primarily on these references and our own experience, we summarize the more important field marks in Table 4.

Among the tundra plovers, the Grey Plover is the easiest to identify in all plumages, having black axillaries contrasting against white wing undersides (see Plate 36), and rarely any yellow in their plumage. Its bill is particularly bulky. Among the three species of golden plover, the Eurasian stands out as having white wing undersides including axillaries, a relatively short bill, and short 'exposed' (i.e. unfeathered) tibia.

So, the difficulties are usually encountered in differentiating between Pacific and American golden plovers, both species having uniform grey-brown wing undersides. Indeed, you need to be aware of varying light conditions, which can influence the appearance of this character, as the feathers have somewhat shiny surfaces and may appear to flash as white feathers at an angle to the light! Wing undersides of Eurasian and American golden plovers are shown in Plate 37. If the birds are not in moult of their tertials, some of the most convenient field marks separating the two are found in the 'primary projection' (i.e. how far primaries project beyond tertial tips), and the tertial tips relative to tail tip (Figs. 4.2 and 4.3). Whereas 4 or 5 primaries are visible beyond the tertial tips in the American Golden Plover, 3 or 4 (sometimes only 2) primaries project beyond tertials in the Pacific Golden Plover. Moreover in Pacific Golden Plovers, the two primaries forming the wing-tip are almost of equal size (Fig. 4.3). The actual number of projecting

PLATE 36. *Eurasian Golden Plover (upper left) showing white axillaries in contrast to Grey Plover (lower) having black axillaries. Both birds are juveniles. (Ingvar Grastveit)*

PLATE 37. *Wing undersides of American (upper) and Eurasian (lower) golden plovers. (IB)*

primaries can, of course, rarely be seen under field conditions, but the visual impression of the relative primary projection makes a good field mark. American Golden Plovers have the two wing-tip feathers of unequal length, which also leads to primaries projecting farther beyond the tail tip than in the Pacific Golden Plover (Fig. 4.2). The tip of the longest tertial ends just beyond the tail basis in the American, but over the outer third of the tail in the Pacific Golden Plovers. But you do need to be careful, because the tertial moult can make Pacific Golden Plovers look like American Golden Plovers (see picture in Golley & Stoddart 1991)! Nevertheless, the long primaries make the rear end of American Golden Plovers look more prolonged than the shorter-looking rear of Pacific Golden Plovers (Larsson 1992).

Good field marks separating Pacific and American golden plovers are also found in:

– long, slender body, relatively short neck and large head in American; plump body, slender neck and smaller (*contra* Larsson 1992) head in Pacific Golden Plover);
– leg length, especially the relative length of tibia – as long as, or, longer than bill in Pacific; shorter than bill in American Golden Plover (Figs. 4.2 and 4.4); and
– bill length relative to head length – projected backwards, the bill reaches well beyond the eye in Pacific, but barely across the eye in American Golden Plovers.

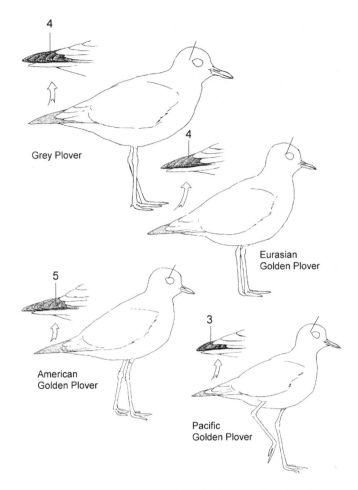

FIG. 4.2.   *Differences in appearance and specific features of tundra plovers, useful for field identification. Numerals on primary tips refer to number of primaries protruding beyond longest tertial. Backward projection of bill on head incicated by line. Further details, see Table 4.*

All of these characters are variable, and the impression they give may change with the birds' posture, but are often more useful for identifying birds in the field (photographs give snapshots of static postures!). In flight, a good field mark separating American and Pacific golden plovers is the extent to which toes project behind the tail: in Pacific golden plovers they do so very prominently, in American Golden Plover very little, if at all.

In breeding plumage, some male Pacific Golden Plovers may show flank feathers almost as dark as those of American Golden Plovers. Yet on closer examination these reveal a grey and black transverse barring, different from the solid black of American Golden Plover males (Fig. 4.5). In juvenile and non-breeding plumages, American Golden Plovers give a pale grey impression and show a dark crown

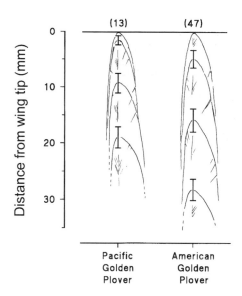

FIG. 4.3. *Relationship between the four outermost primaries in Pacific and American golden plovers, given as the primary tips' average distance (± SD) from wing-tip. American Golden Plovers have more pointed wings than Pacific Golden Plovers, due to the former's longer relative distance between the tip of the primaries 9 and 10 (outermost). Measured from museum skins (number of birds in parentheses).*

contrasting with the white supercilium. Pacific Golden Plovers are far more yellow, and show a less contrasting crown with a yellowish supercilium.

Perhaps the easiest field marks pertain to voice. All four species have differing vocalizations, the most common of which are described at the bottom of Table 4. We explore these in greater detail in Chapter 8. The common alarm call heard from American Golden Plovers on being flushed is a high-pitched, curlew-like disyllabic note with emphasis on the first syllable. Pacific Golden Plovers, on the other hand, utter a note almost identical to the alarm call of the Spotted Redshank, and put emphasis on the second syllable.

MOULTS

After the rigours of the breeding season the plumage of adults is worn, and replaced by a complete moult. In tundra plovers, feather renewal follows a general pattern found in many shorebirds, although there are differences in detail between the four species, and to some degree between populations and even between males and females. Special studies of the moult have been made of the Eurasian Golden Plover (Jukema 1982, 1986; Henriksen 1985; Jukema & Piersma 1987), Grey Plover (Branson & Minton 1976) and the Pacific Golden Plover (Johnson 1977, 1979; Kinsky & Yaldwin 1981; Johnson & Johnson 1983; Barter 1988; Johnson *et al.* 1989). Based on these studies and information from handbooks, various published notes, and our

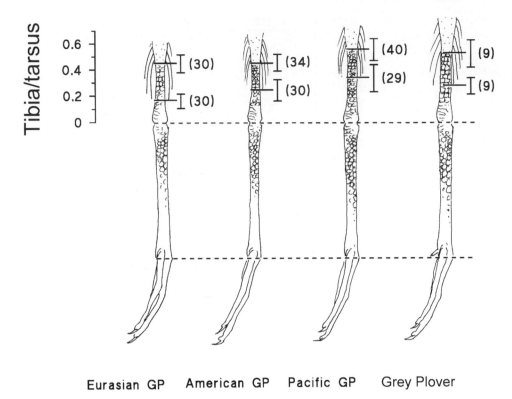

FIG. 4.4.   *Length of unfeathered part of tibia relative to tarsus length, measured from museum skins (number of birds in parentheses). Measurements were taken at front of tibia.*

FIG. 4.5.   *Pacific Golden Plover male showing resemblance to American Golden Plover by having dark flanks, but differing by having black/dark grey barring. Other characteristics were typical of the species.*

own observations, annual moult cycles are outlined in Fig. 4.6. The extent of moulted and non-moulted feathers in the various plumages is shown in Appendix 3.

Downy chicks to juvenile moult

Like other shorebirds (Fjeldså 1977; Chandler 1989), tundra plovers' chicks start growing their contour feathers from the bases of down, so that the downy part of the feathers remains as a tuft at the end of the growing feather, and then disappears gradually, owing to wear. Chick growth has been described for Grey Plover by Hussell & Page (1976). They showed that whereas tarsus and bill started to grow from hatching, primary and tail feather growth was rapid only after the 6th and 10th day. The newly hatched chick is entirely downy. However, three days after hatching, sheaths of juvenile feathers were visible under the skin, and primary sheaths started to protrude. Beyond 6–7 days, feather sheaths protruded from the skin over most of the body, and the 10th primary was 6 mm long (in one specimen examined). Juvenile feathering was noticeable over the whole body at 12–13 days, but the appearance was still that of a downy chick. The juvenile plumage was prominent at 18–23 days, down being found mainly on the nape, rump, and underparts. A 23-day

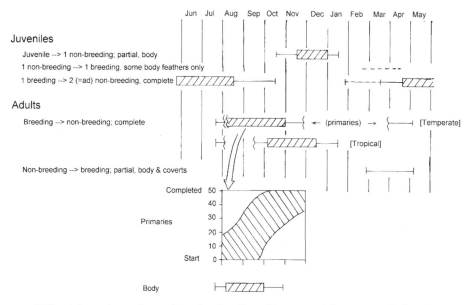

FIG. 4.6a. *Annual moult cycles in Grey Plover, mainly western Palearctic information, based primarily on Stresemann & Stresemann (1966), Branson & Minton (1976) and Cramp & Simmons (1983).*

▨ = main moult period (where known), ⟨ = suspended moult, dotted line – a few birds. Note that first non-breeding plumage essentially moults directly into second non-breeding plumage, by birds spending summer on wintering grounds. Inserted diagram of primary moult stages on date, Britain, adapted from Branson & Minton (1976); scores (0–50) according to Snow (1967). Also, body moult indicated separately (temperate zone wintering birds).

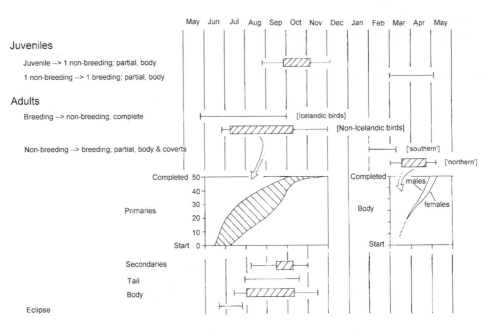

FIG. 4.6b. *Annual moult cycles in Eurasian Golden Plover, based primarily on Stresemann & Stresemann (1966), Jukema (1982, 1986), Cramp & Simmons (1983), Henriksen (1985), Jukema & Piersma (1987), and Byrkjedal (1978a). Legend as in Fig. 4.6a. Inserted diagrams of moult stage on date for post-breeding primary moult of adults (adapted from Jukema 1982) and pre-breeding body moult (average values, adapted from Jukema 1986), all from Friesland, Netherlands. Primary moult scores (0–50) according to Snow (1967) and of body feathers (0–6) according to Jukema (1986). Post-breeding moult of body, tail, and secondaries, also separately indicated.*

old chick could fly 150 m uninterrupted, although the flight feathers were still in growth. No such detailed description of the chick development in the other species of tundra plovers has been published.

Post-juvenile moult

In autumn, juveniles leave the breeding grounds in an entire fresh plumage. Eurasian Golden Plover juveniles moult into their first non-breeding plumage in September–November (Fig. 4.6b), whereas Grey Plovers, and Pacific and American golden plovers attain this plumage later, in November–December (Fig. 4.6a, c and d). The latter three are pronounced long-distance migrants, notably Pacific and American golden plovers. Their post-juvenile moult takes place mainly after the birds have reached their wintering grounds, whereas juvenile Eurasian Golden Plovers are in active post-juvenile moult at a time when they may have to make major movements if the weather turns cold in Europe. In all four species, post-juvenile moult involves a limited number of feathers. The renewed feathers are like those of adults in post-breeding plumage.

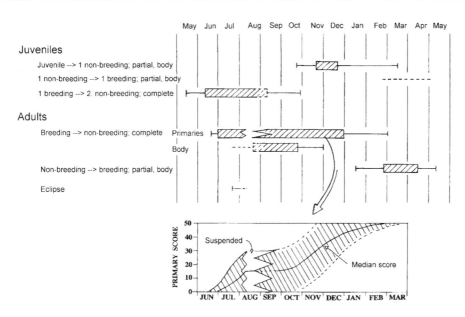

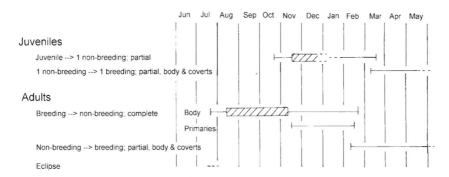

FIG. 4.6c.   *Annual moult cycles of Pacific Golden Plover, mainly for birds that winter on Pacific Islands. Based on Sauer (1962), Stresemann & Stresemann (1966), Johnson (1977), Johnson & Johnson (1983), Cramp & Simmons (1983), and I.B. pers. obs., Yamal. Legend as in Fig. 4.6a. Note that first non-breeding plumage to a large extent moults directly into second non-breeding plumage by birds (majority) spending summer on wintering grounds. One-year old birds spending summer in Arctic claimed to moult on same schedules as adults (Cramp & Simmons 1983). Pre-breeding moult of adults claimed (Cramp & Simmons 1983) to be suspended during migration.*

FIG. 4.6d.   *Annual moult cycles of American Golden Plover, based on Bent (1929), Stresemann & Stresemann (1966), Stout (1967), Cramp & Simmons (1983), and Johnson (1985). Legends as in Fig. 4.6a. Most one-year birds leave wintering grounds for the Arctic. According to Johnson (1985) they occur with fresh primaries in spring and are suspected to have a complete pre-breeding primary moult. Pre-breeding moult claimed by Cramp & Simmons (1983) to be suspended during migration. Post-breeding moult of body feathers continues through autumn migration, while primary moult starts as birds reach wintering grounds.*

PLATE 38. *This Eurasian Golden Plover male trapped on its nest at Hardangervidda has started to moult its primaries, apparent as a notch in the wing and from the contrast between dark new (innermost) primaries and more faded old ones. (IB)*

along their routes, Eurasian Golden Plovers are usually in active primary and body feather moult during their migratory movements. Yet a large number of birds from Fennoscandian and Russian breeding grounds linger for a while in late summer and autumn in Denmark, Germany and the Netherlands, evidently to virtually complete their moult before spreading farther south. Icelandic populations, on the other hand, finish their primary moult before crossing the sea to their wintering grounds in Britain and westernmost Europe, and start their primary moult particularly early (Stresemann & Stresemann 1966; Fig. 4.6b).

Contrary to Eurasian Golden Plovers, Grey Plovers and Pacific Golden Plovers (long-distance migrants) suspend their primary moult before leaving their breeding grounds. Renewal of the innermost 1–3 primaries in the Grey Plover (Branson & Minton 1976), and 1–5 primaries in the Pacific Golden Plover (Fig 4.7a–c) is usually completed on the breeding grounds, and no further primaries are shed before the birds reach their wintering grounds, or, in the case of West Palearctic Grey Plovers when reaching their moulting area in the Wadden Sea and

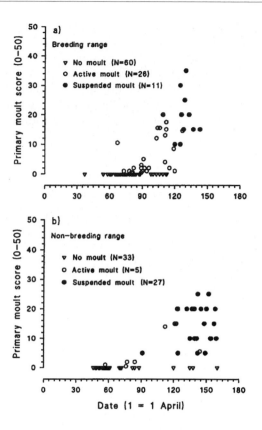

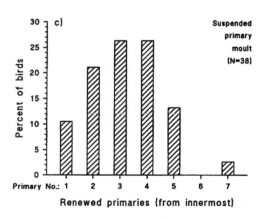

FIG. 4.7. *Primary moult scores (0 = no moult, 50 = all feathers renewed) of Pacific Golden Plovers on Siberian breeding grounds (a), and on Asian migratory flyways (b), showing that moult frequently starts on the breeding grounds but is suspended before or during migration. Lower panel (c) shows the frequency of renewal of specific primaries before suspension of moult. Based on museum specimens in Moscow, St Petersburg, and Oslo.*

eastern England. Increasing in mass from innermost to outermost (see Underhill & Summers 1993), the innermost primaries are energetically the least costly to renew. The birds often arrive in heavy body feather moult, and by late autumn most of the adults have attained a complete post-breeding (winter) plumage (Fig. 4.6a–d). American Golden Plovers, which travel farthest on migration, postpone their primary moult until they reach their wintering grounds, while the renewal of the body feathers is undertaken at an earlier stage, during southward migration (Bent 1929; Stout 1967, Appendix 3F).

MOULT, MIGRATION AND WINTERING: PRIORITIES FOR RESOURCE ALLOCATIONS

Prior to migration from their breeding grounds, tundra plovers, like other shorebirds, must accumulate body fat to fuel their migratory flights. A 'conflict' may arise between the post-breeding moult and pre-migratory fattening, as both processes require energy. For longer imminent flight distances a higher priority should be given to fattening. Interestingly, all four species of tundra plovers carry out their body feather moult during the fattening and migration period, regardless of the flight distances. Yet American Golden Plovers, which have the longest migratory flight distances, do not start to moult their primaries until they have reached their wintering areas. The primaries are the feathers which are most expensive to renew.

However, full-feathered wings are apparently important for long-distance flights, and one way to retain full-feathered wings during migration is to postpone the primary moult until after migration, as seen in American Golden Plovers. In Pacific Golden Plovers a suspended moult keeps intact the complement of full-grown primaries during migration, whereas in ocean-crossing Icelandic Eurasian Golden Plovers the primary moult is completed before migration.

The farther north they spend the winter, the more body fat must be accumulated by the birds in order to endure adverse periods with little available food. Again, the non-breeding moult may conflict with the fattening process. This seems to be the case in Grey Plovers. On temperate zone wintering grounds, where bouts of bad weather prevent sufficient food intake (Dugan *et al.* 1981), a number of Grey Plovers, not having finished their post-breeding moult by the end of November, suspended their moult until late March (Branson & Minton 1976). High body fat levels are necessary to carry Grey Plovers through temperate zone winters, and presumably late moulters reach a stage where they give higher priority to fat accumulation than to their moult. Grey Plovers on tropical/subtropical wintering grounds, admittedly farther from their breeding grounds, face more favourable and stable conditions with high temperatures, leading to less demand for accumulated fat. Starting their primary moult later than those on the northern wintering grounds, these birds finish their primary renewal during the winter, without any suspension (Stresemann & Stresemann 1966; Cramp & Simmons 1983, Appendix 3C). As in Grey Plovers, primary moult suspension at the onset of winter may also be found in a minority of late-moulting Eurasian Golden Plovers (Jukema 1982).

The post-breeding moult results in the complete renewal of feathers, or nearly so. In Eurasian Golden Plovers only about half the secondaries are renewed each year, however, and those not renewed in one year are renewed the next (Jukema 1982; Henriksen 1985). Whether or not this is also so for the other three species warrants study. Secondaries are renewed convergently, starting with the middle ones and proceeding inwards and outwards (Jukema 1982; Henriksen 1985).

BREEDING PLUMAGE PATTERNS: CAMOUFLAGE BY CONTRASTS

We have frequently mulled over the striking plumage patterns of the tundra plovers in spring. During their breeding season, they possess a plumage pattern of a black or dark brown face, breast and belly, bordered by a sharply contrasting, more or less white, line. Among open-nesters, such contrasting patterns may yield camouflage against a variegated background (Cott 1940). In a comparative study of shorebirds, Graul (1973) found a correlation between the presence of breast bands and a discontinuous nest substrate, supporting Cott's suggestion. Although Graul did not score tundra plovers as having breast bands, they do actually possess a contrast-rich breast plumage and, breeding largely on lichen-covered tundra and alpine habitats, occupy a highly variegated habitat. Strong contrasts between black and white is a characteristic feature of ground covered by lichens, especially those of the genus *Cladonia*, typical of mountains and tundra. Sauer (1962) pointed out how well the black and white plumage patterns broke the 'bird outline' of incubating Pacific Golden Plovers nesting on lichen-covered ground. Indeed, American Golden Plovers nesting on such ground avoid nest predation better than do those nesting in more uniform sedge or *Dryas*-dominated habitats (Byrkjedal 1989a).

Eurasian Golden Plovers and timing of breeding

Among the tundra plovers, Eurasian Golden Plovers show most variation in plumage distinctness. IB has already suggested one explanation for the geographical variation in plumage and linked this to 'subspecies' differences, with 'northern' plumage variants occurring in the lichen-dominated montane/alpine and arctic habitats, while 'southern' plumages appear to coincide with more uniform sedge and heather moors and lowland raised bogs (Byrkjedal 1978b).

However, there are alternative possibilities. The less distinct ('southern') plumage, caused by incomplete spring moult, may be an energetic consequence of early breeding (i.e. they cease moulting and shift energy reserves into breeding; Bill Hale pers. comm.; J. Fjeldså pers. comm. in Byrkjedal 1978b). Such a system could represent an adaptation to the 'average' phenology on the different breeding grounds (and show little variation between years), or be a direct response to the phenological situation particular to different breeding seasons ('late or early' years; and be more variable between years). In the latter case, individuals should obtain a more complete breeding plumage and increased plumage distinctness in years when the onset of spring is late and in years when they arrive late on their breeding grounds. This could cause marked year-to-year variations in plumage, notably in the southernmost populations, where the potential overlap between spring moult and breeding is greater. Furthermore, birds born late in 'southern' populations might attain a plumage similar to 'northern' birds if they overshoot their natal grounds and migrate farther north, where they will be as dark as their northern conspecifics.

However, Parr (1980) found that individual golden plovers in Scotland did not change in plumage distinctness over a number of years, but as he did not relate this to spring phenology or the birds' time of arrival, this needs to be examined more carefully.

We have compared plumage scores (given in Appendix 2) of birds from southern Norway with: a) predominant habitat within the territories of the birds for which plumage was scored; b) altitude; and c) date of last vernal frost night (average over 30 years, extracted from Myklebost and Strømme 1963). Habitat was ranked in increasing contrast-richness: grass/sedge < heather moor < *Racomitrium* heath < lichen heath. Spring phenology is associated with both altitude and frost nights.

The results of the analyses are shown in Table 5. The total material from southern and southwestern coastal Norway lends fairly strong support for the hypothesis that plumage distinctness increases with increasingly contrast-rich habitat, whereas spring phenology seems to exert less effect on plumage, particularly when the effect of habitat is controlled for. Breeding occurs earliest along the southwestern coast (i.e. Jæren and Karmøy). Here, spring moult and breeding is most likely to overlap. In the other sampled populations (inland) the birds arrive in almost complete breeding plumage (at least the males do). Any effect of spring phenology on plumage distinctness should be stronger on the southwestern breeding grounds. Hence, we analysed these birds separately but did not find an association with spring phenology here (Table 5).

Considering the coarse scale of habitat contrast, the significant association with plumage distinctness is remarkable. The association between plumage and altitude and vernal frost nights may be even more notable, however, as the latter two variables give only an indirect measure of phenology. We need to relate the plumage scores of a number of individual birds to their arrival and onset of laying over a series of years in a 'southern' population of Eurasian Golden Plovers. Such a study would more accurately demonstrate the effects of spring phenology on plumage development and also indicate the flexibility of the relationship. Intriguingly, on one of its most southern breeding grounds (the Peak District in the UK) golden plovers have very strongly marked plumage (Derek Yalden & James Pearce-Higgins pers. comm.). There, these birds merge well with the contrasting physiognomy of their eroded blanket bog habitat.

Sexual plumage dimorphism

Tundra plovers show sexual plumage dimorphism (Chapter 2). In all four species, females possess the same general plumage patterns as males but are less distinctly coloured. Are these differences due to sexual selection (through female preferences for more distinctly coloured males, or male–male competition) or have the differences arisen from natural selection (e.g. plumage distinctness acting differently on male and female survival and/or nest protection)? In the latter case, this is potentially linked with camouflage during incubation.

Geographical variation in the Eurasian Golden Plover suggests plumage distinctness to be a disruptive (camouflage) coloration feature, related to habitat. As males tend to incubate during daytime (Chapter 9), tundra plover males may be more in need of a contrast-rich (disruptive) plumage, than females, which usually incubate during the night. Although the breeding ranges of tundra plovers fall mainly north of the Arctic Circle, where the difference in light between night and day is only slight, avian nest predators, which are sight-oriented, are chiefly active during daytime (even in the Arctic). This may select for disruptive coloration in males.

In the case of sexual selection, females may choose males on the basis of traits that indicate male superiority, in terms of good genes and/or resources offered that may increase the female's fitness (e.g. discussion by Andersson 1994). Distinctness in males could be a consequence of power or strength (linked to high testosterone levels), which in turn may make them more adept at defending good territories, escaping predators in spite of being more conspicuous, and resisting parasite infections. A link between plumage distinctness and strength is plausible for tundra plover males, as individual differences in plumage distinctness are attributed to differences in the degree of moult completeness (the moult being an energetically demanding process).

Is there any evidence that distinctness in tundra plover males indicates viability, and do females, in fact, prefer distinctive males? According to Edwards (1982) male plumage distinctness in Eurasian Golden Plovers signals dominance. Among 10 males Philip Edwards studied in Scotland, the blacker (more distinct) males won more contests and were able to defend those territories richest in food resources. Edwards (1982) suggested, from anecdotal evidence, that females did prefer the blacker males. Such a system could create a selection pressure for increased male plumage contrasts, which could reliably signal male quality, provided developing a bright (i.e. completely moulted) plumage incurs costs to the males.

The energy a bird can afford to spend on moulting while facing other energetically demanding events (like migration and territorial defence) should be influenced by that individual's body condition, however. This again may be determined by the individual bird's ability to cope with expenditure over the winter, during migration, and from parasite loads. A bright plumage signalling good body condition may also signal dominance (perhaps depending on body size), parasite resistance, ability to avoid predators, and generally higher viability – all attributes which females might look for in a mate. Twenty-two Eurasian Golden Plover males collected at Hardangervidda in mid-May 1974 enabled us to compare plumage scores with body size, body condition, and ectoparasite load. No significant associations were found (r_s = 0.05–0.22; total number of parasites: 1803 feather mites, 17 *Quadraceps charadrii* (Mallophaga).

The population studied by Phillip Edwards was highly unusual among golden plovers in that all feeding seemed to take place inside the territories. Golden plovers (any species) usually feed outside territories, except in some alpine habitats and in the Western Isles of Britain (see Chapters 7 and 9). In western Europe, Eurasian Golden Plovers feed extensively on earthworms on farmland, often up to 10 km from their territories (Chapter 7). We did not find more distinct males on Jæren with territories closer to farmland (Table 5). One problem which arises with Edwards' (1982) idea is that distinct plumage males may also incur costs that could lower the fitness of their females. As already discussed, a distinct plumage offers camouflage against a variegated background but increases conspicuousness against uniform backgrounds. Distinct males incubating in heather or grassland habitats (uniform) could actually increase the risks of nest predation. Studies similar to that by Edwards (1982) ought to be performed on arctic and alpine breeding grounds (for all of the tundra plovers), where the bright plumage of males is less likely to incur costs to females. Furthermore, we should like to repeat Edwards' study (in S. Scotland) to examine plumage darkness/distinctness–social dominance–territory quality associations, and to see if there are also relationships with nest survival.

SUMMARY

1. The key plumage characteristics of the four species are described. For downy chicks, the four species differ in facial, nape and back patterns. Juvenile and non-breeding plumages are fairly similar, though the former have a more pronounced pattern. The breeding plumages contrast markedly. The 'eclipse' plumage (transitional between breeding and non-breeding plumages) has been observed in the golden plovers, but not in the Grey Plover.

2. Field identification features are summarized. The main ones are black axillaries contrasting with white wing undersides (Grey Plovers), white wing undersides including axillaries, a relatively short bill and short exposed tibia (Eurasian Golden Plover), a smaller number of primaries projecting beyond tertials (in Pacific Golden Plover compared with the American Golden Plover – which also has unequal sized primaries forming the wing-tip), and long primaries making the rear end of American Golden Plovers look longer than Pacifics'.

3. Annual moult cycles are summarized: for chick, juveniles and adults. There are several differences between Grey and golden plovers, and between the three long-distance migrants and Eurasian Golden Plovers. Long-distance migrants tend to migrate with full plumage wings (old feathers retained, all feathers renewed, or moult suspended).

4. Breeding plumage patterns may be strongly associated with disruptive colouration in contrast-rich habitats (black-white face, breast and belly contrasts), and timing of breeding (less contrasting Eurasian Golden Plovers breed earliest).

5. Sexual plumage dimorphism is evident in all four species, and may arise from the tendency for males to incubate during daylight (the predation-prone period) when their more distinctive plumage provides camouflage. Plumage differences associated with social dominance and habitat type need to be studied more closely.

CHAPTER 5
Phylogeny and Biogeography
(with Godtfred Anker Halvorsen)

*Pacific Golden Plover chasing
Eurasian Golden Plover*

The waders may well be a polyphyletic group but to those who watch them and work with them they have the singular fascination of a group of birds which has survived several ice ages and tens of millions of years of evolution because of the adaptations they possess. In many ways these adaptations obscure relationships and it is quite possible that we may never know the true origins of these birds.

Bill Hale writing about the evolution of shorebirds in *Waders* (1980)

BIRDS may have been on this planet for almost 140 million years. The first evidence of the plovers' existence, however, dates from around 30 million years ago, when early fossils of *Vanellus* and *Charadrius* were found in Belgium and Colorado, USA, respectively (Piersma & Wiersma 1996). In this chapter, we try to trace the evolution of the tundra plovers. We focus on two issues: phylogeny, namely the genealogical relationships between the species in the genus *Pluvialis;* and biogeography, dealing with both historical and present-day aspects. It must be emphasized at the outset that a phylogeny is a prerequisite for a historical biogeographic analysis.

PHYLOGENY

Background and methods

The discipline of phylogenetic systematics, or cladistics, was developed as a new contribution to systematics by the German dipterist Willi Henning in the early 1950s. Its endeavour was to find a testable and more objective method for determining the genealogical relationships among living beings. The main principle of the method is that only shared derived characters, termed 'synapomorphies', can show relationships between different groups. Shared primitive characters ('symplesiomorphies') do not show relationships. The group that is analysed is termed the 'ingroup', in our case the genus *Pluvialis*. To identify the synapomorphies in the ingroup, the character states have to be compared with the same characters in an 'outgroup'. The outgroup consists of what are shown or believed to be species related to the ingroup, in our case other members of *Charadrius*.

A tree is constructed which connects the species under consideration to the others. The tree is constructed so as to minimize the number of times each character has to change, thus giving the shortest possible tree for all the characters analysed (i.e., we have employed parsimony as the criterion for comparing alternative hypotheses). But characters can conflict, so that species A and B may be related closest for some, but species B and C related closest for others. The actual relationship is determined as that which has the the highest number of possible shared derived characters. The result of the analysis is represented as a 'cladogram', quite similar to a family tree. This method follows that of Forey *et al.* (1992) in the book *Cladistics: a practical course in systematics*. That book discusses the alternatives to parsimony analysis, and lists the references to the major publications concerning the various issues of the method.

Phylogeny for shorebirds

Several workers have attempted to provide a phylogeny for shorebirds, notably Strauch (1976, 1978), Mickevich & Parenti (1980), Bjørklund (1994) and Chu (1995) based on osteological characters, and Sibley and Ahlquist (1990) using DNA–DNA hybridization methods (subsequently re-analysed by Harshman 1994). These studies indicate that the tundra plovers are either the sistergroup of the subfamilies Vanellinae and Charadriinae combined, or they may be the sistergroup of the Charadriinae only. We still do not have a definitive phylogeny for shorebirds.

Proposals for the tundra plovers

Our analysis of the tundra plovers is described in detail in Appendix 4. It was based on 19 characters from the adult, juvenile and chick plumages. The first result of these analyses was a corroboration of the claim that the tundra plovers are a monophyletic group. This means that the four species are more closely related to each other than they are to any other species outside the group. That is, the tundra plovers have a common ancestor which is not shared with any other species. The cladogram is shown in Fig. 5.1. It shows that the Grey Plover is the sister species to the golden plovers, and that the Eurasian Golden Plover is the sister species to the Pacific and the American golden plovers. The vertical component of the cladogram may be read as a time scale. This means that the ancestor of the tundra plovers first split into the Grey Plover and the ancestor of the golden plovers. Later on, the ancestor of the golden plovers underwent a splitting event, where the Eurasian Golden Plover and the ancestor of the Pacific and the American golden plovers (the ancestral 'Lesser' golden plover) was the result. Finally, this ancestor divided into the Pacific and the American golden plovers.

This has confirmed what we had suspected, and what has underlain the traditional classification of tundra plovers. However, we should bear in mind that this analysis is based solely on plumage characters. Johnson & Connors (1996) quote work on mitochondrial DNA by F. Gill *et al.*, which indicates that the Pacific Golden Plover is more closely related to the Eurasian than the American Golden Plover. This work has not been published yet, so we are unable to discuss their results or evaluate the method used. We feel, however, that there is considerable scope for more research in this area, not least in tandem with molecular advances in systematics.

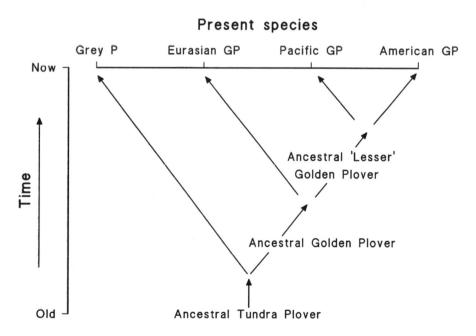

FIG. 5.1. *Proposed lineage of the tundra plovers, shown as a cladogram.*

BIOGEOGRAPHY – SPATIAL AND TEMPORAL PATTERNS OF CHANGE

Given such a picture, biogeographers ask the question 'What lives where and why?' The answer invokes either ecological or historical explanations, or both.

Humphries & Parenti (1986) in their introduction to *Cladistic Biogeography*

The field of biogeography deals with the patterns of distribution of organisms around the world. Our specific questions are: where and when did the tundra plover ancestor originate; and what gave rise to the occurrence of the four species today? However, before we try to give an answer to these questions, we offer some words of caution. What we present below is not a biogeographical analysis in a stringent sense, but some ideas about how the evolution of the tundra plovers may have occurred, and what might have caused this. These ideas are based on the phylogeny as well as present-day distribution and glacial/inter-glacial habitat maps, and as such are narrative rather than strictly analytical.

With the exciting advent of plate tectonic theory, workers have come to realize the implications of whole continents splitting, with fragments moving in different directions with cargos of both living organisms and fossils. As workers began to appreciate the extent of these land mass shifts, two concepts emerged to explain historical changes. First, the original distribution of a species may have been divided by a barrier (a new sea, or a range of mountains, for instance) giving rise to a 'vicariance' event, which accounts for species subsequently evolving some similar and other different traits in two somewhat contrasting environments. Second, there may be dispersal whereby the original species crosses a barrier and expands its range. Here, the extent of expansion may be so great that the species becomes isolated from its ancestor, and develops into a new species. Both concepts have been hotly debated, and need not be mutually inclusive, though it is likely that dispersal provides only occasional aberrances in the biogeographical record (e.g. Cox & Moore 1993).

The tundra plovers' ancestor

When we look back in time at the geography of the world it is intriguing to realize that the disposition of the land masses was different from that of today. In the Eocene world, some 50 million years ago, shortly before shorebirds are believed to have arisen, there was a massive northern super continent of Laurasia (still largely intact with the Old and New Worlds combined) with Africa much closer to it than South America is now. But towards the end of this, around 38 million years ago (moving into the Oligocene epoch), the present-day Palearctic and Nearctic regions had clearly separated, with Greenland part of the latter (e.g. Tallis 1991; Cox & Moore 1993). Moving into much more recent times, some 2.4–1.8 million years ago, we arrive at the beginning of the Ice Ages. Around the advent of these, we suggest that the ancestor of the tundra plover may have arisen.

According to Larsson (1957), fossils of the closely related Kentish Plover and Little Ringed Plover were found in the Pliocene, from up to five million years ago.

Johansen (1958) even went so far as to suggest that the centre of origin of the tundra plovers was in the Eastern Siberian high mountains about 1.8 million years ago. We shall probably never know the truth, but it is likely that the ancestral tundra plover lived before the Ice Age, in the north of the Holarctic, having separated from the common ancestor of *Charadrius.*

Ancestral golden plovers

The ancestral 'Golden Plover' If our cladogram is correct, the ancestral tundra plover gave rise to the Grey Plover and the ancestral golden plover, rather than to the three species of present-day golden plovers (Fig. 5.1). It is noteworthy that both the Grey Plover and the golden plovers (combined) have near-circumpolar breeding distributions; the ancestral golden plover may have parted from its ancestor by occupying more southern reaches of the tundra. It is impossible to say more!

The ancestral 'Lesser Golden Plover' Moving on in time, we then have a further split, with the Eurasian Golden Plover separating from the ancestral 'Lesser' Golden Plover. This time, the split possibly occurred in the western Palearctic, and the marked differences in present-day non-breeding grounds suggest that factors other than on the breeding grounds may have been involved. Whilst the Grey Plover over-winters virtually throughout the southern hemisphere, the Eurasian Golden Plover is confined to the southern and western Palearctic (and the edge of N. Africa), the Pacific Golden Plover to Australasia, and the American Golden Plover to the east-central plains of South America.

There are at least two possible explanations for the evolution of the ancestral golden plover into the Eurasian and 'Lesser' golden plovers. First, there may have been a physical barrier somewhere west of the Ural Mountains in Russia which impeded physical contact between the two species. In the context, we have been excited by Quaternary scientists' recent work. While it is very unlikely that plate tectonic movements have formed landscape impediments, such as temporary high mountains, in the last 1.6 million years, periodic fluctuations in the global climate may have shifted core breeding distributions as glaciations shifted breeding quarters south and then north. The problem, however, is that with each successive glaciation traces of earlier events have been removed (e.g. Andersen & Borns 1995). So, although it is quite possible that massive areas of tundra were carted south during glacial periods, and then moved north to form different spatial arrays during inter-glaciations, we cannot identify the location or extent of these today. For a while it was believed that the Caspian Sea shifted north during an inter-glacial period (which might have provided a minor barrier in Russia), but there is little supporting evidence for this (H.J.B. Birks pers. comm.).

Nevertheless, it seems possible, indeed probable, that one of the many inter-glacials during the last 1.6 million years caused the ancestral golden plovers to part. The last maximum glaciation is tantalizing because there is a very narrow strip of periglacial tundra between what is now mainly France–Germany and western Russia (Fig. 5.2). Did this contribute to the isolation between what is now the Eurasian Golden Plover and the 'Lesser' Golden Plover ancestor, to the west and the east, respectively? It possibly did, but occurs rather too recently so far as the

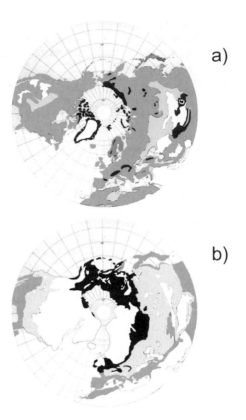

FIG. 5.2. *The rough extent of tundra and montane vegetation (black), forest (dark grey), and steppe (light grey) on the northern hemisphere in the last global a) inter-glacial (approximately 120 000 years ago), and b) glaciation (maximum approximately 20 000–18 000 years ago). In south forest includes savanna. White shows glaciers in the north, deserts in the south. Redrawn from Frenzel et al. (1992).*

phylogeny is concerned (but earlier glaciations may well have had similar configurations). On the other hand, during the preceding inter-glacial period significant divisions may have come into force when some breeding populations inhabited the far north, and others were on the mountain tundra 'refuges' to the south (Fig. 5.2a).

The second possibility is that there was divergence on the non-breeding grounds. There, while the Eurasian Golden Plovers may have spent more time on their western European quarters, the 'Lesser' golden plovers may have travelled much farther south to Australia/S. America. Here, a time barrier forms, because those wintering in the far south arrive on their nesting grounds much later (Chapter 10).

One cannot escape the notion that, over a million years ago, two forces may have been at work in late summer and then late spring. Whereas a fraction of the ancestral golden plovers migrated west into the mild pastoral quarters of Europe, others may have travelled south, much farther, to the southern hemisphere. The Urals may have been sufficient to deflect the latter birds south, and a glacial bottleneck may have served to separate the two 'species'. Once the pattern had been set, and gone to genetic fixation, the ancestral 'Lesser' Golden Plovers possibly returned to breed long after their ancestral congeners (now the Eurasians) had returned to breed from western Europe and even the fringes of N. Africa, so helping form two distinct species.

Evolution of the Pacific and American Golden Plovers

Moving forward further, to the evolution of the two eastern Palearctic/Nearctic species, we are strongly tempted to implicate the latter stages of the Ice Age. Essentially, a barrier seems to have split the two species around the Bering Strait. The most likely explanation for this is the last glaciation, which reached its maximum 20 000–10 000 years ago (Fig. 5.2). Then, a glacier in the western American continent could have divided the ancestral 'Lesser' golden plovers. After all, whereas the present-day extent of ice sheets extends to 1.2% of North America/Greenland, it was considerably greater at 12.4% during the most recent glacial maximum (Tallis 1991). One series of 'Lesser' Golden Plover populations could have remained in Eastern Siberia and indeed over the Bering Strait to Alaska (which was almost all dry at the time) giving rise to the Pacific Golden Plover. The other, eastern, populations might have been taken southwards by the expanding Ice Sheet in the American continent, so developing subtle behavioural and morphological changes which finally gave rise to the American Golden Plover.

However, even further back in time, during the Interglacial period (120 000 years ago), there would have been an inter-glacial barrier (predominantly forests) which divided the ancestral 'Lesser' golden plover populations, corresponding with what are now the Pacific and American golden plovers' distributions (see Fig. 5.2a). During this period, the land mass of tundra was small (and did not include Alaska), with a glacial refuge in central and western USA (also Hale 1980).

No matter, because the two species evolved and occupied different non-breeding ranges. A look at the two species there today suggests some fascinating adaptations. The American Golden Plover has small salt glands, a dull 'winter' plumage, and a tendency to flock inland – all seemingly in tune with their pampas grassland habitats. Fascinatingly, during the last glaciation the pampas grasslands of S. America were composed mainly of sand dune type vegetation (e.g. Tallis 1991; H.J.B. Birks pers. comm.) against which the birds would have been well camouflaged. The Pacific Golden Plover, on the other hand, has more adaptations for the coast. It has larger salt glands than the other golden plovers (Chapter 2), a more golden upper body, and is better adapted for feeding on mudflats as well as coastal saltings. These differences seem to reflect adaptations to quite different environments in the non-breeding season.

Later in the book (Chapter 10) we provide detailed descriptions of the migration routes taken by these birds. We now turn to factors possibly limiting the present-day breeding distributions of the four species.

POSSIBLE FACTORS LIMITING PRESENT-DAY BREEDING DISTRIBUTIONS

At the coarse scale, Grey Plovers are confined to arctic lichen-moss tundra, and the three golden plover species are predominantly found on the dwarf shrub tundra and northern montane (alpine) heaths (Fig 5.3). What factors confine them to these areas, and prevent expansion? Why do golden plovers not breed as far north as Grey Plovers, and why do Grey Plovers not expand southwards to the same extent as golden plovers? Indeed, why are Grey Plovers absent as a breeding bird from apparently suitable terrain on both sides of the Atlantic? Why do each of the golden plovers have such relatively limited east–west distributions? What limits the golden plovers' penetration into the northern forest zones where there are large open spaces? A number of factors may be involved, and of these we briefly consider habitat requirements, climate, interspecific competition, migration and phenology.

In discussing these aspects we assume that populations are at, or near, a 'saturation' level. But they may not be. As we shall discuss in the following chapter, American Golden Plovers reached a very low population level at the turn of the century, after which there has been a population increase. The present distribution of this species may not be at equilibrium (cf. Connors 1983). Observations in arctic Canada indicate a continuing increase (Vink *et al.* 1988; Parker & Ross 1973; Pattie 1990). This has led to the suggestion that American Golden Plovers are actually more typical of arctic areas than previously realized (Pattie 1990). Perhaps a range expansion should be expected in this species over the next few decades, even towards east and west.

Habitat requirements

Confinement of species to different vegetation zones may reflect differences in habitat requirements. Klomp (1954) showed a relationship between leg morphology, locomotion and habitat choice in shorebirds. Hence, plovers (exemplified by the Northern Lapwing) have short legs, a forward-skewed centre of gravity, and a long gait, and are found to be adapted to locomotion in short vegetation. Scolopacids (exemplified by Black-tailed Godwit), on the other hand, with their long legs, more upright stance, and more deliberate gait, are suited to taller and denser vegetation (Chapter 2). Tundra plovers do not differ much in these respects, for they are all adapted to short vegetation. The vegetation in the dwarf shrub zone is generally taller and denser than what is found in the lichen-moss zone. Nevertheless, it is the longer-legged Grey Plover which is found in the latter zone. Evidently, therefore, leg length in the tundra plovers is geared to the amount of time spent food searching in the non-breeding season in the littoral zone (leg lengths: Grey Plover > Pacific > American > Eurasian golden plovers). So, adaptations to locomotion in spring/summer do not seem to explain differences in their breeding distribution ranges.

Habitats provide food, suitable nest sites, and food and cover for the chicks. All four species use nest sites with virtually no cover. Again the largest species, the Grey Plover, is the one found in the zone with the habitats offering least cover. Food is

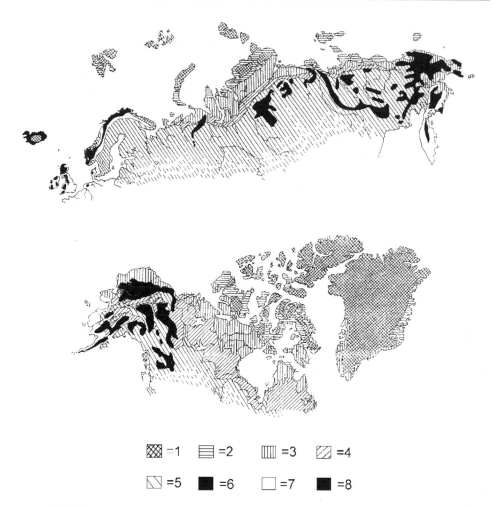

FIG. 5.3. *Principal vegetation regions of northern boreal and arctic areas, from Schmithüsen (1976), modified after Gimingham (1975), Sjörs (1956), Chernov (1985), Sage (1986), CAFF (1994), Thompson* et al. *(1995a), Byrkjedal* et al. *(1997).*
1 = polar deserts and glaciers, 2 = lichen-moss tundra, 3 = dwarf shrub tundra, 4 = forest tundra, 5 = boreal forest, 6 = alpine heath zone, 7 = subalpine and subpolar shrub, 8 = heather moor.

probably a limiting factor in the arctic deserts, as well as on the most barren mountains. Indeed, such arctic areas support only a very limited terrestrial bird fauna. Do the species have special dietary requirements that can be satisfied only within the selected, different vegetation zones? Tundra plovers feed mainly on surface-living and subterranean invertebrates. Berries, which are mainly confined to dwarf shrub habitats (*Empetrum* spp., *Vaccinium* spp., *Rubus chaememorus*), form a substantial component of the golden plovers' diet both on arrival on the breeding grounds (when old berries are available) and in late summer (Chapter 12). How important are berries to golden plovers, and are berries more important to them than to Grey Plovers? The answer seems to be no, for studies of Grey Plovers breeding within the dwarf shrub zone reveal that they, too, do feed on berries when available (Kondrat'ev 1982).

To the south, forests have a profound influence on habitat availability. Being birds of the open, tundra plovers avoid dense growths of trees, as has been shown for the Eurasian Golden Plover, notably in Sweden (Alexandersson 1987). Wet forest bogs are avoided, hence we find expansions of the Eurasian Golden Plover into recently drained forest mires in Finland (Hildén & Hyytiä 1981; a matter we discuss in the next chapter). Wet forest bogs ('muskeg' type of habitat) tend to have taller vegetation than that preferred by plovers. Many of the northern forests have large open spaces. Presumably, therefore, wet bogs and tall vegetation are more significant deterrents than bog size in limiting tundra plover distributions in the northern forest zones. We suggest that habitat structure measurements in relation to plover distribution on a north–south transect, from tundra to taiga, are needed to confirm our inferences here. Vast northern plains would have become available to the Eurasian Golden Plover as forest clearance spread. Fire was probably used by humans as early as 500 thousand years ago, and intensively over the past 20 thousand years (Tallis 1991).

The southward limit of Eurasian Golden Plover distribution in western Europe seems to be set clearly by cultivation of land. The species has not, like Eurasian Curlews, Eurasian Oystercatchers and Northern Lapwings, adapted to breed on cropland and grass fields (Glutz von Blotzheim *et al.* 1975, 1977; Cramp & Simmons 1983). The closest they have come to breeding in cultivated fields was when they colonized fields used in northern Germany in the 17th–19th centuries for growing *Fagopoyrum* (Steiniger 1959). There, the natural vegetation was cut and burnt and seeds were sown in the hot ashes. Crops were grown for only a limited number of consecutive seasons, after which fields were left barren, and then new areas were treated. The abandoned fields had an impoverished soil supporting only a short and sparse vegetation. At that stage, Eurasian Golden Plovers moved in to breed, and this form of land-use created breeding habitat for a considerable number of pairs (Steiniger 1959).

Climatic factors

Climate may influence distributions in a number of ways. Climate ultimately determines the vegetative zones to which the birds are more or less confined. Furthermore, temperature, rainfall and wind may impose limits on the abundance and activity of invertebrate prey, as well as on the metabolic needs of the birds.

So far as tolerances of the birds themselves are concerned, cold-hardiness of young chicks readily springs to mind. The distribution of certain ducks in Europe seems to be influenced by the cold tolerances of ducklings (Koskimies & Lahti 1964). Eurasian and American golden plover chicks appear to have a high tolerance for low temperatures (Myhre & Steen 1979; Visser & Ricklefs 1993), but information about the other congeners are lacking. Although temperature tolerances of chicks may provide a proximate explanation for the distribution of a species, the ultimate cause of such physiological differences remains obscure. Moreover, day-to-day temperatures can vary enormously, even in the arctic and high montane areas, especially at ground level (cf. Geiger 1961; Skartveit *et al.* 1975; Chernov 1985; Sage 1986; Holt & Whitfield 1996). Presumably, the temperature fluctuations have more important impacts on food availability rather than on the physiological tolerances of the chicks (let alone their parents).

Inter-specific competition

As they are very similar morphologically, tundra plovers might be expected to compete for resources in areas where their distributions overlap (e.g. Hutchinson 1959; MacArthur 1972). The critical resource here would seem to be: (i) territorial space in order to avoid density-dependent nest predation (cf. Göransson *et al.* 1975; Thompson *et al.* 1988; Byrkjedal 1989a); and (ii) food. All four species defend very large territories. Although no study has rigorously compared the food of tundra plovers from any one site, general food lists from breeding grounds show a potential high food overlap (Chapter 12). Plovers are visual foragers, tending to take food from the vegetation and ground surfaces and in the upper sub-surface layer of the ground (e.g. Thompson 1983a, 1984; Byrkjedal 1985a). Bill length is usually considered a good indicator of food similarity between species. All three golden plovers have virtually identical bill lengths (Table 6). Body size, though, usually considered indicative of the potential for winning a combat, differs more between the species.

According to the body mass ratios given in Table 6, Grey Plovers should be dominant, and golden plovers should be subdominant. Observations from migration stopover sites indicate that the largest species is the one which indeed wins the contests, though this is not at all so on the breeding grounds (Table 7). On the latter, territory ownership, rather than size, seems to be the decisive factor. As a consequence, the timing of their arrival on breeding territories may be what matters in competition between these species.

Over most of their breeding grounds, Grey Plovers arrive and breed later than sympatric golden plovers, especially in areas overlapping with Eurasian and American golden plovers (Chapter 7). Have these golden plovers, by arriving earlier, managed to exclude Grey Plovers to the lichen-moss zone, away from the presumably more productive dwarf shrub tundra? After all, Grey Plovers breed numerously on dwarf shrub tundra in northeast Asia and in west Alaska, where they tend to arrive before golden plovers.

Competition may also influence the distribution of Pacific and Eurasian golden plovers in west and north central Siberia. Eastwards, Pacific Golden Plovers tend to arrive earlier than Eurasian Golden Plovers, yet westwards the converse is so, with the dividing line apparently situated somewhere near Yenisei. East of this, the Pacific Golden Plovers may have an increasing competitive advantage over Eurasian Golden Plovers. If competitive exclusion does operate between these species, cold springs with a late thaw in west Siberia (preventing Eurasian Golden Plovers from occupying their territories early) should favour a westward expansion of Pacific Golden Plovers, whilst Eurasian Golden Plovers might reinforce their foothold eastwards in years with a late thaw east of Yenisei.

One of the most interesting relationships is that between American and Pacific golden plovers in west Alaska. Both species are said to arrive at the same time (Kessel 1989), and Connors *et al.* (1993) found them breeding on adjacent territories (although American Golden Plovers tended to choose drier upland habitats, compared with the wetter coastal tundra more often used by Pacific Golden Plovers). Inter-specific chases and fights seem to be common between these two species in western Alaska, apparently creating interspecific territoriality (Connors *et al.* 1993).

Although habitat shifts by species at different localities may reflect the outcome of competition (e.g. the Pacific Golden Plover on South Yamal breeds on extremely dry lichen habitat, a habitat chosen by Grey Plovers on north Yamal where Pacific Golden Plovers breed in sedge-tussock tundra), year-to-year studies of numerical responses and habitat use at single localities would be necessary. A decrease in number of Grey Plovers breeding on certain Canadian sites may be a response to increases in numbers of American Golden Plovers (Vink *et al.* 1988; Parker & Ross 1973; Pattie 1990).

Experimental exclusion studies, using tundra plover models or taxidermic mounts and sound playback, would be interesting if carried out during the period of territory establishment. These could be performed both in areas with only one tundra plover species and in those with more than one.

Breeding distribution in relation to migration distances and phenology

With the exception of some of the westernmost Eurasian Golden Plover populations, tundra plovers are long-distance migrants. Alerstam *et al.* (1986) proposed that migration distance and the availability of staging posts on spring migration could constrain the breeding distributions of waders in the Arctic. Insufficient access to staging posts might allow the birds to arrive at their breeding grounds early enough to complete their nesting. This argument depends on the distances the birds would be able to cover before 'refuelling', and how much time they need to 'refuel' before continuing. On migration, tundra plovers cover large tracts of uninhabitable land. They pass over the world's largest forests (Amazonas, Siberian taiga) or extremely large stretches of ocean (Northwest Atlantic, Pacific) evidently without staging.

Could birds with such capabilities for non-stop flight (see Johnson *et al.* 1989, Castro & Myers 1989) be limited in their present distribution by migration distances, as alluded to earlier? The problem seems most relevant to east–west limits to golden plovers, as none of them breed circumpolarly. For Pacific Golden Plovers the distance from their nearest wintering grounds to the mouth of Petchora, about 4800 km, is actually 100 km shorter than it is to Yamal, where they do breed. Moreover, Pacific Golden Plovers fly 3800–4500 km non-stop from Hawaii to reach their breeding grounds in Alaska (Johnson *et al.* 1989). In order to discuss this aspect further, however, we need more information about spring staging sites.

A special case may be the American Golden Plover distribution towards the west. According to Kessel (1989), American Golden Plovers arrive in west Alaska in mid-May. At that time, winter prevails on the west side of the Bering Strait for at least another two weeks. Any American Golden Plovers over-shooting their west Alaskan destiny and finding themselves on the Asian side would probably make a return migration to the American side or, if unable to do so, quickly succumb and die. Thus, dissimilarities in spring phenology may act as a barrier to efficient spreading of American Golden Plovers westwards across the Bering Strait.

A similar situation may prevent tundra plovers from breeding on the apparently suitable tundras of Labrador, Newfoundland and west Greenland. Here, the snow layer is considerable owing to the maritime climate, causing very late springs (e.g. Alerstam *et al.* 1986; Morrison 1984; Montevecchi & Tuck 1987). American Golden and Grey Plovers arriving from northward migrations in May may find it very difficult to survive in these areas for a long time, let alone prepare themselves for breeding there. In fact, relatively few shorebirds breed in these areas (Alerstam & Jönsson 1986; Hayman *et al.* 1986). Eurasian Golden Plovers have occasionally reached Newfoundland and Labrador in spring (Tuck 1968; Mactavish 1988). In 1988 they occurred there in large numbers: hundreds were reported and as many as thousands may have reached Newfoundland and Labrador in April–May (Mactavish 1988). Apparently, these birds represented a wind-drifted flight from Ireland to Iceland. In spite of such large numbers of birds, none appeared to establish themselves for breeding; spring was still many weeks away and the birds must have had problems keeping alive. Over the centuries, such wind-drifted flocks of Eurasian Golden Plovers must have reached Labrador and Newfoundland now and then, but the species has not yet been able to establish itself as a breeder on the North American continent. On less snow-rich Northeast Greenland, however, the species appears to have gained a toe-hold, probably through wind-drifted Icelandic birds (Chapter 6).

One species that could inhabit Northeast Greenland is the Grey Plover. But Greenland is far away from the species' present spring migration routes, so colonization by wind-drifted flocks is unlikely to occur.

SUMMARY

1. The tundra plovers probably emerged in the Pliocene within the last five million years. The chapter explores elements of their phylogeny and biogeography.
2. We propose that a northern tundra plover ancestor gave rise to the Grey Plover and a 'golden plover' ancestor, and that the golden plover ancestor then gave way to the Eurasian Golden Plover and a 'Lesser' golden plover ancestor. From the latter, the Pacific and American golden plovers emerged. We suggest that the last inter-glacial or glacial periods are implicated in the evolution of these two species.
3. Several factors seem to impose limits on the present-day distribution of tundra plovers. Timing of arrival in the breeding grounds may keep the following apart: Grey Plovers from golden plovers; Eurasian from Pacific golden plovers; and Pacific from American golden plovers.
4. Existing migration routes may impose significant limits on the extent of eastward or westward spread in breeding ranges. The Eurasian Golden Plover has started to breed in NE Greenland.

CHAPTER 6

Breeding Distribution, Population Trends and Status

Eurasian Golden Plover nesting in subpolar birch forest

The reason they are not now as abundant as formerly, is, first, the absence of suitable feeding ground, and secondly the eagerness with which they are pursued, allowing them no opportunity to become attached to any one locality. Civilization has encroached upon and absorbed so many of the fields bordering on the coast, to which they used to resort, that there is little room now left for them.

George H. Mackay (1891) writing about the American Golden Plover on passage along the coast of New England, USA.

HAVING discussed some of the factors which may explain the past and present-day distributions of tundra plovers, we now turn to considering the regional and recent historical variations in numbers. We present up-to-date breeding distribution maps, and estimates of the world populations of each species.

Although tundra plovers are fairly conspicuous on their breeding grounds it is, nonetheless, a considerable challenge to provide definitive distribution maps for their breeding ranges. We have resorted to the major handbooks, regional and local works as well as personal observations and communications. Where possible we have distinguished between areas of high and low abundance to provide indications of 'core' and 'marginal' areas, respectively. This distinction was based on statements in the literature, varying from numerical density estimates across different habitats to crude assessments such as 'abundant', 'uncommon', etc. Discrepancies between distribution maps given by different authors have also been used to provide us with a guide to the consistency of core and marginal areas. Hence, the distinction between these two areas should be looked upon as tentative for parts of the range.

SURVEY METHODS AND POPULATION ESTIMATES

We have attempted to estimate the size of each of the four species' world breeding populations (Table 8). Many readers will probably look upon such figures as guesstimates! However, we are reasonably confident that the figures are in the right order of magnitude. Only for Eurasian Golden Plovers were there many older estimates of breeding populations, notably for parts of western Europe.

Methodological issues

Population estimates are often interpolations or even extrapolations based on density estimates multiplied by the extent of what is considered to be suitable habitat. One problem here is that the original density estimates often relate to highly suitable areas of land, or are for high density 'study populations', giving overestimates for population sizes based on interpolation. Census methods vary a good deal, in terms of technique and observer efficiency. Some density estimates are obtained from plots on which passerine territories are being mapped. These are quite unrealistic, because the plots are often smaller than a tundra plover's territory! Many estimates of abundance are based on line transects (see Järvinen & Väisänen 1975, 1983; Buckland *et al.* 1993) which can overestimate breeding densities for two simple reasons. First, golden plovers encountered during the incubation period are usually feeding off-territory, often in loose aggregations away from breeding sites. Second, tundra plovers encountered after the hatch tend to approach the observer. Moreover, pre-hatching and post-hatching records can be widely different owing to changing responses to humans, leading to further erroneous density estimates (for details, see Hildén & Hyytiä 1981; Kålås & Byrkjedal 1984). Single counts during the incubation period may be especially unreliable because tightly sitting birds are easily missed and off-duty birds may be outside territories. Some other pairs may have lost nests to predators and quit (temporarily, until they nest again), though a few Eurasian Golden Plover territories may be taken over by 'sequential breeders' (Parr 1979, 1980). Brown & Shepherd's (1993) 'constant search effort' method, based on two visits, reduces some of these errors, and detected an average of just over 90% of 'known' Eurasian Golden Plover pairs on four study areas in Britain. Their method is now used as part of the terrestrial protocol for monitoring in the UK-wide Environmental Change Network (Thompson & Brown 1992). Stroud *et al.*'s (1987) within-plot line transect observations also seemed to reduce sampling errors. Most recently, a 'distance sampling' methodology has been devised to estimate species, including Eurasian Golden Plover, densities (Buckland, in press).

Breeding density estimates are, in our view, best made from repeated maps of pre-laying observations of territorial birds and their song flights. But this is no small task, for the weather can be poor, preventing decent observations, and successive watches are needed to record all song-flighting birds and other territorial behaviour. Not surprisingly, for most of the regional population estimates encountered in the literature other census methods have been used, or the methods themselves are not clear. Nevertheless, we have used the published estimates, trusting the local experience and judgement of observers.

Breeding densities in various parts of the range are summarized for all four species in Appendix 5. A mixture of accuracies here are amalgamated. Nevertheless, the figures indicate that breeding densities rarely exceed 5 pairs km^{-2}, and only very rarely 10 pairs km^{-2} for any of the species (Ratcliffe 1976, 1990; Thompson & Boobyer 1993, Brown 1993 for Eurasian Golden Plover). Tundra plovers have breeding territories which usually cover 0.20–0.25 km^2, sometimes even more, corresponding to densities of 4–5 pairs km^{-2} (also Maher 1959; Sauer 1962; Bengtson & Persson 1965; Ratcliffe 1976; 1990, Flint & Kondratjew 1977; Kistschinski 1980; Nethersole-Thompson & Nethersole-Thompson 1986). When attempting to assess the size of previously unestimated arctic breeding populations of tundra plovers, we have used 1–2 pairs km^{-2} for the 'core areas' of the distribution maps and 0.1–0.5 pairs km^{-2} for 'marginal' areas (Fig. 6.1). Although vast, the Arctic is in some respects easier to deal with in so far as breeding population estimates are concerned, because it appears much more uniform and is far less altered by human activity than corresponding temperate zone areas (e.g. Byrkjedal *et al.* 1997).

Value of population estimates

What is the value of such estimates? From educational and conservation perspectives they remind us that bird populations are not endlessly large, and often populations turn out to be much lower than expected or even widely believed. Scientifically based wildlife management practices become increasingly important as human activities continue to change the environment. Population size estimates are important in guiding the sorts of action needed, and in providing a basis for monitoring. Accurate estimates are currently available for only a few bird populations – of any species! Such estimates and trends are used to identify those species most vulnerable and in need of protection. Within countries, population estimates are also used to identify and put into context areas of conservation importance, such as Special Protection Areas designated in the European Union under the EC Birds Directive (EC Directive 79/409). The specialist networks of Wetlands International provide the Ramsar Convention Contracting Parties with population estimates of waterbirds (Rose & Stroud 1994). These estimates (and derived 1% thresholds) are used to identify wetlands of international importance, and are updated, where possible, every three years. Full revisions to 1% thresholds, 'benchmarks' against which sites can be assessed, are produced every nine years (Rose & Stroud 1994; formally adopted by Ramsar Resolution VI 4 in 1996).

We have found only a few publications dealing with long-term counts of tundra plovers, most of them from migratory sites or from wintering grounds. There is a dearth of long-term shorebird counts on the breeding grounds, let alone detailed studies (Thompson & Thompson 1991), though some valuable Russian studies have been published recently (Ryabitsev & Alekseeva 1998; Morozov 1998; Gilyazov 1998). Monitoring bird populations on a large geographical scale is, naturally, a very laborious task, especially when species, such as those dealt with here, breed in areas so little inhabited by humans. Yet, even the results from monitoring at single locations, or over limited areas, are problematical because changes caused by local shifts in bird abundance may be hard to distinguish from real population changes.

Below we treat the four species separately, and comment on population changes, status and distribution maps. Our population estimates are generally much higher than others, and we hope this will stimulate a more critical approach to producing such assessments of population sizes of shorebirds.

GREY PLOVER

Distribution and numbers

Unlike the other three species, the Grey Plover has an almost circumpolar arctic distribution, ranging along the northern part of the dwarf shrub tundra and, above all, across the lichen-moss tundra (Fig. 5.3) from the eastern side of the White Sea eastwards across the Bering Strait to Baffin Island (Fig. 6.1a). Over much of its range, in Eurasia as well as in North America, the Grey Plover is closely tied to coastal tundra. The exception seems to be in western and northern Central Siberia, where it appears to be numerous even in the interior of the large peninsulas (e.g. Morozov 1998; Ryabitsev & Alekseeva 1998). But more information on abundance is needed from interior regions of Taimyr, the largest Asian arctic peninsula, which has barren arctic alpine habitats (e.g. Chernov 1985; Sage 1986). Mountain/alpine zone (above the northern tree-line) breeding records have been made in the Chukchi Range, but the species is apparently rare there, and it does not penetrate (anywhere) into the forest tundra zone (Dement'ev & Gladkov 1951; Johansen 1958, 1960). Thus, in Eurasia, the southern limit follows that of the dwarf shrub tundra. Yet, in North America, especially in Canada, the Grey Plover does not even penetrate far into the dwarf shrub tundra, and is almost totally confined to the lichen-moss zone. Perhaps it has disappeared from the former, where it may have been excluded by the American Golden Plover (Chapter 5, and see below).

(a)

FIG. 6.1(a–d). *Breeding distribution of tundra plovers: (a) Grey Plover, (b) Eurasian Golden Plover, (c) Pacific Golden Plover, and (d) American Golden Plover. Core (dark shading) areas are shown separately. Dots (●) provide breeding records outside the normal limits of the breeding range, and ? indicates indirect evidence for breeding (such as injury feigning, etc.). Sources are: Dement'ev & Gladkov (1951), Johansen (1958, 1960), Kozlova (1961), Flint et al. (1968), Godfrey (1979, 1986), Johnsgard (1981), Cramp & Simmons (1983), and Hayman et al. (1986). Modifications to, and further details on abundance, come from: 1. de Korte (1975), 2. de Korte et al. (1981), 3. Thompson & Boobyer (1993), 4. Sharrock (1976), 5. Ratcliffe (1976), 6. Scharringa (1976), 7. Brinkmann (1962), 8. Glutz von Blotzheim et al. (1975), 9. Fabricius & Hald Mortensen (1969), 10. Dybbro (1976), 11. Lepiksaar & Zastrov (1963), 12. Pavel S. Tomkovich (pers. comm.), 13. Kålås & Byrkjedal (1981), 14. Karvik (1964), 15. Sveriges ornitologiska förening (1962), 16. Alexandersson (1987), 17. Nilsson (1977), 18. Bengtson & Persson (1965), 19. Gjershaug et al. (1994), 20. Hyytiä et al. (1983), 21. Merikallio (1958), 22. Tomkovich & Vronskij (1988b), 23. Danilov et al. (1984), 24. Portenko (1972), 25. Tomkovich & Vronskij (1988a), 26. Tomkovich (1988), 27. Walter (1902), 28. Haviland (1915), 29. Kistchinski (1980), 30. Kretchmar et al. (1978), 31. Kiryuschenko (1973), 32. Flint & Kondratjew (1977), 33. Kondrat'ev (1982), 34. Stischov (1989), 35. Holmes & Black (1973), 36. Gabrielson & Lincoln (1959), 37. Kessel (1989), 38. Johnson & Herter (1989), 39. Manning & Macpherson (1961), 40. Porsild (1943), 41. Höhn (1959), 42. Parmelee et al. (1967), 43. Macpherson & Manning (1959), 44. Manning et al. (1956), 45. Montgomerie et al. (1983), 46. Hussell & Holroyd (1974), 47. Renaud et al. (1979), 48. Hussell & Page (1976), 49. Drury (1961), 50. Sutton (1932), 51. Sutton & Parmelee (1956), 52. Frimer & Nielsen (1990), Frimer (1993), 53. Connors (1983), 54. Connors et al. (1993), 55. Maher (1959), 56. Tomkovich & Solov'ev (1988), 57. Sage (1974), 58. Parker & Ross (1973), 59. Renaud et al. (1981), 60. Savile (1951), 61. Jehl & Smith (1970), 62. Peck (1972), 63. Peck & James (1983), 64. Labutin et al. (1988), 65. Haviland (1915), 66. Flint (1976), 67. Walkinshaw (1948), 68. Sauer (1962), 69. Brandt (1943), 70. Swarth (1934), 71. Hildén & Hyytiä (1981), 72. Stischov et al. (1991), 73. Ahlén & Tjernberg (1992), 74. Priednieks et al. (1989), 75. Sage (1975), 76. Murie (1946), 77. Thompson (1967), 78. Boertmann (1994).*

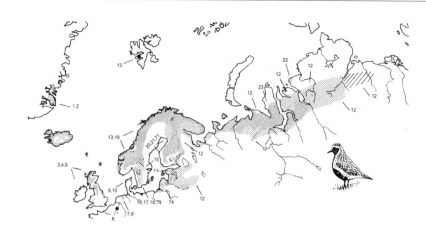

(b)

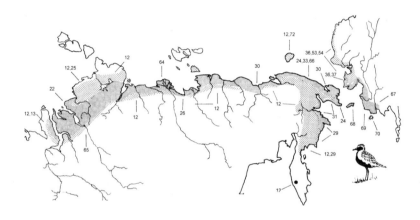

(c)

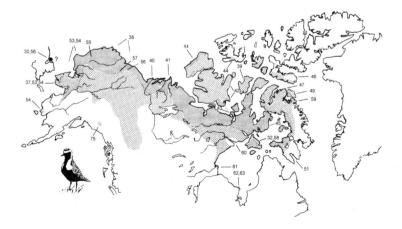

(d)

Northwards, the species is limited by the polar desert zone. In Eurasia, Grey Plovers breed on only a few of the arctic islands (though they are particularly common on Wrangel Island), contrary to the situation in the NE Canadian archipelago. They breed regularly as far north as Bathurst Island, only some 200–300 km south of the present location of the magnetic North Pole. The Canadian arctic polar deserts contain scattered 'arctic oases' (Bliss 1977; Sage 1986) with a comparatively lush vegetation, and here Grey Plovers can breed locally at high densities. The Grey Plover is the most arctic of the four tundra plovers. It is absent as a breeder on both sides of the North Atlantic, however, where the heaths are primarily dominated by dwarf shrubs (arctic, alpine, heather moors, etc.), which seem to be unsuitable. Nevertheless, absences from Greenland and the North Canadian archipelago are puzzling, given that there are some large areas of apparently suitable habitat (e.g. on Ellesmere, D.P. Whitfield pers. comm.).

We estimate that the world breeding population is 1.4–3.2 million pairs (Table 8). This is at least six times higher than the most recent 'official' estimate of a maximum of around 500 000 individuals (Rose & Scott 1994). The core area, which tends to follow the arctic coastal tundra strips, may be narrower than the one used in our calculations, so the lower figure in our estimates is perhaps closer to the real population size. We should remember that the actual extent of the tundra is immense, covering some 8.2% of the global land surface (Tallis 1991; Chapter 5); the high population estimate does not surprise us!

Grey Plovers giving way to American Golden Plovers

On the breeding grounds no large-scale population changes have been detected. Bent (1929) noted that Grey Plovers had decreased notably on passage at many localities in North America over 'the past 75 years' but attributed this mainly to a shift to other localities as a response to heavy hunting pressure. When spring hunting was banned, numbers increased rapidly again on the previously hunted spring passage localities. Over the last few decades, however, observations from some arctic Canadian localities seem to indicate that the Grey Plover is in the process of giving way to American Golden Plovers. A shift in favour of American Golden Plover appears to have taken place at Cambridge Bay (Parmelee *et al.* 1967 cf. Vink *et al.* 1988), possibly at Southampton Island (Sutton 1932 cf. Parker & Ross 1973), and probably at Truelove Lowlands, Devon Island (16 years standardized counts: Pattie 1990). Perhaps this is linked with the tendency for American Golden Plovers to return to their breeding grounds before Grey Plovers (Chapters 5 and 10). Data from more sites are needed to establish whether or not this is a general phenomenon within arctic North America.

Population increases in the Western Palearctic

For the Old World, there is no information to shed light on changes in populations on the breeding grounds. However, long-term counts on migration and wintering sites indicate changes, with the East Atlantic flyway population observed to increase in recent decades (Meltofte *et al.* 1994; Poot *et al.* 1996). Yet, the increase in numbers in the Dutch Delta, in the period 1964–65 to 1978–79, is somewhat difficult to interpret because of the profound habitat changes which took place there (Lambeck *et al.* 1989).

The most extraordinary change has been the huge increase in recorded numbers of wintering Grey Plovers in the British Isles (Prater 1981a; Thom 1986; Townshend 1986; Moser 1988; Tubbs 1991, 1996a; Cranswick *et al.* 1996). Here, an increase by over eightfold appears to have occurred in the short period from 1970–71 (peak winter count of 5570 birds) to the mid-1990s (peak winter count of 47 620 birds in 1991/92), although the increase may actually have started in the 1950s (Moser 1988). As Thom (1986) points out for Scotland, Baxter & Rintoul (1953) gave no records of flocks of more than 50–60 birds, yet many post-1980 counts of more than 50 birds have been made. Furthermore, Colin Tubbs (1996a), who had made an exhaustive study of the published and unpublished literature from the early 19th century onwards, 'can find no suggestion that they occurred anywhere in hundreds, whilst most numerical references are to 50 or less.' It seems that Grey Plovers were comparatively scarce on British estuaries prior to the 1950s and 1960s.

Tubbs (1991, 1996a,b) ascribes some of the increase to a decline in hunting pressure leading to a subsequent shift in the use of wintering sites. Moser (1988), however, favours the idea that an absolute increase in populations has taken place. Mike Moser indicated that European and African counts have shown stable or increasing trends, while the estuarine flats in Great Britain have shrunk as a result of land-claim. From this, he concludes that the observed increase in Britain probably represents an increase on the breeding grounds. Dave Townshend (1986) reinforces this view, proposing that year-to-year variation in numbers arriving in the British Isles in autumn are due to differences in the number of juveniles.

There is no evidence for a substantial increase of the breeding population having taken place on the tundra west of the Urals, however, from where most of the Grey Plovers wintering in Europe appear to originate (Chapter 10, Branson & Minton 1976). And for this to have happened there should also have been an increase in survival or breeding performance. The latter is not supported by long-term counts at migratory sites in Scandinavia, and no corresponding changes are indicated at a stopover site in Denmark (1928–82, Meltofte 1987), in southwest Norway (1947–67), or on passage in south Sweden (1949–89) (Fig. 6.2). Moreover, no changes have been noted in numbers passing the Kola Peninsula over the last couple of decades (I.P. Tatarinkova pers. comm.). So, perhaps the increase in Grey Plovers wintering in Britain is largely due to a shift in their use of wintering sites, possibly precipitated by disturbance or other changes in habitat availability.

Although the Grey Plover has been protected in Great Britain since 1954 (Tubbs 1991), it is still subject to heavy hunting in many European countries. We believe that more of the autumn birds have remained on British estuaries (rather then moving farther south after moulting), because of a reduction in shooting pressure in Britain. This would explain the steady build-up in numbers, with the preferred 'core' estuaries filling up first to reach some sort of carrying capacity (Moser 1988), and then the birds spill over onto other estuaries – as autumn and early winter numbers build up annually.

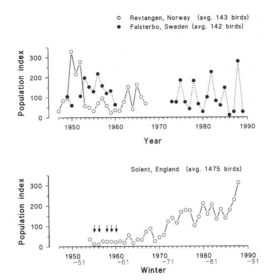

FIG. 6.2.   *Population trends of Grey Plover at two Scandinavian migratory sites and an English wintering site, expressed as % of average annual figures.*
Data and sources: Revtangen: annual totals of daily maximal numbers of staging birds, 20 August–10 October, redrawn from Byrkjedal & Bernhoft-Osa (1982); Falsterbo: annual totals of daily counts (dawn to 1400 h) of migrating birds 11 August–20 November (less standardized 1949–60; average used for 1973–89), from annual reports in Vår fågelvärld *(1949–73) and* Anser *(1974–89); Solent: pooled data for winter counts at Langstone and Chichester Harbours; recalculated from Tubbs (1991). Arrows indicate where there were no counts at Chichester Harbour, and so populations are conservatively given as 100 birds (also, see Tubbs 1996a).*

EURASIAN GOLDEN PLOVER

Distribution and numbers

This species breeds on the heather moors and alpine heaths from the North Sea countries and Iceland, over Scandinavia and along the dwarf shrub tundra east to north central Siberia (Fig. 6.1b). The species is less numerous on the tundra east of Yenesei, and it breeds only sparsely on the Putorana Plateau (Morozov 1998; V. Morozov pers. comm. via P.S. Tomkovich). Nests have been found east of Khatanga, on Taimyr, but summering birds have been seen as far east as Anabar River though breeding there has not been proven (Tomkovich 1992 and pers. comm.), possibly as a result of low ornithological activity in the area (Il'ičev & Flint 1985). To the west, the core area extends to the British Isles and Iceland, and a few pairs have established themselves in east Greenland where they have been described as local breeders (Boertmann 1994).

The Eurasian Golden Plover's distribution typically follows the tundra zone of dwarf shrubs and, to the west, occurs in sub-alpine and alpine heaths and mires. The northern limit usually falls within the northern fringe of this zone, and relatively few birds breed within the lichen-moss tundra zone proper. The distribution extends well into the forest zone, however. In Siberia and northwest Russia, they breed on the forest tundra, and in northern Fennoscandia they are numerous in open, stunted sub-polar and sub-alpine birch forest. In the last of these they nest not only on bogs and in open spaces, but also in between the trees where vegetation growth is open (also Pulliainen & Saari 1993; H.M.S. Blair pers. comm.).

To the south, on both sides of the Baltic, Eurasian Golden Plovers inhabit vast areas of the boreal coniferous forest zone. Here they breed on sloping fens and aapa mires, but also in areas clear-felled of trees. Although local breeding densities on individual mire systems can reach those of densely inhabited open heaths and moorland (Nilsson 1977; Alexandersson 1987; Thompson & Boobyer 1993), the overall density in these bogland areas is far lower, as the birds do not breed in between the trees in this type of forest, which, in contrast to sub-alpine/sub-polar birch forest, has far taller trees forming a more closed forest canopy.

In south Swedish forests, Alexandersson (1987) found that Eurasian Golden Plover densities increased with bog area up to 0.5 km^2 in size, at which the density levelled off at around 4 pairs km^{-2}. Bog areas there should be at least 0.13 km^2 in order to support breeding golden plovers (see also Nilsson 1977). Finland has many Eurasian Golden Plovers within its forest zone, where they are widespread and locally common.

In the British Isles, the breeding distribution at the 10 km^2 level has been described in detail for the late 1960s/early 1970s (Sharrock 1976; Ratcliffe 1976) and for the late 1980s and early 1990s (Thompson & Boobyer 1993, also Brown 1993; Whitfield 1997a). Figure 6.3a gives the latest distribution maps, and Figure 6.3b shows recorded changes between 1968–72 and 1988–81. Highest densities have been recorded on alpine blanket mire or southern sub-alpine blanket mire/wet heath and rough grassland areas, with the mires characterized by much exposure of erosion haggs and bare peat (see Appendix 5). On the Isle of Lewis, part of the Western Isles of Scotland, 14% of the British breeding population occurs on what is predominantly eroded *Racomitrium lanuginosum*-dominated blanket mire (Whitfield 1997a).

Britain has high densities of Eurasian Golden Plovers. At least five factors seem to account for some parts of Britain having these. First, some upland localities have fertile soils, notably where there are limestone grasslands next to moorland (Ratcliffe 1976). Second, in the alpine montane bogs of the Highlands, and throughout the Western Isles and the Pennines, the exposed expanses of eroding blanket mire hold high densities of golden plovers, possibly because prey are more available (or conspicuous) there, and predation pressure is low (there is much pest and illegal predator control in parts of the Pennines). Third, the close juxtaposition of pasture fields and moorland habitats may provide a good combination of habitats for off-duty birds during incubation to the extent that much higher numbers are sustained than in the extensive tracts of tundra or boreal forest open plains. Fourth, the heaths next to wet acid grassland or boggy patches provide an ample range of feeding for adults and chicks (Whittingham 1996a; O'Connell *et al.* 1996). Fifth, the close proximity of breeding to wintering grounds may reduce non-breeding season mortality in some parts. Combinations

changes. Nevertheless, Gibbons *et al.* (1996) found that the Eurasian Golden Plover is one of 26 species to have decreased most in abundance in the UK since 1800.

The most compelling account of a breeding population's decline is provided by Ray Parr (1992). He describes a population at Kerloch, NE Scotland, which went from 85 birds (17 territories occupied) in 1974, up to about 120 birds (15–17 territories) by 1977, and then to zero in 1990. There has been no subsequent recovery (Ray Parr, pers. comm.). Parr (1992) attributed the decline to winter losses (mortality and/or emigration) and, in later years, nest predation (which coincided with afforestation of part of the area). The impact of winter losses *per se* may not have been that great, however (also Harding *et al.* 1993), because breeding success was significantly lower during the 'decline' phase and may have precipitated reduced breeding site fidelity and insufficient recruitment. Indeed, the main decline in number of occupied territories occurred from 1984 onwards, when there was poor breeding.

George Boobyer (1992) and Thompson & Boobyer (1993) discuss a number of possible factors implicated in these diminutions. The recent practice of turning old grasslands (old pastures) into arable land or agriculturally 'improved' pastures may be particularly important. Old grasslands contain a richer soil fauna, in particular more earthworms (Thompson 1984; Edwards & Lofty 1993; Barnard & Thompson 1995; Downie *et al.* 1996), and provide favoured feeding habitat for wintering birds (Fuller & Youngman 1979; Barnard & Thompson 1985; Chapter 11). Losses of these grasslands may well account for sharp declines in numbers of wintering and breeding birds.

Furthermore, there has been a tendency for many of the upland grasslands, not least those re-seeded (having been 'reclaimed' from moorland), to have become rushier and, in parts, wetter. These seem to be less attractive to golden plovers because of their reduced earthworm densities (though are favoured by other shorebirds such as Northern Lapwing, Common Redshank and Common Snipe). Interestingly, *Juncus* rushes can be most prevalent in formerly rich soil fields, and this might explain why adult golden plovers remain faithful to a few of these (such as in the Flow Country). Some of these, as well as lowland 'old' pasture fields, have been used traditionally over many decades (as we discuss in Chapter 8 also), and their deterioration probably accounts for many of the more local declines. Indeed, numbers may have reached a temporary 'high' during the mid-1940–70s era when many of the 'rough grazings' were created. Between the 1950s and 1970s substantial areas of moorland were drained and re-seeded. Later, grant-aid for this was withdrawn and further creation of rough grazings ceased. Figure 6.5 indicates recent declines in the extent of these throughout Britain. It is notable that some of the most marked golden plover declines have occurred in areas where rough grazings/fields are used by off-duty birds (also O'Connell *et al.* 1996; Whittingham 1996a, though see Brown 1993 for the S. Pennines), rather than in the alpine/montane areas or on Lewis, where most off-duty birds feed on territory (also Holt & Whitfield 1996; D.P. Whitfield and K. Shepherd pers. comm.) and numbers are stable or even increasing.

There have been some other recent changes on British moors. Derek and Pat Yalden (Yalden & Yalden 1990) considered recreational disturbance to be

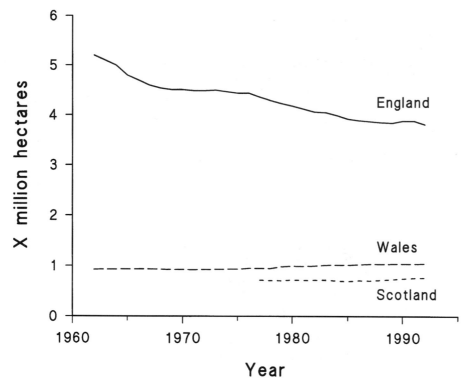

FIG. 6.5.   *Changes in extent of rough grazing (hectares) in Great Britain. These exclude 'common' grazings in England and Wales, and largely embrace moorland areas drained and re-seeded with grass. Data from Ministry for Agriculture and Fisheries, MAFF (England and Wales) and Scottish Office Agriculture, Environment and Fisheries Department, SOAEFD (Scotland), compiled by Rob Fuller and Su Gough, BTO.*

important in the Peak District in keeping some local populations low (but see Brown 1993; Harding *et al.* 1993). Yalden & Pearce-Higgins (1997) detected an effect of severe winter weather (but not breeding season weather) on spring population size in the Peak District. On Derek Ratcliffe's best study area for golden plovers (Mallerstang limestone plateau), where to our knowledge the recorded breeding density of 16.4 pairs km^{-2} (during 1963–75) has not been surpassed anywhere, there has been a substantial decline evidently related to disturbance from hang gliding (D. A. Ratcliffe pers. comm.). Generally, heather moors are nowadays less well 'keepered' for grouse shooting (Haworth & Thompson 1990; Tapper 1992; Boobyer 1992; Thompson & Boobyer 1993; Parr 1992; Thompson *et al.* 1995b,c, 1997; Phillips & Watson 1995), and some workers have linked this with increases in numbers of 'pest' species such as crows and foxes (Hudson 1992, 1995; Tapper 1992). Gamekeeping involves pest control and habitat management practices favourable to Red Grouse, but with many of the practices also benefiting breeding golden plovers (Thompson *et al.* 1995c, 1997; Brown & Bainbridge 1995).

Increasing populations in European boreal forests

Considerable population changes in Eurasian Golden Plover numbers have taken place within the boreal coniferous forest zone during the 20th century (Fig. 6.6), notably in Finland and the eastern Baltic countries. Much of the southern Swedish forest population was censused in 1975–80, when the species was found to be more abundant than had been suspected previously, but numbers did not amount to more than around 3800 pairs (Ahlén & Tjernberg 1992). Finland has a special position in northern Europe as far as bird censuses are concerned. Nationwide surveys based on innumerable line transects had already been published by Merikallio in 1958, and were followed up by Järvinen & Väisänen (1975, 1977, 1983 and in other years!). A breeding bird atlas (Hyytiä *et al.* 1983) and supplement

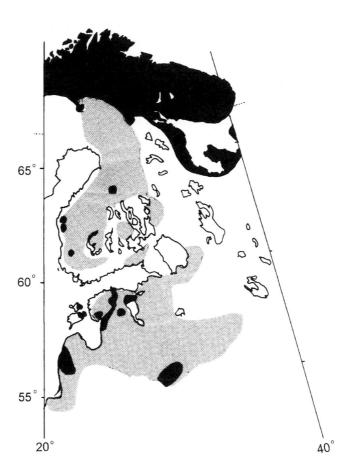

FIG. 6.6.   *Breeding distribution of Eurasian Golden Plover in Finland and adjacent areas, and in the eastern Baltic, around 1950 (black) and present (black and shaded). Sources: Merikallio (1958), Lepiksaar & Zastrov (1963), Hildén & Hyytiä (1981), Cramp & Simmons (1983), Hyytiä* et al. *(1983), Priednieks* et al. *(1989), Tomkovich (1992 and pers. comm.).*

(Koskimies 1989) have been published, and the status of breeding waders was treated in a special account by Hildén & Hyytiä (1981).

From these sources it appears that Eurasian Golden Plovers have had, and still have, their stronghold in the northern alpine (montane) and sub-alpine areas during the 20th century. However, during the beginning of the 20th century a number of locations within the coniferous forest zone also held breeding golden plovers. By the 1950s, however, golden plovers were absent from most of these, though birds subsequently started to re-colonize some of the forest areas and indeed expanded into new ones. They are now more numerous and widespread than ever in the 20th century.

The estimated breeding population in Finland, based on line transect censuses, gives an unduly optimistic impression of the population development over the latter half of the 20th century (Merikallio 1958: 21 000 pairs; Järvinen & Väisänen pers. comm. to Nethersole-Thompson & Nethersole-Thompson 1986: 258 000 pairs!). In their 1981 paper, Hildén & Hyytiä (1981) judged the Finnish Eurasian Golden Plover population to be at 50 000–200 000 pairs, and Koskimies (1989) gives a total population of 50 000–100 000 pairs. While there is no doubt that golden plovers have increased considerably in numbers and expanded their range in Finland over the last few decades, some of the increase may be apparent rather than real, as forest bogs were under-represented in the older censuses (Hildén & Hyytiä 1981).

According to Hildén & Hyytiä (1981) two main factors have favoured breeding golden plovers through creating new habitats in the Finnish forest zone: (i) drainage of mires for improved forest production; and (ii) large-scale clear felling of forests. The effect of these two factors should only be temporary ones, however, as drainage and clear felling are followed by afforestation. But, large clear-cut areas do seem to have produced golden plover habitat of a more permanent character, and over large northern tracts the Finnish forests have not regenerated readily. Clear fells of 10 000 ha were made in many parts in northern and eastern Finnish pine forests, especially in the 1950s. Many of these still remain rather tundra-like. By the early 1970s, 100 000–150 000 ha clearfell areas remained treeless (Hildén & Hyytiä 1981, also Koskimies 1989).

Recently, in the eastern Baltic countries, Eurasian Golden Plovers appear to have expanded their breeding distribution considerably. Though some of this is due to improved knowledge of numbers (cf. Priednieks *et al.* 1989), real range extensions have taken place in the last decade or two, and a population increase appears general (Tomkovich 1992 and pers. comm.). From 1960 to the early 1990s a marked rise in numbers of migrating Eurasian Golden Plovers has been noted in the German Baltic region (Kube *et al.* 1994), presumably reflecting the growing populations in the East Baltic and Finland.

Stable populations in the north?

Alpine/montane Icelandic and Fennoscandian populations, together with those of arctic and sub-arctic Russian tundra, constitute around 95% of the breeding Eurasian Golden Plovers of the world (Table 8). Monitoring bird populations over such a vast and to a large extent inaccessible area is a formidable task. Existing information from these breeding grounds is not sufficient to judge current population trends. Alex Gilyazov (1998) and colleagues have monitored shorebirds in the Lapland Nature Reserve in the western part of the Kola Peninsula. They found no marked overall changes in Eurasian Golden Plover numbers between 1960 and 1991 (with fluctuations between 0.7 and 5.0 individuals km^{-2}). However, numbers fluctuated every 4–5 years in tandem with small rodent cycles (and evidently predation pressure). Interestingly, there are only two records of Eurasian Golden Plovers there in the 1930s, so it has become more common there only in the last 40 or so years (occupying a range of tundra and bog habitats).

Habitat has remained comparatively undisturbed over most of these areas, although oil and gas exploitation on the tundra (e.g. Vilchek & Bykova 1992) and hydroelectric power schemes in the mountains have affected or destroyed considerable tracts of land (Byrkjedal *et al.* 1997). By spending the winter mostly in areas heavily inhabited and manipulated by man, golden plover populations from these northern areas may be more susceptible to factors acting outside the breeding season. The Icelandic population of Eurasian Golden Plover passes chiefly to (and through) the British Isles (Cramp & Simmons 1983; Chapter 10), where recent changes in land-use create impoverished feeding grounds for golden plovers, as discussed above (and in Chapter 11).

However, there is no firm evidence for any population changes in the northern and alpine/montane Eurasian Golden Plover populations of Iceland, Fennoscandia and Russia. In the first few decades of the present century many hunters, gamekeepers, and ornithologists felt that numbers of golden plovers passing on autumn migration declined, notably in Sweden and Denmark (Lönnberg 1924; Fabricius & Hald Mortensen 1969). At least partly, these were thought to represent northern birds, although the north Fennoscandian and Russian birds would have been difficult if not impossible to separate from birds from dwindling Danish, Swedish and Norwegian heather moor populations. No decline is evident from the 54 years of counts of staging golden plovers (1928–82) at Tipperne, Denmark. Indeed, the species has gradually increased in numbers there since around 1950 in spring, as well as in autumn, but that increase might be due to habitat changes at Tipperne (Meltofte 1987). Counts during autumn migration at the southernmost tip of Sweden indicate no changes in numbers in the latter half of this century (Fig. 6.7), with the observed birds probably being of Scandinavian origin.

In Europe, Eurasian Golden Plovers have been popular quarries for gunners since the 19th century, especially in countries such as Denmark, France, Italy, Spain, Portugal and Britain (Lampio 1975; Boobyer 1992). In the Netherlands, mass trapping, 'wilsterflapping', involved the use of large clap nets operated with calls and live as well as artificial golden plover decoys. This practice led to as many as 40 000–80 000 birds *in a season* being trapped and killed for export – which must have been a major mortality factor (Haverschmidt 1943; Eenshuistra 1973; Jukema 1987a)! This activity is bound to have contributed to the rapid decline of middle European breeding populations, but kills of that size, occurring each year over at least half a century, and possibly much longer, could also have had a negative impact on north Scandinavian and Russian populations, for which we have no firm information on trends.

The netting of golden plovers in the Netherlands gradually diminished after World War II. Since 1978 wilsterflapping has been permitted for only ringing (and

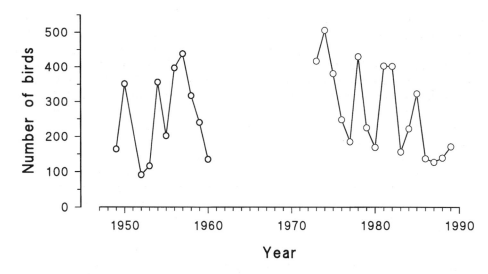

FIG. 6.7. *Variation in numbers of Eurasian Golden Plover counted passing on autumn migration at Falsterbo, Sweden. Source: annual reports in* Vår Fågelvärld *(1949–73) and* Anser *(1974–89).*

for recreation by a few of the 'old' licence holders who still trap birds but release them; Eenshuistra 1973; Jukema 1987a).

PACIFIC GOLDEN PLOVER

Distribution and numbers

The core area of this species stretches from the mainland dwarf shrub and lichen-moss tundras of Siberia, eastwards across the Bering Strait, to the western edge of Alaska (Fig. 6.1c). The southern limit goes along the northern part of forest tundra, but the species only rarely extends into this zone (Dement'ev & Gladkov 1951; Johansen 1958, 1960). In northeast Asia, Pacific Golden Plovers are also found breeding in montane (alpine) zones, in particular in the NE part of the Koryak Range (Kistchinski 1980). It has not been recorded in the mountainous areas between Lena and Kolyma, which ought to hold potential habitat, presumably because these have yet to be surveyed in detail (P. Tomkovich pers. comm., also Il'ičev & Flint 1985)! The southernmost breeding range for the species is found on northern Kamchatka; a breeding record has been made as far south as about 55°N.

In Alaska, the species has its limited core area along the coastal tundra. Unlike the American Golden Plover, it is less abundant in the upland tundras there (Kessel 1989; Connors *et al.* 1993). It is increasingly rare northwards of the Seaward Peninsula, but breeding records have been made north to Barrow (Connors 1983).

The westernmost border of the Pacific Golden Plover range follows approximately 70°E on Yamal Peninsula (e.g. Ryabitsev & Alekseeva 1998). The species has not been found breeding in the northern Urals, nor on the Bol'shesemelskaya Tundra. However, the occasional large numbers recorded in early winter in western Europe are interesting. During the first half of the 20th century many were captured by the 'wilsterflappers' in the Netherlands (Jukema 1987b,c), in contrast to only a few records made by birdwatchers (Pym 1982; Roselaar 1990; Lewington *et al.* 1991). These catches indicate that the species occasionally must have been reasonably abundant autumn and winter visitors in the Waddensee area. From there they were apparently forced on to the grasslands, where the trappers operated, as winter weather set in and made the mudflats inhospitable. Although these may have represented wind-drifted southward-bound flocks from east of the Urals, it is tempting to speculate that such large numbers of Pacific Golden Plovers on the east Atlantic flyway might have originated from westerly breeding range extensions, effectively put to an end by large-scale commercial golden plover trapping in the Netherlands (cf. Haverschmidt 1943; Eenshuistra 1973).

Little information is available on Pacific Golden Plover breeding densities, especially from the core areas (Table 8). However, finding no reason to assume a generally lower density for this species than for its congeners (cf. Haviland 1915), we arrive at an estimated world population of about 1.1–2.6 million pairs (Table 8). The most recent estimate lies between 125 000–2 million individuals (Rose & Scott 1994) – much lower than ours.

Although susceptible to man-influenced habitat changes outside the breeding season, no general increases or decreases in populations are known for this species (Connors 1983; Johnson & Connors 1996). However, Australian wintering site counts between 1986 and 1995 suggest some substantial declines (Harris 1995; but see Marchant & Higgins 1993). Considering the species' range outside the breeding season, shooting is likely to have had only local effects (Munro 1945; see however Parish & Howes 1990; Lane & Parish 1991). The species utilizes marine mudflats as well as grasslands. The creation of grassy airfields on many of the Pacific islands in the early 1940s may have had a positive influence on numbers of birds after World War II!

AMERICAN GOLDEN PLOVER

Distribution and numbers

The breeding distribution of this species extends along the dwarf shrub tundra from the Bering Strait to Baffin Island. It is also found in the lichen-moss zone on the Canadian arctic islands, where it is less abundant (Fig. 6.1d).

The southern limit of distribution extends to some degree into the northern reaches of the forest tundra zone in Canada west of Hudson Bay, and in North Alaska the species breeds abundantly from the Beaufort Sea coast up to the North Slope into the alpine zone of the Brooks Range. In the interior of Alaska breeding has been recorded southwards to about 64°N. We have found little concrete information for these montane (alpine) parts of the northwest, but judging by the topography we tentatively assume the species is less abundant there. Another area of uncertainty is the tundra zone of the Canadian mainland eastwards of Great Bear and Slave Lakes. The southern border of the American Golden Plover range here is drawn differently on distribution maps in the literature (Johnsgard 1981; Godfrey 1979; 1986; Hayman *et al.* 1986; Johnson & Connors 1996; Piersma & Wiersma 1996). This could indicate a low abundance here, and it is noteworthy that Savile (1951) did not find the species breeding near Chesterfield Inlet. Farther down the west coast of Hudson Bay, the species is common in the Churchill area, and it has been found breeding as far south as Cape Henrietta Maria (about 55°N).

To the west, the breeding range stops abruptly at the Bering Strait, in spite of the short distance across to the Siberian side. Only a few records have been made on the latter (Portenko 1972; Kretchmar *et al.* 1978), although in 1988 the species was seen regularly at the mouth of Kolyuchin Bay, where it probably bred (Tomkovich & Solov'ev 1988). It does not breed even sporadically on the tundra of Labrador or Greenland, although it has been recorded many times as a vagrant in west Greenland (Salomonsen 1967b; Montevecchi & Tuck 1987) and as a breeder at least once in north Greenland (Boertmann 1994).

Our estimates give a total population size of 1.0–2.5 million pairs (Table 8), which is at least 20 times higher than the published estimate of 10 000–100 000 individuals (Rose & Scott 1994); Wiersma (1996) gives a total of 10 000–50 000 birds. More of the interior areas northwest of Hudson Bay, as well as the arctic islands of Canada (where numbers are probably increasing, as we discuss below), may turn out to belong to the 'core' rather than 'marginal' areas, in which case even 2.5 million pairs may be on the conservative side. The previously published estimates cited above are clearly wrong. For instance, Erickson (1992) reports spring migration total counts in Benton Co., Indiana, alone, of 8000–25 000 birds – and these counts were made each year in April on one day only!

Population recovery after 19th century game hunting

Throughout the 19th century this species was subject to inexorable hunting pressure in eastern and central North America, both during spring and autumn migration (Bent 1929). It was highly valued for the 'table' and readily bagged in large numbers. Wagonloads, literally, of golden plovers were brought to the game markets. On one day alone, in spring 1821, it was estimated that 200 hunters near New Orleans shot a staggering 48 000 golden plovers (Bent 1929 citing Audubon 1840)! Persecution of this species and Eskimo Curlews in the 1860s intensified due to demands created by the failing supply of the now extinct Passenger Pigeon (Gollop *et al.* 1986). Increasing numbers of golden plovers were also shot on their wintering grounds in South America, although the numbers taken were not comparable with those slaughtered in North America.

Soon a severe decline in numbers on migration in North America was noted. By the end of the 19th century the population level was at its lowest and the species was scarce in places where it once abounded. Early in the 20th century the sale of game was stopped in the USA and Canada, and the American Golden Plover was then removed from the game quarry list. Already, by 1920, there were noted increases in the sizes of migratory flocks on the 'old' sites (Bent 1929). Unlike the Eskimo Curlew, eventually decimated by market hunting, the American Golden Plover recovered and is presently widespread and common again (Connors 1983; Johnson & Connors 1996).

It is not known whether or not population levels changed in all or parts of the species' breeding range in the 20th century. Increases in numbers have been noted on arctic sites visited repeatedly by ornithologists since the early part of the 20th century, such as on Southampton Island (Sutton 1932; Parker & Ross 1973) and Pond Inlet at Baffin Island (Renaud *et al.* 1981). An increase over the last few decades has taken place at Truelove Lowlands, Devon Island (Hussell & Holroyd 1974; Pattie 1990) and possibly in Cambridge Bay at Victoria Island (Parmelee *et al.* 1967; Vink *et al.* 1988).

SUMMARY

1. The estimated world breeding populations of tundra plovers are given, with the Grey Plover the most numerous (1.4–3.2 million pairs) and the Eurasian Golden Plover possibly the least numerous (1.1–1.9 million pairs). Population sizes of Pacific (1.1–2.6 million pairs) and American (1.0–2.5 million pairs) golden plovers are estimated to be quite similar. These estimates are considerably higher than even the most recently published assessments.
2. Grey Plovers have their core distribution on coastal arctic lichen-moss tundra, whereas golden plovers typically breed in sub-arctic and northern alpine (montane) dwarf shrub zones. In contrast to the circumpolar Grey Plover, the American Golden Plover is confined to the Nearctic, the Pacific Golden Plover mainly to the eastern Palearctic, and Eurasian Golden Plovers to the western and north-central eastern Palearctic.
3. An eightfold increase in number of wintering Grey Plovers on British estuaries has taken place since the 1970s, but no evidence indicates a corresponding increase on western Palearctic breeding grounds. A relaxation of hunting may be implicated in this increase, which probably began around the 1960s. A local replacement of Grey Plovers by American Golden Plovers may currently be taking place in arctic Canada.
4. Eurasian Golden Plover populations have declined severely in the heather moor zone of western and continental Europe during the 20th century, and continue to do so. Prime factors involved in this seem to be breeding habitat destruction due to intensive agricultural development and afforestation, and also the transformation of old pasture fields (into arable) which are feeding habitats for many wintering and off-duty incubating birds. Population increases and range expansions have taken place in the European boreal forest zone mainly because of clear felling of forests. The net effect of these changes on western populations is unknown. There is no evidence of changes in the migratory northern alpine (montane) and tundra populations.
5. Population trends for Pacific Golden Plover are unknown.
6. American Golden Plover populations declined dramatically during the 19th century owing to market hunting, but have recovered after protective measures were implemented early in the 20th century.

CHAPTER 7

Breeding Season: Breeding Schedules and Nesting

*Eurasian Golden Plover removing
eggshell from nest*

In contrast to Golden Plovers in high latitudes, British birds typically show a long spread of nesting, over the four months April–July, associated with their wide altitudinal range, and more especially the high failure rate of early nests in many areas and the laying of repeat clutches.

Derek Ratcliffe (1976)

THIS chapter and the next two present an overview of the key features of the breeding biology of tundra plovers. We have concentrated more on drawing comparisons between the four species rather than focusing on one. Derek

Ratcliffe's (1976) *Observations on the Breeding of the Golden Plover in Great Britain* remains a masterful source of information. The reader is directed to this for detailed data on distribution and nesting habitats in Britain (updated in part by Ratcliffe 1990). We have benefited greatly from Derek's more recent observations in Britain and Lapland. We have also included unpublished observations from Phil Whitfield and colleagues for high mountain areas in Scotland, Phil's own observations on Lewis, work by Mark O'Connell, Ian Downie, Chris Thomas, John Coulson and colleagues in Peter Evans' group at Durham, and an unpublished PhD thesis by Mark Whittingham (1996a). The accounts in *The Birds of North America* on Grey Plovers (by Dennis Paulson, 1995) and Pacific and American golden plovers (by Oscar Johnson and Peter Connors, 1996) have been a huge help. Much of our own material given here has not been published before.

We begin with the timing of arrival and onset of breeding. But before going into this we need to comment on the various sources of information, and our assumptions. We have summarized the literature, and drawn on unpublished information from oological collections, nest record card databases, and our own field studies. All three sources of the latter usually require that the laying date for the first egg in a nest has to be estimated by counting back from hatching dates (or from laying dates of eggs subsequent to the first one). We have assumed that egg-laying lasts 6 days, and incubation lasts 28 days (from last egg laid to first egg hatched), based on several detailed studies which we will deal with towards the end of this chapter. The few precise measurements of incubation periods and time intervals between eggs have been made almost solely for the Eurasian Golden Plover. Where nests have been observed for 3 weeks or more without recording egg-laying or hatching dates, we have estimated hatching dates as mid-way between the 'earliest possible' and 'latest possible' dates (the day after last nest inspection and 28 days after first nest inspection, respectively). To check the method we made the same calculations (using a 21 days span) on material with known hatching dates for Eurasian Golden Plovers (8 and 7 nests, respectively) and got estimated hatch dates that were 1.5 ± 1.05 standard deviation, SD, days and 1.4 ± 1.13 SD days from the real hatching dates.

Data slips with museum egg collections frequently give information on the incubation stage of the eggs. All clutches for which these labels state 'fresh' or 'non-incubated' have been considered as newly laid and included in our analysis, and here we have only counted back to the date for laying of egg number one. Embryonic development was apparently often used as the basis for the collectors' assessment of incubation stage. As this is usually hard to detect during the first few days after completion of the clutch, we suspect that the presumed date of laying based on egg collections is later than the actual date. A comparison between nest record cards (with known laying dates) and egg collections from American Golden Plovers at Barrow, Alaska confirmed this suspicion. Oological collections gave egg-laying estimates 4–5 days later than nest record cards (Mann-Whitney U-test, $U = 155.5$, $p<0.005$). Hence, egg-laying estimates from egg collections used in material presented in figures have had 4 days subtracted.

BREEDING SCHEDULE

British Isles and Norway

Figures 7.1–7.4 provide summaries for arrival, egg-laying and departure dates for the four species. When Eurasian Golden Plovers arrive at their North Central Siberian and East Greenland breeding grounds in June, many of those breeding around the North Sea and southern Baltic may have chicks (Fig. 7.2). With their maritime climate and early spring, the latter areas have golden plover populations laying mainly in April and May. The earliest tend to be the British populations, where egg-laying may start as early as late March (Ratcliffe 1976).

Many British golden plover populations winter very close to their breeding grounds and some birds frequent these periodically throughout the winter, and will even make flight displays there (Nethersole-Thompson & Nethersole-Thompson 1961, 1986; Ratcliffe 1976; Parr 1980; Thompson 1990a). But usually they are not regularly back on their breeding territories before late February. Altitude and weather conditions influence the breeding season. In Scotland, an altitudinal difference between breeding grounds of about 300–600 m may mean 2–3 weeks' difference in egg-laying (Nethersole-Thompson & Nethersole-Thompson 1961; Ratcliffe 1976). Indeed, the higher nesting grounds may not be snow-free until April (Holt & Whitfield 1996). In southern Norway, golden plovers at 1300–1400 m elevation breed about 1.5 months later than those 1000 m below (Hardangervidda vs. Jæren, Fig. 7.2). The S. Norway birds breed on a schedule similar to that of north Fennoscandia and the Arctic, and later than northern Icelandic birds.

The Arctic

In the Arctic, the phenology of all four species varies less from one site to another than is the case for Eurasian Golden Plovers in temperate areas: as a rule egg-laying takes place in June. The most notable exception to this is found on the tundra along western Alaska. Here, Grey Plovers and Pacific Golden Plovers arrive in early to mid-May (some Grey Plovers even arrive in late April), and most of the clutches are initiated in mid to late May. Just on the other side of the Bering Strait, these two species arrive and lay eggs some 3–4 weeks later. Western Alaska has a more maritime and milder climate and so spring is earlier (details on climate, e.g. Sage 1986; Kessel 1989).

A particularly late start to the breeding season is found at Taimyr for Grey Plover and Eurasian Golden Plover, and along the North Alaskan coast, and in the NE Canadian archipelago, for Grey Plover and American Golden Plover. In these places, egg-laying mostly starts in the latter half of June. However, American Golden Plovers breeding along the west coast of Hudson Bay, even south of 60°N, do not have a breeding schedule much different from those along the Arctic Sea at around 70°N. The continental low arctic climate and relatively late springs characterize the western Hudson Bay coast (Sage 1986).

End of egg-laying

The end of egg-laying tends to differ less between populations than does the onset. This seems evident both in Grey Plover, American and Eurasian Golden Plovers (Fig. 7.5a,b,d; Pacific Golden Plover material comprises far fewer nests, Fig. 7.5c).

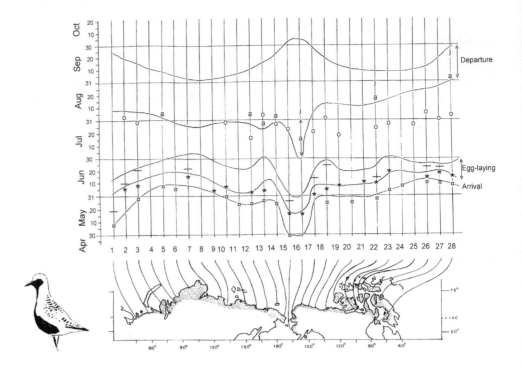

FIG. 7.1. *Arrival, egg-laying, and departure of Grey Plovers. Symbols for Figures 7.1–7.4 are as follows:*

◻ = *First recorded arrival*
* = *First recorded egg-laying (first egg)*
── = *Median*
○ = *Last active nest*
a = *adults*
j = *juveniles.*
Localities: 1. White Sea, 2. Bol'shezemelskaya Tundra, 3. Yamal Peninsula, 4. Gol'shika, 5. Dickson, 6. north-western Taimyr, 7. northeastern Taimyr, 8. Lena Delta, 9. Buor-Khaya Bay, 10. Indigirka, 11. Kolyma Lowlands, 12. Chaun Bay, 13. Wrangel Island, 14. Chukchi Peninsula, 15. Yukon-Kuskokwim Delta, 16. Seward Peninsula, 17. Barrow, 18. Prudhoe Bay, 19. Kaktovik, 20. Mackenzie-Tuktoyaktuk, 21. Banks Island, 22. Cambridge Bay, 23. Jenny Lind Island, 24. Prince of Wales Island, 25. Bathurst Island, 26. Truelove Lowlands, 27. Bylot Island and Pond Inlet, 28. Southampton Island.
Sources, and localities covered: Belopol'skij et al. (1970), 1; Seebohm (1901), 2; Dement'ev & Gladkov (1951), 2,10,12,13,14; Danilov et al. (1984), 3; IB (pers. obs.), 3; Haviland (1916), 4; Tomkovich & Vronskij (1988b), 5; Walter (1902), 6; Underhill et al. (1993), 7; Tomkovich (1988), 9; Flint & Kondratjew (1977), 10; Kondrat'ev (1982), 11,15; Portenko (1972), 13; Brandt (1943),15; Walkinshaw (1948),15; Holmes & Black (1973),15; Kessel (1989), 15,16,17; North American oological collections (corrected, see text),15,17; Johnson & Herter (1989), 18,19,20; North American nest record schemes, 18,26,28; Bent (1929), 20; Manning et al. (1956), 21; Parmelee et al. (1967), 22,23; Manning & Macpherson (1961), 24; Mayfield (1973), 25,26; Hussell & Page (1976), 26; 26, Hussell & Holroyd (1974), 26; Drury (1961), 27; Renaud et al. (1981), 27; Sutton (1932), 28.

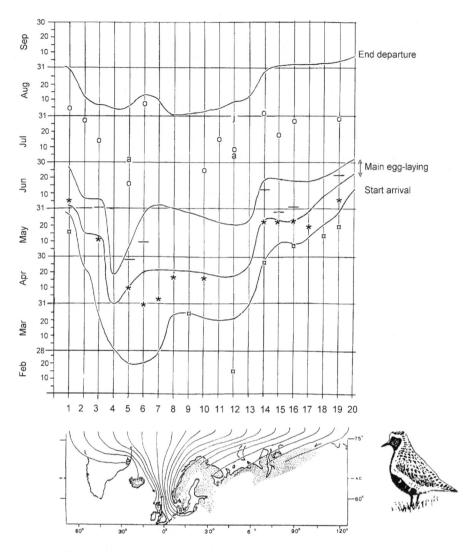

FIG. 7.2. *Arrival, egg-laying, and departure of Eurasian Golden Plovers. Symbols as in Fig. 7.1.*

Localities: 1. Scoresbysund, 2. Iceland, 3. Faroes, 4. Orkneys, 5. Kerloch, 6. Wales, 7. Netherlands, 8. northern Germany, 9. Estonia, 10. Öland, 11. Skåne, 12. Jæren, 13. south-western Sweden, 14. Hardangervidda, 15. interior Finnmark, 16. Finnish Lapland, 17. White Sea, 18. Timan Tundra, 19. Yamal Peninsula, 20. Yenisei.

Sources, and localities covered: de Korte et al. (1981),1; Glutz von Blotzheim et al. (1975), 2,7,9,14,18; Williamson (1948), 3; Nethersole-Thompson & Nethersole-Thompson (1986), 4; Parr (1980), 5; Thomas et al. (1983), 6; Thomas & Hack (1984), 6; Scharringa (1976),7; Brinkmann (1961), 8; Lammers (1969), 8; Rittinghaus (1969), 10; Bengston & Persson (1965), 11; Collett (1921), 12,15; Byrkjedal (1978a)12,14; IB (pers. obs.), 12,14,15,19; Alexandersson (1987), 13; Pulliainen & Saari (1993), 16,18, Belopolskij et al. (1970), 17,18; Dement'ev & Gladkov (1951), 18; Danilov et al. (1984), 19; Johansen (1960), 20.

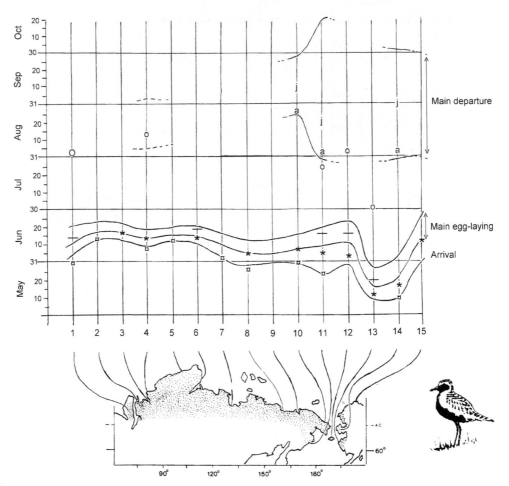

FIG. 7.3. *Arrival, egg-laying, and departure of Pacific Golden Plovers. Symbols as in Fig. 7.1.*
Localities: 1. Yamal Peninsula, 2. Gydan Peninsula, 3. Yenisei, 4. Dickson, 5. north-western Taimyr, 6. northeastern Taimyr, 7. Buor-Khaya Bay, 8. Kolyma Lowlands, 9. Chaun Bay, 10. Chukchi Peninsula, 11. Koryak Mountains, 12. St. Lawrence Island, 13. Yukon-Kuskokwim Delta, 14. Seward Peninsula, 15. Barrow.
Sources, and localities covered: Danilov et al. (1984), 1; IB (pers. obs.), 1; Dement'ev & Gladkov (1951), 2; Johansen (1960), 2; Haviland (1915), 3; Tomkovich & Vronskij (1988b), 4; Tomkovich & Vronskij (1988a), 5; Underhill et al. (1993), 6; Tomkovich (1988), 7; Kondrat'ev (1982), 8,9,10; Portenko (1972), 10; Kistchinski (1980), 11; Sauer (1962), 12; Bent (1929), 13; North American oological collections (corrected, see text), 13; Kessel (1989), 15.

Almost nowhere are there active nests of any of the tundra plovers in August (Figs 7.1–4). However, even the populations with the earliest egg-laying (e.g. North Sea area) may have a few birds sitting through July (Fig. 7.2). Although eggs of Eurasian Golden Plovers may be found during 5 months in Wales and other southern low-

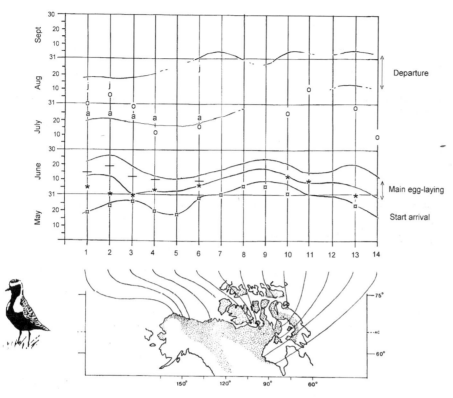

FIG. 7.4. *Arrival, egg-laying, and departure of American Golden Plovers. Symbols as in Fig. 7.1.*

Localities: 1. Barrow, 2. Prudhoe Bay, 3. Kaktovik, 4. Mackenzie-Tuktoyaktuk, 5. Banks Island, 6. Cambridge Bay, 7. Jenny Lind Island, 8. Adelaide Peninsula, 9. Truelove Lowlands, 10. Bylot Island and Pond Inlet, 11. Melville Peninsula, 12. Southampton Island, 13. Churchill, 14. Cape Henrietta Maria.

Sources, and localities covered: Bent (1929), 1; Johnson & Herter (1989), 1, 2, 3; North American nest record schemes, 1,2,3,4,13; North American oological collections (corrected, see text), 4,9; Höhn (1959), 4; Porsild (1943), 4; Manning et al. (1956), 5; Parmelee et al. (1967), 6,7; Macpherson & Manning (1959), 8; Hussell & Holroyd (1974), 9; Drury (1961), 10; Renaud et al. (1981),10; Montgomerie et al. (1983), 11; Sutton (1932), 12; Parker & Ross (1973), 12; Jehl & Smith (1970), 3; IB (pers. obs.), 13; Hagar (1966), 13; Peck (1972), 14.

lying areas in Britain, in the Taimyr population this period can be telescoped to 1.5 months or less. Thus, the short potential egg laying-incubation seasons of late-laying alpine (montane) and northern populations gives rise to a more synchronous pattern of laying within a population, and fewer opportunities for re-nesting.

Re-nesting and sequential breeding

Although re-nesting can take place if egg losses occur shortly after laying in arctic Grey Plovers (Parmelee *et al.* 1967; Flint & Kondratjew 1977) and possibly Pacific

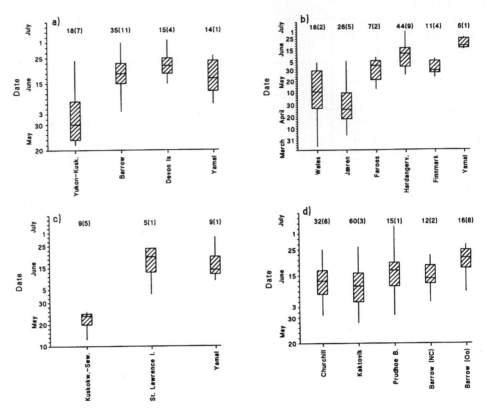

FIG. 7.5.   *Dates of laying of the first egg (medians, upper and lower quartiles, and ranges) in some populations of a) Grey Plovers, b) Eurasian Golden Plovers, c) Pacific Golden Plovers, and d) American Golden Plovers. Number of nests are given above the bars (number of years in parentheses).*
Localities and sources:

a)   – *Yukon-Kuskokwim Delta, western Alaska; North American oological collections*
     – *Point Barrow, North Alaska; North American oological collections*
     – *Truelove Lowlands, Devon Island, NWT; North American nest card schemes*
     – *Yamal, northwestern Siberia; IB*

b)   – *Elan Valley, Wales; Thomas* et al. *(1983), Thomas & Hack (1984)*
     – *Jæren, southwestern Norway (350–400 m elevation); IB*
     – *Faroes; Williamson (1948)*
     – *Hardangervidda, south Norway (1300–1400 m elevation); IB*
     – *Kautokeino, interior Finnmark, northern Norway (400 m elevation); University of Bergen nest card scheme and IB*
     – *Yamal, northwestern Siberia; IB*

c)   – *Kuskokwim Bay – Seward Peninsula, western Alaska; North American oological collections*
     – *St Lawrence Island, Bering Sea; Sauer (1962)*
     – *Yamal, northwestern Siberia; IB*

d)   – *Churchill, Manitoba; North American nest card schemes, IB*
     – *Kaktovik region, Northeast Alaska; North American nest card schemes*
     – *Prudhoe Bay region, North Alaska; North American nest card schemes*
     – *Barrow, North Alaska; North American nest card schemes*
     – *Barrow, North Alaska; North American oological collections*

Oological collections distributed over later dates than nest card data, Mann-Whitney U=155.5, p<0.005.

Golden Plovers (Sauer 1962), re-nesting in the northern areas is uncommon in tundra plovers (reported cases, see Sauer 1962 (Pacific Golden Plover); Parmelee *et al.* 1967; Flint & Kondratjew 1977 (Grey Plover)). Only in the early breeding populations of Eurasian Golden Plovers around the North Sea do replacements appear to be commonplace, though many of these may be laid by 'sequential' breeders.

Among the early nesting British golden plovers, birds may give up breeding after failure despite there still being time for replacement clutches. (Some may move to breed elsewhere, but there is no evidence of this). Their territories can then be taken over quickly by other (sequential) pairs (Parr 1979). Ray Parr's observations indicate that those who took over territories came from a 'floating' population of birds which had not taken territories earlier in the season. Whether or not those who take over these territories are the younger, less experienced, less dominant, or smaller birds, is unknown. Possibly the younger or less experienced pairs which have managed to secure territories early in the season are more likely to quit after nest predation. In any case, such sequential breeding is probably the exception rather than the rule for most populations.

Departure from the breeding grounds

In all four species adults tend to leave the breeding grounds a week or two before the bulk of the young (Figs. 7.1–7.4). This seems to be more pronounced in the arctic populations but, as for so many shorebirds, departure from the breeding grounds has been less well documented than arrivals and egg-laying. Whereas most of the birds tend to leave correspondingly earlier in 'early' than in the 'late' breeding populations, it does seem that breeding is carried on later in the season in the populations which have the early phenology.

FACTORS INFLUENCING TIMING OF EGG-LAYING

In matters of timing, therefore, it is useful to distinguish between 'ultimate' factors, such as food supply, which provide the reason for breeding at a particular season, and 'proximate' factors, which bring the birds into condition at an appropriate early date. Some proximate factors, such as daylength, provide the primary stimulus, while others, such as food availability at the time, may bring about minor modifications in laying dates. In this case, food acts as an ultimate and as a proximate factor in the timing of breeding.

> Ian Newton (1986), writing about the Eurasian Sparrowhawk, which has been thoroughly studied in relation to factors influencing timing of breeding.

For a number of reasons, early breeding in birds is considered advantageous, especially in areas with a short potential breeding season, such as in the mountains and at northern latitudes (e.g. Price *et al.* 1988; Carey 1988).

Early nesting may improve breeding success by increasing the survival of chicks, and juvenile survival may be greater from early nests. Few studies have actually managed to examine this, though there is evidence for such success in early breeders for Eurasian Oystercatchers (Harris 1969), Northern Lapwing (P.S.

Thompson and J. Coulson, pers. comm.) and Eurasian Dotterel (Holt & Whitfield 1996). Even adult survival may be improved by early breeding, as more time becomes available for the birds to prepare themselves for migration and overwintering. Ironically, one of the most important reasons for breeding early might be to leave for the south as soon as possible!

Tundra plovers spend at least 1–2 weeks in pre-laying 'preparations', 1 week in egg-laying, about 1 month incubating, and at least another 1 month before the chicks can fly fully. With a potential span in breeding season of 3–4 months in the arctic and alpine areas, the birds can be on a tight schedule. Even a short delay in egg-laying could reduce the fledging season for the young, forcing them to migrate before they have attained a sufficiently good body condition.

However, even Eurasian Golden Plovers breeding in the maritime North Sea climate, where the potential breeding season spans 5.5–6 months, might benefit from breeding early. Early hatched broods should have a competitive advantage by being the first to reach the best food patches (territorial boundaries break down post-hatch). The availability of the favoured prey, earthworms, probably declines later on in the season, as drier weather causes them to occupy deeper parts of the soil (e.g. Edwards & Lofty 1993). The vegetation gets more rank later on, and this may impede movement between food patches and impair adult–chick visibility (though the provision of more cover may offer some more security from predators). An early end to breeding reduces overlap with the energy demanding post-breeding moult (Chapter 4). However, perhaps most importantly in these southern populations, early breeding increases the time available for replacement clutches following nest losses.

Spring weather

So, do tundra plovers nest as early as they can? We look at a number of factors which serve as constraints or restraints on timing of breeding.

Parr (1980) found no correlation between dates of arrival and start of egg-laying in Eurasian Golden Plovers in NE Scotland. Evidently, therefore, conditions during the pre-laying period constrained the onset of egg-laying. Nevertheless, the start of egg-laying in Eurasian Golden Plovers has not been found to correlate with temperature, rain or wind in the pre-laying period, and only snow cover seems to have an effect. Parr (1980) found a correlation between the start of egg-laying and number of days with snowfall in April (representing the pre-laying period), as had previously been suggested by Nethersole-Thompson & Nethersole-Thompson (1961).

Golden plovers in southern Norway breeding at 1300–1400 m elevation, however, showed no such correlation, although timing of egg-laying was significantly associated with the rate at which the winter snow disappeared from the ground ($r_s = 0.31$, $p<0.05$; for date of 50% snow cover versus first egg date for 42 nests). The latter association was also found in NE Canadian Grey Plovers ($r_s = 0.71$, $p<0.001$; data for 13 nests given by Hussell & Page 1976). This seems to confirm statements by Parmelee *et al.* (1967) and Holmes & Black (1973) that Grey Plovers sometimes postpone their egg-laying until vast areas of bare grounds are snow-free and available. This is a situation likely to be found for alpine and northern populations, which arrive on more or less snow-covered breeding grounds.

Indeed, snow cover may prevent some birds from breeding altogether. Montgomerie *et al.* (1983) found that fewer American Golden Plovers bred at Melville Peninsula, NWT, when snowfalls occurring in their pre-laying season caused prolonged periods of complete snow cover. Such a situation in the egg-laying period also apparently caused postponed laying in Eurasian Golden Plovers at Hardangervidda, S. Norway, in one of the seasons they were studied by IB. In some arctic areas there is little snow in spring, yet still there is variation in laying date. Perhaps the birds respond to local weather conditions experienced during their early days of arrival, and of course to food availability. Hussell & Page (1976) found that Grey Plovers started their egg-laying when the snow cover had contracted to 70–50%, which also seems to be the case for Eurasian Golden Plovers breeding in S. Norwegian mountains.

Food availability

Although snow conditions may be a factor to which the pre-laying birds respond directly, food availability is important and, of course, is initially limited by snow cover and cold weather. The importance of rich food supplies for the rapid formation of eggs has been pointed out by Perrins (1979), shown for raptors and passerines by 'supplementary feeding' experiments (e.g. Dijkstra *et al.* 1982; Ewald & Rohwer 1982; Davies & Lundberg 1985; Birkhead 1991), and in shorebirds demonstrated for Lapwings by Högstedt (1974).

In the breeding season, tundra plovers feed mainly on invertebrates (Chapter 12). Presumably, these are better sources of protein than vegetable matter during egg-formation (e.g. Krapu & Swanson 1975). Persistent snow cover, and certainly pre-laying season snowfalls, will reduce the availability of invertebrates as well as berries.

At Hardangervidda (1300–1400 m), S. Norway, Eurasian Golden Plover females in the pre-laying period spend about 60–90% of their time feeding (Byrkjedal 1985a), 1.5 times the duration of that of their mates, a difference presumably indicating the extra effort required to produce eggs. Hence the laying date may be determined by the time it takes the female to find enough food to form eggs, which is bound to be affected by snow conditions. Yet, snowy conditions during the pre-laying period could conceivably postpone the start of egg-laying more indirectly, by a) reducing the amount of food available later for chicks, b) producing melt water that could cause heat leakage from, and damage to, nests, and c) influencing nest predation rates. Let us look at each of these in turn.

Snow cover and food availability for chicks Lack (1954, 1968) suggested that birds time their breeding season so that their young hatch when food is most plentiful. Support for this has been found in classic studies of tits feeding their young extensively on lepidoptera larvae (Perrins 1979). In temperate and northern shorebirds, however, site or annual variations in timing of egg-laying do not seem to be explained by variation in seasonal peaks in prey for the chicks (Green *et al.* 1977; Meltofte 1985; Thompson *et al.* 1986; but see Holmes 1966a; Holmes & Pitelka 1968; Nettleship 1973). Yet, shorebird chicks do hatch mostly during the part of the season when arthropods are most numerous (e.g. Holmes 1966a, 1972; Galbraith *et al.* 1993). This is apparently not a fine-tuned co-occurrence, as pre-laying conditions do not seem to be a reliable predictor of arthropod activity later in the year (Thompson *et al.* 1986). Rather, weather conditions throughout the first part of the summer have important effects on when the peak occurrence of arthropods occurs (MacLean & Pitelka 1971). The phenology of arthropod hatching and activity schedules are therefore presumably determined by some conditions which occur after the birds have laid their eggs.

Tundra plover chicks take adult insects and insect larvae (Chapter 12). Inferring from the diet of Eurasian Dotterel chicks (Byrkjedal 1989c; Galbraith *et al.* 1993; Holt & Whitfield 1996) and recent studies of Eurasian Golden Plovers in N. Scotland (O'Connell *et al.* 1996b; Downie *et al.* 1996) and N. England (Whittingham 1996a), the diet of tundra plover chicks and adults should be similar by about 1 week post-hatch. Mark Whittingham (1996a) found that hatching tends to occur during the peak of food availability. However, we still cannot say whether or not tundra plovers time their breeding to maximize use of available food for their chicks.

Snow melt and flooding of the nest Naturally, thawing snow soaks much of the ground and small temporary streams are created around almost every tussock. This may flood nests, destroying eggs and preventing incubation. The cold, soaked ground will also cause 'heat leakage' through the nest cup, resulting in increased energetic costs for the incubating birds. Shorebirds nests are usually scantily lined, though tundra plovers tend to be an exception, with a layer of lichens in many northern nests, presumably providing insulation (also, see Sauer 1962; Ratcliffe 1976; Owens 1981; Kålås & Løfaldli 1987; Whittingham 1996a). Dotterel, for instance, selectively line their nests with the tubular *Cladonia uncialis*. Eurasian Golden Plovers also do this and manage to select nest sites where the nest cup remains dry (Ratcliffe 1976).

Flooding of the ground during the thaw may be most pronounced in flat areas with permafrost, where drainage is minimal. To the best of our knowledge, however, only one case of nest loss as a result of flooding has so far been reported for tundra plovers (one Grey Plover nest out of 16, NE Asian tundra, Flint & Kondratjew 1977). By tending to nest on the drier ridges and more elevated ground (e.g. Sauer 1962; Ratcliffe 1976; Parr 1980; Kondrat'ev 1982; Byrkjedal 1989a,b) problems posed by melt-water seem to be minimized.

Snow cover and nest predation A far more serious cause of nest losses for these plovers is predation (e.g. Ratcliffe 1976; Parr 1980; Kondrat'ev 1982; Langslow 1983; Nethersole-Thompson & Nethersole-Thompson 1986; Byrkjedal 1987a, 1989a; O'Connell *et al.* 1996). Nesting on small snow-free patches in a predominantly snow-covered landscape may increase nest predation risk, as the predators can then restrict their search to small patches of bare ground (Byrkjedal 1978a; Pienkowski 1984; Meltofte 1985). IB showed this experimentally by exposing artificial nests to predation under different snow conditions (Byrkjedal 1980b). Nest predation in relation to snow cover should be less of a problem in flat plains such as those in much of the arctic tundra, however. Here, winter snow depth is minimal, as the wind sweeps away the snow (Chernov 1985), and the 'melt' rapidly uncovers large areas. But where winter snow accumulates in depressions, as in the more undulating alpine areas (such as where IB did his experiment) the effect of snow cover on nest predation risk may persist over a much longer proportion of the season. Unfortunately, data for shorebirds, let alone tundra plovers, are insufficient to test more critically the effects of snow cover on nest predation rates, predator activities and timing of nesting.

THE NESTS

Having dwelt on arrival and timing of breeding, we now turn our attention to the nests and their contents, and details of incubation. During the pre-laying phase, the birds work on a number of nest scrapes (Steiniger 1959), with the male making most of the initial unlined scrapes (Nethersole-Thompson & Nethersole-Thompson 1939, 1943, 1986), though even unused ones can be well lined. A pair of Eurasian Golden Plovers watched for 229 min (distributed over 3 days) in the heather moors of Jæren, SW Norway, visited at least 12 different scrapes. Apparently it is the female that, during her nest scrape inspections, finally settles for one. However, little is known about the factors governing her choice. Where scrapes are made in the soil, rather than in litter or vegetation, they persist from year-to-year and may be renewed (e.g. at Mallerstang, D.A. Ratcliffe pers. comm.). No study has yet compared the charactcristics of rejected and accepted nest scrapes, though this should be highly revealing. Has the choice of scrape, or nest site, an element of randomness? Possibly, because a pattern of preference might be learnt by predators (also Ratcliffe 1976).

Nest site position

Information on nest site location and habitat selection/avoidance gives some insight into factors of importance. The choice of nest site is probably influenced by four factors: the need to keep eggs warm and safe from destruction; proximity to feeding areas for adults/chicks, and minimized risks to adult survival. There is a general consensus in the literature that tundra plovers, like most plovers for that matter, nest on drier ground. This is supported by the available data presented in Appendix 6a–d. Protection from flooding as well as reduced heat leakage from the nest may well be important factors here. Furthermore, the dry habitats offer tundra plovers the best protection against nest predation. Dry, windswept hummocks and ridges of northern and alpine heaths are typically covered by lichen communities (e.g. Ahti 1961; Thompson & Brown 1992), and the blending in with this variegated background by eggs and the sitting bird has impressed several authors (Bent 1929; Sauer 1962; Portenko 1972; Kondrat'ev 1982).

On moorland, heather (*Calluna vulgaris*) stands are more typical on the drier ridges (hence the term 'dry heath') and alpine slopes. These also offer a distinctly fine-spangled background which, although far less contrasting than the lichen communities, can merge well with the dorsal plumage of Eurasian Golden Plovers. As nesting habitat, the lichen-dominated and heather-dominated habitats are frequently used, and preferred, by tundra plovers (Appendix 6) (see also Sauer 1962; Hussell & Page 1976; Ratcliffe 1976; Kondrat'ev 1982; Montgomerie *et al.* 1983; Danilov *et al.* 1984; Byrkjedal 1989a,b). But in Britain, with so much heather moorland in the eastern uplands, the most favoured habitat is blanket bog or wet

PLATE 39.   *Nest of Grey Plover, Rowley, Canada. Note almost no nest lining.*
(William J. Sutherland and Nicola Crockford)

heath with cotton grasses (*Eriophorum vaginatum* and *E. angustifolium*) rather than
the drier heather moors. Although heather can be co-dominant, the cotton grasses
are most prominent around the nest. Where the bog surfaces are eroded or dried
out there can be a high cover of *Racomitrium* or *Sphagnum*.

Nests do survive better in lichen-rich habitat than in the less variegated and more
uniform green non-lichen habitats, though different age classes of breeders may
have occupied these (Fig. 7.6; also Byrkjedal 1989a,b). Heather does not appear to
influence nest survival in Eurasian Golden Plover breeding on moorland. On some
moors, birds show a preference for recently burnt areas (Parr 1980; Whittingham
1996a). Interestingly, in one alpine study area in the Cairngorms, Eurasian Golden
Plovers preferred to nest in alpine *Racomitrium*-dominated mossy heaths rather than
dwarf-shrub dominated heaths (which are less broken, but more lichen-rich) (Holt
& Whitfield 1996). The birds are particularly cryptic when sitting on these mossy
heaths when moist.

An approaching predator causes incubating Grey Plovers to leave the nest at a
long distance, and many golden plovers respond similarly in the presence of
ground-hunting predators (for flying nest predators golden plovers crouch on their
nests: Drury 1961; Sauer 1962; Parmelee *et al.* 1967; Flint & Kondratjew 1976;
Byrkjedal 1987a, 1989d; Chapter 9). An unimpeded view from the nest might allow

PLATE 40. *The hatch in a Grey Plover's nest, Sabettayakha, Yamal Peninsula, northwest Siberia. (IB)*

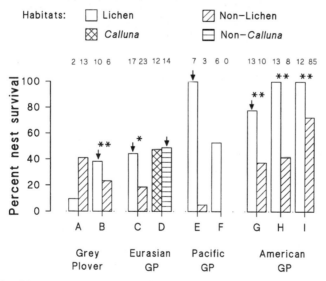

FIG. 7.6. *Nest survival (Mayfield 1975) in relation to nest habitat. A, Alaska; B and E, Yamal; C, Hardangervidda; D, Jæren; F, West Alaska northwards to Barrow; G, Churchill, non-defined study area; H, Churchill, defined study area; I, North Alaska eastwards from Barrow. Number of nests are given above the bars. Significance levels (χ^2 tests on exposure days, Mayfield 1973); * p <0.05, ** p <0.001. Arrows indicate positively selected habitats.*

PLATE 41. *Nest of Eurasian Golden Plover in heather moorland, Britain. (Derek Ratcliffe)*

the incubating bird to act early should a predator appear, and this could be why tundra plovers typically breed in such short vegetation (Rittinghaus 1969; Ratcliffe 1976; Parr 1980; Parmelee *et al.* 1967; Drury 1961; Sutton 1932; Mayfield 1973; Köpke 1971; Flint & Kondratjew 1977; Hussell & Page 1976; Sauer 1962; Kondrat'ev 1982). Available data show that American and Pacific golden plovers and Grey Plovers tend to breed in vegetation 1.5 cm tall; Eurasian Golden Plovers in NE Scotland and S. Norway breed in somewhat taller vegetation, especially on heather moors (10–12 cm) (Fig. 7.7). We have occasionally seen some of the latter's nests in deep heather to the extent that nests are hidden. On the Moorfoots, nests are in heather up to 25 cm high (D.A. Ratcliffe pers. comm.). However, as a general rule, it appears that tundra plovers prefer to nest in open, dry areas with short vegetation, against which the eggs and adults are well camouflaged. There may be a serious difficulty in reaching firm conclusions on the topic of nest site position and habitat use. Some areas will have relatively small populations relative to the availability of

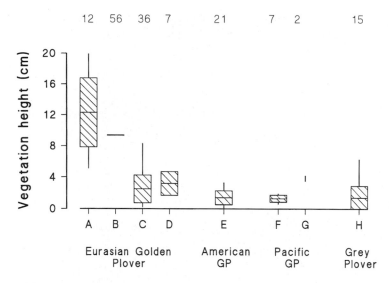

FIG. 7.7. *Vegetation height around nests (measurements at 6 random points 5 cm from nest averaged for each nest; for B, see Parr 1980). Data are given as means, standard deviations, and ranges. A, heather moor, Jæren; B, heather moor, Scotland; C, low alpine heath, Hardangervidda; D and F, sub-arctic tundra, Yamal; E, sub-arctic tundra, Churchill; G and H, arctic tundra, Yamal. Sources: B, Parr (1980); others, IB (pers. obs.).*

PLATE 42. *Nest of Eurasian Golden Plover, on montane lichen heath, Hardangervidda, Norway, in typical sparse cover of vegetation. (IB)*

PLATE 43.   *Newly hatched chick of Eurasian Golden Plover, Hardangervidda,*
Norway. (IB)

favoured habitat, with virtually all birds nesting in 'near ideal' situations; some
others may have birds dispersed to the extent that a proportion of them occupy
inferior habitats or situations.

The nest cup

The nests of tundra plovers are fairly shallow scrapes in the ground. Of the four
species, American Golden Plovers have the smallest nests, Eurasian Golden Plovers
have the deepest, and Grey Plovers have the widest nests. Nest dimensions are not
therefore merely a function of egg dimensions or body size.

In all four species the nest cup is usually made in the vegetation mat. Some nests
are scratched out in bare ground (gravel, soil), significantly more so in Grey Plovers
(18%) than in golden plovers (6%; $\chi^2 = 5.34$, p<0.02; data for 51, 43, 27 and 55 nests
of Grey, Eurasian, Pacific and American golden plovers, respectively; described for
North American egg collections, on nest record cards, or examined by us). A few
nests contain no lining, again more often in Grey (24%) than in golden plovers

PLATE 44.   *Nest of American Golden Plover on variegated lichen tundra, Churchill, Manitoba, Canada. (IB)*

(6%; χ^2 = 12.24, p<0.001), yet all nests examined by us on bare ground have had lining. The amount of lining seems to be influenced by the stage of incubation (Ratcliffe 1976; Nethersole-Thompson & Nethersole-Thompson 1986), as the incubating bird spends a considerable part of its non-sleeping time adding bits of vegetation to the nest (Fig. 7.8). Nevertheless, material can be blown out of the nest, and some is even pushed out by the sitting bird during the course of incubation.

A variety of plant material is used to line the nest, but lichens, dry grasses, sedges, and leaves of *Salix* spp., *Betula nana*, or *Vaccinium* spp., are most commonly used (Fig. 7.9). The composition of this largely reflects whatever dry plant material is available nearby (Nethersole-Thompson & Nethersole-Thompson 1961; Ratcliffe 1976). However, several authors have pointed out the selective use made of lichens (Sutton 1932; Walkinshaw 1948; Sauer 1962; Mayfield 1973; Flint & Kondratjew 1977; Kondrat'ev 1982). As we have mentioned already, lichens probably insulate the nests especially well and seem to offer protection from predators through improved camouflage when the eggs are exposed. But there may be a cost to adding too many lichens, to the extent that the eggs become more conspicuous from the air. Hence,

FIG. 7.8.   *Incubating female Grey Plover picking bits of lichen for nest lining. This is a common behaviour of incubating tundra plovers.*

tundra plovers may be compelled to squat over their eggs when predators fly over to reduce this risk. Figure 7.9 shows that lichens are indeed selectively used for nest lining, except by Eurasian Golden Plovers in heather moors. On the other hand, mosses occur less often than expected. Eurasian Golden Plovers on heather moors

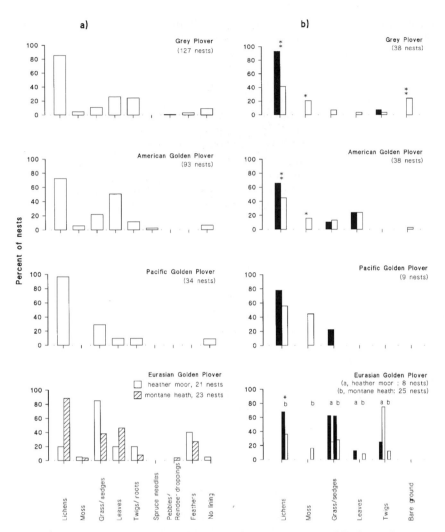

FIG. 7.9.   *Material used as nest lining; a) shows constancy, and b) the single most dominant material in nest cups (filled bars) and immediately surrounding nest cups (open bars).*
Significance levels for statistical differences between observed and expected (in b) are: * p<0.05, ** p<0.001 (Fisher's exact tests and χ^2 tests). Sources: Walkinshaw (1948), Sutton (1932), Sauer (1962), Kondrat'ev (1982), North American oological collections, North American nest record cards, IB.

seem to prefer dry grass and sedges over the more commonly available heather, as indicated also by Ratcliffe (1976), but data are available for only a few nests.

We have no data to evaluate the insulating effect of lichens compared with other material, but nests lined with lichens do seem to survive better, at least in the American Golden Plover, the only species for which we have relevant data. In this species survival was 84% (Mayfield's [1973] method) for nests lined with lichens compared with 49% for those that were not (36 nests, 517 nest days; Fisher's test on nest days: p<0.01). Compared with those of the three golden plover species, Grey Plover nests are scantily lined, as detailed above (see also Sauer 1962a; Parmelee *et al.* 1967; Mayfield 1973; Flint & Kondratjew 1977; Kondrat'ev 1982). Often only a few *Thamnolia* spp. fragments are found in Grey Plover nests, and frequently less than 50% of the nest cup is covered by lining in spite of the parents' constant endeavours to add lining while they incubate. This small amount of lining can hardly offer much insulation, but a few pieces of vegetation may help break the outline of the eggs (*cf.* Lind 1961) and thus act as camouflage. In spite of their skills at driving away nest predators, Grey Plovers may experience severe nest predation pressure, and so may benefit from nest camouflage just as well as the more 'timid' golden plovers. Clearly, the effects which nest habitat and lining have on nest survival and heat balance need further study involving simple field experiments.

THE EGGS

Dimensions

The majority of shorebirds do not carry reserves for egg-laying into the breeding grounds, but instead use food taken immediately before laying to produce eggs (Erckmann 1983). Like most plovers, tundra plovers lay large eggs with a single egg constituting 18–20% of the females' body weight (e.g. Lack 1968; Ratcliffe 1976; Nethersole-Thompson & Nethersole-Thompson 1986). No wonder the females concentrate so ardently on feeding shortly before egg-laying. Amongst the four species, Pacific and Eurasian golden plovers lay the largest eggs relative to the female's mass (Table 9).

Egg dimensions within Eurasian Golden Plover populations have been reported to be smaller in late than in early clutches (Byrkjedal & Kålås 1985; Pulliainen & Saari 1993), a possible consequence of later-laying first-time breeders and/or replacement clutches. Only Eurasian Golden Plovers at Jæren (*contra* Byrkjedal & Kålås 1985), however, show a significant decrease in egg volume over the season, primarily owing to a declining egg length. But we have no data to show whether or not females actually lay smaller eggs in replacement clutches. It is interesting that the other three species show no seasonal trend in egg dimensions.

Historically, it seems that egg sizes of Eurasian Golden Plovers in the central Welsh uplands have increased in the 20th century (Ferns *et al.* 1983). This may be explained by the increased use of fertilizers on 'in-bye' agricultural grasslands and rough grazings used by pre-breeding flocks. After all, Murton and Westwood (1974) found the mean weight of Northern Lapwings' eggs was higher in more fertile farmland.

Pattern and colour of shell markings

Grey Plover eggs are usually much darker than those of the golden plovers. While the former tend to be buffy brown or pale brownish-olive with black or blackish-brown spots and blotches, golden plover eggs are pale green, cream coloured, or pale flesh coloured with blackish-brown or black, and greyish-violet to fuscous marks. However, some clutches cannot be distinguished between the four species on egg patterns and colours alone.

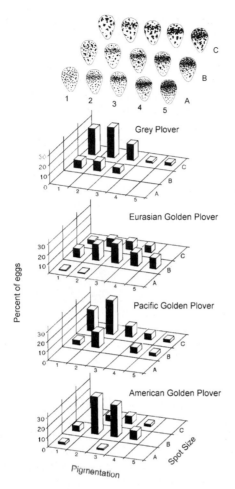

FIG. 7.10. *Frequency distribution of eggs of the four species, according to egg pigmentation and spottedness, based on photo archive of clutches (IB). For Eurasian Golden Plover, data from Hardangervidda (192 eggs), Jæren (51 eggs) and Yamal (16 eggs) were pooled; data for American Golden Plover are from Churchill (87 eggs); and data for Pacific Golden Plover and Grey Plover from Yamal (35 and 52 eggs, respectively). Grades of pigmentation: A, Primarily small dots; B, Dots and blotches more or less in equal amounts; and C, Primarily larger blotches. 1, Spots more or less evenly distributed; 2, Spots faintly forming a ring around the blunt end; 3, Spots forming a distinct but broken ring; 4, Spots forming a bold and more or less unbroken ring; and 5, Cap heavily pigmented.*
Interspecific differences explained 63%, 55%, 79% and 58% of the variance in spot size (A–C) in Grey Plovers, Eurasian, Pacific and American golden plovers, respectively (Non-parametric ANOVA). For degree of pigmentation (1–5) the figures were 76%, 39%, 60% and 23%.

Egg patterns vary considerably, both within and between the species. Some eggs have predominantly small spots, others large blotches. Usually the marks are concentrated around the blunt end (Fig. 7.10). Large blotches are, on average, found most often on the eggs of Grey Plovers, followed by Pacific, Eurasian and then American golden plovers (Fig. 7.10). For each of the species, egg patterns vary within as well as between clutches. Only egg spot size in Pacific Golden Plovers and the degree of pigmentation in Grey Plovers seem to be fairly constant within clutches (legend to Fig. 7.10). In the Eurasian Golden Plover the greyish-violet 'shell marks' are buried deep in the shell. Some clutches have attractive reddish-brown surface marks.

Intriguingly, Fig. 7.10 suggests that the more northern tundra plover species lay eggs with larger blotches. Is it possible that these birds form eggs more rapidly resulting in more continuously pigmented shells? Probably not! After all, in Britain, Derek Ratcliffe (pers. comm.) found that of the 377 clutches examined by him, the most heavily blotched were in the Pennines (especially on his Mallerstang study area). In Lapland, he has seen 16 clutches and none was particularly heavily blotched. Nevertheless, we feel there is scope for more detailed work on egg shell patterns (see also Thomas *et al.* 1989).

PLATE 45.   *Tundra plovers normally lay four eggs. In this nest of American Golden Plovers at Churchill, Manitoba, Canada, eight eggs had probably been laid by two females. (IB)*

INCUBATION AND HATCHING

Egg-laying intervals

Generally, single eggs are laid at 1–3 day intervals; the interval between the third and fourth eggs being longer than between the others (Fig. 7.11). The clutch of four eggs is usually completed within 4.5–7 days. Few direct observations of egg-laying have been made in these species. Nethersole-Thompson & Nethersole-Thompson (1939, 1961) stated that Eurasian Golden Plovers laid eggs at any time of

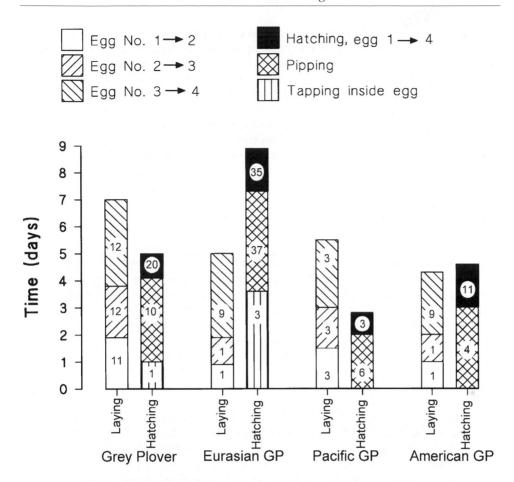

FIG. 7.11. *Average time it takes to lay (L) and hatch (H) a clutch of four eggs. No information could be found about tapping inside eggs of American and Pacific Golden Plovers. Number of clutches are given on the bars. Sources: Williamson (1948), Drury (1961), Sauer (1962), Parmelee et al. (1967), Oring (1967), Rittinghaus (1969), Mayfield (1973), Flint & Kondratjew (1977), Parr (1980), Kondrat'ev (1982), North American nest cards, and IB.*

the day, until 2000 h, whereas eggs were laid at around 0730–0800 h in two nests observed by Oring (1967). For Grey Plover, Hussell & Page (1976), who observed 7 nests, concluded that eggs were laid within 3 hours of midnight and 3 hours of noon, yet Flint & Kondratjew (1977) recorded laying at around 0100–0300 h and 0700–0800 h for two eggs in a continuously monitored nest.

Hatching intervals

Although the time between hatching out by the first and the fourth chick is usually between 1 and 1.5 days, the hatching process itself is almost as long as the laying. It takes about 3–5 days from pipping of the first egg until the last chick has emerged (Fig. 7.11). In fact, the chick may start to tap inside the egg days before pipping. In the Eurasian Golden Plover and Grey Plover, chicks have been reported to call inside the egg even before any sign of fracture, and in the former the sitting bird responds by calling (Nethersole-Thompson & Nethersole-Thompson 1961; Flint & Kondratjew 1977). Flint & Kondratjew (1977) suggested that all this noisy activity within the eggs contributed to synchronize the hatching, and there is some indication that the hatching process is accelerated for the fourth egg. However, the main factor synchronizing hatching must surely be the pattern of incubation.

Incubation

Firm incubation is not established before the last egg has been laid. Flint & Kondratjew (1977) and Kondrat'ev (1982) found that Grey Plovers sat for 5.6% of the period between the first and second eggs, 12.8–17.4% between the second and third eggs, and 35.4–45.8% between the third and fourth eggs (13 nest days). Consequently, the temperatures Kondrat'ev measured inside an artificial egg in the nests were close to ambient temperatures for much of the time, and usually fell far below the temperature necessary for embryonic development in eggs of the domestic chicken (Harrison & Irving 1954). Eurasian and American golden plover nests checked during laying are often unattended but attentiveness for these has not been measured: some are covered by parents, but others are not.

As in most monogamous shorebirds (*cf.* Kondrat'ev 1982; Løfaldli 1985), tundra plover nests are usually covered for more than 95% of the day and night. This is maintained throughout the incubation period (Fig. 7.12), starting just after laying of the last egg. However, by the end of the incubation period the temperature in the eggs may fluctuate more, due to the increasing restlessness of the incubating bird (Flint & Kondratjew 1977; Kondrat'ev 1982). Flint & Kondratjew (1977) suggested that this temperature fluctuation actually speeded up hatching.

The duration of incubation has been measured variously by different observers, and surprisingly few precise measurements seem to have been made. The time elapsing between when the last egg is laid and when the first egg has hatched is usually within 26 to 28 days, and is rarely outwith the range 25–30 days (Appendix 7d provides a summary of raw data). Available information indicates a day or two longer incubation in Eurasian Golden Plovers than in the other tundra plovers, but more data are needed before conclusions can be reached on this. Nethersole-Thompson & Nethersole-Thompson (1961) considered that incubation periods for some nests of Eurasian Golden Plover in the Cairngorms were extended by up to 4 days owing to disturbance.

In spite of the relatively high degree of hatching synchrony within clutches (given the long duration of egg-laying), the time between when the first chick hatches and all chicks are out of the nest (1–1.5 days) is longer than in the smaller Palearctic *Charadrius* plovers and the Northern Lapwing (0.2–1 days) (Cramp & Simmons 1983; Glutz von Blotzheim *et al.* 1975). Sometimes, the first hatched chick leaves the nest before the last one has hatched out (Grey Plover – Mayfield 1973; Hussell & Page 1976; Kondrat'ev 1982; Eurasian Golden Plover – Williamson 1948; Parr 1980; Thomas *et al.* 1983; Pacific Golden Plover – Sauer 1962; and American Golden

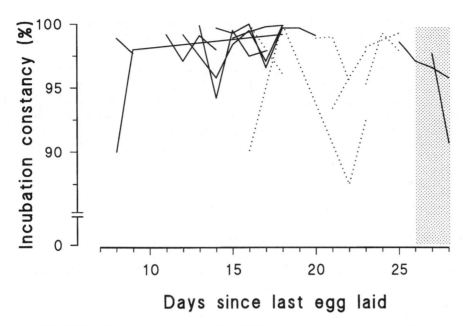

FIG. 7.12. *Incubation constancy (% of 24 hours that the nest is covered) for Eurasian (solid lines) and American (dotted) golden plovers. Lines connect data for the same nest. The shaded area is the hatching period (i.e. at least 1 chick emerged).*
Material: Thermistor, pointing up amidst the eggs, connected to a continuously recording thermograph, or visual observations through spotting scope from long distance, sometimes both methods combined. American Golden Plover: 7 nests, 170 hours, Churchill; Eurasian Golden Plover: 9 nests, 488 hours, Hardangervidda and Jæren.

Plover – Parmelee *et al.* (1967): and our own observation for all except the Pacific Golden Plover). In this case the clutch may be temporarily split between the two parents (Williamson 1948), but the brood is reunited when the last chick leaves the nest. However, we need to be careful in reaching definitive conclusions here, because we suspect that prolonged disturbance at the nest may induce parents to take early hatching chicks from the nest sooner than might naturally be the case. Usually though, the older siblings return to the nest to be brooded as long as the youngest one is still there (Nethersole-Thompson & Nethersole-Thompson 1961; Parr 1980). However, as soon as the latter is dry, they all leave the nest; but in the late evening all chicks may be brooded in the nest overnight before the final departure (also Drury 1961).

Eggshell removal

Like many birds, tundra plovers quickly remove their empty eggshells from the nest. The first person to suggest that eggshell removal is an anti-predator tactic was F. Menteith Ogilvie (1891) in his essay on the Stone Curlew, cited in F. Poynting's (1895–96) *Eggs of British Birds*. Tinbergen *et al.* (1963) performed a classic

PLATE 46.   *Newly hatched chick of American Golden Plover, Churchill, Manitoba, Canada. (IB)*

experiment, precipitated by earlier trials by Nethersole-Thompson & Nethersole-Thompson (1942) and others, revealing that eggshell removal could be an adaptation to minimize nest predation (the white inside surfaces of large eggshell fragments may catch the attention of predators).

In several species, however, Derrickson & Warkentin (1991) found that if they were not removed, shells from hatched eggs could 'cap' eggs still in the process of hatching, preventing the young from emerging efficiently from the egg (and presumably exposing the nest to predators for longer, at a time when the contents are more conspicuous). Tundra plovers fly with the larger eggshell fragments and drop them 30–300 m from the nest (also Williamson 1948; Steiniger 1959; Nethersole-Thompson & Nethersole-Thompson 1942, 1961; Sauer 1962; Mayfield 1973; Hussell & Page 1976). Grey Plovers not only fly with the fragments but also tuck some into crevices and underneath vegetation (Flint & Kondratjew 1977). We believe that, as with so many aspects of breeding, predation risk has given rise to these tactics of eggshell removal.

SUMMARY

1. Eurasian Golden Plovers around the North Sea and in southern Baltic regions are on their breeding grounds in February–March and lay eggs in April–May. Alpine (montane) and northern populations arrive in late April/May–June and

PLATE 47. *Nest of Pacific Golden Plover near Nurmayakha, Yamal Peninsula, northeast Siberia. A thick lining of lichens is apparent. (IB)*

    lay eggs chiefly in June. The latest start to breeding is found in East Greenland and North Central Siberia.

2. Along the Arctic Coast, Grey Plover, Pacific and American golden plovers arrive in May–June and lay eggs in June, but later on the North Alaskan coast, in the North East Canadian islands and at Taimyr. Along the west coast of Alaska, where the climate is somewhat milder, most Grey Plovers and Pacific Golden Plovers arrive and lay eggs in May.

3. The breeding season spans 5–6 months in the North Sea area (for Eurasian Golden Plover), providing time for replacement clutches following nest failures, but not much more than 3 months in the Arctic, where re-nesting is uncommon. Termination of nesting, and departure, vary less between populations than does the start of nesting. Some so-called 'replacement clutches' may actually have been laid by 'sequential' breeders, which failed to occupy territories in early spring, but took over the territories of failed breeders.

4. Early spring snow conditions, other weather conditions and possibly available food, influence timing of egg-laying. In Eurasian Golden Plovers breeding in

PLATE 48.   *Summer snowfalls can occur on the breeding grounds of tundra plovers in the Arctic as well as in the mountains. Here 'Camp Hanovey' at Nurmayakha, Yamal Peninsula, northwest Siberia, has a white cover of snow in early June. (IB)*

Norway, and Grey Plovers breeding in Canada, laying is delayed by a slow disappearance rate of winter snow, while egg-laying of Eurasian Golden Plovers in Scotland is set back by frequent snow-falls in the pre-laying season. Much more work is needed to tease apart the factors influencing timing of laying.

5. Tundra plovers nest mainly on dry, well drained habitats that are free from snow early in the season. On tundra and alpine heaths they tend to select lichen-dominated habitats for nesting, and show a preference for lichens in their nest lining, both of which reduce nest losses to predators.

6. Of the four species, Pacific and Eurasian golden plovers lay the largest eggs relative to female body mass. Eurasian Golden Plover eggs are more pointed in the northern and eastern parts of the range, without notable changes in volume.

7. Some differences in eggshell patterns are found, with the more northern tundra plovers having larger pigmented blotches.

8. The clutch is usually completed in a week, after which nest attendance is high with the parents incubating for 95–98% of their time. The eggs are incubated for 26–28 days. The post-hatch period spent in the nest is long in comparison with many other plovers.

CHAPTER 8
Breeding Season: Social Behaviour

Pacific Golden Plover in 'torpedo run'

The wind birds [shorebirds] are not credited with the ability to sing, a disgrace that they share with all nonmembers of the Passeriformes, or perching birds – the so-called songbirds. Yet the calls of shorebirds are often more melodious than the songs of songbirds.

Peter Matthiesen writing about North American shorebirds, in Stout (1967)

ALL four species hold large territories, are monogamous and have equal sharing of parental duties. Most of the information presented in this chapter concerns mating and territoriality. Virtually all of the data were collected and analysed by us, and have not been published before.

THE FIRST WEEK

Only 2–3 days, and usually less than a week, elapse from when the first birds are seen until individuals disperse over the breeding grounds. Then there is a hive of social activity. Territories are occupied and defended, old pairings are re-established (although some may have re-formed earlier on), new pairings are formed, and preparations for nesting begin. And only a couple of days after the first birds have arrived the first flights of song are heard. For us, few other bird sounds capture the wildness and fresh beauty of the moors, heaths and tundras.

Although males tend to arrive before females in all four species, the first pairs are seen only a few (3–6) days after the first birds' arrival (also Drury 1961; Manning & MacPherson 1961; Hagar 1966; Portenko 1972; Hussel & Page 1976; Sutton 1932; Parmelee *et al.* 1967; Flint & Kondratjew 1977; but cf. Sauer 1962). The time differences between when the first bird is observed and when most birds are on territories seem to vary only slightly between species (2–4 days: Pacific Golden Plover; 2–7 days: American Golden Plover; 0–13 days: Eurasian Golden Plover; 4–11 days: Grey Plover; above references and Porsild 1943; Hagar 1966; Sauer 1962; Hussel & Holroyd 1974; de Korte 1975; Parr 1980; Renaud *et al.* 1981; Danilov *et al.* 1984). The first song flights tend to be seen or heard just before the majority of birds have spread out, typically 1–7 days (Pacific Golden Plover), 2–3 days (but 3–7 days in high Arctic, American Golden Plover) and 2–7 days (Grey Plover) after the first pair is observed (above references).

While still performing their loud and spectacular flight displays, the birds now begin to engage in quiet and intimate acts with their partners. Females inspect the many nest scrapes offered by their mates, before choosing one. A male must make sure that he, and only he, fertilizes his mate, and the female must find sufficient food for egg production. Naturally, the four species have many features in common. But there are differences, and the most striking ones early in the breeding season pertain to communication, especially song and other vocal utterances of importance for pair formation.

SONG FLIGHTS

Bird display is comparable, not to a silent film nor to broadcast music, but to a play in which form, colour, movement and sound combine to impress and move the observer.

Edward A. Armstrong (1965) writing about song-flights in bird

As in most shorebirds, male tundra plovers perform song flights over their breeding grounds. Song flights are among the very first social activities engaged in after the spring arrival (also Drury 1961; Sauer 1962; Parmelee *et al.* 1967; Portenko 1972; Hussell & Holroyd 1974; Hussell & Page 1976; Flint & Kondratjew 1977; Renaud *et al.* 1981; Montgomerie *et al.* 1983; Danilov *et al.* 1984). Before discussing the functions of these flights, we present a description of their visual as well as vocal components. The latter includes the 'song', which constitutes the most far-carrying and obvious part of the song flight. Yet the movement patterns, such as the stereotyped wing-strokes, also convey long-distance signals.

Descriptions of song flights are given in varying degrees of detail for the American Golden Plover (Drury 1961; Parmelee *et al.* 1967), Pacific Golden Plover (Walkinshaw 1948; Sauer 1962; Kondrat'ev 1982; Connors *et al.* 1993; Eurasian Golden Plover (Steiniger 1959; Nethersole-Thompson & Nethersole-Thompson 1961, 1986; Glutz von Blotzheim *et al.* 1975; Cramp & Simmons 1983) and Grey Plover (Drury 1961; Parmelee 1967; Flint & Kondratjew 1977; Kondrat'ev 1982). Few of the descriptions contain enough detail for a close comparison between the species, so the present account is based mainly on our own field observations. IB made a particular effort to study as many song flights as possible in 1989 and 1990 at Jæren, Hardangervidda and Yamal.

Birds in song flights were followed through binoculars, with relevant information dictated simultaneously on a tape recorder. A tape recorder with a parabolic reflector and mounted microphone was used to record the songs. Flight paths and patterns were sketched in a notebook immediately afterwards, and discussed later by us both in Bergen. The song flight is usually first noticed whilst the bird is in the air. Special observation sessions on individual birds were therefore also necessary in order to describe complete song flights, from its beginning on the ground to the end.

Description of song flights

Figures 8.1–8.3 show lateral views of song flights for the Grey Plover, Eurasian and Pacific golden plovers, and Table 10 gives quantitative details. Song flight patterns of American Golden Plovers are known in far less detail (Fig. 8.4; Table 10).

Common to all four species is a strong, rapid, and increasingly fluttering ascent. At 15–100 m above the ground the bird levels out and enters the main phase of the song flight. Now the bird cruises back and forth over its territory, in irregular circles or as a figure-of-eight, flapping wings in a slow, stiff and jerky manner while singing. This is referred to as the 'butterfly flight' (e.g. Cramp & Simmons 1983), because of the butterfly-like wingbeats (though of course they are far slower than those of any butterfly!). Eurasian Golden Plovers and Grey Plovers have the shallowest butterfly flight wingbeats, rarely extending below the horizontal on the downstroke. In contrast, Pacific Golden Plovers lift and lower their wings considerably; in fact, their wings sometimes seem almost to meet above the back and below the belly. American Golden Plovers have deep wingstrokes, but less so than in Pacific Golden Plovers (Fig. 8.4). In the two latter species, the body dips up and down with the wingbeats, making the flight undulating and tern-like. In the Eurasian Golden Plover, and especially in Grey Plover, the butterfly flight is strikingly level without any undulations.

In a few cases butterfly flight wing-flapping frequency was recorded while tape-recording song (by tapping the rim of the parabolic reflector for each downstroke, and then measuring the time between downstrokes on sonagrams!). The deep wingbeats of Pacific Golden Plovers take longer to perform (0.55 ± 0.12 s; time between downstrokes) than the shallower wingbeats of Eurasian Golden Plover (0.47 ± 0.10 s) and Grey Plover (0.38 ± 0.6 s). Steiniger (1959), Glutz von Blotzheim *et al.* (1975) and Cramp & Simmons (1983) claim that Eurasian Golden Plovers beat their wings in rhythm with their song utterances. We found, however, that neither Eurasian nor Pacific golden plovers do so: downstrokes could occur anytime in relation to the song notes.

In all three golden plover species, but apparently not in Grey Plovers, butterfly flights are frequently interrupted by rapid 'fluttering flights', during which the birds continue to circle over their territories. In these the wings are relatively little extended, appear somewhat curved when seen from the front or rear, and the wingtips not beaten above the horizontal plane.

The planing, circling phase of the song flight can last for almost 20 minutes, at

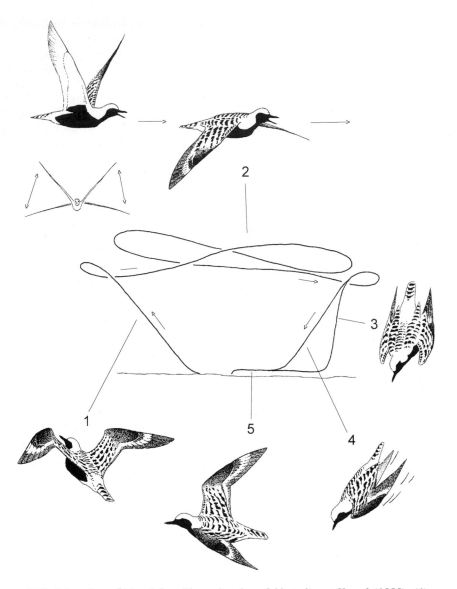

FIG. 8.1. *Song flight of Grey Plover, based on field studies at Yamal (1989). (1) Ascent in strong flight, (2) butterfly flight, (3) perpendicular descent, (4) sloping descent, half-closed wings fluttering, and (5) skimming low.*

least in the Eurasian Golden Plover, but usually within 10 minutes the song flight ends and the bird descends to the ground. Several variants of the descent have been observed, even for the same individual, but usually Eurasian Golden Plovers and Grey Plovers swoop down with wings half closed, 'peregrine falcon-like' fashion, or in a fluttering dive, whereas Pacific Golden Plovers descend very smoothly – floating down in butterfly flight almost to the ground. Unlike Pacific Golden Plovers,

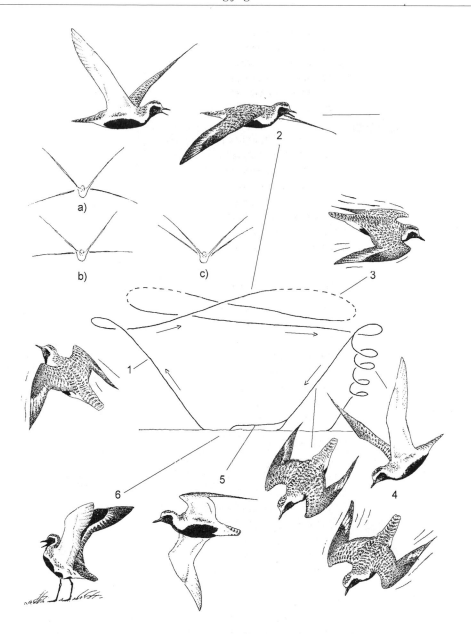

FIG. 8.2. *Song flight of Eurasian Golden Plover, based on field studies at Jæren (1972–91) and Yamal (1989). (1) Fluttering ascent, (2) butterfly flight, a) or b) show ordinary shallow wingbeats of the butterfly flight, c) shows wingbeats alternative to a) or b) when two birds display simultaneously over territory borders) (3) fluttering flight, (4) spiralling descent gliding with wings in V above back, alternatively sloping descent in falcon dive or rapid fluttering, (5) skimming low, and (6) wings high with trill after landing.*

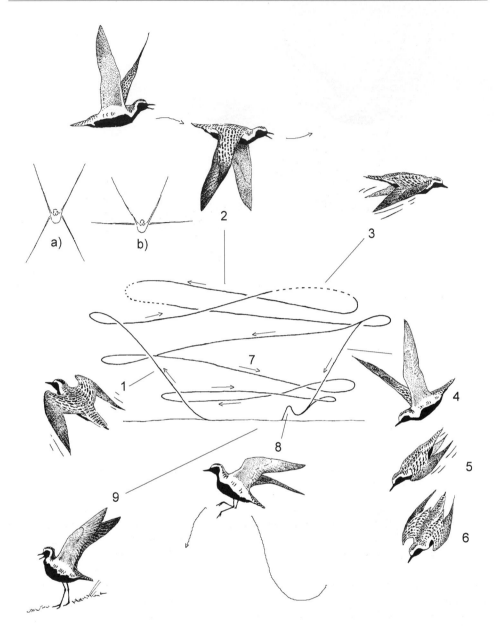

FIG. 8.3. *Song flight of Pacific Golden Plover, based on field studies at Yamal (1989). (1) Fluttering ascent, (2) butterfly flight a), the usual deep wingbeats in; b), shallow wingbeats, (3) fluttering flight, (4) gliding descent, (5) fluttering descent, (6) diving descent, (7) gentle descent in butterfly flight, (8) stall before touch-down, and (9) wings high with trill after landing.*

FIG. 8.4. *Butterfly flight of American Golden Plover, based on field observations at Churchill (1986).*

American Golden Plovers descend steeply and rapidly, but details are lacking (see also Parmelee *et al.* 1967). Grey Plovers often descend at a very steep angle, appearing to drop almost like a stone. Eurasian, and sometimes Pacific, golden plovers may descend in a steep glide with the wings held in a V above the back. In the Eurasian Golden Plover this was typically seen when two birds had been duelling in song flights 2–3 m apart above their territory boundaries. In that situation the butterfly flight itself was partially performed with the wings in the V-position, barely beating and, on two occasions, followed by a sharply spiralling descent.

At the end of their descent, Grey Plovers skim 1.5–2 m above the ground at a tremendous speed covering 50–100 m before landing. Eurasian Golden Plovers may also do this, as can Pacific Golden Plovers. On landing, the 'wings high' posture is adopted – as a rule in the Pacific Golden Plover, commonly in the Eurasian Golden Plover, but not seen in the Grey Plover. Interestingly, a peculiarity of Pacific Golden Plovers, just before touch-down, is the 'stall', in which the bird, wings out-stretched above the back and legs dangling, swoops up (about 0.5–1.5 m high, depending on its speed), before gently settling to the ground. This dainty finale provides a superb finishing touch to a flight display which is delicate and ethereal throughout, in sharp contrast to the heavy, forceful and speedy performance of the Grey Plover.

Vocalizations during song flights

It is a thankless and also a futile task to reduce the calls of birds to syllables.

Maud Haviland (1915)

Tundra plovers are highly vocal during much of the breeding season. While the strong remonstrations to a human passing near their offspring can be quite maddening, the pure, whistling songs with their bubbling trills used during the song flight are surely the paeans of the north in early spring. To our ears, the Grey Plover is the master, followed closely by the Pacific Golden Plover. Having a more modest song than the others, American Golden Plovers emit trills just as evocative as those of the Pacific Golden Plover.

Song flight vocalizations of tundra plovers have been described phonetically in a number of publications (e.g. Höhn 1957; Steiniger 1959; Drury 1961; Nethersole-Thompson & Nethersole-Thompson 1961, 1986; Parmelee *et al.* 1967; Ratcliffe 1976; Kondrat'ev 1982). However, such descriptions really are limited, and have not enabled people even to distinguish between Pacific and American golden plovers (though Höhn 1957 did notice and describe the differences in song). So far, sonagrams of song flight vocalizations have been published for the golden plovers by Cramp & Simmons (1983) and Connors *et al.* (1993). Our descriptions are based almost entirely on tape recordings made by IB. Eurasian Golden Plovers were recorded at Jæren in 1989 and 1990, Pacific Golden Plovers and Grey Plovers at Yamal in 1989, and American Golden Plovers at Churchill, Manitoba in 1986.

Our analytical methods We should mention in detail the equipment and methods used. American Golden Plovers were recorded on a Sony TCM-2 recorder with an internal microphone; the others were recorded on a Sony TC-55B recorder equipped with a cardioid dynamic microphone (Sony F-27S) mounted in a 33 cm parabolic reflector (Sony PBR0330). The sound recordings were analysed on a Uniscan II sonagraph, but the sonagram printouts were made on a Voice Identification Series 700 sound spectrograph with a 300 Hz filtering band width. The sonograph allowed digital reading of time and frequency levels and intervals.

The standard method of illustrating and analysing calls or song is based on the sonagram (sound spectrogram). The horizontal scale shows time (seconds), the vertical axis shows frequency (kHz), and the density of the shading indicates the relative loudness (amplitude). Each block of shading is referred to as an 'element'. Crudely speaking, birds hear variations in others' sounds in terms of loudness and pitch (frequency) over time. On the sonagram, a sound varying only slightly in frequency appears as a straight black line (frequency-unmodulated); a whistle dropping or rising in frequency has the black line falling or rising with time (frequency-modulated). As a rule, sounds designed to travel far are structurally simple, low in frequency with little modulation. These are least susceptible to background interference such as wind, and for ease of location tend to be highly repetitive. Now let us examine the four types of song.

Wailing song/main song Figure 8.5 shows sonagrams for wailing songs from different individuals of each of the four species, and quantitative information on durations and frequencies of tonal elements is given in Figs. 8.6 and 8.7.

In Eurasian Golden Plovers this song consists of two tonal elements, in Grey Plover and Pacific Golden Plover of three, and in American Golden Plover of four following each other in a fixed sequence, which forms the 'song unit'. These units are repeated at a fairly constant rate during the butterfly flight. The song units of Grey Plovers have first and last tonal elements of about equal duration (ca 0.4 s) and equal frequency (2.0–2.3 kHz). The middle element is shorter (0.16 s), higher pitched and with more frequency modulation than the other two elements (2.6–3.1 kHz). There are no intervals between the tonal elements, so the whole unit sounds like a yodelling 'too^lee^oo'.

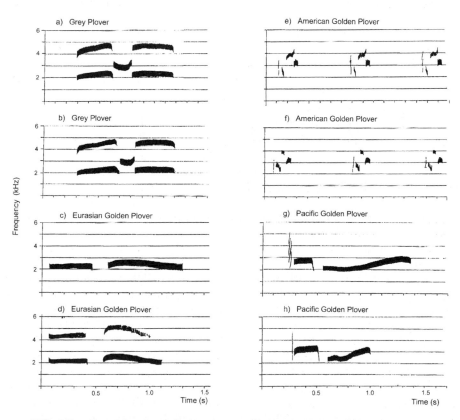

FIG. 8.5. *Broad band sonagrams of wailing song performed in butterfly flight by tundra plovers. Examples from two individuals are shown for each species. a, b, Grey Plovers recorded at Yamal, July 1989; c, d, Eurasian Golden Plovers, Jæren, April 1989; e, f, American Golden Plovers, Churchill, June/July 1986; g, h, Pacific Golden Plovers, Yamal, June 1989.*

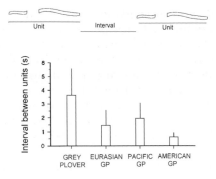

FIG. 8.6.   *Song rhythm expressed as time interval between song units. Song units are the sequences of tonal elements repeated during wailing song; upper panel indicates two units and one interval in a sonagram of Eurasian Golden Plover song.*

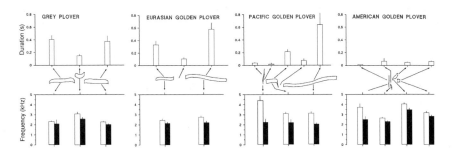

FIG. 8.7.   *Average rhythm and pitch (±SD) of the wailing song of tundra plovers. Averages of both upper (open bars) and lower (filled bars) frequency limits for each tonal element are shown. The structures between the two graph sets are tracings of tonal elements from broad-band sonagrams. The analysis was done using 10 song units for each individual bird. Frequencies and times were analysed on a Uniscan II sonagraph.*

Pacific Golden Plovers start their song with a short (0.04 s) element of abruptly rising frequently (from 2.2 to 4.4 kHz). In Fig. 8.5 (g), harmonic over- and undertones make this element on a sonagram look almost like a sharply falling tremolo. There is a short interval (0.01 s) before the next tonal element, which is also a short one (0.21 s), although of much longer duration than the first. At the end of the second element the frequency drops rapidly from an average of 3.1 to 2.2 kHz, and then there is an interval (0.07 s) before the long-drawn (0.65 s) final whistle, which increases gently in frequency from 2.0 to 3.1 kHz. Onomatopoetically, the song units sound like 'ptee$_{oo}$leeee'. The first of the three tonal elements appears to be less forceful than the others, and it tends not to show up on sonagrams of long distance recordings.

American Golden Plovers sing quite differently from the others. The closely related Pacific Golden Plover sings more like the Eurasian than the American golden plover. The most notable difference is that all four tonal elements are of very short duration (0.04–0.06 s) in American Golden Plover compared with the others. Except for the first element it is difficult to find any structural similarities with the song of the Pacific Golden Plover, and the pitch is slightly higher (Fig. 8.5e,f). The song of the American Golden Plover can hardly be called 'wailing', but rather sounds almost like a clicking: 'tulick' or 'p'tulick'. The two-syllable song units of the Eurasian Golden Plovers, however, definitely deserve the term wailing, with the first element sounding like that of the Grey Plover both in pitch (2.1–2.5 kHz) and duration (avg. 0.33 s), and the other a long-drawn (0.57 s) whistle (frequency increasing-decreasing between 2.5 and 2.7 kHz), resulting in a mournful 'poo-peeooo'.

We have compared variation in duration of song units between and within males using Analysis of Variance on data for key song elements. For Pacific Golden Plovers, in particular, there is highly significant variation between males (F = 253.1, p<0.01, df 1,45; for elements 1, 2 and 3; see Figs. 8.5–8.7). Between-male variation is also highly significant in Eurasian Golden Plover (F = 55.5, p<0.001, df 8,126; for elements 1 and 2) and Grey Plovers (F = 21.8, p<0.001, df 6,45; for elements 1, 2 and 3), but not in American Golden Plovers (F = 0.4, ns, df 6,63 for elements 1, 2, 3 and 4). The intervals between the song units also seem important part of the signal. Being very stereotypic, these largely determine the auditory impression of the song's tempo. Whilst Eurasian and Pacific golden plovers repeat their song units with intervals of 1.80–1.96 s, Grey Plovers have extremely long intervals between their song units (average 3.65 s), and in American Golden Plovers the repetition is very fast (only about 0.06 s between song units). Thus, American Golden Plovers appear to sing in a great hurry, compared with the more staid performances of the others!

Trilling song This consists of a series of sounds with a bubbling or yodelling quality, not only used more or less regularly by all four species during song flights or when landing after song flights, but also on the ground in communication between mates and in aggression. This is the sound referred to as the 'complex whistle' by Connors *et al.* (1993). In song flights, trills accompany periods of fluttering flights between bouts of butterfly flights, especially if there are other conspecifics flying nearby – either in song flights or just passing.

Sonagrams of trills containing all basic tonal elements are shown in Fig. 8.8. At first sight, the differences between the species may be more striking than the similarities. Grey Plover trills are first and foremost characterized by long whistles with abrupt changes in frequency, and by a rolling initial tremolo. The tonal elements usually follow each other in the sequence shown in Fig. 8.8 (but sometimes they are slightly shuffled, or even lacking some of the elements). The Grey Plover trill is a fantastic sound which, phonetically, can be rendered 'pee-rrrrrrwit-poo-plluuuee-poolee-pooooee'.

Golden plover trills differ from those of Grey Plovers by having more rapidly frequency-modulated elements instead of abrupt frequency shifts. Of the four species, the Eurasian Golden Plover has the most constant trill: two initial tonal elements are followed by a third (Fig. 8.8), the latter being repeated 3–4 times (range 1–11 times). Although there is a tremolo section in the middle of the third tonal element, the sound bears no resemblance to the tremolo part of the Grey

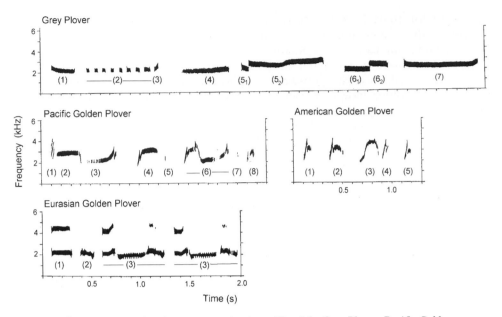

FIG. 8.8.　*Broad-band sonagrams showing trills of the Grey Plover, Pacific Golden Plover, American Golden Plover, and Eurasian Golden Plover. The figures in parentheses within the graphs denote the tonal element numbers (arranged in sequence, and referred to in Appendix 8). Recording dates: Grey Plover, Yamal, July 1989; Pacific Golden Plover, Yamal, June 1989, American Golden Plover, Churchill, June 1986; Eurasian Golden Plover, Kautokeino, North Norway, June 1988.*

Plover's trill. Giving an intense and somewhat grating impression, the trill of the Eurasian Golden Plover sounds like 'poo-pee-pyuyu-pyuyu-pyuyu . . .'

In the field, trills of American and Pacific golden plovers sound fairly similar. Both have strongly frequency-modulated elements (Fig. 8.8), giving them a distinct rhythmic and warbling quality. Trills of Pacific Golden Plovers may contain eight different tonal elements, compared with only four in the American Golden Plover. In both species, the tonal elements usually occur in certain sequences (Appendix 8), although there are shuffles and reductions now and then. Also, certain repetitive patterns of tonal elements within a trill are evident, although less fixed and more complex than in the Eurasian Golden Plover.

With some practice, field ornithologists with a good ear should be able to tell the 'witt-wee-wyu-witt-witt' of the American Golden Plover from the 't'wee-witt-wiy-wyu-witt-wju' of the Pacific Golden Plover! A closer comparison between the trills of these closely related species should be of special interest, as homologous tonal elements can be recognized (Fig. 8.8). These elements are compared in Fig. 8.9. American Golden Plovers have significantly higher pitched and shorter duration trill elements than those of Pacific Golden Plovers.

Hysterical whistle This is a sound typical of Eurasian Golden Plovers when singing birds meet in mid-air and the flights develop into chases or rapid pursuits. No

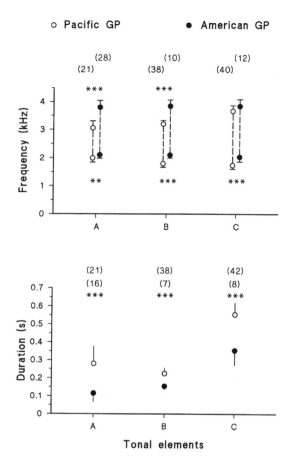

FIG. 8.9. *Upper and lower frequencies, and duration (averages, horizontal bars; ±1 SD vertical bars), of homologous tonal elements in trills of Pacific and American golden plovers. ** = p<0.01, *** p<0.001, t-tests. Number of elements in parentheses. With reference to the identified numbers of elements in Fig. 8.8, the elements compared are: A, Pacific Golden Plover (PGP) element No.3 and American Golden Plover (AGP) No. 1; B, PGP No.4 and AGP No.2; C, PGP No.6 and AGP Nos. 3 + 4.*

corresponding sounds are known for the other golden plovers or Grey Plover. Hysterical whistles (Fig. 8.10) are outbursts of plaintive cries, resembling the second element of the Wailing Song (Fig. 8.5, c, d), and sounding like a very intensive or hysterical' 'piie-piie-piie. . .'

High intensity song For the Eurasian Golden Plover, Veprintsev (1982) recorded a sound, stated to be very rare, which he called 'high intensity song'. In the field we have never heard this sound. Unfortunately, no information about its context is given on Veprintsev's LP record sleeve, so we do not know whether or not the sound was performed during a butterfly flight or on the ground, or indeed near the mate or in a territory dispute. The sound is an 'endless' series of bubbling

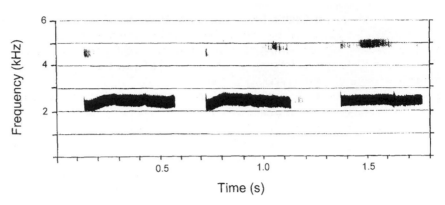

FIG. 8.10. *Hysterical whistles during the song of the Eurasian Golden Plover.*

notes, on sonagrams looking like 'distorted' versions of element No. 3 of the trill (in Fig. 8.8).

Functions of song flights

The song flights, with their wonderful sounds, constitute a long-distance self-advertisement by the performing males. Going on for many minutes uninterrupted, the butterfly flight, with its wailing song, forms the main phase. Movements and sounds in connection with ascent, descent, and landing, although striking and conspicuous enough, can only convey momentary signals, presumably aimed chiefly at nearby individuals, notably mates or neighbouring males. The descent and landing phases, in particular, seem to convey (or enforce) messages about the location of an occupied territory, judging by the conspicuous nature of the dives and wing-high postures.

Although song flights, at least in the Eurasian Golden Plover, may be carried out over neutral feeding grounds in spring or even in passage flocks, song flights are typically performed by males over their breeding territories (Cramp & Simmons 1983; Nethersole-Thompson & Nethersole-Thompson 1986; Connors *et al.* 1993). Song flights apparently serve to mark the bounds of territories in addition to having self-advertisement functions, and may be an invitation to potential mates as well as a signal to other males to 'keep out'. Both functions have been implied for all four species (Flint & Kondrat'ev 1977; Cramp & Simmons 1983; Connors *et al.* 1993). For Eurasian Golden Plovers Steiniger (1959) proposed that the song flights' chief function was for mate acquisition, as did Sauer (1962) for Pacific Golden Plovers.

There can be little doubt about the territorial defence function. In all four species, song flights have been seen to occur almost throughout the breeding season (Drury 1961; Nethersole-Thompson & Nethersole-Thompson 1961; Parmelee *et al.* 1967; Ratcliffe 1976). Moreover, many individually recognizable males of all four species have been observed by us to sing spontaneously throughout the period of incubation, and for Eurasian Golden Plovers also for a while after their chicks have hatched. But we have to be careful in reaching conclusions. Song flighting is much reduced after egg-laying, and the odd unmated male which continues singing well into the nesting season can mislead one into thinking that more birds are singing than is actually the case.

Apart from roughly circling their territories, neighbouring males often sing simultaneously, only metres apart, in parallel flight over apparent territory boundaries. The territorial defence function of song flights is also indicated by the fact that males, having chased off intruders, return to their territories in song flight. Neighbours do intrude on one-anothers' territories, and even challenge the territorial boundaries, during all parts of the breeding season, although the needs for territorial demarcation and defence may be greatest early in the season.

So, do song flights attract females to male territories? The particularly high rate of song flights immediately after male arrival for all four species (Nethersole-Thompson & Nethersole-Thompson 1961, 1986; Sauer 1962; Parmelee *et al.* 1967; Drury 1961; Flint & Kondratjew 1977; Kondrat'ev 1982; Cramp & Simmons 1983) may be interpreted as mate attraction, although they may also reflect the high needs for territorial defence at that time. However, lone male Eurasian Golden Plovers at Jæren and Pacific Golden Plovers at Yamal had significantly higher rates of song flights than neighbouring paired males at the same time (Pacific Golden Plovers: lone male song flight median rate of 3.5 h^{-1}, paired male median rate of 0.5 h^{-1} ($n=5$ and 4 males); Eurasian Golden Plover: lone male median rate of 0.4 h^{-1}, paired male median rate of 0.1 h^{-1} ($n=4$ and 5 males); Mann-Whitney U-tests, combined probability test , $p<0.01$). This strongly indicates a mate attraction function of song flights. Pacific Golden Plover and Grey Plover males have sometimes been seen to sing only a few metres above standing females (Flint & Kondratjew 1977; Kondrat'ev 1982). At Yamal, on two occasions singing unmated male Pacific Golden Plovers encircled females that flew in over their territory, appearing to entice them down to the ground.

Thus, song flights may well function both in territorial defence and female attraction, at least in Eurasian and Pacific golden plovers, but probably also in the other two species. Connors *et al.* (1993) considered the large differences in song to contribute strongly to the absence of mating between Pacific and American golden plovers in the zone of overlap.

Individual variation in the length of the song 'units' (i.e. the tonal elements following each other in repeated sequences during the song) in Grey Plover, Eurasian and Pacific golden plovers is substantial and readily perceived by the human ear. Among nine Eurasian Golden Plovers at Jæren, and seven Grey Plovers tape-recorded at Yamal, the longest average individual song unit was 1.4 times greater than that of the individual with the shortest average song unit length. Among five Pacific Golden Plovers the difference was as much as 1.7 times greater, but only 1.1 times greater among seven American Golden Plovers recorded at Churchill. In the three former species, 74–99% of the variation in song unit length was due to individual differences compared with only 6% in American Golden Plover (Analysis of Variance; Grey Plover: 52 song units, 7 individuals; Eurasian Golden Plover: 135 song units, 9 individuals; Pacific Golden Plover: 50 song units, 5 individuals; American Golden Plover: 70 song units, 7 individuals). Male Pacific and Eurasian golden plovers that arrived later and seemed to have trouble getting a permanent territory and/or a mate tended to have shorter song units.

Social status may, one way or another, be connected with song unit length in these species. Whether or not song unit length is correlated with body size, condition or age, or with any other fitness-related traits, is not known. We need research to explore this in detail, and to test whether or not females use song flights to compare and judge potential mates on their territories.

COURTSHIP AND COPULATION

At least in the Eurasian Golden Plover, pairing activities are considered to have begun in spring flocks, before the birds have dispersed onto territories (Rittinghaus 1969; Cramp and Simmons 1983; Glutz von Blotzheim *et al.* 1975; Nethersole- Thompson & Nethersole-Thompson 1961, 1986; Parr 1980; Edwards 1982). Some pairs, even new ones are already established then (Parr 1980). However, many males spend a number of days on territory before they appear together with their mates. Connors (1983) and Connors *et al.* (1993) point out the difficulties in obtaining relevant information, and maintain that pair formation in Pacific and American golden plovers probably takes place on breeding territories. This is reinforced by Johnson & Connors (1995), and is also indicated for Grey Plovers (Flint & Kondrajew 1977; Paulson 1995). Pair formation in spring flocks is perhaps more likely in populations that have short distances to travel between wintering and breeding grounds, notably for Eurasian Golden Plovers breeding in Britain. There males chasing females in 'torpedo runs' have been seen among flocks in Nottinghamshire, in early March, and in the North Pennines from mid-February onwards (P.S. Thompson pers. comm.). In American Golden Plovers such chases have been seen in late April as far south as Indiana (Johnson 1941).

Although copulations may occur in spring flocks, the typical inter-sexual behaviour consists of 'torpedo runs' (term coined by Connors *et al.* 1993; *cf.* 'hunched run' used by Cramp & Simmons 1983), winglifts, and trills, all of which are also components of aggressive situations. The males seem to isolate females and fend off other males. Neither of us has been able to recognize the difference said to exist between 'aggressive' and 'courtship' types of torpedo run in Eurasian Golden Plovers (as observed in Britain by Edwards 1982, and mentioned by Cramp & Simmons 1983).

The interpretation of observations from spring flocks of these birds near their southwestern breeding grounds is difficult for two reasons. First, many males resemble females, and the chances are that observed aggression is mistaken for courtship, or *vice versa*. Second, the already established pairs can sometimes leave their territories during pre-laying to feed on farmland for a considerable part of the day (8–10 h per day at Jæren), and if these join other Eurasian Golden Plovers there they may easily be mistaken for migrants. Here, what is considered to be courtship may actually be mate-guarding by males.

Pairing behaviour on the territory

In the initial phase of the breeding season, communication between the sexes serves three main goals: (i) initial establishment or re-establishment of the pair; (ii) choice of nest scrape; and (iii) fertilization. Postures as well as vocalizations are involved. However, most of the communication between pair members when they are 'alone together' is extremely quiet and evidently intimate. Tundra plovers actually lack many of the more vigorous and noisy displays of the ringed plovers and lapwings (*cf* Glutz von Blotzheim *et al.* 1975, Cramp & Simmons 1983, Phillips 1980).

Table 11 summarizes the behaviour used in communication between the sexes during the pre-laying period. More information is available for Eurasian Golden Plovers than for the others, and least is known about the American Golden Plover. Torpedo or hunched runs (Fig. 8.11) are part of the communication between the pair members only during their first day or two on territory. Both pair members assume a hunched posture, feathers on their back and belly often ruffled, while they run after each other (male usually chasing the female) or run more or less in parallel. This behaviour seems to be initiated by the male. The frequent use of torpedo runs could indicate a certain initial aggressiveness by males towards females, as torpedo runs are also used in aggression against other males (as we shall discuss shortly). However, in the pair formation context this behaviour more likely signals a 'possessive' attitude, as males isolate (or even mate-guard) females in spring flocks by torpedo runs. Whatever its signal, the torpedo run is reciprocated by the female.

Soon, however, as the pair spend longer together, hunched runs are replaced by what appear to be more co-operative acts. The males now start to look for nest sites. Typically, they walk about in a distinctive forward-tilted posture with slow deliberate gaits (Fig. 8.12a). Often, the female adopts this posture and just stands and watches the male. She also walks about in the same manner, though our observations indicate that this is much less frequent (male: 70–80%; females: 30–40% of time observed in forward tilted walk about 1 week before egg-laying). During this walk they now and then cautiously approach each other, increasingly upright, until they stand bill-to-bill for up to a minute or so (Fig. 8.12b).

The male frequently changes from forward-tilted walk to bouts of nest-scraping, with his breast pressed to the ground, tail pointing almost vertically, and feet scratching the ground vigorously (Fig. 8.13). The scratching is frequently interrupted as the bird picks up and tosses bits of vegetation back over his shoulder, sometimes he even walks a few steps out of the scrape to obtain such material. Meanwhile, the female stands and watches 2–30 m away, or walks about in the forward-tilted posture. After a while she may enter the scrape for inspection. Unlike many *Charadrius* plovers and lapwings (Glutz von Blotzheim *et al.* 1975; Phillips 1980; Cramp & Simmons 1983), however, female Eurasian and Pacific golden plovers and Grey Plovers do not enter the scrape while the male is in it (Flint & Kondratjew 1977); instead, she waits until he has walked 0.2–2 m away. While the female inspects the scrape, pecking at the nest cup, sitting, turning, scraping and tossing nest material, the male Eurasian Golden Plover often continues his forward-tilted walk to another nest scrape. He may even stand in a tail-up posture facing away from the female, which meanwhile is in the scrape (Fig. 8.13c).

During the forward-tilted walk, the birds, especially the males, constantly utter

FIG. 8.11. *Variety of torpedo runs made by male Eurasian Golden Plovers, apparently directed at other males. (From colour slides and field sketches; Yamal and Jæren).*

soft, simple 'pyt' notes (Fig. 8.14a–c). This sound does not carry far, and is most frequently used when the pair is less than 8–10 m apart. At longer distances (20–30 m), the pair members signal to each other by an occasional 'chewit' (Fig. 8.14d) and a plaintive whistle (Fig. 8.14e), both of which are louder than the 'pyt' sounds, yet much weaker than song and alarm cries. A peculiar soft warbling-like constant

FIG. 8.12a.   *Male Eurasian Golden Plover in forward-tilted walk. (From field sketch, Jæren).*

FIG. 8.12b.   *Female and male Eurasian Golden Plover in bill-to-bill posture. (From field sketch, Jæren).*

stream of distorted 'pyt' notes is emitted by the scraping male Eurasian Golden Plover (and apparently by Grey Plovers, Flint & Kondratjew 1977) as his mate stands watching less than one metre from the scrape (Fig. 8.14f). Now and then the mates also communicate with trills. All the vocalizations, except the trills, are noticeably quiet, presumably attuned to short-distance communication and affording minimum attention from predators or potential male competitors.

Copulations

Copulations, although not infrequent, constitute only a tiny fraction of the time spent in social interactions between the pair members. Copulations do not seem to

FIG. 8.13a.   *Nest-scraping by male Eurasian Golden Plover, scratching vigorously with feet (upper) and tossing nest material over shoulder (lower). (From field sketches, Jæren)*

FIG. 8.13b.   *Scrape inspection by female while male adopts tail-up posture. (From field sketches, Jæren).*

follow a very elaborate ritual, though it has to be admitted that information is minimal for the American Golden Plover, and lacking altogether for the Pacific Golden Plover.

In 12 copulations observed in the Eurasian Golden Plover, the male approached

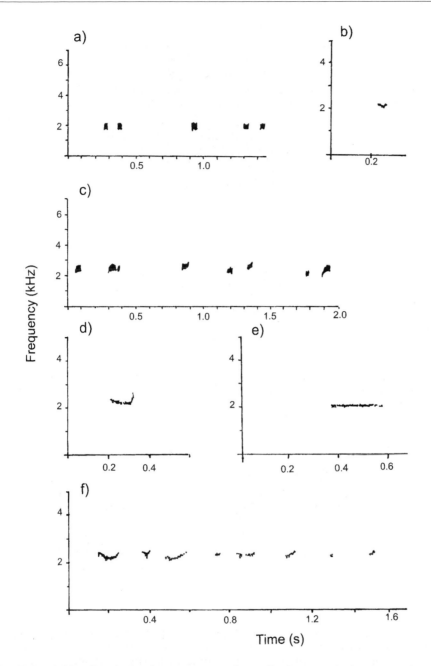

FIG. 8.14. *Broad band sonagrams of vocalizations used in intra-pair communications during pre-laying. 'Pyt' sounds of a) Grey Plover, b) Eurasian Golden Plover and c) Pacific Golden Plover; other sounds are of Eurasian Golden Plover d) 'chewit' sound, e) plaintive whistle and f) warbling 'pyt' notes. Grey Plovers and Pacific Golden Plovers were recorded at Yamal 1989, the former in July and the latter in June; the recordings of Eurasian Golden Plovers were obtained at Jæren, April 1989.*

the female in a torpedo run with lowered tail (7 cases) or in a normal run (5 cases). Before running the males preened (7 cases), performed 'wings-high' display (3 cases), or nest-scraped (1 case). Preening and wings-high have also been observed in American Golden Plovers before copulation, and the tail-canting run in male Grey Plovers (Parmelee *et al.* 1967; Hussell & Page 1976; Flint & Kondratjew 1977). In the 12 Eurasian Golden Plover copulations, females solicited the copulation in a forward bent posture (8 cases; a behaviour seen also in Grey Plover; Flint & Kondratjew 1977), whilst in 4 cases they were feeding and in one case carrying out a nest scrape inspection. Hussell & Page (1976) reported nest scrape inspections in female Grey Plovers before copulation. After copulation, Eurasian Golden Plover males flew off the female's back (9 cases) or they just walked away (3 cases); they then started to preen (6 cases), stood alert (4 cases), performed 'wings-high' display (1 case), or bathed (1 case). Grey Plover males also fly off the female's back (Hussell & Page 1976). Eurasian Golden Plover females, after copulation, began feeding (4 cases) or preening (4 cases), bathed (1 case), or stood inactive for several minutes (3 cases).

In Eurasian Golden Plovers a typical copulation sequence is shown in Fig. 8.15. The female is mounted for 6–35 s (n=8), with the male sometimes keeping balance with a few wingbeats. Coitus lasts 1–2 s. Before running toward the female, the male may utter a trill, but usually he is silent.

Observations of Eurasian Golden Plovers about one week before egg-laying showed a rate of one copulation each 4 hours (5 pairs pooled, 4 copulations in 964 minutes of observation, Hardangervidda; 1 pair, 2 copulations in 516 min, Jæren). If copulations are equally distributed over the day (and at Hardangervidda they seemed to be), the observations indicate a daily minimum of four copulations at that time of the season. Closer to egg-laying (i.e., in the most fertile period), this rate may even increase (e.g. Owens *et al.* 1995 and our observations of Eurasian Dotterel).

Birkhead *et al.* (1987) compared copulation rates in many bird species, and found high copulation rates in birds with a high risk of extra-pair copulation with females. Their study suggested sperm competition to be a strong evolutionary force selecting for a high copulation rate (also Birkhead & Møller 1992). For the Grey Plover, the only tundra plover in their analysis, they gave a copulation rate of less than two per day, yet Birkhead *et al.*'s source, Hussell & Page (1976), did not provide an observation duration for any such estimate. Our observations of Eurasian Golden Plovers indicate a fairly high copulation rate in terms of criteria set by Birkhead *et al.* (1987). Nevertheless, we consider mate guarding to be very effective in tundra plovers. Males defend large territories from which they vigorously repel trespassing conspecifics. During pre-laying, mates mostly keep within a few metres of each other (Eurasian and Pacific golden plovers). So long as the pair is on territory, an intruding male has minimal chances of obtaining extra-pair copulations. However, in areas with a high breeding density, males will spend more time in territorial defence and less time guarding their mates. In dense populations of Black-tailed Godwits and Northern Lapwings, males often copulate as they return from song flights, chases or fights (also Byrkjedal 1985b, Parish 1996; see Birkhead *et al.* 1987 for non-wader examples); most attempts at extra-pair copulations with neighbouring females were observed in these species when their mates were engaged in territorial defence.

FIG. 8.15. *A typical behavioural sequence in copulating Eurasian Golden Plovers. Male preens breast before approaching female, which adopts stiff horizontal posture. During approach male assumes torpedo run with tail increasingly tilted; turns in a semi-circle behind female, tail half spread and now tilted towards female; mounts from side, balances, copulates, and then flies off (2–20 m), and (not shown) preens, and feeds. (From field sketches, Jæren).*

An interesting situation arises in Eurasian Golden Plover populations in which pre-laying pairs feed in flocks on neutral ground outwith their territories. More frequent attempts at extra-pair copulations within the 'confusion' of a flock are likely (and may have been observed in N. Sutherland, though we could not distinguish between intra- and extra-pair copulations), and this may well lead to higher copulation rates on territories of these populations. The observed copulation rates at Jæren (extra-territorial feeding on farmland) and Hardangervidda (all feeding within the territories during pre-laying) did not differ; we hope that comparable data on other such contrasting populations will be collected soon.

ANTAGONISTIC BEHAVIOUR

In the Eurasian Golden Plover, aggression frequently takes place in the spring flocks, where males appear to be fighting over females (Nethersole-Thompson & Nethersole-Thompson 1961; Edwards 1982; Cramp & Simmons 1983). We have watched the bustle in these flocks, with the males appearing to try and isolate females from other males. We do not know to what extent these contests are part of the pairing activities, or simply concerned with mate guarding during extra-territorial feeding. Perhaps already-paired local males are defending their mates against extra-pair copulations from males on passage (*cf.* Köpke 1971) as well as paired/unpaired males? Most observations have been made on non-marked birds, and remember that this is at a time of the year when even sexing the birds may be a problem owing to incomplete moult of passage northern birds (Chapter 4).

Chases and attacks

The most common aggressive behaviour in spring flocks is the 'torpedo run' (Fig. 8.11), in which males rapidly approach each other until 1–2 m apart. Usually one of them turns and retreats, with the other following closely over a few metres' distance. If neither retreats, one 'leap-frogs' (Fig. 8.16) the other before a collision seems imminent. This may be repeated several times (also Edwards 1982; Cramp & Simmons 1983). Frequently, an antagonist approaches another bird by flying at it very close to ground level, then leap-frogging it, after which the birds follow each other in a torpedo run. Torpedo run sequences are often followed by the wings-high posture (bottom left of Fig. 8.2). According to Edwards (1982) the latter posture is usually given laterally to the opponent, with the neck and body in a horizontal posture, though our own observations suggest that the displays are more diagonal in alignment. Torpedo runs may also result in overt flights or even 'pursuit flights'; more rarely, males may remonstrate by 'breast-to-breast' or 'bill-to-bill' displays whilst singing (also Nethersole-Thompson & Nethersole-Thompson 1961, 1986; Edwards 1982; Cramp & Simmons 1983). The torpedo run is also used in aggression by the other tundra plovers (also Connors *et al.* 1993), but far less is known about their aggressive behaviour.

For territorial defence, the song flight appears usually to be sufficient. But neighbours occasionally trespass on each others' territories. Driving off intruders

FIG. 8.16. *Eurasian Golden Plover males leap-frogging (from colour slides and field sketches, Jæren).*

may be carried out by both pair members, but males are more often involved than females. Only Eurasian Golden Plover males have been recorded aggressively chasing females or pairs (Nethersole-Thompson & Nethersole-Thompson 1961; Parr 1980; Cramp & Simmons 1983). On their territories, Eurasian Golden Plovers usually show much less complex aggressive behaviour than they do in spring flocks. During pre-laying, trespassers are usually just approached on wing and promptly chased away (also Parr 1980). Philip Edwards (1982, and also in Cramp & Simmons 1983), however, reported many of the more complex behaviours also on the territories. His study site must have been special, if not unique, as the birds there gradually took up breeding territories on fields used by the spring flocks. It is a pity that Edwards' study area is now largely over-grown with deep Purple Moor Grass (*Molinia caerulea*), as it would have been instructive to develop the study.

The sight of Grey Plovers chasing trespassers off their territories is spectacular! The intruder is harried closely (the birds are only a few centimetres to a metre apart) at an astounding speed, both birds twisting and turning sharply. In passing the territory boundary, the chaser, while trilling, shoots up to stall ca 3–10 m behind the intruder, as if giving the latter a final 'kick', before returning to his territory. Immediately before and/or after this stall, the owner of the territory glides with wings held in a shallow V above the back, emitting his far-carrying trill. Sometimes, immediately afterwards, the resident male climbs to some height and enters a regular song flight. At Yamal, such chases were performed by Grey Plovers throughout the incubation period, and always by males.

Despite some thorough studies of Eurasian Golden Plovers, there are still large uncertainties about pairing behaviour and aggression, especially in spring flocks and in relation to extra-territorial foraging. Quantitative studies of individually marked birds, are needed.

Post-hatch antagonism

As hatched broods begin to wander, they frequently enter neighbouring territories. In fact, territory boundaries break down after hatching, but a certain degree of spacing is nevertheless maintained through aggression and displays at least in American and Eurasian golden plovers (for information on brood movements in the four species, see Haviland 1915; Sutton 1932; Drury 1961; Parmelee *et al.* 1967; Mayfield 1973; Hussell & Page 1976; Flint & Kondratjew 1977; Parr 1980; Kondrat'ev 1982; Byrkjedal 1985a; Yalden & Yalden 1990).

The most prolonged and vigorous disputes take place when broods enter territories of incubating birds. The incubating male defends his territory persistently (this may last for several hours in Eurasian and American golden plovers) by 'parallel walks' with the intruding male (Fig. 8.17a), 'upright frontal threats' (Fig. 8.17b), and even vigorous fights. The latter involves pecking, beating with carpal joints, and jumping at the opponent. Torpedo runs and other kinds of behaviour typical of the early season hostilities appear not to be used. The evident rawness and viciousness of these encounters, compared with some of the more stereotyped encounters during the pre-laying period is curious.

SUMMARY

1. We provide detailed descriptions of displays and postures on the breeding grounds, many of which have not previously been recorded in the field or in the literature.
2. In all four species, the 'butterfly flight' (with slow, jerky, and stiff wingbeats) comprises the major component of the male song flight. Signals may also be conveyed in other phases of the song flight, especially during the descent and on landing. There are consistent differences between species.
3. Song (wailing song) is uttered during butterfly flights and differs between

FIG. 8.17.   *American Golden Plover males in a) parallel walk, and b) upright frontal threat (from field sketches, Churchill).*

species in: (i) number of tonal elements sequentially repeated; (ii) structure of tonal elements; and (iii) rhythm. A 'trill' is uttered when males meet in song flight, after landing from song flights, and by either sex in communication between birds on the ground. Trills differ markedly between Grey Plovers and Eurasian Golden Plovers, but those of American and Pacific golden plovers are strikingly similar.

4. Possible functions of song flights are discussed and we suggest these serve both to attract females, and to demonstrate territorial boundaries.
5. Much social activity is observed in spring flocks of Eurasian Golden Plovers; to what extent pairing takes place in these is still uncertain.
6. Pre-laying pairs of Eurasian Golden Plover, on territories, communicate with soft vocalizations and subtle postures, and much time is spent nest scraping.
7. Territorial males immediately chase off intruding males, but persistent fighting, at least in Eurasian and American golden plovers, is most apparent after hatching when broods enter territories of pairs still incubating.
8. Copulations in Eurasian Golden Plovers (detailed information is lacking for the other tundra plovers) follow certain sequences of behaviour but there are no particularly elaborate ceremonies. Copulations occur during the week before laying, and mate guarding is tight.

CHAPTER 9

Breeding Season: Sex Roles and Parental Behaviour

A family of Eurasian Golden Plovers

Your progress across the tundra in July is heralded and attended by a chorus of plaintive cries. Both birds meet you a quarter of a mile from the nest, and never leave you until you are at the boundaries of their own territory, and they can safely hand you over to their next neighbours for espionage. . . . The suspiciousness and patience of the Golden Plovers are the same all the world over; and I will not dwell upon them to those who themselves have no doubt walked vainly for half a day about the birds' breeding grounds in this country, and listened to its maddening but at the same time most musical protests.

Maud Haviland (1915) commenting on the Pacific Golden Plover near the Yenisei.

ALTHOUGH monogamy and biparental care is usual in more than 90% of bird species (e.g. Lack 1968; Perrins 1987), shorebirds exhibit an extraordinary range of mating systems and forms of parental care (e.g. Oring 1982; Piersma *et al.*

1996). This final chapter on the breeding season deals with division of parental care between the sexes. Special attention is paid to the two major components of parental care: incubation/brooding, and anti-predator behaviour. As in the previous chapter, most of the data presented here have not been published before.

The extent to which a bird can maximize its fitness by leaving parental care to its mate, and engage in polygamy, depends on the availability of sufficient resources for uniparental care, certainty of parenthood, options for multiple matings, and the costs of reduced parental care (e.g. Oring 1982; Erckmann 1983; Lenington 1984; Clutton-Brock & Godfray 1991; Whitfield & Tomkovich 1996). It is tempting to assume that the costs of single parent care in altricial birds, which bring food to their young in the nest, are considerably greater than for a single parent shorebird caring for its young outside the nest. And indeed when one thinks of an adult Blue Tit taking a food item to its nest every minute of daylight (this can amount to more than 1000 visits in a 16 hour day, Perrins 1987), the brood caring requirements of parent shorebirds may seem small. However, they have to find good food patches, look out for predators, and brood young at night or when it is cold and wet. We shall develop the argument that parental care in tundra plovers is actually very demanding, something which is readily overlooked by many workers.

TIME BUDGETS AND PARENTAL CARE

One convenient way of comparing male and female efforts involves recording their time budgets. Classical optimality models in behavioural ecology assume that the various activities birds perform have individual costs and benefits, and contribute to fitness to different degrees (e.g. foraging: Barnard & Thompson 1985; mating behaviour: Bateson 1983; territorial defence: Davies & Houston 1984). Maintenance activities, such as feeding, preening and resting can influence a bird's chances of survival to the next breeding season, while incubation and alertness are more immediately important for breeding success and parental survival. Many of the birds' activities cannot be performed simultaneously, hence the birds have to 'budget' their activities. Studies of time allocation to these can therefore give valuable insights into the trade-offs between different behaviours involved in parental effort.

Breeding season time budgets of tundra plovers are, as yet, available only for the Eurasian Golden Plover, recorded at Hardangervidda in the summers of 1980 and 1981 (Byrkjedal 1985a), and the results are summarized in Fig. 9.1. Recently, researchers have used radio-telemetry to track Eurasian Golden Plovers in their breeding grounds in Sutherland (Whitfield 1997b; O'Connell *et al.* 1996) and in the north Pennines (Whittingham 1996a,b). As we shall see later (Chapter 11), this time budget approach has also improved our understanding of social behaviour in the non-breeding season.

Pre-laying period

In the pre-laying period the female clearly gives feeding a high priority, as already commented upon in Chapters 7 and 8, while the male spends relatively more time

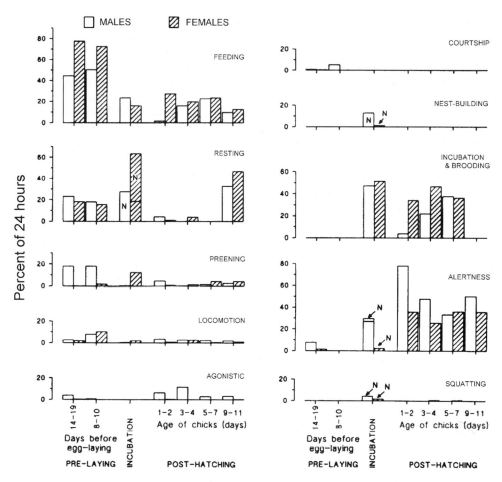

FIG. 9.1. *Estimated time-activity budget of Eurasian Golden Plover at Hardangervidda 1980–81, redrawn from Byrkjedal (1985a). N= activities performed on nest; Ns adds up to the percentage of time spent incubating. Nest building during the pre-laying period could not be separated from courtship. Alertness includes alarm situations. 'Squatting'= bird lying prostrate when overflown by Common Raven.*

preening and keeping watch. When other Eurasian Golden Plovers intrude, the male, sometimes joined by his mate, chases them off their ground. This suggests a sentinel function of the male from the beginning of the breeding season, which might account for distances of hundreds of metres between pairs. Such spacing may benefit the male in three ways: extra-pair copulations should be rare, thus increasing his confidence about his own paternity; the risk of predators being attracted to a given area should be smaller; and the female is protected from harassment by unpaired (and paired) males, and so she ought to be able to concentrate on feeding, presumably resulting in high quality eggs (cf. Galbraith 1988a; Parish 1996). Pre-laying females spend much time feeding, but also feed more on highly profitable, though less accessible, sub-surface prey, which probably requires more attentive feeding (Byrkjedal 1980a, 1985a, 1989c; Thompson 1983a, 1984).

The situation in the pre-laying season for Eurasian Golden Plovers breeding near pastures and cultivated fields may be different from that described above, as they feed mostly extra-territorially near others on farmland, even in the pre-laying period (cf. Chapter 7, also Nethersole-Thompson & Nethersole-Thompson 1961; Köpke 1971; Ratcliffe 1976; Parr 1980; Whitfield 1997a; Whittingham 1996a; O'Connell *et al.* 1996). Here, the males may spend considerably more time mate-guarding (cf. Chapter 8) than they do in the northern tundra, alpine, peatland areas (where fields do not seem to be used) and the Scandinavian mountains, where all their pre-laying activities take place with the pairs well spaced on their breeding territories.

Incubation

As the eggs are laid and incubation starts, the males continue to act as sentinels. However, incubation itself is fairly equally divided between mates. Looking at incubation schedules in more detail, we find that the sitting spells are extremely long, lasting around 12 hours. This applies both to the American Golden Plovers (male average of 626, range 541–673 min; female average of 817, range 681–836 min) and Eurasian Golden Plovers (males average 660 minutes ± 68 minutes (SD; n=18), females average 738 minutes ± 69 minutes (SD; n=14) for which continuous automatic recordings of incubation schedules have been done. These recordings, coupled with our observations of the birds, have shown that the males tend to sit during the day and females during the night, with changeovers taking place in the morning and in the evening. This pattern is supported by observations of the incubating sex during nest inspections at various times of the day (Fig. 9.2). Information on incubation schedules of Eurasian Golden Plovers in Great Britain is, however, conflicting. Whereas Whittingham (1996a) in N. England, and Parr (1980) and O'Connell *et al.* (1996) in Scotland found a pattern similar to the above, observations by Nethersole-Thompson & Nethersole-Thompson (1961) indicated more variation, and in NW Sutherland many males exchanged in the evening before incubating through the night. On mountain tops in the Cairngorms, many off-duty birds seen during the day were males (Holt & Whitfield 1996). These remarkable exceptions to the rule deserve closer study.

Automatic recordings of incubation schedules of Pacific Golden Plovers (incubation stints of 270–480 min) and Grey Plover (90–780 min) indicate less regular patterns in these two species (Kondrat'ev 1982), but details on sex differences and variation are lacking. Pacific Golden Plovers seem to have a schedule similar to that found in Eurasian and American Golden Plovers (Fig. 9.2).

Off-duty birds during incubation phase

In all four species, females spend most of their off-duty time outside the territory (Fig. 9.3). Female Eurasian Golden Plovers at Hardangervidda congregated in loose

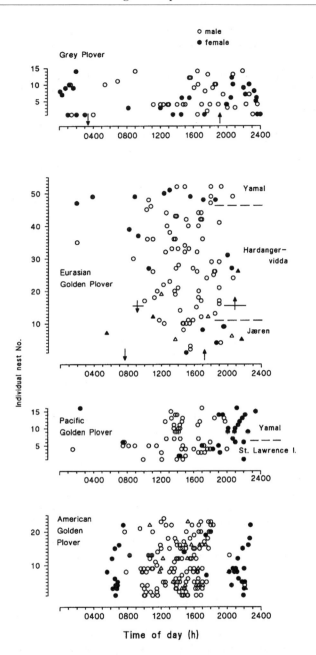

FIG. 9.2. *Sex of the incubating bird during nest visits at various times of the day. Only data for completed clutches are included. Filled symbols: females, open symbols: males. Data collected when eggs were pipping are shown by triangles. Arrows give recorded changeovers (visual observations and/or machine recordings), ↑: female relieved by male, ↓: relieved by female. Where there are several observations the horizontal arrows mean ± 1 SD.*
Sources: Sauer (1962) for St Lawrence Island, others IB.

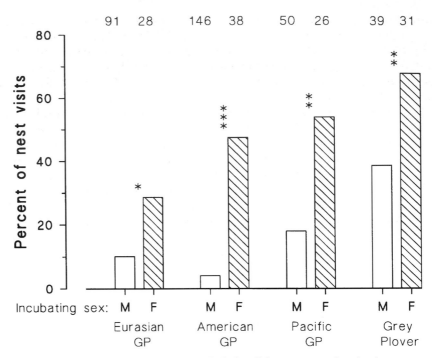

FIG. 9.3.   *Proportion of nest visits at which the off-duty mate was found to be present on territory.*
Sources as for Fig. 9.2. Chi-square tests for differences between males and females:
*p <0.05, ** p<0.01, *** p<0.001.

flocks on 'neutral' ground on the edge of bogs and on *Salix herbacea* heaths (Byrkjedal 1989b), where they spent most of their time feeding, preening and sleeping. In the Cairngorms, off-duty birds during the day tended to feed on or close to their territories, showing a preference for alpine blanket bog (also Holt & Whitfield 1996). As on the Hardangervidda, small flocks feed on neutral ground. American Golden Plover females at Churchill fed along the Hudson Bay coast, in the saltmarsh zone immediately above the high tide mark. Off-duty female Pacific Golden Plovers and Grey Plovers at Yamal were often encountered feeding and resting along floodplains and in small flat stream valleys (see also Sauer's 1962 observations for Pacific Golden Plovers involving 'inner' territories and extra-territorial feeding grounds).

Off-duty males of all four species also frequently feed outside their territories, but spend considerably more time than their mates on territories. The males, particularly those of the golden plovers, tend to be present on the territories at dawn and dusk. This is the time when most ground-living nest predators (e.g. foxes) are active. Compared with flying predators, foxes must be more difficult to detect by the incubating bird, not only due to darkness, but also due to their furtive movements along the ground. The importance of a sentinel, which may give early warning to the incubating bird, is likely to be of particular significance around dawn and dusk. During daytime, however, silence characterizes golden plover territories, and as a rule no warning mate is present. In the Eurasian Golden Plover the combination of extremely inconspicuous behaviour by the incubating birds and lack of off-duty mates on the territory most of the day makes censusing of breeding birds during the incubation period almost impossible (Ratcliffe 1976; Kålås & Byrkjedal 1984; Chapter 6).

In Sutherland, radio-tracking of individual Eurasian Golden Plovers on blanket bogs has revealed that off-duty birds have overlapping 'home ranges', with a mean area (± standard deviation) of 1.06 ± 0.92 km^2, range 0.14–3.93 km^2 (Fig. 9.4). Distances moved from nest sites by off-duty birds vary between 10 m and 2.3 km (this excludes longer-distance movements to farmland outwith these ranges, discussed shortly), with an overall mean of 480 ± 31 m (data for 4 areas; O'Connell *et al.* 1996b). On the Mallerstang study area in N. England where Eurasian Golden Plovers breed at very high density on limestone grassland-moorland mosaics, home range overlap occurs during incubation/brood rearing (Thomas 1986; D.A. Ratcliffe pers. comm.).

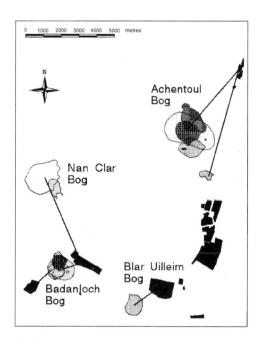

FIG. 9.4.   *Home ranges and movements of Eurasian Golden Plovers in Sutherland, Scotland, 1995. The map shows overlapping and separate individual home ranges (different shadings), and pasture fields (black blocks) used during trips from territories. Within a bog complex, off-duty birds used the same fields throughout the season. Home ranges were calculated as 95% harmonic mean isopleths of adult activity (from beginning of incubation to end of fledging period) based on radio-tracking data.*
Sources: Mark O'Connell and Chris Thomas (pers. comm.) and O'Connell et al. *(1996).*

One important function of the extra-territorial existence in daylight during the incubation phase may be to reduce nest detection by avian nest predators, which are sight oriented. Birds present on territory might induce a nest search by the predator. Against this function, however, is the absence of early warning to the incubating bird. Furthermore, on both the peatlands of Lewis and N. England, off-duty birds tend to feed on territories (D.P. Whitfield pers. comm.; Whittingham 1996a). Interestingly, Grey Plovers, which defend their nests very aggressively (also Drury 1961; Hussell & Page 1976; Flint & Kondrat'ev 1977), have females off the nest chiefly during the day, but they are present on their territories for significantly longer than golden plover females (Fig. 9.3). Indeed, Grey Plovers may actually benefit from the off-duty bird fending off aerial predators and so avoiding the need for the sitting mate to leave the nest (Flint & Kondratjew 1977). However, if the anti-predator function is so important, it is males rather than females which should be off-duty during the day. Nevertheless, there does seem to be a tendency for the more northern breeding birds to spend more time on territory.

Extra-territorial use of farmland and fields

Extra-territorial life may serve at least two other functions, both tied up with food. First, food resources inside the territory may be reserved for the chicks and attentive parents. Second, the parent birds may be exploiting areas good for feeding but unsuitable for nesting and chick-rearing. The nutrient levels in food from farmland compared with acidic moorland is much higher (Thompson 1984; Downie *et al.* 1996). Whichever is most important is unknown, but broods do seem to make limited use of resources within breeding territories. Indeed, all four species often move broods well beyond their territory boundaries (which have now broken down) within a few days (also Haviland 1915; Sutton 1932; Drury 1961; Parmelee *et al.* 1967; Mayfield 1973; Hussell & Page 1976; Flint & Kondratjew 1977; Parr 1980; O'Connell *et al.* 1996; but see Kondrat'ev 1982 for a different statement about Pacific Golden Plover).

Intriguingly, off-duty Eurasian Golden Plovers can travel considerable distances to feed extra-territorially in agricultural fields (Nethersole-Thompson & Nethersole Thompson 1939, 1961, 1986; Ratcliffe 1976 and Parr 1980; Thompson 1984, 1993; Whittingham 1996a). O'Connell *et al.* (1996) recorded mean distances flown to fields of 2.69±0.26 km, range 0.36–10.70 km from nests. Some of these birds passed over fields closer to their nests but used by other golden plovers throughout the spring! Only a small proportion of fields are used, and these tend to be old, large, grazed (and used for lambing) and have some stands of *Juncus* spp. (other shorebirds such as Eurasian Curlew, Northern Lapwing and Common Redshank are much less selective, using these and other fields not used by golden plovers). Flocks of golden plovers on these fields consisted of up to 150 birds, and many were even faithful to particular parts of fields (avoiding areas within 100 m of the edge). Moreover, birds from one bog catchment area tended to use the same fields; there was little or no mixing of catchment populations. Overall, 56% of off-duty radio-telemetry fixes were of golden plovers on fields. While on fields, they allocated their time to feeding (55% time), vigilance (30%), preening (14%) and interactions (1%). As we shall see in Chapter 11, such fidelity to a few large, old pastures, and even to parts of these, is a feature of habitat use by Eurasian Golden Plovers in the non-breeding season as well.

Post-hatch period

In the Sutherland study, after the hatch, use of fields by off-duty birds virtually ceased (with only 3% of 'fixes' of radio-tagged birds in fields). Instead, while one bird guarded the brood, the other spent just over 30% of its time 0.97±0.62 km (range 0.38–4.0 km) away from the brood feeding largely on bog habitats. For the home ranges shown in Fig. 9.4, the off-duty birds moved to feed 0.80±0.45 km from the brood. The broods moved progressively farther from the nest site (0.30±0.10 km from the nest during 1–10 days after hatching, up to 0.45±0.24 km during 21–30 days after the hatch; data for 12 broods), with the furthest distance recorded being just under 1 km. Daily, broods tended to move 0.21±0.17 km (1–10 days post-hatch) to 0.27±0.19 km (21–30 days post-hatch). The only main difference in habitat use by adults (besides the declining use of fields) during incubation and chick-rearing periods was relatively more use of grassland when with broods, though *Erica tetralix–Sphagnum papillosum* blanket bog (with pools) was the preferred habitat throughout the two periods (O'Connell *et al.* 1996) and on this, breeding densities were highest. In the N. Pennines, Mark Whittingham (1996a) found relatively more use of fields during brood-rearing (and indeed during incubation).

Returning to the time budgets of Eurasian Golden Plovers at Hardangervidda (Fig. 9.1), hatching brings about a marked change for the parent birds. Anti-predator behaviour changes abruptly, as do time budgets and division of labour. Now the males do little else but stay alert. During the first few days they hardly feed: only now and then do they hastily take one or two items from the surface (Byrkjedal 1985a). Mostly, they stand on a slightly elevated point from which they have a good view of the brood and the surroundings. From there they constantly communicate with the chicks, using weak plaintive notes emitted at a rate of 15–25 per minute, audible only over a few tens of metres. At the slightest sign of danger the males warn their chicks loudly (see Appendix 9 for description of alarm calls). Tall hummocks, or even peat mounds, are preferred for these watches, and are often used in successive years (these may well be modified by enrichment from the birds' droppings over decades of use).

The first week after hatching, and especially the first two days, seem to require concentrated parental effort by the males. During this time their body mass drops (Fig. 9.5). Although females, too, spend a fair amount of the time being alert, they seem to be far more relaxed than males. The time spent feeding by females is just as high as during the incubation period. Yet the females do almost all the brooding in the first couple of days. Thus, in the first couple of days post-hatch, parental care takes place according to marked sex roles, males being alert almost all of the time while females either brood the chicks or feed. Gradually, however, the males start to feed more, and even share some of the brooding. Within a week the differences in male and female behaviour have largely disappeared.

At the age of 9–11 days the chicks can evidently thermoregulate (cf. feather development, Chapter 4). Now they are presumably less vulnerable to predators and do not need to stay as close to each other or their parents. So, the parents seem inclined to spend more time resting (Fig. 9.1). However, parents still respond

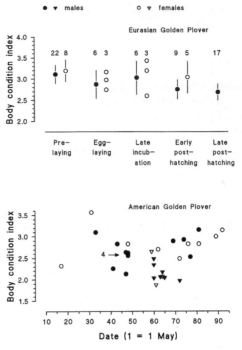

FIG. 9.5.   *Body condition through the breeding season for Eurasian Golden Plovers at Hardangervidda, and for American Golden Plovers at North Alaska and Churchill, expressed as weight/(wing length)³.*
Sources: Upper graph recalculated from Byrkjedal (1985a); lower graph data from skin collections in USA and Canada for Alaska and Canadian Arctic (○) with information about wing length given by P. Connors pers. comm. (see Connors 1983 for method), and obtained by IB for Churchill (▽). The values for skin collection materials are biased upwards compared with the data from live birds at Churchill, as no correction has been made for shrinkage. Mean ± 1 SD, with numbers giving number of birds measured.

promptly to predators at a very long distance (Byrkjedal 1987a; Yalden & Yalden 1990), and the males lose more weight as the chicks develop (Fig. 9.5).

Towards the end of the chick-rearing period females of many monogamous waders tend to depart and leave the chicks entirely to the males (Pitelka *et al.* 1974; Piersma & Wiersma 1996). This is also so in the Eurasian, and probably American golden plovers, especially in late broods (Figs. 9.6, 9.7, also Parr 1980), and in Grey Plover (Parmelee *et al.* 1967). Perhaps this is a result of a shift in the trade-off between female investment in the brood (immediate reproduction) and in its own survival (and future broods). It would be interesting to see research that compares the extent of female desertion of broods across ranges with and without use of pasture fields. Interestingly, on the Isle of Lewis, where a large proportion of the British golden plover population breeds (Chapter 6), and where fields are seldom used by off-duty birds, brood desertion by females is also earlier than in males (D.P. Whitfield pers. comm.).

By leaving early, females may be exploiting willingness of the males to care for the

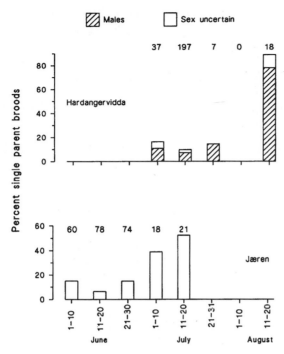

FIG. 9.6.   *Frequency of Eurasian Golden Plover broods attended by a single parent at Jæren and Hardangervidda. Numbers above bars denote total number of broods observed.*

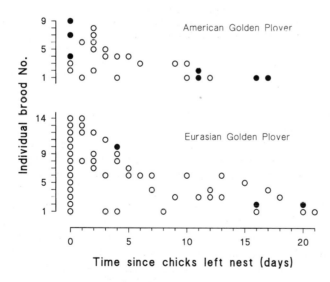

FIG. 9.7.   *Brood attendance within individually recognizable pairs of Eurasian and American golden plovers (Hardangervidda and Churchill, respectively) when resighted after hatching. Both parents attending (○), or a single parent attending (●, males in all cases) are shown.*

brood un-aided as the season progresses beyond the point at which other matings would be feasible. Female Eurasian Golden Plovers do not seem willing or able to continue singlehanded if their mates disappear during incubation (Byrkjedal 1985a), which is hardly surprising considering the equal share of lengthy incubation stints. Apparently though, there are individual differences between the females in their willingness to stay with the brood. Additional research relating body condition of females to their parental effort would be very valuable.

NEST AND CHICK DEFENCE: ANTI-PREDATOR BEHAVIOUR

Nest predation and anti-predator tactics

Tundra plovers lose a considerable number of nests to predators. In Eurasian Golden Plovers breeding at Hardangervidda the average nest predation rate is close to 78% (Byrkjedal 1987a). Lower nest predation rates are usually found elsewhere, but 40–50% is not uncommon (Ratcliffe 1976; Parr 1980; Holt & Whitfield 1996; O'Connell *et al.* 1996). In the Arctic, nest predation may fluctuate strongly in relation to cyclic population fluctuations of small rodents, with predators switching to alternative food, including eggs and chicks, as rodent populations crash (Hagen 1952, 1969; Stenseth *et al*, 1979; Underhill *et al.* 1993). At Yamal, tundra plovers and other ground-nesting birds are subject to such fluctuations. Nearly all their nests survive in lemming 'peak' years, whereas most nests are lost to foxes and skuas in lemming 'crash' years (N.S. Alekseeva and V.K. Ryabitsev pers. comm.). We believe that such high losses have exerted a very strong selection force on nest and chick defence behaviour, as well as the evolution of adaptations to avoid predators (discussed already, Chapters 6 and 7).

To a European reader, the anti-predator behaviour of breeding shorebirds may be best exemplified by the aggressive 'dive-bombing' of Northern Lapwings and the persistent broken-wing antics of Common Ringed Plovers. While the lapwing drives away the predator, the ringed plover lures the predator from the nest, behaving like an easy prey, which diverts the hunting behaviour of the predator (Gochfeld 1984).

In tundra plovers both attacks and distraction displays are given. In addition, they use two types of anti-predator behaviour that are even more widespread among birds: circling/scolding and surreptitious behaviour. The four species differ in how they protect their offspring, and there are changes over the season, geographical differences, and individual differences. Before going into some of the factors accounting for this variation, we first look at the diversity of anti-predator antics. Fairly detailed descriptions are given in a few publications. But without quantitative information, it is often difficult to judge which types of behaviour are the most common and important ones – we suspect a bias towards reporting the more dramatic variants (also Gochfeld 1984). The following description is therefore drawn mainly from our own data.

Responses to ground-living predators: our methods

Our descriptions are based on recording the responses of adult birds to our own approaches to their nests and broods. Our approaches were made in a straight line towards the nests, at normal walking speed. Responses were dictated on a tape recorder, and response distances were subsequently determined by pacing. These approaches were considered to simulate approaches of ground predators. As a variety of responses to different avian predators were observed (as we shall see shortly), there may also be much variation in response to ground predators. We have some observations of birds responding to live and stuffed foxes, and in some cases we have seen incubating birds' responses to trained dogs (Byrkjedal 1987a; 1989d). These observations have led us to conclude that the responses to us are similar to those used towards ground predators (see also arguments by Armstrong 1956; Thompson & Barnard 1983).

Responses to ground-living predators: at the nest

Types of response The complex responses can be divided into four types (Fig. 9.10): (a) leaving the nest early or stealthily, and remaining hidden or inactive at long distance; (b) leaving the nest by an 'explosive' departure, i.e. the bird leaves the nest in a display, giving the impression of impeded flight while disappearing hastily; (c) the bird leaves the nest and continually exposes itself, circles the intruder (more or less fully) and gives loud alarm cries (scolds); and (d) remains exposed during the whole approach, as in (c), but in addition performs one or more distraction displays ('injury feigning'; see Fig. 9.8). These four categories reflect a complex interaction between predator and tundra plover involving detection (is plover

PLATE 49. *When a human appears suddenly near the nest of a Eurasian Golden Plover, the incubating bird squats on the nest. (IB)*

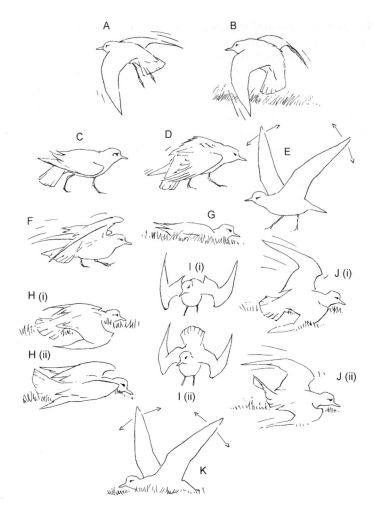

FIG. 9.8.   *Distraction displays given by tundra plovers when an observer approaches their nests (frequencies in Fig. 9.9):*
A = Weakly impeded flight; B = Strongly impeded flight; C = Tail down run (tail canting, head lowered) [Grey Plover showed less canting of the tail than golden plovers]; D = Rodent run (tail canting and half spread, wings drooping and quivering, back feathers more or less ruffled); E = Wings erect run (running with wings stretched upwards and beating stiffly in narrow arc); F = Mobile broken wing display (bird moves along ground with one or both wings flapping irregularly as if broken). [Grey Plover performed with slightly erect tail (ii), golden plovers with erect, straight, or depressed tail (i)]; G = False brooding (bird sits on the ground as if incubating); H = Spread-eagled (bird lies prostrate on the ground, wings held motionless) [Grey Plover often with more or less erect and/or tilted tail (ii)]; I = Stationary wing spread (bird standing or lying on breast, wings held immobile, half spread, joints depressed, tips elevated) [Grey Plover with erect tail (ii), golden plovers with more or less depressed tail (i)]; J = Stationary broken wing (as in F but performed on the same spot) [Erect tail in Grey Plover (ii), varying tail position in golden plovers]; and K = Stationary erect wings display (as in E but performed on the same spot).

cryptic or exposed?), distraction (is plover circling and scolding, or fluttering on the ground?), and pursuit response (does predator pursue plover or search for nest?).

Differences and similarities between species Figure 9.9 shows American and Pacific Golden Plovers to have very similar responses, with circling, scolding and distraction displays being most often used as nest defence behaviour, though stealth is also employed. Eurasian Golden Plovers differ strongly from these two, by relying more on stealth and, above all, by their frequent use of explosive departures, a

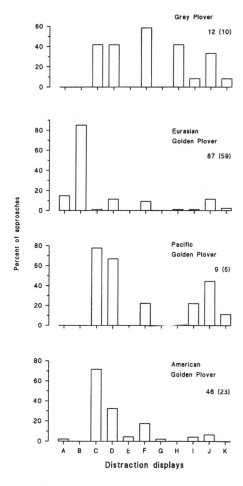

FIG. 9.9.   *Frequency of distraction displays (A–K refers to categories in Fig. 9.8) given when nests were approached in a standardized manner by the observer. Shown below the species names are the number of approaches and number of individual birds (latter in parentheses).*
Data from Yamal for Grey Plover and Pacific Golden Plovers; Churchill for American Golden Plovers; and Jæren, Hardangervidda, and Yamal for Eurasian Golden Plover.

response not recorded for the others. Scolding and distraction displays are rare in Eurasian Golden Plovers during the incubation period (even in the north, *contra* Williamson 1948), and when scolding, they do this far less intensively than any of their congeners. Grey Plovers bear a similarity to the Eurasian Golden Plover in their frequent use of cryptic responses, but resemble Pacific and American golden plovers in their use of circling and scolding behaviour. Compared with these two, distraction displays are less often used by Grey Plovers during the incubation period.

Functions of the responses Tundra plovers approached by a human usually leave their nests at a long distance (Fig. 9.11). When staying cryptic the birds tend to leave when the intruder is still more than 100 m away; leaving at short distances would ruin a cryptic 'ploy'. Whether or not they should leave at long or short distances appears to depend on the distance at which the incubating bird sees the intruder (at least for Eurasian Golden Plovers; Ratcliffe 1976; Byrkjedal 1987a). Presumably detectability is influenced by the predator-to-nest distance at the moment the bird sees the predator. Thus, there might be a threshold distance within which it pays the bird to sit tightly and hope the predator passes by without noticing the nest (see Byrkjedal 1987a for a suggested model). If, on the other hand, the bird has to leave at a short predator-to-nest distance, a distraction response should be performed. This is exactly what happens! Departures at less than 10–15 m usually result in 'injury feigning' behaviour. The 'explosive departures', so typical of Eurasian

PLATE 50.   *Grey Plover male performing 'Tail Down Run' in presence of a human near its nest. (IB)*

PLATE 51.   *American Golden Plover male in intense 'Broken Wing Display' near its nest. (IB)*

Golden Plovers, are almost always performed when the birds are flushed from their nests less than 10 m from the intruder; perhaps this type of behaviour, more than any, has its maximum effect within a certain distance (Byrkjedal 1987a).

By leaving the nest early and remaining concealed, the birds keep visual conspicuousness to a minimum, and also decrease the scent from the nest site. When pointing dogs have been used to find nests of Eurasian Golden Plovers the dogs tended only to react to nests with a sitting bird. When a bird departed from its nest well in advance, the dogs took no notice of the nest!

Responses to predators close to the nest may fail to fulfil their 'purpose', and thus actually incur a risk to the nest. A better solution would be for the bird to leave the nest earlier on, approach the predator, and then perform distractions before the predator gets close. The bird could then display at a sufficiently short distance to distract or deter the predator, and at the same time avoid the risk of letting the predator close in on the nest. Again, this is what we frequently see in Grey Plover and sometimes in American and Pacific golden plovers (Fig. 9.11). The latter two, however, tend to depart from the nest to one side or the other while scolding or injury feigning, without approaching the predator.

These patterns of ground predator responses are, to varying extents, confirmed by other sources. However, the more conspicuous and spectacular categories of behaviour are frequently over-represented in the literature (Table 12). Although responses can vary from one nest visit to the next, no consistent changes through the incubation period have been found. So, the main behavioural categories may be arranged according to increasing conspicuousness from (a) to (d) given earlier. None of the species seem to show any significant change in conspicuous behaviour with date, day of incubation, and number of nest visits.

Responses to ground-living predators: hatching and post-hatching

As soon as the eggs start pipping, the situation changes. Now there are changes in favour of more exposed behaviour – increasingly so as hatching proceeds. Distraction displays become increasingly important, even in the cautious Eurasian Golden Plover (Fig. 9.10). Now the off-duty mate is more often found on territory as a sentinel. Data for the period after broods have left the nests are available for Eurasian and American golden plovers (Fig. 9.12). Response distances are now extremely long, and the exposed behaviour seen during hatching is maintained. Information from the literature confirms the long response distances after hatching, with scolding and circling as the most important response, turning into

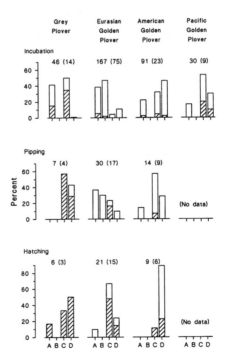

FIG. 9.10.   *Responses to an approaching observer by incubating birds. The four behavioural categories were obtained from recorded behavioural sequences. Hatched bars: off-duty mate present on territory; open bars: off-duty mate absent or not seen. A = leaving nest secretly or at long distance and staying hidden or inactive at a distance; B = 'explosive' departure, i.e. the bird flies off the nest in an 'impeded' flight and disappears; C = bird circles the intruder (flying or running) and scolds; D = the bird performs some form of distraction display ('broken wing trick', 'rodent run', etc.) while the intruder approaches the nest.*
Sources as for Fig. 9.9.

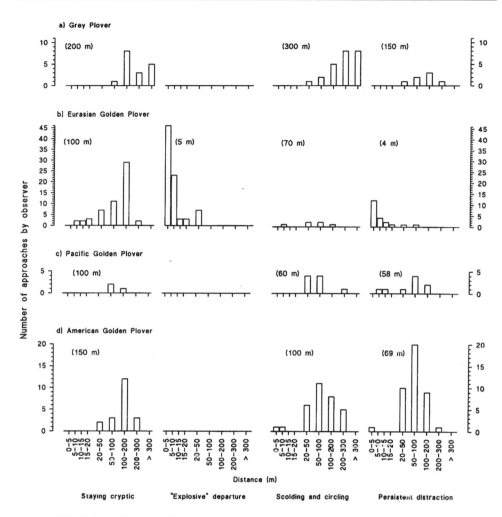

FIG. 9.11. *Response distances (i.e. distance between intruder and bird on nest) in relation to the four main responses made by a sitting bird having sighted the observer walking straight toward its nest. Median distances in parentheses within the graphs. Sources as for Figs 9.9 and 9.10.*

distraction displays as the intruder closes in on the brood (also Sutton 1932; Williamson 1948; Sutton & Parmelee 1956; Steiniger 1959; Sauer 1962; Yalden & Yalden 1990).

Responses to flying predators

Ground-living and flying predators pose very different threats. Whereas most of the former are scent-orientated mammals, the latter are acutely sight-oriented.

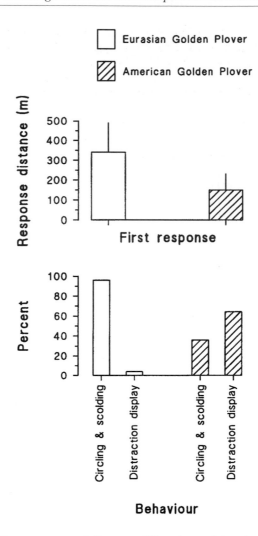

FIG. 9.12.   *Response type and distances of Eurasian and American golden plovers tending chicks (23 broods and 25 approaches; 9 broods and 25 approaches, respectively). Sources as for Figs. 9.9 and 9.10. The behaviour categories are circling and scolding, and distraction displays.*

Naturally, therefore, tundra plovers respond differently to flying and ground-living predators. Table 13 summarizes responses to avian predators. Depending on the type of flying predator, we observed golden plovers to rely mainly on crouching or squatting immobile on the nest until the predator had departed from the area. However, Pacific Golden Plovers, and in particular American Golden Plovers, have been reported to aggressively chase predators in parts of their range (Table 12). Grey Plovers forcefully drive off flying predators, even those as large as Snowy Owls and Rough-legged Buzzards. The plover flies swiftly towards the predator whilst calling, and swoops up towards the latter's belly, its bill nearly coming into contact! In the case of gulls and skuas, one or two swoops are sufficient to see off the predator. Snowy Owls are more sedate, however, and seem less affected by the plovers' efforts. Indeed, raptors and owls are not normally considered important as nest predators, but at Yamal Snowy Owls plundered nests, including those of Grey Plovers, when the lemmings disappeared.

In the case of raptors, American and Eurasian golden plovers seem to respond differently. Whereas American Golden Plovers left their nests and stood quietly 100 m away until the predator had passed, a single observation suggests that Eurasian Golden Plovers are capable of aggressively chasing birds of prey.

SOME FACTORS AFFECTING ANTI-PREDATOR BEHAVIOUR

Anti-predator behaviour is supposed to divert predators from nests or broods (cf. Sauer 1962; Gochfeld 1984 but see Sonerud 1988). How efficient are the various types of behaviour described? What factors govern their use and their effects? A popular tenet of classical ethology, persisting for many decades, was that birds' responses to approaching predators were merely governed by conflicts between drives to attack and escape from the predator, and to incubate the eggs and care for the young (Friedman 1934; Tinbergen 1952; Simmons 1952, 1955; Hinde 1966; and see Lack 1941). We now know that the context is much more complex. There are trade-offs between the risks to the parents and their eggs (and the probability of re-nesting, which is low anyway and declines with incubation period), and there is variation depending upon whether or not the sitting bird is seen (or possibly senses it is seen) by the predator.

Anti-predator drives

IBs earlier study of American Golden Plovers showed that responses to him approaching nests were more than just a mechanistic compromise of drives (Byrkjedal 1991). Being carried out in full view, and reasonably slowly along the ground, their responses were excellently suited for study. Because the nests were approached by IB directly (straight on and without him following the bird) two outcomes were possible: (a) the birds moves along the intruder–nest line away from IB, 'leading' him to the nest site (according to the drive conflict hypothesis); or (b) the bird acts conspicuously, running out from one of the sides of the line of approach, 'leading' him away from the nest site (the adaptive response hypothesis). The latter was observed. Moreover, many of the birds engaged in 're-entrapments' (Gochfeld 1984), i.e. birds repeatedly approached IB, as if trying anew to capture his attention. In such situations American Golden Plovers departed from IB while performing increasingly intensive distraction displays (Byrkjedal 1991), opposite from what would be predicted from the drive conflict hypothesis.

Nest defence intensity in birds can be considered by cost/benefit models (e.g. Montgomerie & Weatherhead 1988 and references therein), in which fitness gains from defending a given brood are weighted against the risks to the parents, both of which are assumed to increase with defence intensity. The optimal level of nest

defence intensity is likely to vary with time of season (Barash 1975; Andersson *et al.*
1980), size of the bird (Sordahl 1981a; Larsen *et al.* 1996) and predator regime
(McCaffery 1982). Nest defence intensity may well influence the parental care
system (Larsen 1991; Larsen *et al.* 1996).

Whereas Barash (1975) predicts an increase in anti-predator intensity with season
owing to decreased chances of successful replacement clutches, Andersson *et al.*
(1980) predict that the intensity of anti-predator behaviour should increase with
offspring age because offspring become increasingly valuable to their parents owing
to their increased chances of survival. Tundra plovers fit neither of these model
propositions. Defence intensity (conspicuousness of behaviour) does not increase
until hatching, and then remains at a high level for a limited period while the chicks
are small (at least in the Eurasian Golden Plover) before becoming somewhat more
relaxed (presumably because the young are better able to avoid the attentions of
predators). Similar patterns have been found in Killdeer (Lenington 1980; Brunton
1990). Apparently their defence intensity is at a height when the chicks are young
and vulnerable. Chick predation is difficult to assess in shorebirds, but mortality
appears to be highest in the days just after hatching (Galbraith 1988b; Holt &
Whitfield 1996).

Differences within tundra plovers

Despite broad similarities in appearance and habitats used for nesting, the tundra
plovers nevertheless adopt quite different anti-predator tactics. Perhaps each
species has evolved adaptations to different predator regimes. For instance, high
densities of ground predators could select for elaborate distraction displays in one
region, while a preponderance of avian predators could lead to cryptic behaviour in
another. Avian predators might even impose constraints on the behaviour used
against ground predators in favour of more cryptic strategies, as conspicuous
behaviour used against ground predators could betray the nest site to avian
predators (Sauer 1962; Byrkjedal 1987a, 1989d).

Having the most southern breeding range, Eurasian Golden Plovers encounter a
higher risk of predation (also Erckmann 1983). Their more 'cryptic' behaviour may
be a result of this, or of a high ratio of bird:mammal predators on their breeding
grounds compared with that for their more arctic congeners. Sufficient quantitative
information is not available to evaluate this, but there are some notable qualitative
differences in predator assemblages. While foxes and mustelids occur universally on
the breeding grounds of tundra plovers, as do gulls and to a large extent skuas,
corvids (crows, ravens) are absent from most of the arctic tundra (because there are
insufficient nest sites). Skuas and gulls hunt on the wing, and the latter in particular
miss many nests, passing by very rapidly. Crows and ravens, on the other hand, are
very clever and persistent predators (e.g. Holt & Whitfield 1996; Ratcliffe 1997).
They may spend long intervals half concealed watching the surroundings
(Byrkjedal 1989d) and are therefore much more likely to capitalize on conspicuous
ground predator responses. At Yamal, where corvids are exceedingly rare (Danilov
et al. 1984), Eurasian Golden Plovers did not use non-cryptic behaviour
(circling/scolding or distraction-displaying) significantly more often than on the
'raven-infested' heaths in southern Norway ($\chi^2_1 = 0.4$–0.9, ns). This may not be

entirely surprising, however, considering the long evolutionary history Eurasian Golden Plovers must have had in forested and montane areas (Chapter 5), where corvids are common. The fact that anti-predator behaviour of Eurasian Golden Plovers at Yamal was the same as that used in Norway, and that all three tundra plovers at Yamal showed markedly different anti-predator behaviour there, indicates, however, that the local predator regime may not have an immediate impact on anti-predator tactics.

Variety of responses: some explanations

It is costly to chase a predator (by attack and pursuit; sometimes referred to as mobbing – an incorrect term, as the birds often act solitarily), not least because the bird may incur the considerabe cost of injury or death (Sordahl 1990). Not surprisingly, attacking tends to be used by the larger waders, especially curlews and Whimbrels (Sordahl 1981a; Larsen *et al.* 1996). Considering their size, tundra plovers should attack predators. Yet, strangely enough, only Grey Plovers do so regularly. Pacific and American golden plovers attack nest predators only in some populations (also McCaffery 1982; Sauer 1962; Kondrat'ev 1982; Byrkjedal 1989d), and Eurasian Golden Plover do so only very rarely. Why are golden plovers, and especially the relatively large Eurasian Golden Plover, so reluctant to attack predators? Vigorous attacking of a Peregrine Falcon by the latter (Tables 12 and 13) demonstrates that they are at least capable of this action! McCaffery (1982) found that American Golden Plovers in Alaska attacked only Artic and Long-tailed skuas, and not the larger Pomarine Skua. He thought that attacking might have little effect on the Pomarine Skuas and expose the plover to a high mortality risk (one attacking bird was actually grabbed by the wing by a Long-tailed Skua). Derek Ratcliffe (pers. comm.) has seen an Arctic Skua, attacked by a Whimbrel, turn on its pursuer and knock feathers out!

Attacking can also reveal nest sites to Pomarine Skuas (see Sauer's 1962 example of a skua attracted to a Pacific Golden Plover nest site by the plovers' alarm calls). What prevented American Golden Plovers from attacking predators at Churchill, where there were no Pomarine Skuas (Byrkjedal 1989d)? Hen Harriers, which were common and elicited cryptic responses, as well as some Common Ravens, might have played a role similar to that of the Pomarine Skua in Alaska (i.e. increasing the net cost of attacking), if not the explanation lies in the presence of other aggressive species. Tundra plovers often share their breeding grounds with curlews, godwits, Northern Lapwings and other highly vigilant waders. Gulls and even skuas aggressively drive off predators. Breeding near aggressive species may provide early warning of predators as well as protection (Dyrcz *et al.* 1981; Göransson *et al.* 1975; Larsen & Moldsvor 1992). Hence the less aggressive nesting species may obtain the benefits of attacking without having to incur the costs themselves. At Churchill most golden plover territories overlapped with territories of Whimbrel. To what extent this could explain the virtual lack of attacking in golden plovers requires further study.

At Mallerstang, where Eurasian Golden Plovers nest at high density with Northern Lapwings (at even higher densities), the goldies show a strong tendency to leave the nest early and stealthily on approach of humans, evidently using the lapwings to signal danger (D.A. Ratcliffe pers. comm.). This long-distance response is much more pronounced than in other populations without lapwings. Even in winter, Eurasian Golden Plovers use lapwings to give early warning of danger, and tend to take off after lapwings have done so (Thompson & Barnard 1983; Chapter 11).

SUMMARY

1. Tundra plovers are monogamous, and both sexes care for eggs and young.
2. Males and females share incubation almost equally. In golden plovers males usually sit during the day and females during the night, relieving one another at about 12 h intervals. The Grey Plover shows a less regular pattern.
3. During incubation, the birds feed largely outside territories within overlapping ranges, or even away from these. Some off-duty Eurasian Golden Plovers fly up to 10 km from their nests to feed in fields.
4. Eurasian Golden Plover males attend to most of the vigilance and territorial defence, whilst females brood more than males. Males are extremely vigilant during the first few days post-hatch, and feed sparingly thus resulting in a marked drop in body condition.
5. Female Eurasian Golden Plovers and Grey Plovers tend to leave the unfledged broods in the care of their mates, and depart from the breeding grounds, especially when nesting late in the season.
6. Anti-predator behaviour is detailed. Eurasian Golden Plovers either leave their nests early and surreptitiously, or sit tight and perform an 'explosive' departure at a short distance, in response to an approaching human. Grey Plovers also leave early and secretly, but then often approach the intruder giving alarm calls. American and Pacific golden plovers tend to perform 'injury feigning' as well as scolding and circling displays. Grey Plovers and Pacific Golden Plovers can act aggressively toward foxes.
7. In response to avian nest predators, golden plovers squat on the nest, while Grey Plovers attack them. Aggression toward avian nest predators by American and Pacific golden plovers has been observed in only a few populations.
8. Nest defence behaviour remains at a stable level throughout incubation and does not increase in intensity before the eggs start to pip and hatch.
9. Given their large size, golden plovers, especially Eurasians, are unusual for shorebirds in being non-aggressive and resorting instead to 'cryptic' anti-predator tactics.

CHAPTER 10
Migration and Non-breeding Distributions

Eurasian Golden Plovers

These plovers make some of the longest migrations in the world; they often make extensive nonstop flights over water. Annual travels extend from tundra breeding grounds to winter ranges on grasslands, coastal wetlands, and other habitats in temperate (Southern Hemisphere) and tropical regions.

Oscar Johnson & Peter Connors (1996)

OVER most of their range, tundra plovers are long-distance migrants, members of the 'globe-spanners' which, as Derek Ratcliffe reminds us, is a term coined by Abel Chapman in 1924. Pacific and American golden plovers are famous for their ocean crossings, representing tremendously long non-stop flights. No less impressive are the crossings of vast tracts of forest and barren mountains in Asia and the Americas, and the latest research reveals that they may be capable of non-stop flights of at least 7000 km (Johnson & Connors 1996). In this chapter we pull together published accounts and unpublished information to summarize the picture of migration routes and non-breeding season distributions.

SOURCES OF INFORMATION

The literature represents a mixture of information, from analyses of ringing recoveries, quantitative counts of migration stopover sites in larger or smaller parts of the wintering range, to local avifaunas. While the former report with a very high degree of precision, local avifaunas often give only very brief and general statements. However, the latter are invaluable in helping us trace migration corridors or identify important non-breeding/wintering, or stopover, sites.

There are problems with the way the phenology of migration is reported. Some sources give information only about earliest arrival at a site area, while others report the period of the main passage and, not infrequently, distinctions between these categories are not made explicit. Thus, information is not always comparable from one locality to another. In an attempt to obtain more uniform information, we have resorted to examining museum collections. We wrote to a large number of museums and asked for information about the locality, date, age and sex of all their *Pluvialis* specimens. Museum collections may be biased in favour of the more unusual material in terms of location and season of sampling. However, from our personal experience of museums, we felt that the bulk of the specimens would originate from places where the species in question is more common, and that most birds would find their way to museums at times when they are most abundant. Most of the museums responded overwhelmingly to our enquiries and sent us all the information they had. In total, we received information for over 4400 skins.

Isophenes

When we plotted the specimen localities on maps, we found that they often grouped into clearly defined clusters (Appendix 10). For each cluster in either spring (February–May inclusive) or autumn (August–November inclusive) we calculated the median date of collection. We considered this to be indicative of the time for main passage, and median dates for clusters of five or more specimens formed the basis for isophenes shown on our migration charts. A huge foundation of information in the literature (Appendix 11) modified the isophenes slightly (but more typically confirmed these). By and large we based most of the timings of passage on the dated museum specimens. Spring migration in tundra plovers, as in other shorebirds, is more rapid and less protracted than the autumn migration. Isophenes can therefore give a better description of the migration phenology for spring than autumn.

Adults compared with juveniles

Having studied the literature and the museum specimen lists, we found that adult and juvenile birds sometimes showed different migration schedules and routes, and even different non-breeding season ranges. However, too few of the museum specimens contained information about the birds' age. As a world-wide museum tour was out of question, and even borrowing skins from museums on such a large scale was not feasible, we asked the museums to photocopy particular specimens taken during autumn–winter, showing the dorsal, ventro-lateral, and ventral aspects. Soon photocopied specimens piled up, and virtually all of them were sufficiently clear to enable us to age the birds confidently! Furthermore, because we had the museum specimen information we could also look for differences between males and females, for museum specimens were usually sexed (from gonads). This was ideal for our purposes, because sexing tundra plovers in the field is not readily done outwith the breeding season, and published material based on field observations given scant information on the differential migration of sexes).

Age and sex differences in migration

> Males and females and adults and juveniles often have different migration routes. Although it is possible that this is related to differences in competitive ability, the evidence suggests that other factors, such as the need for the sex that competes for mates to return early to the breeding grounds may be more important.
>
> Bill Sutherland (1996)

Three hypotheses are currently considered in discussing differences in migration between the sexes and older and younger age groups (Myers 1981; Gauthreaux 1982; Ketterson & Nolan 1983; Pienkowski *et al.* 1985; Reynolds *et al.* 1986; Meltofte 1996). All of these assume migration to be costly and that it should therefore be made to the nearest suitable wintering habitat. One hypothesis, the 'Body Size Hypothesis', claims that birds with the larger body size endure fasting, or at least harsher weather, better than smaller individuals, and are thus less in need of a long migration. The second hypothesis, known as the 'Social Dominance Hypothesis', relates migration to social dominance. Here, it is hypothesized that subordinate individuals are relegated to poorer habitats due to intraspecific competition, and should be the first to move if conditions get more difficult, and so over-winter farther south (e.g. Gauthreaux 1982; Evans & Townshend 1988). Finally, the 'Arrival Time Hypothesis' proposes that the sex which establishes the breeding territory should migrate the shortest distance in order to achieve early access to its territory in spring (Gauthreaux 1982; Reynolds *et al.* 1986).

In tundra plovers, males and females do not differ significantly in size (Chapters 2 and 3), so differences in migration are not expected according to the body size hypothesis. However, adults should be more efficient foragers than juveniles (Townshend *et al.* 1984; Marchetti & Price 1989; Whitfield 1990; Goss-Custard 1996), and thus be better able than juveniles at enduring fasting on more northern wintering grounds. So far as social dominance is concerned, differences between the sexes are not known, but adults should be dominant over juveniles. Consequently, juveniles should be expected to over-winter south of adults. In all four species, breeding territories are established by the males, hence the arrival time hypothesis predicts males will winter farther north than females.

Below, we provide species-by-species accounts of migration and non-breeding season distributions of the tundra plovers. We are the first to admit that the picture drawn may be preliminary and coarse-grained. Clearly, there is a need for more studies of all four species, especially involving ringing and tracking in various parts of their ranges, and also morphometrical and biochemical methods to identify different populations.

GREY PLOVER

Autumn

Many Grey Plovers spend the boreal summer on their wintering grounds and some even along their migration routes (e.g. Bent 1929; Smit & Wolff 1981; Cramp & Simmons 1983; Dijk *et al.* 1990; Meltofte 1996). Observations of Grey Plovers south of their arctic breeding grounds in early July probably represent summering, non-breeding individuals. The autumn migration starts in late July and early August, and by early September most Grey Plovers have left the Arctic (Fig. 10.1). The autumn migration is a protracted affair: Grey Plovers are on the move over most of the temperate zone flyways from late July until November. Yet, the main passage can be represented by isophenes for parts of the migratory routes (Fig. 10.1).

A particularly early main passage seems evident on the Atlantic coast of North America and in the Baltic. Although Grey Plovers start to appear on their subtropical and tropical wintering grounds by August (Grimes 1974; Glutz von Blotzheim *et al.* 1975; Cramp & Simmons 1983; Urban *et al.* 1986), the bulk of the birds seem to reach their destinations during November onwards. Numbers continue to build up on some wintering grounds towards mid-winter, especially when birds face severe weather on their more northern wintering sites. Grey Plovers tend to move from the Wadden Sea area to the milder British Isles during colder spells in winter, causing peak numbers there in January–February (Prater 1981a; Evans *et al.* 1984; Townshend 1986; Moser 1988; Cranswick *et al.* 1996; Exo & Wahls 1996).

Generally, adult Grey Plovers migrate several weeks before the bulk of the juveniles (e.g. Bent 1929; Jehl & Smith 1970; Glutz von Blotzheim *et al.* 1975; Meltofte 1987, 1993; Landing 1991; Tubbs 1991). In a cumulative distribution (Aug.–Nov.) of museum specimens (78 males, 62 females), collected between 30° and 60°N, and which had been sexed from examination of gonads, there were 2–10% more adult females than adult males at any given time from August through October. This is as expected from the tendency for females to leave their broods before males (Chapter 9).

On migration, Grey Plovers are usually confined to marine or fresh water mud and sandflats and sandy beaches for staging. Less often, they are found on pastures or ploughed fields (e.g. Bent 1929; Michael 1935; Storer 1951; Meise 1952; Dolgushin 1962; Gerstenberg 1979; Cramp & Simmons 1983; Hicklin 1987; Paulson 1995). They are far less gregarious than migrating golden plovers; often single or a few Grey Plovers are seen accompanying other shorebird flocks. Rarely more than a few tens of birds are found together, and while feeding, these birds tend to space out (Chapter 11).

Migrating Grey Plovers are found on suitable sites almost world-wide. Yet, the main migration routes adhere to certain major flyways. One of these, presumably carrying birds almost exclusively from western Alaskan breeding grounds, extends down the Pacific seaboard to wintering grounds from southern British Columbia to Chile (Fig. 10.1a). A much larger flight, from northern Alaska and western Canadian Arctic, proceeds on a broad inland front mainly northeast of the Great Plains. It passes quickly across the Canadian forest region and heads for the Great Lakes. Another passage route, presumably mainly from the Canadian Archipelago, goes down the coasts of Hudson Bay, heading for James Bay. From the Great Lakes and James Bay, birds partly funnel down the Mississippi Valley to wintering grounds in the Gulf of Mexico and farther south, and partly slant southeast and east, hitting the Atlantic coast from New England to Newfoundland. From there they proceed south along the coast to wintering grounds in the Atlantic northern end of South America, and farther south there, as well as into the West Indies. Some birds could

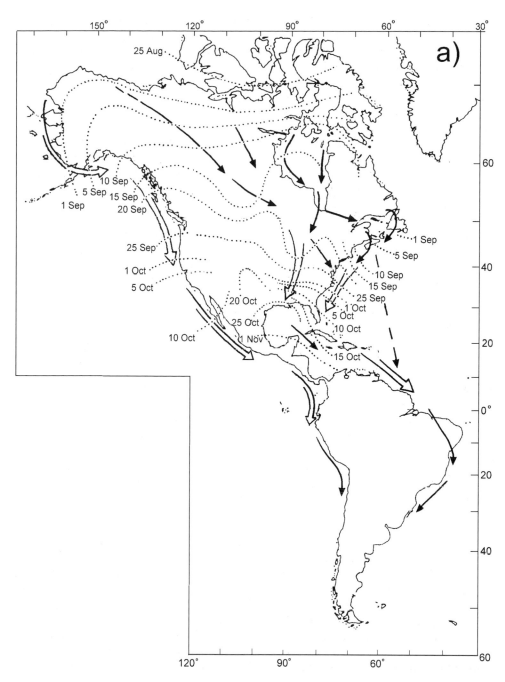

FIG. 10.1a. *Autumn migration of Grey Plovers in the Americas (a) and elsewhere (b). Dotted lines (isophenes) are based on median dates for clusters of museum specimens (the data are given in Appendix 10), supplemented by the literature (Appendix 11). Arrows indicate migration routes (broad arrows show the most important routes).*

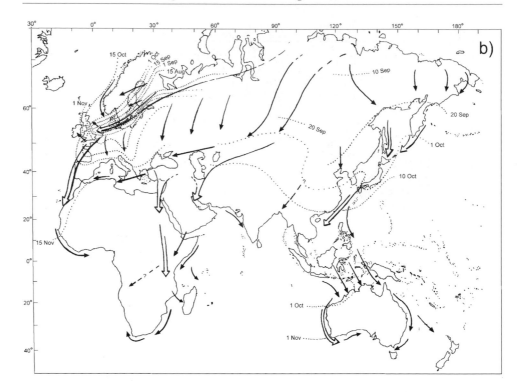

FIG. 10.1b.   *Autumn migration of Grey Plovers outside America (b). Dotted lines (isophenes) are based on median dates for clusters of museum specimens (the data are given in Appendix 10), supplemented by the literature (Appendix 11). Arrows indicate migration routes (broad arrows show the most important routes).*

even make a West Atlantic crossing from northeast America to their South American wintering grounds (Glutz von Blotzheim *et al.* 1975; Paulson 1995). Grey Plovers are rare in the South American interior (Fjeldså & Krabbe 1990; Hayes *et al.* 1990; Stotz *et al.* 1992), but an inland autumn migration cuts the eastern corner of Brazil (Antas 1983).

In eastern North America, adults and juveniles differ to some degree in their choice of routes on their flights from inland to the coast, the bulk of the juveniles appearing to hit the Atlantic coast farther south than the adults (Fig. 10.2). The proportion of adults seems to be particularly large in the Gulf of St Lawrence area (cf. also Hicklin 1987, reporting peak numbers of juveniles representing only 21% of adult peaks in the Bay of Fundy). Presumably, an eastward passage of adults takes place to this area also. Passage over Labrador is probably very slight, with birds arriving in the Gulf of St Lawrence area from the west (Godfrey 1986). James Bay and the eastern part of the Great Lakes region (east of 85°W) seem to be particularly important staging areas for juvenile Grey Plovers subsequently heading for the Atlantic as well as for the Mississippi flyways (Fig. 10.2).

In the western Palearctic, Grey Plovers follow two major routes: the Baltic–East Atlantic, and the Mediterranean flyways (Fig. 10.1b). A strong early autumn

a)

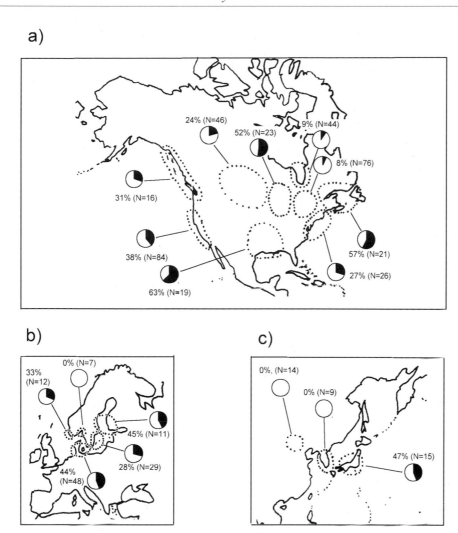

b) c)

FIG. 10.2. *Distribution of Grey Plover adults (filled sectors) and juveniles (open sectors) in autumn (August–November), from regions (encircled) in a) North America, b) northern Europe, and c) around the Sea of Japan, according to museum specimens. Percentage adults are given, along with the total number of specimens examined.*

migration, to a large extent consisting of adult birds (also Salomonsen 1967a; Glutz von Blotzheim *et al.* 1975; Branson & Minton 1976; Cramp & Simmons 1983; Tubbs 1991; Kube & Struwe 1994; Exo & Wahls 1996; Meltofte 1996; Poot *et al.* 1996), follows a narrow line from the Gulf of Finland along the southern part of the Baltic, to important moult areas in the German Waddensee and southeast England, notably the Wash (Glutz von Blotzheim *et al.* 1975; Branson & Minton 1976; Prater 1981a; Evans *et al.* 1984). Having finished their moult, adults disperse to their West European wintering grounds or proceed as far as West Africa, as do some even without finishing their moult (Branson & Minton 1976; Evans *et al.* 1984; Meltofte

1996). Later in the season, juveniles follow on a broader front, along the Scandinavian Peninsula as well as across continental Europe (Glutz von Blotzheim 1963; Glutz von Blotzheim *et al.* 1975; Byrkjedal 1980c).

As confirmed by ringing recoveries (Fig. 10.3), Grey Plovers from the West Palearctic and West Siberian breeding grounds may follow the Baltic–East Atlantic seaboard route, and end up on West European and West African wintering grounds, even as far south as the Gulf of Guinea (also Exo & Wahls 1996).

The Mediterranean flyway delivers birds to the wintering grounds around the Mediterranean coasts as well as to Western Africa. Measurements of Grey Plovers wintering in Guinea Bissau seem to indicate that even birds from the far eastern breeding grounds may be involved, contrary to analyses of measurements from birds wintering in Mauritania, which indicate the presence only of North European and West Siberian birds (Wymenga *et al.* 1990). The Mediterranean flight arrives via the Black Sea, the northwestern Kazakhstan area, where the species is common in autumn (Dolgushin 1962). This is an area of vital importance to migrating Grey Plover, providing good staging sites. Seen rather scarcely in the interior of Russia during migration, Grey Plovers seem to reach the Black Sea–Kazakhstan area in rather long non-stop flights, contrary to what is indicated by the isophenes from museum material (Fig. 10.1b). More material is needed to verify this. From this area, birds go westwards over the Mediterranean flyway, but also down the East African flyway, mainly along the interior over the Nile–Rift Valleys, and to some extent along the Arabian and Somalian peninsulas (Dement'ev & Gladkov 1951; Dolgushin 1962; Smart *et al.* 1983; Wymenga *et al.* 1990; Hirschfeld 1994). Ringing recoveries link the Black Sea and southern African wintering grounds (Fig. 10.3). Whether or not Grey Plovers cross Africa to reach their wintering grounds along the coast of Lower Guinea is not known. There seems to be no evidence for a trans-Saharan route in autumn (Wymenga *et al.* 1990).

While easternmost populations migrate along Kamchatka and the Kuriles, North-central and East Siberian Grey Plovers appear to reach the Sea of Ochotsk along the large river valleys of Lena and Kolyma (cf. Labutin *et al.* 1988). A flight also crosses the Manchurian Plain to reach the coasts of Korea and North China, and crossings of the Central Asian mountains also occur (Vaurie 1972).

Japan may hold particularly important staging areas for the northeastern Palearctic Grey Plovers, perhaps especially so for adults. Migration proceeds to the South China Sea and Australasia, and relatively large number of birds migrate along the west coast of Australia (Lane 1987; Parish *et al.* 1987).

Winter

Virtually absent from the Pacific islands (Mayr 1945; Munro 1960; Holyoak 1980; Holyoak & Thibault 1984; Lane 1987; Marchant & Higgins 1993), Grey Plovers otherwise winter world-wide along the coasts between 40°N and 40°S (Fig. 10.4). However, in western Europe the wintering grounds extend to about 60°N (Fig. 10.4b), because of the milder oceanic climate. The centre of the winter distribution is generally found on tropical and subtropical mudflats and beaches, although considerable numbers spend the winter in temperate zone Europe (Appendix 12).

'Christmas Bird Counts' have shown that in North America the most important

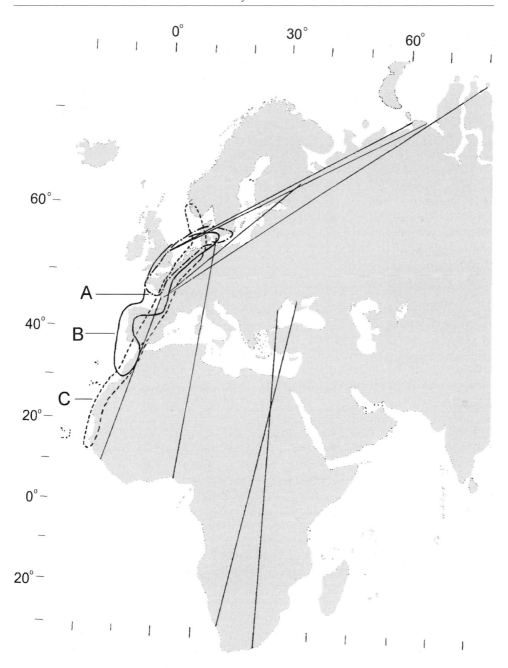

FIG. 10.3. *Distribution of ringing recoveries (encircled) for Grey Plovers ringed in (A) South Sweden, Denmark, Heligoland, and the Netherlands, (B) British Isles, and (C) Norway. Straight lines connect ringing and recovery sites for single recoveries of special interest. Data from Glutz von Blotzheim et al. (1975) and Korzukov (1991); n=127 recoveries.*

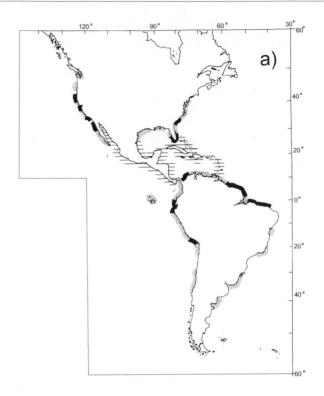

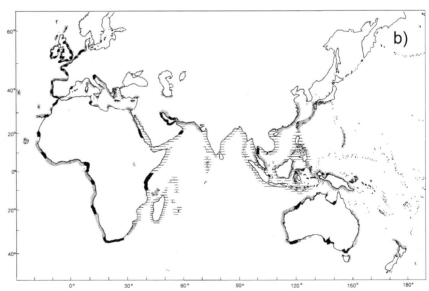

FIG. 10.4.   *Winter distribution of Grey Plovers in the Americas (a) and outside the Americas (b). Areas of highest abundance are shown in black, less abundance are shaded, and regular wintering areas without information about abundance are hatched. Sources in Appendix 11.*

wintering grounds are in central California and South Carolina (Root 1988), but many birds may also over-winter in southern California and northern Mexico (Schick *et al.* 1984).

Shorebird air surveys covering most of the South American coasts (Morrison & Ross 1989), show that about 87% of the Grey Plovers wintering there are found along the northern Atlantic and the Caribbean shorelines, with the Brazilian coast between Belem and Sao Luis accounting for 54% alone. Only around 2% of the birds were found along the southeastern coast of South America, and 11% along the Pacific side (Appendix 12).

In Europe, although many Grey Plovers spend the winter along the Iberian Peninsula, the most important wintering grounds consist of southern North Sea coasts (including the Wadden Sea), British estuaries, and the Atlantic coast of France (Poot *et al.* 1996; Exo & Wahls 1996). The wintering population within that area may amount to no less than 80 000–100 000 birds (Appendix 12), and on the coast of the British Isles, with over 50% of these birds, numbers have been increasing steadily over the last decades (Chapter 6). The rise has been phenomenal with British winter count indices rising by 17% per annum in the mid-1990s (Cranswick *et al.* 1996; Chapter 6). Numbers in the Wadden Sea have also shown a marked increase (e.g. Poot *et al.* 1996), and the East Atlantic flyway population as a whole has increased in recent decades. This population may now consist of 166 000 birds (Meltofte *et al.* 1994).

In the Mediterranean basin wintering grounds, Grey Plover seem more scattered (Smit 1986). Numbers are generally fairly low, except along the Tunisian coast where there are more than 20 000 birds (Appendix 12), most of which are found along the Gulf of Gabés (Dijk *et al.* 1984).

Along the Atlantic coasts of Africa particularly important areas are in Morocco and, above all, in Mauritania, the latter with perhaps 24 000 birds (Appendix 12). Fairly large numbers have also been reported from Sierra Leone, Namibia, and South Africa. Due to a lack of field surveys and counts along much of the Gulf of Guinea and southwards, Tye (1987) used maritime charts to judge the suitability of the various stretches of coast for wintering shorebirds. He inferred from these that the stretch from Niger River Delta to Cape Lopez in Gabon may hold important numbers of Grey Plovers. This has been confirmed by recent surveys of the area. Van Dijk *et al.* (1993) estimated a total of 6700–7500 Grey Plovers on the Gabonese coast (in key sites). Piersma & Ntiamoa-Baidu (1995) reported peak numbers of 2370 at two Ghanian lagoons monitored between 1986 and 1994.

From the east African coast information about the abundance of wintering Grey Plovers is more fragmentary. However, the coasts of Tanzania and Kenya appear to hold particularly high numbers, the former perhaps having 17 000–21 000 birds.

Important wintering grounds for Grey Plover may exist around the Arabian Peninsula; at least there are high numbers in Oman and along the Persian Gulf (Appendix 12). Again, survey work is sorely needed to identify important wintering areas along the coasts of India and Southeast Asia (Fig. 10.4b). In Australia, the highest numbers are found in the west and south (Lane 1987; Marchant & Higgins 1993).

According to Cramp & Simmons (1983) about 90% of the Grey Plovers wintering in the temperate zone of Europe are males, and in the Afrotropical zone 90% are females. A similar trend was said to be present in Asia and the Americas. We pooled latitudinal data for age and sex in winter, according to museum specimens from all continents. These data confirmed that the proportion of males:females decreases to the south (60°–40°: 65% males; 40°–20°: 58% males; 20°–0°: 43% males; 0°–20°: 24% males), although less dramatically than suggested by Cramp & Simmons (1983). The difference in wintering grounds of male and female Grey Plover therefore possibly accords with the arrival time hypothesis outlined in the introduction to this chapter. Surprisingly, juveniles seem to be more numerous on the northernmost wintering grounds, but more material is needed to conclude on this aspect.

Spring

> Most authors, writing from the north temperate zone, have stressed only the advantage of the southward autumn journey, but for migration to develop there must presumably also be an advantage in the return spring journey, giving a net benefit to the two-way movement.
>
> Ian Newton in his Presidential address to the British Ecological Society, published in 1995.

Although Grey Plovers start moving northwards from their southernmost wintering grounds in early March, most seem not to be on the move from tropical and subtropical regions before late April and early May. As they depend on marine and freshwater littoral invertebrates for food Grey Plovers, unlike the golden plovers, may be constrained by ice, harsh weather conditions, and competition with other littoral-feeding shorebirds on their northern staging sites. On their northern staging sites, Grey Plovers have been reported in cultivated fields more often in spring than in autumn (Mumford & Keller 1984).

To a large extent spring migration is a reversal of autumn flights, but there is some evidence that birds may use routes different from those in autumn (e.g. Exo & Wahls 1996). In the Americas, the Grey Plover migration is on a particularly early schedule along the Pacific coast (Fig. 10.5a). In early May the bulk of the Grey Plovers along the Pacific flyway seems to be 20–25% north of those on the Mississippi and Atlantic flyways. Presumably there is negligible, if any, exchange of birds between the Pacific and more eastern flyways in North America; to what extent birds from the west coast of South America cross Central America to the southern states of USA is unknown. In South America, Fjeldså & Krabbe (1990) suspect a trans-continental crossing over the Andes from the southeast in spring.

Grey Plovers migrate abundantly up the Mississippi Valley in late April–early May (Bent 1929; Maestri 1931; Oberholser 1938), to the Great Lakes region, fanning out across the southern Canadian prairie region in late May, and proceeding rapidly to their arctic breeding grounds. Birds wintering on the north coast of Atlantic South America proceed up along the West Indies to the Atlantic coast of USA. The migration continues upwards along the coast, but turns inland towards the Great Lakes and James Bay. Generally, Grey Plovers are less abundant in southeastern Canada in spring than in autumn (Peters & Burleigh 1951; Godfrey 1986), and although common in Massachusetts and in the Bay of Fundy (Bent

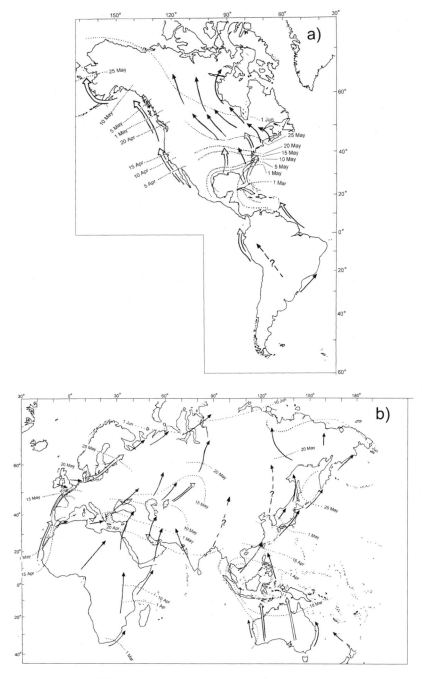

FIG. 10.5. *Spring migration of Grey Plovers in the Americas (a) and elsewhere (b). Dotted lines (isophenes) are based on median dates for clusters of museum specimens (the data are given in Appendix 10), supplemented by the literature (Appendix 11). Arrows indicate migration routes (broad arrows show the most important routes).*

1929; Hicklin 1987), the species mainly appears to leave the coast on the stretch from Virginia to New Jersey, though some may have already headed northwest at the coast of South Carolina (Bent 1929). In spring, the Great Lakes and the northern prairie regions are apparently more important for Grey Plover than are the coasts of Hudson Bay, which remain ice covered for a long time, and food resources there may be at a seasonal low, as in the Canadian Maritime Provinces (Morrison 1984).

Grey Plovers along the East Atlantic flyway begin their main departure from northwestern Africa in late April, continue up the West European coast, and along with conspecifics wintering on the coasts of western Europe head for the Wadden Sea in May (Fig. 10.5b), where the German Wadden Sea in particular constitutes an important staging area (Pienkowski *et al.* 1985; Meltofte *et al.* 1994; Poot *et al.* 1996). From there, the plovers continue northeastwards along the Baltic Sea and up to their Russian breeding grounds. Along the East Atlantic flyway Grey Plovers follow a more narrow corridor in spring than in autumn. In spring they are far less common than in autumn over inland western Europe (Glutz von Blotzheim 1963; Glutz von Blotzheim *et al.* 1975), almost absent from the Scandinavian Peninsula, except southernmost Sweden (Haftorn 1971), and scarce in inland Russia (Dement'ev & Gladkov 1951).

Birds on the Mediterranean flyway and partly those on the East African flyway presumably head for staging areas on the Black Sea. Radar observations indicate a northeast trans-Saharan crossing from the Gulf of Guinea in spring (Grimes 1974). Important staging areas in Uzbekistan and central and western Kazakhstan (Dement'ev & Gladkov 1951; Dolgushin 1962; Glutz von Blotzheim *et al.* 1975) probably receive birds from the East African flyway as well as from wintering grounds in the Middle East and India. To what extent this area brings together these birds and these from the Mediterranean flyway is not known.

Northbound Grey Plovers may cross the Central Asian mountain region (Glutz von Blotzheim *et al.* 1975), and these are presumably from the Bay of Bengal. However, an equally likely route for these birds might be northwestward up the Ganges Valley and then to the Uzbek and Kazakhstani staging areas. Clearly, far more information is needed.

Some Grey Plovers leave Australia by moving up the coasts, but many seem to fly directly north across the continent and then proceed to southeast Asian staging sites without stopping on the North Australian coast (Lane 1987). Following the coast from Southeast Asia, some Grey Plovers apparently turn inland over Korea and Manchuria, while others proceed up the coasts of Japan as well as the mainland. From the Sea of Ochotsk the migration clearly turns inland along the river valleys to the central and east Siberian Arctic (e.g. Labutin *et al.* 1988). No doubt migration along the Kuriles and Kamchatka (Bergmann 1935) proceeds to breeding grounds on the Chukchi Peninsula.

Male Grey Plovers tend to arrive a few days earlier on the breeding grounds than females (Chapter 7). Information from a good number of sexed museum specimens from spring were available only for North America (278 males, 220 females). At any given time we found no clear differences in the migration schedules of males and females (from examination of cumulative time distributions between 30° and 60°N).

EURASIAN GOLDEN PLOVER

Autumn

The migration patterns deduced from museum specimens and the literature are shown in Fig. 10.6. The movements of birds of different geographical origins are reasonably well documented by ringing recoveries (Fig. 10.7). The species is partially migratory in Britain and Ireland and wholly migratory elsewhere (Cramp & Simmons 1983). British and Irish wintering populations are to a certain extent overflown by birds from more northern (Icelandic) breeding grounds; thus there is a tendency towards leapfrog migration, at least in the westernmost populations (Pienkowski *et al.* 1985). We consider that around three quarters of the autumn birds in Britain are from Iceland, but some may also be of Russian origin (having arrived via the Netherlands).

Information from museum specimens and the literature (Fig. 10.6) indicates more of a broad-front migration of this inland meadow-bird, compared with Grey Plovers. Nevertheless, there is apparently a particularly strong migration on a narrow front along the White Sea (Belopolskij *et al.* 1970), the Gulf of Finland, through the Baltic Sea area to Denmark, northern Germany and Netherlands. Furthermore, birds from the Scandinavian Peninsula go down to the Denmark–

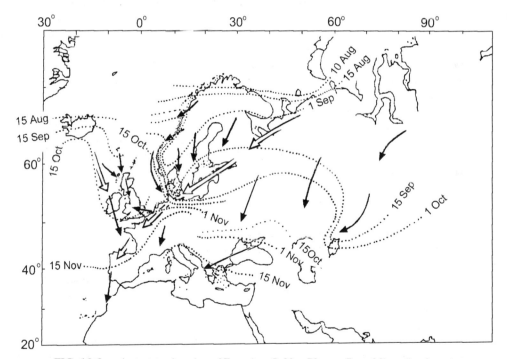

FIG. 10.6. *Autumn migration of Eurasian Golden Plovers. Dotted lines (isophenes) are based on median dates for clusters of museum specimens (the data are given in Appendix 10), supplemented by the literature (Appendix 11). Arrows indicate migration routes (broad arrows show the most important routes).*

Germany–Netherlands area, and ringing recoveries show that only a few go from Norway directly to the British Isles (Fig. 10.7). An important moult area for adults is found from Denmark to Schleswig-Holstein; here moulting adults are found from mid-July until September/October (Glutz von Blotzheim *et al.* 1975; Meltofte 1993; Rasmussen 1994; Poot *et al.* 1996). Birds from the Scandinavian and Russian flights, having reached the eastern North Sea countries, spread farther west, and then south, fairly slowly, depending on the severity of the approaching winter weather (cf. Jukema & Hulscher 1988; Meltofte 1993). Although some Eurasian Golden Plovers gradually leave the southeastern North Sea countries during cold weather and head for Britain, most of them seem to proceed to France, the Iberian Peninsula, and northwestern Africa (Figs. 10.6, 10.7). Poot *et al.* (1996) point out that birds of Scandinavian origin moult in Jutland, whereas those of more eastern populations (e.g. Russia) moult further to the east, and are presumed to pass through the Wadden Sea later in autumn (Meltofte 1993; Meltofte *et al.* 1994).

While one autumn migration of Eurasian Golden Plovers passes over interior Middle Europe (some possibly for the Mediterranean countries, Blaszyk 1939; Glutz von Blotzheim 1963), a larger broad front inland migration appears to go over western Russia and Poland (Dement'ev & Gladkov 1951), presumably delivering birds both to the Mediterranean and East Atlantic flyways. The birds also cross the West Siberian Plain to northwestern Kazakhstan (Dement'ev & Gladkov 1951; Kozlova 1961; Dolgushin 1962), and from there southwestwards to the Mediterranean flyway.

Adult migration peaks several weeks ahead of the juvenile migration (Salomonsen 1967a; Glutz von Blotzheim *et al.* 1975; Byrkjedal 1980c; Cramp & Simmons 1983; Garðarsson & Nielsen 1989; Meltofte 1993). Isophenes indicate relatively early migration waves over the Baltic areas and northern Kazakhstan (Fig. 10.6), suggesting a preponderance of adults here. Juveniles tend to migrate on broader fronts than adults also in this species. According to Glutz von Blotzheim *et al.* (1975), adults are generally few in the flights through interior Middle Europe, compared with juveniles. Yet, museum specimens of aged Eurasian Golden Plovers available to us were not sufficiently geographically spread to give information about differential adult/juvenile migration.

As for Grey Plovers, adult females commence migration somewhat earlier than the adult males (from cumulative time distributions of 36 adult males and 24 adult females, 30°–60°N), in accordance with the tendency for females to be the first to leave broods (Chapter 9). This may be why a bimodality in the peak adult migration is observed on the German Baltic (Kube *et al.* 1994), one peak occurring in August and the next along with the juveniles in September. The latter peak might consist mainly of males. In the Netherlands adult males do not start to become numerous before September (Jukema 1989).

Winter

Eurasian Golden Plovers winter from the British Isles and the southern North Sea countries to North Africa, eastwards along the Mediterranean Sea, to the Middle East and areas south of the Caspian Sea (Fig. 10.8). Small flocks may also be found on the northeast side of the Arabian Sea (Ali & Ripley 1969). During migration and

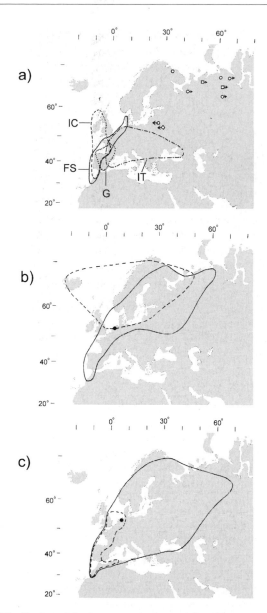

FIG. 10.7.   *Distribution of ringing recoveries (encircled) of Eurasian Golden Plovers
(a) ringed in Iceland (IC) (winter recoveries; a few in SE England and the Netherlands
excluded), Fennoscandia (FS), Germany (G), Italy (IT). Single recoveries of birds
ringed in Belgium ○, Denmark □, and France ◇. Arrows indicate spring (→) and
autumn (←); no arrows = summer;
(b) ringed in the Netherlands (●), ···· recovered in summer (June–July), _____
recovered in autumn (August–November);
(c) ringed in the Netherlands (●), ···· recovered in winter (December–January), ____
recovered in spring (February–May). Sources: Glutz von Blotzheim et al. (1975), Speek
(1978), Viksne & Mikhel'son (1985).*

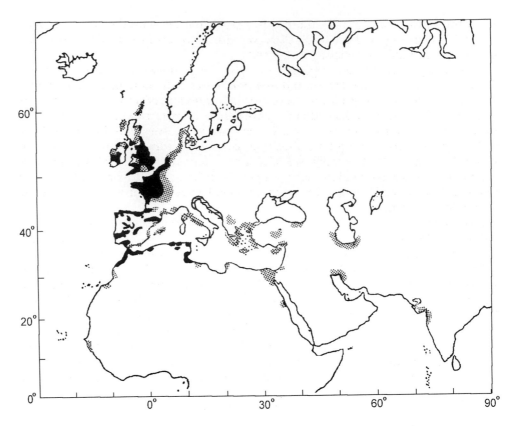

FIG. 10.8. *Winter distribution of Eurasian Golden Plovers. Areas of highest abundance are shown in black, less abundance are shaded, and regular wintering areas without information about abundance are hatched. Sources in Appendix 11.*

wintering Eurasian Golden Plovers are chiefly found on grass meadows and cultivated land (e.g. Eerden & Keij 1979; Fuller & Youngman 1979; Thompson 1984; Barnard & Thompson 1985), but also in saltmarshes and on mudflats (Kersten & Smit 1984; Rasmussen 1994; Cranswick *et al.* 1996) and in Hungary on alkali *puszta* grassland grazed by sheep (Gábor 1985). Mudflats and ploughed fields tend to be used by resting flocks, whereas grassland and some types of cropland are used primarily for feeding (Fuller & Youngman 1979; Eerden & Keij 1979; Fuller & Lloyd 1981; Barnard & Thompson 1985; Straka 1991).

In Denmark, in autumn, adult golden plovers are reportedly found primarily on grassland whereas juveniles are more frequent on mudflats (Meltofte 1987). In Britain and Ireland only about 10% of the wintering golden plovers are found in coastal habitats (numbers in Glutz von Blotzheim *et al.* 1975 cf. those in Appendix 13), though Cranswick *et al.* (1996) report data for 1993–94 which suggest around 15% of the birds may be coastal. Nevertheless, numbers of Eurasian Golden Plovers using marine mudflats during migration and winter can be significant, as revealed by recent counts along the Wadden Sca (Meltofte *et al.* 1994; Appendix 13), and along the British coast, notably on the Humber Estuary, and on the Solway, Ribble, Lower Derwent Ings and the Wash. However, the majority of the golden plovers do stay on inland habitats (Kirby & Lack 1993).

Although golden plovers regularly occur in large flocks, the birds are more dispersed over large inland tracts and therefore more difficult to count than typical coastal waders like Grey Plover. Nevertheless, figures produced in recent years (Appendix 13) clearly indicate that the core area is in westermost Europe, from the British Isles to the Iberian Peninsula, and in northwest Africa. On the British Isles, 650 000 golden plovers spend the winter, just over half of which are found in Ireland (Kirby & Lack 1993). The latter are to a large extent Icelandic birds as shown by ringing recoveries. No golden plovers ringed as chicks in Great Britain have been found in Ireland, and the breeding population in Ireland amounts to only 600 pairs (Hutchinson 1989).

In farmlands and coastal habitats from Denmark to the Netherlands more than 500 000 golden plovers have been counted in November (Appendix 13). The extent to which golden plovers spend the winter there depends largely on the frequency of cold spells (Glutz von Blotzheim *et al.* 1975; Eerden & Keij 1979; Jukema & Hulscher 1988). Ringing recoveries show that cold weather any time from November to January causes birds to fly to the milder British Isles, and, above all, to Belgium, France and the Iberian Peninsula (Fig. 10.7: Jukema & Hulscher 1988; Glutz von Blotzheim *et al.* 1975). Furthermore, golden plovers wintering in Britain may fly to milder regions, usually Ireland and France during cold spells (Kirby & Lack 1993). Even French birds move about during winter, according to the severity of the weather, and the winter presence of golden plovers in Seine-et-Marne depends a good deal on the temperature (Balanca 1984). Around Vienne, variations in the winter weather have been associated with 20-fold changes in winter numbers (Yeatman-Berthelot & Jarry 1991).

Compared with the large populations on the Atlantic side, numbers in the Mediterranean areas and in the Middle East may be small (Cramp & Simmons 1983; Mainardi 1987). However, much more information is needed from areas around the Adriatic Sea.

Spring

Eurasian Golden Plovers are already on the move in their African, Iberian, and west Mediterranean wintering grounds by mid-February (Fig. 10.9). Although the largest numbers of birds pass the North Sea countries in April and May, a smaller peak in March probably belonging to the early breeders in the heather moorland regions (cf. Chapters 6 and 7) of Germany, Denmark, and southernmost parts of Sweden and Norway (Brinkmann 1941; Jukema 1989; Meltofte 1993).

The migration passes over Europe on a broad front. Nevertheless, as in autumn, the majority of birds passes through the maritime countries of western Europe, up Belgium, Netherlands, Germany, and Denmark, spreading out to Fennoscandia, and through the Baltic region to Russian breeding grounds. Apparently, a larger proportion in spring than in autumn flies over the Mediterranean basin to the south Russian plains. Birds ringed in the Netherlands are more often recovered on the Mediterranean flyway in spring (6.7% of 112 recoveries) than in autumn (0.98%

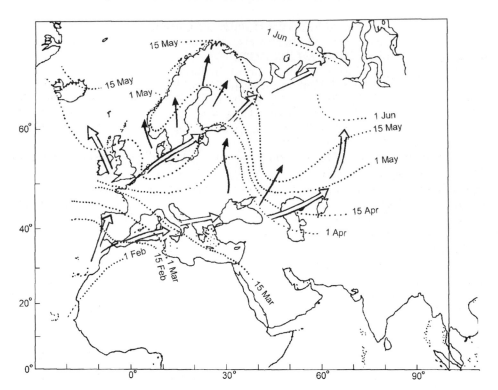

FIG. 10.9.   *Spring migration of Eurasian Golden Plovers. Dotted lines (isophenes) are based on median dates for clusters of museum specimens (the data are given in Appendix 10), supplemented by the literature (Appendix 11). Arrows indicate migration routes (broad arrows show the most important routes).*

of 165 recoveries: $\chi^2 = 5.4$, $p<0.05$, birds found within 1 year from ringing excluded, see also Fig. 10.7). Thus, there is a sort of elliptical migration system in Eurasian Golden Plovers.

Birds on the Mediterranean route in spring clearly use the south Russian plains as a staging area, lingering there in April and much of May (Fig. 10.9) before crossing the forests up to the breeding grounds in the European sub-arctic. Judging by the extent of the staging areas, this passage probably takes place on a broad front. A considerable migration goes over northwestern Kazakhstan, probably on a narrower front, up along the farmlands in the forest steppe region east of the Urals, and finally across the taiga forest zone to the Siberian breeding grounds. Golden plovers ringed in Italy as well as in Denmark have been recovered east of the Urals (Fig. 10.7), indicating that birds from the easternmost breeding populations may be on either flyways.

Cumulative time distributions of museum specimens (79 males, 50 females) from the spring migration in western Europe revealed no differences for males and females for any given date, although males often arrive on their breeding territories a few days before the females (Chapters 7 and 8).

PACIFIC GOLDEN PLOVER

Autumn

As for the Grey Plover, the winter range of this species is immense, and with few ringing recoveries the migration routes to and within the Pacific islands are far from obvious (Johnson & Connors 1996). Nevertheless, on the basis of museum specimens and published information we propose the outline of migratory movements given below (Fig. 10.10).

A very small number of birds, from western Alaska, follow the Pacific coast of North America, but the vast majority of the birds from these breeding grounds appear to enter a flight across the Aleutians (mainly east of Rat Islands), down to the Hawaiian islands, and a fraction continues to Central and Eastern Polynesia (cf. Salomonsen 1967; Kenyon 1961; Sauer 1963; Johnson 1979; Morrison 1984; Paulson 1993; Johnson & Connors 1996).

To what extent birds from the Siberian side of the Bering Sea enter this route is uncertain. Flocks of young birds observed leaving easternmost Chukchi Peninsula in late August actually headed east and southeast toward the American side (Tomkovich & Sorokin 1983). On the other hand, the only long-distance ringing recovery known to us, is of a bird ringed in early autumn on Pribilof Islands, and

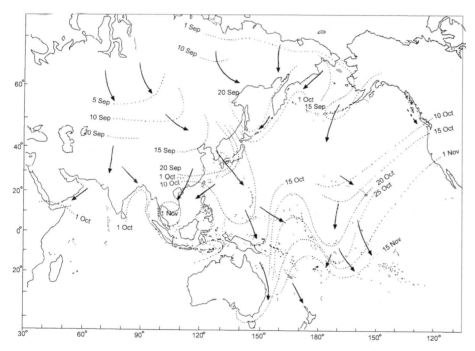

FIG. 10.10. *Autumn migration of Pacific Golden Plovers. Dotted lines (isophenes) are based on median dates for clusters of museum specimens (the data are given in Appendix 10), supplemented by the literature (Appendix 11). Arrows indicate migration routes.*

found 6 weeks later at Hokkaido, Japan (McClure 1974). The Pribilof Islands are on the Alaskan side, and their position would suggest that they should be crossed by birds heading for the Hawaiian route. Northeast Asian birds seem to be on a later time schedule than those on the West Alaskan–Hawaiian flight. This may indicate that Alaskan and northeast Asian birds fly on separate routes, and that a majority of the latter follow southwest along the Asian coastlines. However, the distribution of museum specimens indicates a high proportion of juveniles on the northeast Asian side (Fig. 10.11), and since juveniles tend to be several weeks behind adults, differential migration of adults and juveniles might be responsible for the different time schedules on each side of the Bering Sea.

Laboratory experiments showed that Pacific Golden Plovers taken as chicks at St Lawrence Islands (170°W) and displaced east of the Hawaiian flyway, not only compensated for this displacement during their subsequent spring migration

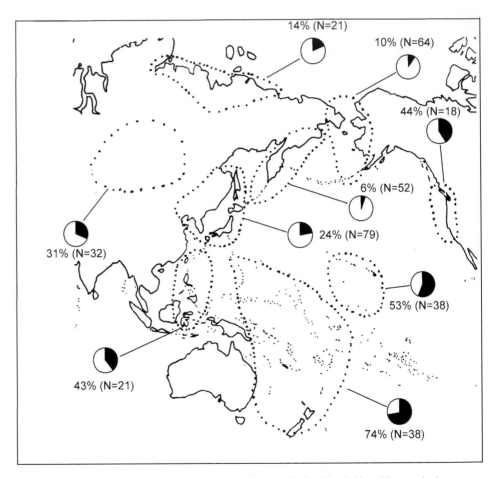

FIG. 10.11. *Distribution of adult and juvenile Pacific Golden Plovers during autumn migration, according to museum specimens. Percentage adults are given, along with the total number of specimens examined.*

orientation, but also became imprinted on their 'new' wintering grounds, showing an orientation that would have taken them east of the Hawaiian route in autumn (Sauer 1963a,b).

A flight path passes down along Kamchatka and the Kuriles to Japan (Bergman 1935). Many large marine mudflat areas, highly suitable for staging waders in general, are found in this region (P.S. Tomkovich pers. comm.). However, in Korea and Japan these areas are subject to extremely rapid rates of land claim and even degradation (e.g. Melville 1997). During migration Pacific Golden Plovers, like the two other species of golden plover, are often found on short grass fields and cultivated land for feeding grounds, but apparently to a much larger extent than the others they use intertidal and associated habitats, like mudflats, lagoons, and beaches (Smythies 1953, 1960; Henry 1955; Munro 1960; Lane 1987; Kinsky & Yaldwyn 1981; Marle & Voous 1988; Williams & Williams 1988; Sampath & Krishnamurthy 1990). Japan, as well as the mainland coastlines of Asia, also receives golden plover flights that have reached the Sea of Ochotsk along the large river valleys from north central and east Siberia. These valleys offer staging areas primarily along waterbodies but also on farmland (Labutin *et al.* 1988, Kretchmar *et al.* 1991).

An inland flight over the Manchurian plains and Korea apparently hits southern Japan. Thus mainland and insular coasts of the Japan Sea appear to receive golden plovers from a number of flights representing birds from many parts of the species' breeding range. Numerous estuarine areas in the west coast of Korea and along the coast of Japan (Gore & Pyong-Oh 1971; Piersma 1985; Brazil 1991) provide important staging areas for golden plovers and other migrating shorebirds. From Japan migration probably continues along two main routes, one going southeastwards to Micronesia, Melanesia, and probably to eastern Australia and New Zealand, and the other southwestwards along the mainland and islands of the South China Sea (cf. Johnson 1979; Parish *et al.* 1987). To what extent birds on the Japan–southeastern route come into contact with those on the Hawaiian–east Polynesian route, is unknown. Body size measurements of birds from Wake in the northwest and Niue in the southeast indicate a Siberian origin for Micronesian birds (small birds; Johnston & McFarlane 1967; Kinsky & Yaldwyn 1981). On the other hand, among golden plovers wintering in southeastern Australia, birds large enough to be of Alaskan origin have been found (Barter 1988). Yet, these may also have come from the breeding grounds in Kamchatka, where birds are particularly large (Chapter 3).

Pacific Golden Plovers migrate in reasonably high numbers through eastern Kazakhstan (Dolgushin 1962), apparently an important staging area for birds from western Siberia *en route* to their wintering grounds along the Arabian Sea, the Bay of Bengal, and down to Indonesia. Whether birds from this flight reach as far as Australia, is more uncertain, as is the degree to which they meet birds coming down the South China Sea from the northeast. An analysis of the body sizes of golden plovers wintering in Southeast Asia would clearly be interesting.

Adults migrate earlier than the juveniles, often begin to appear on the flyways by July, and may be 5–6 weeks ahead of the first juveniles (Henshaw 1910; Munro 1960; Wishart *et al.* 1981; Johnson *et al.* 1981a,b; Paulson 1993). Presumably the adults, especially males, are on a tighter schedule than juveniles in order to reach their wintering grounds, where they may hold territories in successive winters. Cumulative time distribution of museum specimens between 60° and 30°N (54 adult males, 53 adult females) revealed no consistent differences in timing of the male and female migration, even though the females leave the broods earlier than the males (Chapter 9).

Observations in the Yukon-Kuskokwim Delta, Alaska, of what must have been chiefly this species, shows that migrating adults are found feeding terrestrially more often than juveniles, the juveniles being more frequent on intertidal habitats (Gill & Handel 1990). This is in accordance with observations on the other two golden plover species.

Winter

The winter habitat of Pacific Golden Plovers is similar to that used during migration. Frequently found on pastures and cultivated fields, they also have a fondness for air fields, golf courses and big lawns (Belcher 1929; Sibley 1951; Manson-Bahr 1953; Smythies 1960; Johnson *et al.* 1981b; Williams & Williams 1988; Johnson *et al.* 1989). Over much of the Pacific such habitats may be of relatively recent origin, and intertidal habitats are therefore thought to be the 'original' winter habitat of this species on the Pacific Islands (Johnson 1985). In eastern Polynesia and Australasia the birds are often found along beaches, lagoons, and reefs (Holyoak & Thibault 1984; Marchant & Higgins 1993).

The wintering range is mainly found south of 20°N and stretches from easternmost Africa and the Arabian Peninsula to southeastern Polynesia and California (Fig. 10.12). Although reported to be quite common in Somalia in winter (Ash 1980; Urban *et al.* 1986), the core wintering areas are in eastern India, Bangladesh, Southeast Asia, the Pacific islands, and eastern Australia (Mayr 1945; Smythies 1960; Munro 1960; Ali & Ripley 1969; King *et al.* 1975; Lane 1987). The species also occurs regularly in New Zealand (Falla *et al.* 1970; Lane 1987), and has recently been found wintering in small numbers in Oman as well as in Bahrain (Green *et al.* 1994; Hirschfeld 1994). Indeed, Pacific Golden Plovers may turn out to be even more widespread along the southern and eastern coast of the Arabian Peninsula.

Interestingly, Dijk *et al.* (1993) observed small groups of Pacific Golden Plovers on the coast of Gabon during January–February 1992 and estimated a total of 20–25 birds for the northern intertidal areas. Further observations are needed to establish whether the species winters regularly on the Atlantic coast of Africa.

Large-scale counts have only been made for coastal Australia, totalling 4800 birds for the 'top twenty zones' (Lane 1987). Marchant & Higgins (1993) give an estimated total of 9000 birds. This is a modest quantity compared with an estimated 5000 birds for one estuary alone in Singapore. The wintering population of Pacific Golden Plover in East Polynesia numbers several thousand birds (Holyoak & Thibault 1984), while fewer than 100 winter along the Pacific coast of North America (Paulson & Lee 1992). Other available counts of Pacific Golden Plovers from the wintering grounds are from a few mudflat complexes.

Although adults arrive on the wintering grounds long before the juveniles, there is no evidence for a north–south difference in the wintering distribution according to age. Males are, however, more numerous than females among birds wintering

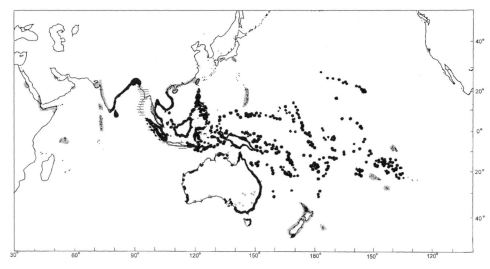

FIG. 10.12. *Winter distribution of Pacific Golden Plovers. Areas of highest abundance are shown in black, less abundance are shaded, and regular wintering areas without information about abundance are hatched. Sources in Appendix 11.*

north of 20°N (68.6% males), compared with south of 20°N (46.7% males) ($\chi^2 = 5.2$, $p<0.05$, $n=45$ birds) which is as we should expect according to the arrival time hypothesis.

Spring

On the Hawaiian flyway, the bulk of the golden plovers are apparently on the move up the Tuamotu Archipelago in early April (Fig. 10.13). The major flights from the Hawaiian Islands occur in late April and early May, arriving in the Aleutians and on the Alaska Peninsula (Henshaw 1910; Munro 1960; Sauer 1962; Gill & Jorgensen 1979; Johnson *et al.* 1981a). Oscar Johnson and colleagues are now using radio telemetry to track birds moving north. They recently tracked three birds caught in Hawaii, in late April 1996, to their breeding grounds in Western Alaska (Johnson *et al.* 1997).

From New Zealand, most birds leave in late March (McKenzie 1967) and from southeastern Australia in late February–March (Lane 1987). A number of birds proceed from southeastern and eastern Australia up the east coast, but many cross north over inland Australia without even a stopover in northern Australia (Lane 1987).

Migration up SE Asia and the Philippines proceeds from late March through most of April (see also Dement'ev & Gladkov 1951; Sauer 1963a,b; Lord Medway & Wells 1976; Verheugt *et al.* 1990), and by the end of April through to the beginning of May the migration peaks in the Japanese–Korean area. From there, in mid–late May, one migration corridor seems to slant inland over Korea and the Manchurian Plain to north central Siberia, and another one continues to north Japan and proceeds on both sides of the Sea of Ochotsk. In the Maritime Territory,

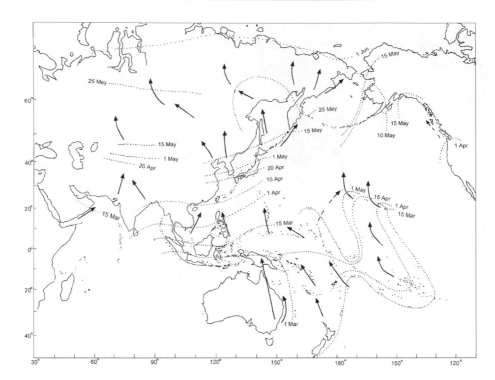

FIG. 10.13.   *Spring migration of Pacific Golden Plovers. Dotted lines (isophenes) are based on median dates for clusters of museum specimens (the data are given in Appendix 10), supplemented by the literature (Appendix 11). Arrows indicate migration routes.*

southeasternmost Russia, Pacific Golden Plovers are only seen in the autumn, not in spring (Dement'ev & Gladkov 1951). The bulk of the birds arrive in the tundras of central and east Siberia and Northeast Asia in the beginning of June.

The populations wintering around the Bay of Bengal, as well as those in Somalia, have been reported to depart in late April–early May (cf. also Smythies 1953; Henry 1955; Urban *et al.* 1986; Sampath & Krishnamurthy 1990). However, Hirschfeld (1994) found a small passage of birds in Bahrain in March, indicating an earlier start of northbound movements in these westernmost wintering populations. In east Kazakhstan, the main flights start to appear in late April, although small numbers may already be seen in late March in the southernmost parts (Dement'ev & Gladkov 1951; Dolgushin 1962). Peak numbers in northern Kazakhstan in mid–late May indicate that the birds use Kazakhstan as a staging area, before continuing to northwestern Siberia, where they arrive on the breeding grounds in early–mid-June. Passage of birds inland might also take place from the South China Sea, but we have not been able to find any information about this.

Many, if not most, of the one year old Pacific Golden Plovers spend the summer on their wintering range (Smythies 1960; Johnson 1973, 1977; Kinsky & Yaldwin 1981; Johnson & Johnson 1983; Holyoak & Thibault 1984). This is in contrast to the two other golden plover species, which tend not to be found on the wintering grounds during the boreal summer (Bent 1929; Cramp & Simmons 1983; Johnson 1985).

Cumulative time distribution of museum specimens (158 males, 106 females) between 30° and 60°N revealed no differences in the migration schedules of males and females.

AMERICAN GOLDEN PLOVER

Autumn

In autumn American Golden Plovers migrate from the Arctic to the northern prairie regions, and from there southeastwards (Fig. 10.14). Most continue to the Atlantic coast and leave for northern South America, perhaps on a great circular route (Morrison 1984; Johnson & Connors 1996). Some birds, however, follow the Mississippi Valley to the Gulf of Mexico, and then move down to northwestern South America (Cooke 1912; Bent 1929; Allen 1939; Stout 1967). There have been some disagreements over where the birds leave the Atlantic coast of North America. Early in the 20th century the departure was mainly considered to take place from Labrador to Nova Scotia (Cooke 1912; Bent 1929; Allen 1939). However, there is no contemporary evidence for major departures from the Maritime Provinces of Canada. Instead, the majority leave the coast farther south, from northeastern USA to Virginia, though a shift during the 20th century towards a more southerly departure from North America may have taken place (Todd 1963; Stout 1967; Godfrey 1986). By 1949, Peters & Burleigh had reported the species to be only accidental in Newfoundland!

According to Bent (1929) and Stout (1967) the adults migrate to the Atlantic coast of North America, while the Mississippi Valley flights are dominated by juveniles. Stout (1967) goes further in postulating an adult migration over a narrow corridor, leaving the coast for South America between Delaware and New England, and a juvenile movement that hits the east American coast on a broader front. Available museum specimens largely confirm this picture (Fig. 10.15), and the proportion of adults is significantly higher from the Midwest prairies over the Great Lakes region east to the Atlantic coast, compared with the Pacific coast, northern Canadian prairies, James Bay and the Gulf of Mexico ($\chi^2 = 16.8$, p<0.001). The low proportion of adults among museum specimens from the north Canadian prairies and James Bay may, however, indicate a fast passage by adults from the Arctic to staging areas eastwards from the Midwest prairies.

On the north coast of South America the major landfall is made in Guyanas-Suriname (Fig. 10.14; Bent 1929; Stout 1967; see also Morrison 1984), evidently consisting of a high proportion of adults (Fig. 10.15). American Golden Plover flights pass the Bermudas without landing and they do not usually land on the Bahamas unless encountered by southerly winds (Bent 1929). The migration then proceeds over central Brazil and along the Amazonian–Pantanal flyways to the wintering grounds, from southern Brazil to Argentina (Antas 1983). A flight, largely of juveniles, seems also to follow the Andes, turning southeast and crossing Bolivia

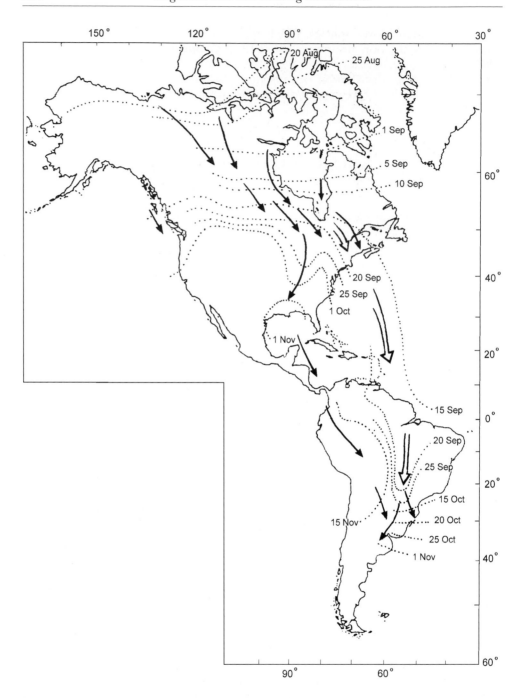

FIG. 10.14. *Autumn migration of American Golden Plovers. Dotted lines (isophenes) are based on median dates for clusters of museum specimens (the data are given in Appendix 10), supplemented by the literature (Appendix 11). Arrows indicate migration routes (broad arrows show the most important routes).*

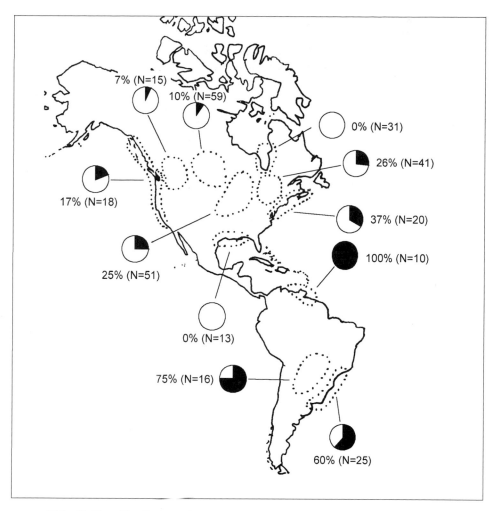

FIG. 10.15. *Distribution of adult and juvenile American Golden Plovers during autumn migration (south of 60°N), according to museum specimens. Percentage of adults are given, along with the total number of specimens examined.*

(Antas 1983). This may consist of birds from the Mississippi flyway crossing the Caribbean Sea. Thus, also in South America, adults and juveniles do not seem to follow identical routes.

It is generally stated (Cooke 1912; Bent 1929; Landing 1991; Paulson 1993) that the migration of adult American Golden Plovers peaks several weeks before that of juveniles. Cumulative time distribution of museum specimens (60°–30°N) reached the 50% level for adults to occur 28 days before juveniles (56 adults, 200 juveniles). Contrary to Cooke (1912), adult females tend to migrate slightly earlier than adult males (cumulative distribution of females found to be 2–6% ahead of males on any one date; 29 adult males, 28 adult females), as we should expect from their tendency to leave their broods earlier than males (Chapter 9).

During migration, American Golden Plovers are found feeding on grasslands and ploughed fields, in much the same way as the Eurasian Golden Plover, but birds are also found on mudflats and along shallow lagoons (e.g. Rowan 1923; Bent 1929; Belcher & Smooker 1935; Wishart *et al.* 1981; Morrison & Ross 1989; Hicklin 1987; Hayes & Fox 1991; Stotz *et al.* 1992). They are far more terrestrial than Grey Plovers, but probably somewhat less so than Eurasian Golden Plovers. During autumn migration in Paraguay, Hayes & Fox (1991) found about 18% of the birds to be on freshwater habitats, while around 64% and 18% were on wet and dry terrestrial habitats, respectively. As in Eurasian and Pacific golden plovers, juveniles seem to be found more often on mudflats than adults (Stout 1967).

Winter

American Golden Plovers are regularly found wintering in small numbers on the Gulf of Mexico, the Caribbean islands and on the north coast of South America (Bond 1974; Voous 1983; Root 1988; Morrison & Ross 1989; Fig. 10.16). To the south the species regularly reaches Tierra del Fuego (Fjeldså & Krabbe 1990), and to the east Fernando de Norhona and Trinidade Islands (Jorge Bruno Nacinovic pers. comm.). The species is also recorded in small numbers on the Pacific Coast of South America (Morrison & Ross 1989).

The main wintering grounds of this species, however, are found on the grasslands from Mato Grosso to Uruguay and Argentina, with the core area apparently from the Buenos Aires Province and northwards in Argentina, over Uruguay to maritime regions of Rio Grande do Sul (Fig. 10.16). We have not been able to find any extensive counts for the wintering grounds on the grasslands. However, counts of coastal waders in South America, which embrace only a tiny part of the wintering populations of American Golden Plover, reflect the general picture of winter abundance (Appendix 14).

Spring

American Golden Plovers are on the move from their core wintering areas by late February (Fig. 10.17). Rather than just reversing the autumn flights, the northward migration goes northwest over the Andes. The species is very numerous in March–April on *altiplanos* at 4000 m elevation in northwestern Argentina, Bolivia and Peru (Fjeldså & Krabbe 1990). From there, the migration may continue to the north side of the Gulf of Mexico in one jump, as the species has not been recorded as common anywhere between Peru and Texas (Bent 1929; Imhof 1950; Loetscher 1955; Andrle 1966).

In Texas the birds appear to pause on the grasslands for a while, before continuing up by the Mississippi, where the main passage goes along the prairie region on the west side of the river (Bent 1929; Stout 1967). Here food seems to be abundant, and the birds pass 'leisurely' northwards over the prairies (Bent 1929). In spring American Golden Plovers are rare on the Atlantic coasts of both South and North America. The passage up the Mississippi Valley continues over the southern and western parts of the Great Lakes Region, fanning out to the Canadian prairies,

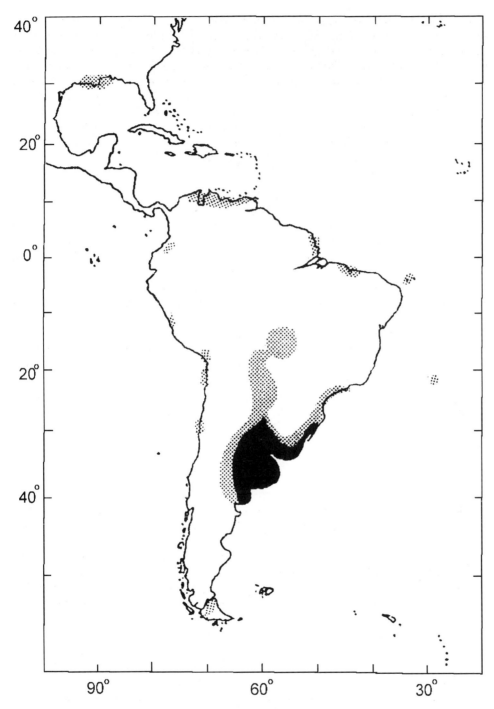

FIG. 10.16. *Winter distribution of American Golden Plovers. Areas of highest abundance are shown in black, less abundance are shaded. Sources in Appendix 11.*

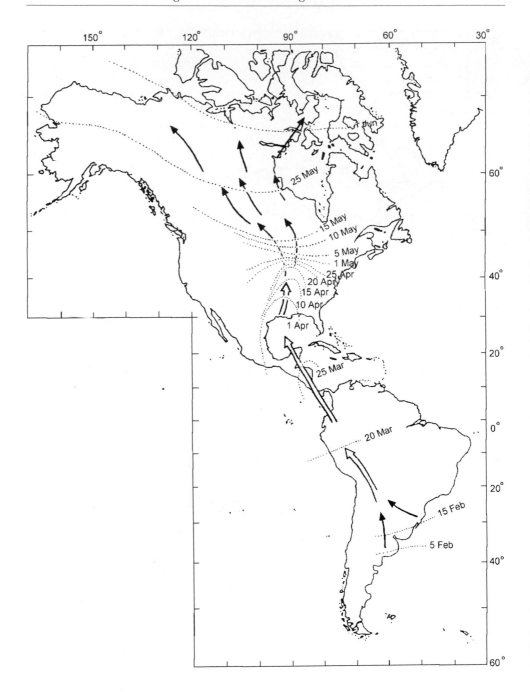

FIG. 10.17.   *Spring migration of American Golden Plovers. Dotted lines (isophenes) are based on median dates for clusters of museum specimens (the data are given in Appendix 10), supplemented by the literature (Appendix 11). Arrows indicate migration routes (broad arrows show the most important routes).*

where the birds linger for about 10 days (Stout 1967; Fig. 10.17) before heading for the Arctic across the forest zones.

A few birds regularly pass up the Pacific coast of North America (Paulson 1993), but the species is lacking on spring migration over Labrador and Newfoundland (Godfrey 1986), and contrary to the situation in autumn, James Bay does not hold staging golden plovers in any numbers.

American Golden Plovers thus perform a pronounced elliptical movement during their annual cycle. The explanation for their use of different routes in autumn and spring was, early on, founded on the differences in prevailing wind directions (Cooke 1912; Bent 1929). If leaving the east coast of Canada after the passage of a cold front (as shorebirds commonly do in autumn) the birds should start out with a convenient tail wind and then encounter northeasterly winds which bring them to the north coast of South America (Hale 1980; Morrison 1984). Tail winds will also be frequently experienced by spring migrants on a central route through North America. However, the choice of a different route in spring for this predominantly terrestrial shorebird might be governed by constraints arising from regional shifts in rainfall seasons in South America (Antas 1983), as well as from persistent winter conditions during spring in maritime provinces of Canada (Morrison 1984). So, the availability of staging areas with plenty of food may be an important factor here in determining the migration routes (Johnson & Connors 1996).

The cumulative time distribution of museum specimens (132 males, 115 females; 30°–60°N) did not indicate any differences in the migration schedules of males and females, although males seemed to arrive on the breeding grounds slightly before females (Chapter 9).

SUMMARY

1. The migration systems of the four species have been deduced from the literature, ringing returns and the analysis in space and time of over 4000 museum specimens. Migration ranges from relatively stationary (Eurasian Golden Plovers in the British Isles) to long distance (arctic breeders).

2. Grey Plovers, the most maritime of the four, winter along beaches and on mudflats from the temperate zone to the tropics, almost world-wide. Eurasian and American Golden Plovers are chiefly terrestrial and confined to grasslands of Europe and South America, respectively. The Pacific Golden Plover is found wintering on marine mudflats as well as on grasslands from the Arabian Sea to the Pacific.

3. Adults tend to migrate south several weeks before juveniles and follow narrower corridors. Females tend to precede males.

4. Grey Plover and Pacific Golden Plover males tend to winter farther north than females, perhaps in order to reach the breeding grounds early to compete for territories there.

6. Ringing recoveries are available for Eurasian Golden Plovers and West Palearctic Grey Plovers. These identify population-specific wintering grounds at

least for the West European Eurasian Golden Plovers. More material is needed to reach conclusions about differential adult-juvenile wintering.

7. American Golden Plovers, and to some extent Grey Plovers and Eurasian Golden Plovers, follow routes in spring which are different from those used in autumn.

CHAPTER 11
Behaviour and Ecology in the Non-breeding Season

Eurasion Golden Plover and Black-headed Gull

Away from the areas where long-term territories were held, Grey Plovers sometimes occupied territories for short periods.... It is clear that Grey Plovers show great variation, both within and between individuals, in the way that they utilise a feeding area.

Dave Townshend, Pat Dugan and Mike Pienkowski (1984)

MANY of the most northern shorebirds spend up to 10 months of the year away from their breeding grounds. In the previous chapter, we contrasted the migration routes, passage areas and over-wintering grounds of the four species. In this chapter, we look at features of their ecology and behaviour away from their breeding grounds. As we shall see, while some birds are highly territorial others are strongly gregarious.

GREY PLOVERS

Whereas the first Grey Plover's nest was discovered on 26 June 1843 by the German explorer Middendorf on the Taimyir Peninsula, these birds had been noted on the coast centuries earlier. As we have discussed in the previous chapter, Grey Plovers are widely distributed during the non-breeding season. On the tidal flats of San Fransisco Bay on the central coast of California they feed on sandflats and mudflats (high above the tideline where there is little surface water) and in marshy areas (Recher 1966). A fairly similar distribution was found in the Bay of Fundy (which has one of the highest recorded tidal maxima in the world, 17 m), where as many as 10 000 birds 'stage' on the sand/mudflats, beaches and saltmarshes before migrating to South America (Hicklin 1987). In Britain, they tend to be on the larger and muddier estuaries, and are absent from many parts of coastal Scotland.

The Grey Plover exhibits winter territorial behaviour throughout much of its winter range. Territory sizes vary: Cramp & Simmons (1983) give a size range of 200–600 m² for birds in Europe. In America, mean distances between territorial birds have been given as 96 m (Florida), 125 m (California) and 269 m (Georgia) (Stinson 1977, 1980; Michael 1935; Myers *et al.* 1979). Two particularly detailed studies have been made of non-breeding behaviour in Grey Plovers, and these are summarized below along with some other major studies.

Grey Plovers in Northeast England

Grey Plovers in Britain originate from nesting grounds in W. Siberia, with numbers building up rapidly in July and August to reach a peak in October. Later on, into winter, there is a small southerly movement of post-moult birds to SW Europe and W. Africa; in January there is a small influx of birds that have spent autumn moulting in the Wadden Sea. From February onwards, there is a gradual decrease in number as birds leave to breed. The non-breeding individuals present in summer are probably first-year immatures (Chapter 10).

The Tees Estuary Between 200 and 300 Grey Plovers over-winter in the Tees Estuary, NE England. This population has been studied in detail since 1975 (Pienkowski 1982, 1983; Dugan 1981, 1982; Townshend *et al.* 1984; Townshend 1985; Evans & Townshend 1988; Evans *et al.* 1991). Like most areas favoured by Grey Plover in winter, the Tees is characterized by large stretches of nutrient-rich mudflats. Birds feed on the exposed tidal flats, detecting their main prey (the ragworm *Nereis diversicolor*) by sight. They employ a highly characteristic fixed feeding method of 'run-stop-search' (Baker 1974; Pienkowski 1983; Turpie & Hockey 1997). This seems to impose a limit on the density at which birds can feed (e.g. Turpie & Hockey 1993, 1997): they need to avoid disturbing prey temporarily available on the mud surface (Townshend 1986). Individuals space out in three ways: (i) on territories defended over long periods (measured in months); (ii) on territories defended over short periods (measured in days); and (iii) non-territorially, over a broad feeding range within the estuary. Dave Townshend and colleagues studied over 200 uniquely marked birds to tease apart the costs and benefits of feeding in the above three ways.

Long-term territories included creeks which afforded sheltered feeding in harsh weather conditions, whilst short-term territories enabled occupants to feed without disturbance. Non-territorial birds, however, may have gained anti-predator benefits from feeding with conspecifics and other shorebirds. Approximately one third of them held long-term territories. Short-term defence of territories occurred most often when birds were most numerous (in October and mid-winter) whereas long-term territoriality tended to begin immediately after birds arrived in August. Birds built up fat reserves gradually, with a peak in December–January (Pienkowski *et al.* 1984).

Interestingly, individuals feeding in any of the above three ways as juveniles did not then change in their adult years; hence they took 'decisions for a lifetime' (Townshend 1985). Juveniles showed two basic patterns of seasonal movement: some stayed and remained all winter; others moved on (with some migrating farther south) 3–8 weeks after arrival. The juveniles that stayed throughout the winter tended to be larger; these may have hatched earlier or had superior growth prior to fledging. There was competition between juveniles and adults for the main territorial areas, and at least in the first weeks of autumn defence of a feeding territory appeared to be the favoured strategy. However, as Townshend (1985) put it: 'In winter there seems to be a fine balance between the two strategies, long-term territoriality and non-territoriality'.

Other British estuaries Studies of Grey Plovers on other British estuaries reveal interesting comparisons. At Lindisfarne, some 130 km north of the Tees, the substrate is sandier. There, aggression and territorial behaviour are rare. Severe weather is responsible for less prey being available, and birds feed further apart (see Pienkowski 1981, 1983). Two factors seem to account for the lack of territoriality at Lindisfarne. First, there are no defendable gullies and creeks. Compared with the ragworm *Nereis diversicolor*, the main prey present – the worms *Notomastus latericeus* and *Arenicola marina* – appear to be more conspicuous at the mud surface and less vulnerable to bad weather. Second, potential competitors – Common Ringed Plovers, Bar-tailed Godwits and Dunlin – are present at Lindisfarne where Grey Plovers feed. All take the same prey so the exclusion of conspecifics would result in only a marginal improvement in food intake.

Evans *et al.*'s (1979) study of Grey Plover in the Tees in 1973, prior to that by Townshend *et al.* (1984), provided yet another interesting difference. The former study was undertaken prior to extensive reclamation producing the mid-1980s situation on the Tees (a 60% reduction in area of tidal flat). In the early 1970s, fewer birds were territorial and bird density was considerably lower. Perhaps, therefore, an increase in bird density played an important role in promoting territoriality.

It remains to be seen whether or not mortality and breeding success differs between territorial and non-territorial birds, and if territoriality and density-dependent regulation in non-territorial areas can limit winter population size. Low ranking juveniles, for instance, may be deterred from remaining on good wintering grounds. This could give rise to greater juvenile mortality and, in turn, smaller local breeding populations in some of the following years.

Grey Plovers in South Africa

On the Zwartkops Estuary on the southern edge of South Africa, Jane Turpie and Philip Hockey have studied Grey Plovers since 1990. There, Grey Plovers are among the commonest shorebirds on the estuary during the non-breeding season, their 'austral summer' (Turpie & Hockey 1993, 1996, 1997; Turpie 1995). Approximately 65% of the birds defend feeding territories, with territories established during the arrival period (September) when foraging densities exceed around 4.6 birds ha^{-1}. Territories ranged in size between 490 and 2800 m^2, larger than in temperate regions.

Numbers of birds studied by Turpie and Hockey were somewhat larger than those on the Tees Estuary, ranging from a winter minimum of 21 birds to a late summer maximum of 603 (though 810 birds had been recorded previously). Bird densities were correlated with prey biomass (largely consisting of the mudprawn, *Upogebia africana*).

Interference and territories Throughout the 'summer', territories were retained and defended vigorously. Food intake rates were influenced largely by bird density, rather than the pattern of prey availability, suggesting that interference or competition played a role in regulating the feeding preferences (Turpie & Hockey 1996). Compared with any of the northern hemisphere estuaries, recorded feeding densities on the South African estuary were higher. As numbers of Grey Plovers built up on the estuary, they progressively spread out from the richest to the poorer areas, the former being occupied first. The interference between birds when feeding at high density probably occurred because the mudprawns were more likely to re-enter their burrows when there was more disturbance from birds (interestingly, in order to complete its life-cycle, a parasite seems to induce the tendency for mudprawns to come to the mud surface). The Grey Plovers therefore need space to locate, run at and take prey, and at high densities there is interference of their searching behaviour and possibly even direct competition for the same prey.

Aggression between birds This was high in early 'spring', but as densities rose, territories got smaller. However, territorial encounters decreased in frequency from September to March, probably because birds became more familiar with their neighbours and indulged in more 'avoidance' behaviour. Much of the aggression consisted of running up to an encroaching neighbour in a 'head-down, tail-fanned posture', with the pair then walking parallel to one another along the territorial boundary some 0.3–1.0 m apart (*cf.* breeding season behaviour, Chapter 8). These encounters were periodically interrupted by birds tail-fanning, wing-dropping and low crouching or even sitting postures (Turpie 1995). Despite the aggression, Turpie & Hockey (1996) concluded that the Grey Plovers 'satisfy their daily energy requirements with ease, even when their foraging performance is at its lowest'.

For most of the non-breeding season, variation in average territory size was explained by changes in the population density of Grey Plovers, rather than by densities of their prey. There was even a suggestion that the birds feeding on the richer areas, which defended smaller territories, actually experienced the highest levels of aggression, implying that owners of large, but poorer quality territories, were better off in terms of time available for feeding (Turpie 1995). Interestingly, the non-territorial birds spent between 8% and 24% more time foraging than territorial birds, and in March foraged for nearly twice as long. These non-territorial birds had a higher frequency of aggressive encounters than territorial birds, though the duration of their encounters was much lower than that of territorial encounters.

West Africa: the tropics

On the Banc d'Arguin, on the atlantic coast of Mauritania (19°20'), northwest Africa, Bruno Ens and colleagues (1990) made a detailed study of wintering shorebirds. There, many Grey Plovers fed on the tidal flats at high densities (0.5–1.5 birds ha^{-1}). A few individuals stole prey (Fiddler Crab *Uca tangeri* and Giant Bloody Cockles *Anadara sentilis)* from Whimbrels and Eurasian Oystercatchers, respectively (Zwarts *et al.* 1990a). Indeed, the Grey Plovers were classed as 'scavengers', though they fed mainly for themselves on polychaetes, and to a lesser extent bivalves and crabs (Engelmoer *et al.* 1984).

Two factors may have accounted for the high densities of these and other shorebirds here: environmental stability and high production of (small) benthic prey. Large falcons were present and took shorebirds (mainly Dunlin) and possibly attacked birds at a sufficient rate to cause the Grey Plovers and other birds to flock.

Night feeding

Night feeding in Grey Plovers is common. As discussed in Chapter 2, Rojas de Azuaje *et al.* (1993) sampled birds in Venezuela and found a high rod:cone ratio and other adaptations in the eyes of Grey Plovers that equip them well for night feeding. On the Tees Estuary, birds foraged on the nocturnally active *Nereis virens* outside their normal feeding areas (Townshend *et al.* 1984). Andy Wood (1986) compared the diurnal and nocturnal territorial behaviour of Grey Plovers on the Tees, using radio telemetry, and found that their night-time activities were at least as important as day-time in terms of feeding time. Feeding territories were used both by day and night, though as mentioned above, other areas were also used at night, possibly in response to extreme weather conditions (notably cold weather). Yet in the South African study area, prey availability did not differ between day and night anywhere, and the territorial birds occupied the richer areas throughout a 24-hour period (Turpie & Hockey 1993). Even on the Great Barrier Reef, Grey Plovers have been observed to feed by day and night (Domm & Recher 1973).

Grey Plovers feed on pasture fields in addition to the coast. Colwell & Dodd

(1997) suggest that Grey Plovers are more likely to use these when it rains and nearer the 'new' moon. This may be because earthworms are more active and/or more visible at such times than on darker nights (also Milson's 1984 study of Northern Lapwings; and Pienkowski *et al.* 1984). There may even be a lunar cycle in invertebrate surface activity (e.g. Thibault & McNeil 1994).

We still have a great deal to learn about the predilection for nocturnal feeding. Prey activity may be higher at night, predation pressure may be lower, and there is less disturbance from people (e.g. Mouritsen 1994). It is not simply the case that birds feed at night because they have to (e.g. during short days in mid-winter), and the interchange between intertidal areas and pastures may yet prove telling.

A few reports focus on the importance of fields. Rottenborn (1996), for instance, studied shorebird flocks on coastal croplands on the eastern shore of Virginia near Chesapeake Bay. He found that substantial numbers of Grey Plovers fed on fields, showing a strong preference for ploughed fields (along with 19 other shorebird species) and avoiding tall grass (>10 cm) vegetated fields (along with 20 other shorebird species!).

EURASIAN GOLDEN PLOVERS

An English writer who is presumably a very good naturalist has lately advocated the opinion . . . that every sentient being is an incarnate fragment of the All Mind; hence the members of a flock act in unison because they are directed by a common intelligence.

R.C. Miller (1921)

Unlike the other tundra plovers, the Eurasian Golden Plover exhibits a strong tendency to feed in flocks in winter. In Britain and Ireland they are found throughout substantial parts of the lowlands, often in association with Northern Lapwings (the two species together are called 'grassland plovers'). Throughout most of their wintering range they feed on agricultural land, and grasslands are preferred. Detailed assessments of distribution and abundance across particular parts of Britain, or the British Isles as a whole, are provided by Fuller & Youngman (1979), Fuller & Lloyd (1981), Fuller (1986), Kirby and Lack (1993) and Gillings & Fuller (1996).

Preferences for lowland pasture

A common thread running through studies of over-wintering Eurasian Golden Plovers is a marked preference for pastures in winter. These show a particularly strong preference for 'permanent' pastures, some of which may not have been ploughed in over 100 years. Furthermore, there appears to be a preference for feeding in large fields; Barnard and Thompson (1985) rarely saw golden plovers in fields smaller than 4 ha (Fig. 11.1). These older pastures have a higher abundance of earthworm prey than fields ploughed in the last 4–5 years, and arable. Yet in the autumn and early spring golden plovers spend more time in cereal fields. There they are much more cryptic, and during milder weather at these times their energy

PLATE 52. *Juvenile Eurasian Golden Plover ringed and released at Giske Bird Observatory, western coast of Norway. (Jan Rabben)*

requirements are lower and prey are nearer the ground surface. Curiously though, Gregory (1987) found a preference for winter cereal fields in mid-winter. He found that short sward vegetation tended to be preferred (as did Barnard and Thompson 1985), presumably because prey are more readily seen in closely grazed fields. Simon Gillings and Rob Fuller (pers. obs.) of the British Trust for Ornithology have been studying Eurasian Golden Plovers and Northern Lapwings on arable farmland in East Anglia. The flocks there have been massive and usually dominated by Eurasian Golden Plovers (76%–98% of individuals). For instance, on 15 December 1996 they observed a flock of 2500 goldies and 300 lapwings on sugarbeet stubble.

The general preference for older pastures is also observed in France, Netherlands, and Germany and similar to that described on the breeding grounds (Chapter 7). Thompson (1984) found that earthworm prey were more patchy but predictable in old pastures, and birds achieved significantly higher rates of energy intake in these compared with young pastures. As we shall see in Chapter 14, agricultural pastureland, and in particular permanent grasslands, are among the most vulnerable habitats in Britain. These habitats sustain grassland plovers throughout the winter, particularly during periods of cold weather. If conditions are very frosty, or snow cover lasts more than several days, then the birds will move temporarily to more sheltered wintering grounds (e.g. Fuller 1986; Kirby & Lack 1993; Gillings & Fuller 1996).

PLATE 53.   *Pasture complex used occasionally by Eurasian Golden Plovers in winter and spring, in Culrain, North Scotland. Much of the surrounding moorland has been afforested since the 1960s. (DBAT)*

Gulls and plovers: mixed-species flocks

In 1985 Chris Barnard & DBAT produced *Gulls and Plovers: the Ecology and Behaviour of Mixed-Species Feeding Groups,* which presents a detailed account of the complex associations between grassland plovers and Black-headed Gulls on farmland in the English Midlands. We summarize the key points relating to Eurasian Golden Plovers arising from that study (see also Barnard *et al.* 1982; Thompson 1983a, 1984, 1986; Thompson & Barnard 1983, 1984; Thompson & Lendrem 1985).

Where to feed? Eurasian Golden Plovers virtually always fed in mixed species flocks with Northern Lapwings. Indeed they appeared to use lapwings as a guide to where to feed. Despite day-to-day variation in the location of the richest areas of earthworms within fields, lapwings somehow managed to land on the best parts of the field. Golden plovers then joined them, tending to land where the local density of lapwings was highest. As the lapwings were concentrated where earthworms were abundant, golden plovers initially landed on good feeding patches. This marked preference for feeding with lapwings has been remarked on by most of the workers mentioned above, as well as by those who have carried out more detailed studies of plover behaviour within flocks (e.g. Källander 1977; McLennan 1979; Cramp & Simmons 1983). Fuller & Youngman (1979) found few single-species golden plover flocks and these were in only one out of their six study winter ranges (evidently

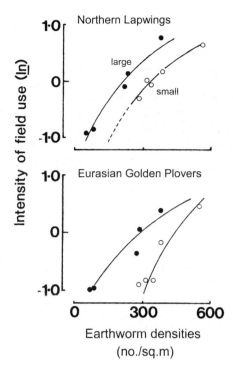

FIG. 11.1. *Relationship between pasture earthworm density and intensity of pasture use by Eurasian Golden Plovers. Large (>4.0 ha, ●) and small (≤ 4.0 ha, ○) fields are compared (other details in Thompson, 1994).*

because Lapwings sometimes failed to return after prolonged cold weather movements). On coastal areas, however, golden plovers sometimes feed without lapwings on mudflats and saltmarsh areas. In arable fields, in autumn, it is not so unusual to see large flocks of golden plovers without Lapwings.

Food intake and interference While feeding, the golden plovers had to balance benefits against the costs. Within flocks, both species tended to move into areas where companions had just taken bill-lengthed earthworms. Moreover, they achieved highest rates of energy intake when the overall density of grassland plovers, rather than just golden plovers, was high. As you watch a flock of plovers in a field you cannot help but form the impression that the birds' movements are geared to the rate at which surface earthworm density replenishes. In this respect there are some parallels with the feeding behaviour of territorial Grey Plovers.

Inter-specific and intra-specific aggression was observed. There were 'chases' with one bird being displaced by another, and 'food thefts' where worms were taken, typically as the victim was pulling it out of the ground. Only 11% and 9% of observed attacks against lapwings and conspecifics, respectively, were connected with food stealing. Following relatively cold nights, or during cold days, rates of inter-specific aggression were high, presumably reflecting higher priorities for feeding on earthworms (which were deeper in the turf then). Golden plovers were more likely to attack lapwings when their own densities were highest, presumably reflecting strong competition (lapwings took slightly larger earthworms than golden plovers). Neighbour–neighbour distances of around 1 m on pastures seemed to be crucial in determining aggression; birds closer together than 1 m were more likely to attack one another.

So, although the golden plovers tended to gravitate towards areas with high earthworm densities, they could pay a cost if they fed too close together. In flocks of grassland plovers, lapwings attacked golden plovers around five times more frequently than *vice-versa*. Recent field and theoretical studies have taken a particular interest in relationships between energy intake and population density, and the different forms of any interference (e.g. Dolman and Sutherland 1997). For winter flocks of grassland plovers, a series of experiments and detailed observations revealed that prey depletion was not a significant factor; depression of earthworm availability through birds feeding at high density did not seem to occur; but birds were more likely to 'area copy' one another at high density (i.e. they moved towards an area where a companion has just foraged successfully), and therefore interfered with one another's searching and feeding. Golden plovers even showed more of a tendency to move towards nearby companions when they were handling bill-sized rather than small or less profitable large worms.

There were interesting differences in the types of flocks observed in fields. Whereas around one third of lapwing flocks tended to oscillate in equilibrium, with birds coming and going at similar overall rates (thus keeping the flock fairly constant in size), only around 3% of golden plover flocks were maintained in this way, with almost 90% being variable in size throughout the day.

Food stealing gulls Many of the mixed species flocks were joined by Black-headed Gulls, and some large flocks had 40–50 gulls, each attempting to steal large earthworms (at which the adults were more adept than immatures, Hesp & Barnard 1989). Gulls joined approximately 15% of flocks with lapwings and 30% with golden plovers. Intriguingly, gulls often arrived in flocks with golden plovers, having joined them in pre-feeding assemblies. Perhaps they exploited the ability of golden plovers to find those lapwing flocks on rich food patches?

Once in the flock, golden plovers fared better than lapwings against gulls (Thompson & Lendrem 1985; Thompson 1986); whereas on average 72% of gull attacks launched at lapwings were successful, only 38% of attacks at golden plovers were successful. Table 14 shows that there seem to be broad similarities in these success rates across different areas (in Barnard & Thompson's Midlands study area by the mid-1980s few flocks contained golden plovers). Golden plovers fared better than lapwings largely because they were faster and more manoeuvrable. However, lapwings did tend to spend longer 'crouching' and then handling earthworms, so were more susceptible to undetected gull attacks.

There was even a benefit to plovers in having these marauding gulls, because gulls appeared to provide them with early warning of alarm. When there was disturbance and the gulls rose, the grassland plovers tended to rise; if the gulls stayed put then so did the plovers. In small fields, where predators can approach from cover more rapidly, birds were more likely to rise in response to disturbance, with golden plovers being particularly wary. Even in grassland plover flocks golden plovers took off after lapwings, suggesting that even lapwings served as early warners.

This study of grassland plovers has revealed how the behaviour of each species is affected markedly by variations in flock size and species composition. Naturally, a range of other environmental factors also influence the formation and behaviour of flocks, not least earthworm density, temperature, day length and field size. Within these dynamic associations, the plovers struggle to meet their energy demands, avoid predators and get what they can out of the gull pirates.

PACIFIC GOLDEN PLOVERS

The wintering population was composed of territorial and non-territorial birds in approximately equal proportions.

Oscar and Patricia Johnson, and Philip Bruner (1981b) announcing the beginnings of their comprehensive study of Pacific Golden Plovers on the island of Ohu, Hawaii in August 1979.

Again, we find some striking differences between the Pacific Golden Plovers and the other tundra plovers in the non-breeding season. Most of our knowledge comes from work by Oscar Johnson and colleagues who have worked in Hawaii (e.g. Johnson *et al.* 1981a,b, 1989; Johnson & Connors 1996). Their work has shown that the non-breeding grounds are extremely varied with a variety of coastal and inland habitats occupied, not least grassy fringes around airports, cemeteries, residential lawns, golf courses, roadside verges, clearings in heavily wooded areas, and even flat roofs (for nocturnal roosting, and day-time loafing and preening). The plovers even occupy grasslands up to an altitude of 2500 m asl, and appear to have expanded their range on Hawaii as a result of extensive forest clearance. However, in other parts of their range a preference for coastal habitats is more apparent (Chapter 10; e.g. Marchant & Higgins 1993; Rohweder & Baverstock 1996). Domm & Recher (1973) mention that they feed on 'reef crests', consisting of boulder tracts, on One Tree Island in the Great Barrier Reef complex, where they take crabs, gastropods and small crustaceans. In Eastern Polynesia the majority of birds fed on beaches, reefs and coastal saltings/shore pastures, though some were on mountain grasslands (up to 800 m asl); they also occupied marshes and root vegetable fields there (Holyoak & Thibault 1984).

As in Grey Plovers, aggression and displays involved in the establishment and defence of territories occur more frequently in early autumn as the territories are being established. Johnson & Connors (1996) describe four behaviours, from least to most aggressive, used at territorial boundaries (similar to behaviour in the breeding season, see Chapter 8): (a) 'confrontational challenge', when birds watch one another at distances of less than 1 m, and alternately stand then walk with slow, deliberate actions; (b) 'parallel marching' which can switch with the previous behaviour; (c) 'crouch-running' at intruders, with the head down and back feathers ruffled while attempting to peck at its opponent; and (d) 'contact fights' in which the birds peck at each other, sometimes on the ground, but usually while fluttering or during brief, erratic and sometimes violent flights. These confrontations go on,

PLATE 54.   *Wintering Pacific Golden Plover among breeding Laysan Albatrosses, Hawaii. (Bryan Sage)*

notably during (c) and (d), and can persist for up to 3 h. Territories are held by male and female adults and juveniles, with males appearing to predominate over the choicest habitats (notably lawns). Birds are highly faithful to territories between years, and throughout the winter they quit them only to roost at night. Interestingly, non-territorial birds are also site-faithful to the same communal grounds (Johnson & Connors 1996), and sometimes substantial aggregations of birds may form on areas safe from disturbance.

Unlike Grey Plovers in the southern hemisphere, the Pacific Golden Plovers in Hawaii do not appear to share their territories readily with other species, and will frequently attack them (Johnson & Connors 1996). In New South Wales, Australia, Rohweder & Baverstock (1996) studied Pacific Golden Plovers on the Richmond River Estuary. There, Pacific Golden Plovers fed with numerous species of shorebirds, and fed on mudflats and ocean beaches (feeding at high densities on moist sandy mudflats at night). Interestingly, Rohweder & Baverstock found a tendency for more plovers to be present on mudflats during night-time 'quarter moons', suggesting that light *per se* is not a limiting factor in controlling nocturnal habitat use (though there was an artificial light from a nearby township). Rohweder (1996) gives details of a more intensive comparison of habitat use and foraging behaviour of Pacific Golden Plovers during day and night. He found that during the day they tended to feed on polychaetes in muddy or seagrass sites, but at night they tended to move to sandier sites to feed on larger (more active) prey, particularly soldier crabs *Mictyris longicarpus*. Higher densities of plovers occurred on those mudflats at night which received artificial light from urban areas. Intriguingly, the use of radio telemetry revealed differences in roost-use between day and night.

There do indeed appear to be very marked similarities between the over-winter behaviour of Pacific Golden Plovers and Grey Plovers.

AMERICAN GOLDEN PLOVERS

Their emphasis on territoriality in uplands produced a relatively even population dispersion over the entire set of suitable grasslands at Ea. Medaland.

Pete and Lois Myers (1979) writing about their seventeen month study of shorebirds near Buenos Aires, Argentina.

Of the tundra plovers, we know least about the American Golden Plover in its non-breeding grounds. Rather like the Eurasian Golden Plover, it shows a preference for grasslands over intertidal habitats – both during migration (Hicklin 1987; Rottenborn 1996) and on their wintering grounds (e.g. Myers & Myers 1979; Johnson & Connors 1996). The majority over-winter on the grassy, treeless plains of eastern (central) Argentina, Uruguay and South Brazil. Some over-winter on the coast, towards the north of their wintering range, but these are in the minority (e.g.

PLATE 55. *Pampas south of Buenos Aires used by wintering American Golden Plovers. (Jan Rabben)*

Morrison & Ross 1989). According to Dabbene (1920) they prefer open grasslands with sparse grass, especially in places with small pools, lakes and marshes.

American Golden Plovers appear to be predominantly territorial on their non-breeding grounds in South America (e.g. Myers & Myers 1979; Myers *et al.* 1979). Territories are held on grasslands and by long streams, each with an extent of up to 0.3 ha. Myers & Myers (1979) describe how territorial and non-territorial birds formed large flocks of 100–300 birds wheeling between foraging areas and wetlands for daily, mid-afternoon bouts of drinking and bathing. Myers *et al.* (1979) describe what little is known about territorial interactions, including 'parallel marching' – rather similar to that described in Pacific Golden Plovers above and in the breeding season (Chapter 8). Both Myers & McCafferty (1984) and Wishart *et al.* (1981) mention inter-specific interactions between American Golden Plovers and Grey Plovers, which the latter won.

There are exciting prospects for undertaking a detailed study of the American Golden Plover in South America, not least to determine factors influencing territorial behaviour. In some ways this bird is reminiscent of Eurasian Golden Plovers flocking on rough grasslands – but it is territorial!

TERRITORIAL VERSUS NON-TERRITORIAL BEHAVIOUR: SOME OBSERVATIONS

Why defend territories?

The differences in the extent of territoriality in the non-breeding tundra plovers intrigues us. It is particularly puzzling why Eurasian Golden Plovers are not territorial. Studies of shorebirds in the non-breeding season have found a fairly consistent pattern of territoriality: some individuals are territorial and others are not (e.g. Myers & Myers 1979; Myers *et al.* 1979, 1981; Townshend 1985; Turpie 1995; Piersma & Wiersma 1996). In their reviews of territoriality in non-breeding shorebirds, Myers *et al.* (1979) and Myers (1983, 1984) pointed out that shorebirds: (a) tend to abandon territories when predation risk increases; (b) may be 'practising' for breeding season territorial defence (though species with male-defence mating systems can also be territorial in winter); and (c) may be behaving in a non-adaptive way as a carry-over from the breeding season (though juveniles and females, which do not defend territories on the breeding grounds, subsequently defend them on their wintering grounds). The most likely explanation for territorial behaviour is that there is a net energy gain to defending a territory.

Myers (1983, 1984) critically assessed these suggestions and others. He pointed out that territories tend to be defended at intermediate resource levels, with defence disappearing when food is scarce or abundant. Many studies support this. He pointed out that predation risk is probably one of the threats to territorial defence, and that territoriality is more common in non-tidal areas (or in tidal sites with relatively little movement of the waterline). Townshend *et al.* (1984) argued that territorial behaviour in Grey Plovers might mediate in the regulation of local population sizes. In other words, with the establishment of territories in autumn, and the subsequent prevention of settlement by juveniles arriving slightly later, juvenile mortality might increase.

However, there are few studies of shorebirds which have critically assessed the costs and benefits of territorial behaviour, not least in relation to winter survival and short-term versus long-term benefits. Jane Turpie's (1995) study of Grey Plovers is important because she was able to conclude that territorial birds do indeed occupy richer areas both by day and night, and achieved higher energy intake rates than non-territorial birds. She found that non-territorial birds indulged in more aggressive encounters. Oddly though, it was not the case that all early arriving birds took up territories (which could have conferred an advantage on birds which leave their breeding grounds first). Instead, some late arrivals ousted established territory owners. Turpie (1995) suggested that territory establishment was dependent on an individual's competitive ability; territories were not considered to be limiting.

Why do Eurasian Golden Plovers not defend territories?

Eurasian Golden Plovers seem to derive many benefits from feeding in flocks (notably with lapwings). Yet Barnard and Thompson's work on gulls and grassland plovers revealed a highly predictable element in the earthworm populations in pastures. Moreover, some grassland plovers were highly faithful to particular fields, and to particular parts of fields. Whereas some lapwings in small fields (where predation risk was highest) were possibly territorial (Thompson 1984) neither they nor golden plovers were observed to be territorial in larger fields.

Given that golden plover populations on the wintering grounds fluctuate in response to harsh weather conditions, notably in their north-western wintering grounds, there may be little advantage to establishing territories which might later be abandoned and then difficult to acquire again. The flocks themselves can be quite labile to the extent that there is a high turnover of individuals, though Parr's (1980) and Whittingham's (1996a) studies do not suggest this, at least in late winter.

On the more southern wintering grounds (such as in the southern part of the Iberian Peninsula or northern Africa), we would not be surprised if Eurasian Golden Plovers defend territories throughout the winter, particularly where predation pressure is low. In this context, it is of course tempting to reach the simple conclusion that the more northern wintering quarters of Eurasian Golden Plovers, compared with the other tundra plovers, have higher predation pressure (and periodic spells of harsh weather, when the birds quit temporarily), giving rise to tendencies to flock rather than defend territories.

SPENDING THE WINTER IN THE SOUTH COMPARED WITH THE NORTH

While there is a massive literature on shorebird migration, one simple question still begs a clear answer: why do some birds fly farther south than others? There seem to be at least three possible answers related to food resource distribution (also Chapter 10).

Competition for food

There is more competition for food on the more northern coastal non-breeding grounds, so some birds have to move farther afield. It has been suggested that one consequence of this is that subordinate juveniles are forced south (e.g. Myers 1981; Pienkowski *et al.* 1985; Evans & Townshend 1988). However, several studies are beginning to refute this (e.g. see Meltofte 1996).

More food in the south?

Perhaps food resources are actually greater in the south. Kalejta & Hockey (1994) found that invertebrate production estimates declined with distance south from the equator (see also Moreira 1997). Furthermore, Grey Plovers in the South African Zwartkops Estuary met their energy demands with 'relative ease' (Turpie & Hockey 1996). Energy intake rates there were high compared with those recorded on more temperate estuaries. Indeed, foraging densities of Grey Plovers were higher on the Zwartkops Estuary during the austral 'summer' than recorded anywhere in the northern hemisphere at the same time (Turpie & Hockey 1996).

Juvenile mortality in the north

There may be differences between adult and juvenile mortality. If mortality is density-dependent on the non-breeding grounds (e.g. Goss-Custard & Sutherland 1997), and higher in more temperate areas, then there would be an advantage to individuals travelling south. We know of no data supporting or refuting this for tundra plovers. However, the chances of harsh weather (and some prey being out of reach) is greater in the north (e.g. Piersma 1987) and this may well contribute to more mortality there. If competition on the winter grounds is an important factor limiting the dispersion of shorebirds, then territorial species should perhaps exhibit the greatest span of north–south distribution. On the other hand, it may simply be the case that birds breeding farthest north leave their breeding grounds last (Chapter 10) and are compelled to over-shoot their northern winter range (because birds are already present) for the south.

   If there is more density-dependent winter mortality in juveniles towards the north in winter we might expect two outcomes. First, southern breeding populations will display more irregular year-to-year fluctuation in populations size (due to variability in numbers of juveniles and weaker adults returning to breed). Second, northern breeding populations should remain relatively large, so long as local conditions during migration are not harsh.

SUMMARY

1.   Tundra plovers spend most their lives on their non-breeding grounds. Of the four species, only the Eurasian Golden Plover appears not to be territorial.
2.   Grey Plover non-breeding populations have territorial and non-territorial individuals, with the latter consisting of relatively more females and juveniles.

Territorial encounters tend to decline during the winter period, and non-territorial birds tend to spend more time feeding than territorial ones. Night feeding is common, and territories can be defended at night as well.

3. Eurasian Golden Plovers feed in flocks on pasture fields, though in milder weather they prefer arable. Single species flocks are not common. Benefits of flocking include greater feeding efficiency and earlier warning of danger. Many flocks are attended by kleptoparasitic gulls which steal a small fraction of the plovers' prey and appear to act as sentinels.

4. Both Pacific and American golden plovers defend territories on their non-breeding grounds, with the Pacific Golden Plover showing a more marked tendency to feed on the coast. Detailed work on Pacific Golden Plovers on Hawaii has found them occupying a range of grasslands, where males appear to hold territories over the best habitats. Both territorial and non-territorial birds appear to be site faithful.

5. There are many affinities in the non-breeding behaviour of Grey Plovers and Pacific Golden Plovers.

6. We can find no evidence indicating disadvantages to tundra plovers over-wintering in the south compared with more northern areas (notably in Grey Plovers). Critical, cost-benefit studies of territorial behaviour are needed, notably those which measure adult and juvenile survival.

CHAPTER 12
Diet: Food and Feeding

Eurasian Golden Plover feeding on Crowberries

I am of a constitution so general, that it consorts and sympathiseth with all things. I have no antipathy, or rather idiosyncrasy, in diet, humour, air, anything.

Sir Thomas Browne (1605–1682) in *Religio Medici* (1643)

W HAT an animal eats tells us a great deal about its behaviour, ecology and evolution. In this chapter we develop some of our comparisons between the tundra plovers by focusing on their diet. We have already commented on their feeding habits (notably in Chapters 2, 6 and 11), but not so much on their food.

METHODOLOGICAL ISSUES

The logical place to begin a study of diet is to examine the stomach contents. The method is a reasonably good one, provided efforts are made to reduce biases. The stomach contents are constantly grinded and digested. Soft items are digested more quickly than hard items. For instance, insect larvae can disappear in minutes, while insect cuticula may persist for hours (e.g. Custer & Pitelka 1975). Food items in the stomach continue to dissolve after a bird is dead (Koersveld 1951), i.e. 'post mortem digestion'. Stomach samples therefore tend to under-represent soft items. Quantification as well as identification of prey is often done on micro-structures, such as mouth parts, legs, corners of elytrae, etc. A minimum number for each prey taxon can be obtained from each stomach by counting the structure of a taxon which occurs in highest number. For certain prey classes, such as earthworms, quantification on the basis of stomach material (by number of prey) is virtually impossible. On the other hand, Diptera larvae reveal their presence, even in much dissolved stomach contents, by their chitinized spiracle openings, appearing as microscopic doughnuts (each larva has two of them).

Identification from small fragments poses special problems, as ordinary identification keys cannot be used. The necessary optical aids and an extensive 'key' of comparable material of possible prey taxa must be at hand. Initial assistance from persons with a first hand knowledge of the important taxa is of invaluable help in familiarizing oneself with the various microstructures of insect and other prey remains!

One way to stop the disintegration of food items is to flush formalin solution down the oesophagus of newly shot birds. Yet some of the food items have already been in the alimentary canal for a while and are thus affected by digestion. An unbiased sample can be obtained only from the oesophagus, where no digestion has taken place and the material is less disintegrated. However, the oesophagus contains a very limited number of prey items, often only one or two at the most. Thus, a large number of birds have to be killed in order to yield a sufficient sample of food items, making this oesophageal method impractical to use. Sometimes, the disintegration rate of various items can be estimated from oesophageal contents compared with stomach contents. Alternatively, examination of birds killed after controlled feeding in captivity can provide estimates of digestion rates (Goss-Custard 1969; Custer & Pitelka 1975), and these can help correct biases in food analyses based on stomach samples.

Stomach and oesophagus examinations in the classical manner destroys the birds, a clear disadvantage. A non-destructive method is to examine faecal dropping contents. These are severely disintegrated, and many of the fragments are too tiny for accurate identification. However, in an insectivorous passerine, the Skylark, faecal samples of nestlings yielded results comparable with unbiased samples from the nestlings' gapes (Poulsen & Aebischer 1995). Another non-destructive method is actually to observe what the birds are eating. This method is used in studies of intake rates (e.g. Pienkowski 1983; Barnard & Thompson 1985). However, prey taxa can be correctly identified only under good observation conditions (good light, short distance, and good telescope) and small items may not be identified, or may even be mis-identified.

There are also various ways to quantify the information on diet, such as the commonly used 'constancy' (% of samples, e.g. stomachs, containing an item), % by numbers (based on estimated number of individual prey), % by volume (measured), % by estimated dry or wet mass, or even energy content. All of these methods have been employed in studies of tundra plover foods. They convey different information of the relative importance of the various food items, and the measures are not always readily comparable. For example, small seeds may be numerous in the diet of a bird but comprise a tiny fraction of the diet in terms of mass or volume; and the biomass of a few earthworms may totally overshadow that of a large number of insects. Often, biomass, volume or energy content are the preferred units used to express the importance of foods. In order to obtain such measures, the numbers of prey of different classes must be determined, and for these measurements are made on intact prey in order to convert the numbers into the mass, volume or energetic contents they represent in the diet. This typically involves breaking the identification down to the lowest possible taxonomic level, preferably that of species. For some prey classes, however, such as insect larvae and earthworms, individual sizes must be estimated first before conversion to biomass, or biovolume can be carried out.

As we browsed the literature for information on food of tundra plovers, we encountered most of the sampling and analytical issues mentioned above! Nevertheless, in order to present an outline of diet, we arbitrarily considered proportions of 20% of the number of items in a sample, 20% biomass, or 20% biovolume as a 'major proportion' of the food. Hence, studies showing a given food class to constitute more or less than 20% of the diet are shown in Fig. 12.1.

INSECTS AND BERRIES IN THE BREEDING SEASON

Throughout most of their breeding range tundra plovers arrive in spring to a more or less winter landscape. Low temperatures keep insect activity to a minimum. Marine and freshwater mudflats are frozen over. Indeed, much of the ground may not even be available for food searching as it is covered by snow. However, over much of the arctic and northern montane tundras a rich resource of berries is available. Most common are crowberries (*Empetrum* spp.), often occurring in dense stands on mounds and ridges – places which emerge first from the snow. As they are

---

FIG. 12.1 (opposite). *Food classes of tundra plovers reported as important (≥ 20% by biovolume, biomass, number of items, or number of stomachs) and less important (<20%) in various quantitative studies. Also included are a few 'semiquantitative' studies, in which the relative amount of food classes were given anecdotally ('major food', 'less important food', etc.), food classes stated to be 'important' were included in the ≥20% category. In studies giving no statement about importance, all food classes are in the <20% class. Number of studies are indicated in parenthesis. 'Non-annelid w.' denote Non-annelid worms (Priapulids, Nemeritini).*
Sources [b=breeding; n=non-breeding; G=Grey Plover, E=Eurasian Golden Plover, P=Pacific Golden Plover, A=American Golden Plover; note: one source may report several studies]: Andreeva (1989) [Eb]; Baker (1974) [Gn], (1977) [Ab]; Belopol'skij et al. (1970) [Gn]; Bengtson et al. (1979) [Eb]; Bent (1929) [Gn, Abn, Pn]; Boehm (1964); cited from Glutz von Blotzheim et al. (1975) [Gn]; Brooks (1967) [An]; Burton (1974) [Gn, En]; Byrkjedal (1978c) [En]; Byrkjedal (1980a) [Eb]; Byrkjedal (unpublished: 9 faeces, saltmarsh, Churchill, Manitoba, 10–17 July, 48 prey consisted of 65% (by numbers) ad. Coleoptera, 13% ad Tipulidae, 13% small Nematocera, 6% insect larvae, 4% araneae; method as Byrkjedal 1989c) [Ab]; Campbell (1935) [En], (1936) [En], (1946) [En]; Collett (1894) [Gn]; Dabbene (1920) [An]; Danilov et al. (1984) [Gb, Eb]; Dement'ev & Gladkov (1951) [Gn, En, Pn]; Domm & Recher (1973) [Pn]; Downie et al. 1996 [Eb]; Dugan (1982) [Gn]; Durell et al. (1990) [Gn]; Engelmoer et al. (1984) [Gn]; Fennell (1965) cited from Glutz von Blotzheim (1975) [Gn]; Garðarsson & Nielsen (1989) [En]; Glutz von Blotzheim et al. (1975) [Gb]; Goss-Custard et al. (1977) [Gn]; Groppali (1992) [En]; Hanson et al. (1956) [Gb]; Hicklin & Smith (1979) [Gn]; Höfmann & Hoerschelmann (1969) [Gn, En]; Holyoak & Thibault (1984) [Pn]; Johnson & Connors (1996) [Pn]; Kalejta & Hockey (1994) [Gn]; Kersten & Piersma (1984) [Gn]; Kistjakovski (1957) cited from Glutz von Blotzheim et al. (1975) [Gn]; Kondrat'ev 1982 [Gb]; Kovačević & Danon (1959) and Cvitanić & Novak (1966) cited from Cramp & Simmons (1983) [En]; Kretchmar et al. (1991) [Gn]; Kumari (1953) [Ebn]; Kumari (1958) [Eb]; Labutin et al. (1988) [Pn]; Lane (1987) [Pn]; Lange (1968) cited from Glutz von Blotzheim et al. (1975) [Gn]; Marks (1993) [Pn]; McGregor (1902) [Pn]; Musacchia (1953) [Ab]; Norlin (1965) [Gn]; Payne & Howe (1976) [Gn]; Pienkowski (1978/79) [Gn]; Pienkowski (1981) [Gn]; Pienkowski et al. (1984) [Gn]; Portenko (1972) [Gb]; Preble (1923) [Pn]; Ratcliffe (1976) [Ebn]; Recher (1966) [Gn]; Rohweder (1996) [Pn]; Schneider (1985) [Gn]; Schneider & Harrington (1981) [Gn]; Sutton (1932) [Ab]; Thompson & Barnard (1984) [En]; Turpie & Hockey 1997 [Gn]; Warnock (1989) [Gn]; Wishart et al. (1981) [Gn, An]; Witherby et al. (1940) [Abn, Pn]; Zwarts et al. (1990a) [Gn].

frequently frozen, and then snow-covered just when they are fully ripe in the autumn, these berries hold an astonishingly high quality in spring. Newly thawed-out they are delicious to eat, even for humans, although after a few days' exposure to wind and sun they shrink and dry up.

Berries in early spring, and throughout the breeding season

Crowberries have been found in the diet of all four tundra plovers on their breeding grounds. Only in Eurasian Golden Plover, however, have quantitative food

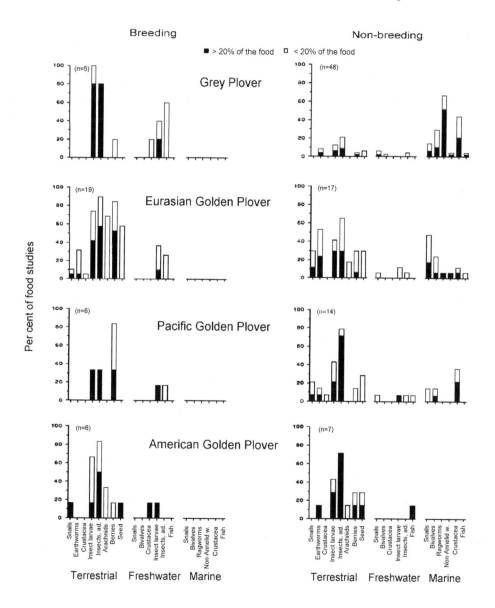

studies been carried out early enough in the year. At Hardangervidda, crowberries make up about one third of the diet (in terms of both number of food items taken and estimated dry weight) of Eurasian Golden Plovers after their arrival, during territory establishment and pairing-up (Byrkjedal 1980a); a similar proportion (by volume) was found on the subarctic tundra at Yamal (Andreeva 1989). Berries other than *Empetrum* may be important, depending on availability. For instance, on raised bogs in Estonia after their spring arrival Eurasian Golden Plovers feed extensively on craneberries (*Oxycoccus* sp.) (Kumari 1953, 1958). In Siberia, cloudberries (*Rubus chamaemorus*) are sometimes found in stomachs of Grey Plovers and Pacific Golden Plovers (Kondrat'ev 1982).

Presumably berries provide a rich source of carbohydrates which may help the birds maintain a high activity level after arrival, even though their body resources may be depleted after the spring migration. Furthermore, by growing in high densities, berries can provide ample food, as the bird can fill its stomach quickly without having to perform costly and time-consuming searches. Berries are undoubtedly much sought by these plovers. At Hardangervidda, Eurasian Golden Plovers start to harvest the new and unripe crowberries around mid-summer. At this time the berries are still green and hard. From then on, they make up between a fifth to more than half of the diet of breeding Eurasian Golden Plovers (Kumari 1953, 1958; Byrkjedal 1980a; Andreeva 1989).

Records of berry-eating in Grey Plover, and American and Pacific Golden Plovers, however, have been made chiefly from the latter part of the breeding season (Bent 1929; Witherby *et al.* 1940; Kondrat'ev 1982). As well as Eurasian Golden Plovers, they continue to include berries in their diet as they encounter berry-rich areas on their southbound autumn migration, especially just south of their breeding grounds (Bent 1929; Belopol'skij *et al.* 1970; Byrkjedal 1978c; Garðarsson & Nielsen 1989).

Earthworms

Despite the importance of berries, the staple food of tundra plovers during the breeding season consists of insects and their larvae, and earthworms where available. Earthworms are most in evidence for Eurasian Golden Plovers breeding near farmland, such as in the British Isles and Iceland (e.g. Ratcliffe 1976; Bengtson *et al.* 1976; Thompson 1984; Downie *et al.* 1996; Whittingham 1996a). Earthworms are large prey and, being without a chitinized cuticula, offer much digestible matter. In terms of both biomass and volume, earthworms make up a dominant portion of the diet, whenever they are available. Nevertheless, their importance in the diet is probably underestimated in most studies, due to the problems of counting such worms in stomachs containing more or less dissolved material. Arthropods in stomach samples are much easier to quantify.

Problems with finding earthworms in stomach samples may explain their absence from most studies of tundra plover diet during the breeding season. In studies where special care has been taken to stop post mortem digestion, earthworms have been found in the diet of Eurasian Golden Plover even on the subarctic tundra (Andreeva 1989). Downie *et al.* (1996) compared faecal and pellet samples of Eurasian Golden Plovers feeding on bogs and pastures in N. Scotland. Earthworms (chetae remains) were recorded in 31% of bog samples but 81% of pasture samples. Admittedly though, parts of the bog samples may well have derived from pasture feeding, particularly in April and May. Pacific Golden Plovers at Yamal (subarctic) have been seen to pull up earthworms from the tundra (IB pers. obs.), and freshwater oligochaete worms were found in stomachs of Pacific Golden Plovers breeding at Lower Kolyma, where they were thought to play a more important role in the diet of these birds than could be demonstrated by stomach samples (Khlebosolov 1983). Interestingly, oligochaete worms have not been recorded in stomach samples from any other of its breeding grounds (Fig. 12.1).

Beetles

Of the insects taken by tundra plovers on the breeding grounds, adult beetles, notably carabids and weevils, and to some extent also byrrhids, are well represented. Among the carabid beetles available, the Eurasian Golden Plovers at Hardangervidda seemed to prefer the large *Carabus problematicus* (ca. 2 cm long) over smaller (ca. 1 cm long or smaller) species (Byrkjedal 1980a). Yet, the smaller species were more numerous in the golden plovers' diet (notably *Patrobus* spp.), as they occurred much more commonly in the area.

Being very heavily chitinized, beetles, notably byrrhids and weevils, are probably over-represented in stomach or faecal samples. At Hardangervidda, weevils made up 10–50% by numbers in the diet of Eurasian Golden Plovers (Byrkjedal 1980a). Downie *et al.* (1996) recorded a high prevalence of chrysomelid beetles (*Plateumaris discolor*) in the faecal and pellet samples of birds collected on bogs (51% of samples) and pastures (12% of samples). These chrysomelids have been found to be prevalent in faecal and pellet contents of Greenshanks (Nethersole-Thompson & Nethersole-Thompson 1979; Downie *et al.* in press). They are leaf beetles and tend to be attached to *Eriophorum* spp., rather than in the ground or in water. In pastures, the main beetles taken were dung beetles (Scarabaeidae), weevils (Curculionidae) and click beetles (Elateridaei). Of course, pellet and faecal samples are biased towards these hard beetles, but their importance should not be underestimated.

Tipulids: one and two year life cycles

Diptera: Nematocera (mosquitoes, chironomids, tipulids) occur in profusion in the tundra, and are well represented in tundra plovers' diet. However, adults of these insects may occur only during relatively short periods after their hatch. Thus, at Hardangervidda Eurasian Golden Plovers take adult tipulids after mid-summer (Byrkjedal 1980a). However, in Britain, adult tipulids are taken throughout May and the first half of June (e.g. Whittingham 1996a). Tipulids are probably preferable to the smaller nematocerans, but the latter can occur in quite high numbers in the diet of both Eurasian (16% by numbers, Bengtson *et al.* 1976) and American (13% by numbers in 9 faecal samples, Churchill, Manitoba) Golden Plovers, apparently as a result of their enormous abundance on the tundra.

However, it is first and foremost the larvae which make dipterans such a valuable food for these plovers on the tundra. Frequently dipteran larvae make up >20%, sometimes even >50% of the diet, by items, dry weight or volume

(Baker 1977; Byrkjedal 1980a; Kondrat'ev 1982; Andreeva 1989). Diptera larvae in alpine and arctic areas can take more than a year to develop into adult insects (Armitage *et al.* 1995). So, more than one larval generation tends to occur simultaneously, which means that the food resource does not vanish when the insects hatch. On some of the mountain tops in Scotland, the tipulids (*Tipula montana*) hatch on a two-year cycle, and this is reflected in the diet of the Eurasian Dotterel (Galbraith *et al.* 1993; Thompson & Brown 1992; Thompson & Whitfield 1993; Holt & Whitfield 1996). Here, on some sites more tipulids are taken in alternate years.

Diptera larvae are nutritionally rich (Armitage *et al.* 1995). While adult coleoptera may contain more than 30% indigestible exoskeleton, diptera larvae are almost totally utilizable by the birds (e.g. Zach & Falls 1978). Considering their energetic content and size, Byrkjedal (1989c) found tipulid larvae at Hardangervidda to be 3–6 times more profitable energetically, prey-for-prey, than adult insects. The Eurasian Golden Plovers feed extensively (ca. 20–50% by items and dry weight) on soil-living tipulid larvae throughout the summer (Byrkjedal 1980a), and these larvae are also important food for all four species on their arctic breeding grounds (Baker 1977; Danilov *et al.* 1984; Kretchmar *et al.* 1991). Yet, in the Arctic, freshwater dipteran larvae (tipulids and especially, chironomids) seem to increase in importance. While such larvae made up only 1–3% or less by numbers in the diet of Eurasian Golden Plovers at Hardangervidda, and on Estonian raised bogs (Byrkjedal 1980a; Kumari 1958), they amounted to 21% by items and 30% by volume in this species feeding on tundra marshes at Yamal (Danilov *et al.* 1984; Andreeva 1989). In Churchill, limnic chironomids and tipulids have been found to represent more than 20% by items in the diet of American Golden Plovers (Baker 1977), and at Wrangel Island, Grey Plover diet contained 12% such larvae (Portenko 1972). At Chukchi Peninsula Pacific Golden Plovers gradually turn to limnic invertebrates (largely dipteran larvae) in the course of the summer, as the ice melts away from waterbodies and wet ground (Kondrat'ev 1982).

Interestingly, in Britain much more adult than larval tipulids are taken, notably *Tipula subnordicornis* (Whittingham 1996a). Whittingham found that the majority of nests in his two study areas hatched in late May/early June when adult tipulids were most numerous. If these tipulids went through a two-year, rather than their typical one-year cycle (Coulson 1988; Coulson *et al.* 1995) many more larvae than adults would be available to the birds. Nevertheless, even in Britain there seem to be differences in the pattern of tipulid emergence. In the north of England the adult emergence is pronounced (Coulson 1988; Whittingham 1996a) but in the blanket bogs of the north of Scotland it is not (Coulson *et al.* 1995; Downie *et al.* 1996), possibly because emerging tipulid species densities are lower and weather conditions are milder (resulting in different emergence periods for the three principal species). As Coulson *et al.* (1995) state '. . . it seems unlikely that it will be possible to explain the exceptional avifauna of the Flows in terms of exceptionally high densities of insect food. Obviously there are adequate numbers of insects to allow the wading birds to breed successfully in most years, but it may be necessary to look to other factors, such as low predation rates to explain richness in bird species.'

Other insects

Sometimes insect larvae other than Diptera play a prominent part in the diet of tundra plovers. On Estonian breeding grounds, Eurasian Golden Plovers had coleopteran larvae in their diet in proportions similar to Diptera larvae found in studies from breeding grounds elsewhere (Kumari 1958). In most studies, caterpillars of Lepidoptera and Hymenoptera are found, but only in small quantities.

Spiders

Spiders, a potential prey class abundant in alpine and arctic regions, are barely taken by tundra plovers. Yet these are much less chitinized and less digestible prey than the frequently taken Coleoptera. In all food studies, spiders are represented in only negligible quantities. At Hardangervidda, spiders were six times more abundant on the mountain heaths than adult Coleoptera, yet their occurrence in the diet of Eurasian Golden Plovers was a fraction (0.006:1 in favour of Coleoptera; Byrkjedal 1980a). Similar results have been found in Britain (e.g. Downie *et al.* 1996; Whittingham 1996a). Presumably, spiders are well protected from avian predation by their agility as well as their crypticity. Furthermore, many of the spiders on mountain and tundra are too small to be of much interest to birds as large as the tundra plovers. In contrast, the opilionid *Mitopus morio*, a fairly slow-moving arachnoid comparable in size to carabids, was taken about 18 times more frequently than spiders by Eurasian Golden Plovers, in spite of being outnumbered 6:1 by spiders on the heaths of Hardangervidda.

WORMS, SMALL CRABS AND MOLLUSCS IN THE NON-BREEDING SEASON

Earthworms

Outside the breeding season, annelid worms become a prime food source for tundra plovers. Frequently, worms totally dominate the recorded diet of these birds. Earthworms tend to be under-represented in stomach samples, yet proportions as high as 70% (estimated dry weight) have been found in stomach samples thought to be highly affected by post mortem digestion (Byrkjedal 1978c). Field observations of feeding birds, however, have suggested that earthworm proportions in the diet can get close to 100% (Payne & Howe 1976; Wishart *et al.* 1981; Barnard *et al.* 1982; Thompson 1983a, 1984; Thompson & Barnard 1984). Indeed, Thompson and Barnard (1984) found that Eurasian Golden Plovers showed a preference for 16–32 mm length earthworms, the size range predicted to be most profitable (in terms of net rate of energy intake). Furthermore, it was this size class of earthworms which declined most over a three-month winter period in two pastures used by flocks of lapwings and golden plovers (some areas were netted to prevent predation, and then comparisons were made between enclosures and exclosures). In the presence of food stealing Black-headed Gulls, the Eurasian

Golden Plovers took smaller earthworms (as predicted, because of the risks attached to large worms being stolen; Chapter 11).

Mudflats: worms and small crabs

The choice of prey, whether earthworms or ragworms (Polychaeta), depends on the birds' use of terrestrial or marine habitats. The most maritime of the four species, the Grey Plover, feeds most consistently on ragworms, which constitute a substantial part of the fauna living in the upper layer of the substrate of muddy coastal flats. Many studies have found the relatively large nereid *Nereis* spp. worms to be the most important non-breeding season food of Grey Plovers in many parts of their range, often constituting more than 75% of the prey items taken (Norlin 1965; Höfmann & Hoerschelmann 1969; Baker 1974; Pienkowski 1978/79; Kersten & Piersma 1984; Durell & Kelly 1990; Kalejta & Hockey 1994). Selection for large worms is reported by Kalejta & Hockey (1994), and even a minor number of the largest ragworms, such as *Arenicola* (Höfmann & Hoerschelmann 1969; Durell & Kelly 1990), may provide a substantial part of the diet in terms of energy contents (Pienkowski *et al.* 1984). In some studies of Grey Plover diet, however, small ragworms (e.g. *Notomastos*) have proven much more important than large worms (Pienkowski 1982; Engelmoer *et al.* 1984). In nine study areas ranging from equatorial east Africa, islands in the western Indian Ocean, to mainland temperate South Africa, Turpie & Hockey (1997) found crustaceans (small crabs *Thalamita macrophthalmus*, *Dotilla* and in some sites mudprawns *Upogebia*) to be more important prey than polycheates (*Murphysa*, *Nereis*), particularly in terms of the birds' net energetic intake.

On migrational stop-over sites inland Grey Plovers may feed extensively on earthworms on arable land (Collett 1894; Wishart *et al.* 1981), as do all three species of golden plovers (e.g. Burton 1974; Thompson & Barnard 1984; Labutin *et al.* 1988). Golden plovers, on the other hand, feeding on coastal mudflats, do not seem to prey upon ragworms to any notable extent; in fact, we have not found any records of ragworms in published diets of American and Pacific golden plovers! One would expect such worms to be taken, especially by the latter, on account of their frequent use of marine shoreline habitats. Recent studies in Australia, not yet published in detail, indicate that Pacific Golden Plovers do prey on ragworms (Rohweder 1996). Surprisingly, the more terrestrial of the golden plovers, the Eurasian, has been found to take some ragworms and similar worms (priapulids) while staging on marine mudflats (Garðarsson & Nielsen (1989). However, the usual food taken by these and evidently also by American and Pacific Golden Plovers, feeding on shoreline habitats, is molluscs, especially littoral snails and to a lesser degree bivalves, and arthropods, notably insects and amphipods (Bent 1929; Kumari 1953; Burton 1974; Ratcliffe 1976; Holyoak & Thibault 1984; Garðarsson & Nielsen 1989; Marks 1993). These food items are also taken by Grey Plovers to a varying extent, and they seem to take more bivalves than do golden plovers (Höfmann & Hoerschelmann 1969; Goss-Custard *et al.* 1977; Durell & Kelly 1990 but see Turpie & Hockey 1997). Grey Plovers pull and dig them out of the muddy substrate in a manner similar to that used for their favoured ragworms.

SOME COMPARISONS BETWEEN TUNDRA PLOVERS

Being much more heavy-billed, Grey Plovers are more adept at digging for prey than the finer-billed golden plovers, which to a larger extent feed on prey picked from the surface, although they vigorously extract subsurface earthworms when available. Grey Plovers thus seem more capable of taking preferred prey, while golden plovers seem to be more of 'jack-of-all-trades' feeders. Eurasian Golden Plovers demonstrate this when feeding on moorland habitat compared with farmland. On the former, a much wider food niche consisting of snails, arthropods and berries is utilized, whereas on farmland the preferred earthworms are available and taken mainly (Byrkjedal 1978c; Downie *et al.* 1996).

The American Golden Plover is the golden plover apparently most inclined to take prey from the surface, as Bent (1929), who undoubtedly had information based primarily on stomach material, did not report a single case of feeding on earthworms (he even placed a special emphasis on crickets being taken during autumn migration). Yet we now know that this species feeds extensively on earthworms (Wishart *et al.* 1981). Outside, as well as during the breeding season, Pacific Golden Plovers seem to feed on freshwater invertebrates more than do Eurasian and American golden plovers. In a sample of stomachs from the Lena Valley (about 65–67°N), Siberia, in autumn, freshwater insect larvae (Plecoptera, Chironomidae, etc.) made up 26% of the diet (by items; Labutin *et al.* 1988).

Whereas the diet of Eurasian Golden Plovers and Grey Plovers is fairly well known from the non-breeding season, much less information exists for American and Pacific Golden Plovers. Of the two latter species, a couple of more substantial studies have been done during migration (Wishart *et al.* 1981; Labutin *et al.* 1988), and the winter diet of Pacific Golden Plovers has recently been studied in detail on Hawaii (Johnson & Connors 1996). The latter emphasize the importance of insects (69–91%) on grassland as well as on saline mudflats. On mudflats crustaceans were important (18–47%), as were snails (17%). The winter diet of the American Golden Plover on the South American pampas is known only from anecdotal information, indicating mainly insects, but apparently also to a certain extent seeds of a Compositae (Dabbene 1920). Undertaking further food studies of these two species would be especially worthwhile.

FOOD DIFFERENCES BY AGE AND SEX

Chicks

Little information seems to be available on the chick diet of tundra plovers, except for a small sample of stomachs (5 birds) from Lower Kolyma, Siberia, of Pacific Golden Plovers (Khlebosolov 1983), the contents of 7 Eurasian Golden Plover chicks' stomachs and 8 broods' faecal samples, examined by Whittingham (1996), and faecal samples from 4 Eurasian chicks studied by Yalden & Yalden (1991). Most of the Pacific Golden Plover chicks had eaten large quantities of adult Coleoptera and Hymenoptera, while only small quantities of earthworms and adult Diptera (non-Tipulidae) were recorded. In comparison, all the adults (*n*=10) had eaten large quantities of Coleoptera, about 40% of the stomachs contained medium quantities of tipulid larvae, and less than a quarter of the birds contained adult diptera, earthworms, larvae of non-tipulid diptera, and plant remains. Thus, chicks seem to take more surface-living prey than the adults. The Eurasian Golden Plover chicks' stomachs consisted almost entirely of dipterans (932/998 items). The faecal samples also consisted mainly of dipteran remains (2568/2624 items) and coleopterans (49 items). However, Whittingham then applied a conversion factor to these data (after Galbraith 1989). After all, many of the tipulid eggs found in faecal samples belonged to one female adult (some 79 eggs represented 1 adult female). The conversion factor indicated that the chick diet consisted (by % of number of items taken): 47% (coleopterans), 44% (adult dipterans, mainly tipulids), and a small number of spiders, true bugs (hemipterans) and oligochaetes.

Whittingham (1996a) found broadly similar diets of adults and chicks. In the Eurasian Dotterel, Galbraith *et al.* (1993) found that adult and chick diets were more similar in years when adult tipulids were abundant (when they were the main prey); in years of low tipulid abundance, adults tended to take a lot of sawfly (Hymenoptera) adults, and chicks took many coleopterans (*Byrrhus, Otiorrhynchos* spp).

Juveniles compared with adults

At Hardangervidda, stomach samples of juvenile Eurasian Golden Plovers were compared with adults at the end of the breeding season (the juveniles being around fledgling age; re-analysis of data used by Byrkjedal 1980a are given in Table 15). These juveniles took more surface prey than the adults, and fewer berries. They also ingested less material than the adults in terms of estimated dry weight and number of prey items. Furthermore, the food niches of the juveniles were broader than those of the adults, the latter being much more specialized on *Empetrum* berries than the juveniles (Table 15). However, the difference between adult and juvenile food may have largely gone by early–mid-autumn, judging by a sample of migrating Eurasian Golden Plovers from farmland on Jæren (Table 15). We should note, however, that adult and juvenile golden plovers may differ in their diet in the non-breeding season as they may be found on different habitats. In American and Eurasian golden plovers, juveniles seem to be found more often on littoral habitats, whereas adults are more frequently seen on grasslands and arable land (Stout 1967; Meltofte 1987). In Grey Plovers and possibly even American Golden Plovers, the diet of territorial non-breeding birds should be different from non-territorial individuals (more preferred prey, narrower food niche, higher intake rate in territorial birds), because the former are more probably younger birds (Chapter 11).

Sex differences

There are few studies comparing the food of male and female shorebirds. During the breeding season at Hardangervidda, the diet of Eurasian Golden Plover males and females is similar through the early part of the season (May and June), while in July (chick period) females take significantly more subterranean prey, much of which is composed of tipulid larvae, than the males, and they take less surface-active prey (to a large extent consisting of adult coleopterans; Table 15). Furthermore, numbers of prey items in the stomachs, as well as estimated dry weights of stomach content items, indicate that females tend to eat more than males. These differences between the sexes may be ascribed to the vigilance burdens assumed by the males (Chapter 9). Then, males may be less able to feed attentively for the more inconspicuous, but nutritionally profitable, soil-living larvae. Similar differences are expected to be present between males and females of the other tundra plover species on their breeding grounds.

One important difference between male and female diets on the breeding grounds relates to the ingestion of rodent bones. At Hardangervidda, microtine bones, chiefly from Norway Lemmings (*Lemmus lemmus*), were found in 63% of the females' stomachs in May and 33% in June, while none of the males had eaten bones. Later in the season, bones did not occur in the golden plover diet (Byrkjedal 1975). This was interpreted as a means for females to obtain calcium supplies for their eggshell formation. Lemming carcases are readily available on the tundra in certain years, providing the birds with a ready access to bones. Downie *et al.* (1996) found bone remains of frogs/newts in a few faecal/pellet samples from Eurasian Golden Plovers on bog, but not on pasture.

The bones are apparently not eaten as grit to aid grinding of the food, as they should then also turn up in male stomachs – and throughout the season. The tundra plovers do eat grit for this purpose though; for instance, at Hardangervidda Eurasian Golden Plover stomachs contained on average 11 gastroliths per stomach (Byrkjedal 1980a). Ingestion of lemming bones as a source of calcium is also practised by *Calidris* sandpipers in Alaska, and dietary calcium supplementation may be relatively widespread among birds before egg-laying (Brenninkmejer *et al.* 1997 and references therein).

CASES OF OPPORTUNISTIC FEEDING

Clearly, tundra plovers show a certain ability to change their diet according to particular circumstances. The diet niche breadth of Eurasian Golden Plovers on migration, feeding in heather moor, is about twice that of conspecifics feeding in farmland, where the birds can specialize on a preferred diet of earthworms (Byrkjedal 1978c). This demonstrates that there is room for opportunistic feeding, with birds taking advantage of favourable occurrences of food.

At the Pribilof Island commercial seal 'killing grounds', migrating Pacific Golden Plovers fed extensively on blowfly maggots, presumably occurring in offal (Bent 1929). From such a feeding habit the next step to scavenging may not be far off! Yet scavenging is not reported for any of the tundra plovers, except for a case of Grey Plover feeding on a dead crab (Bent 1929; live crabs are taken). Interestingly, Zwarts *et al.* (1990a) classified the Grey Plover as a scavenger on the Banc d'Arguin, although it is not clear how much scavenging actually took place.

Food theft

A more remarkable feeding tactic has been alleged for Pacific Golden Plovers on the Pacific islands, where the species is said to steal eggs from incubating seabirds, a habit shared with the Bristle-thighed Curlew and Ruddy Turnstone (Stout 1967, p. 34). The occurrence of this feeding in Pacific Golden Plovers needs further confirmation and study. The step to egg-eating could be short for a bird that would be likely to go for maggots found on cracked eggs, usually present here and there in seabird colonies.

Tundra plovers are frequently kleptoparasitized by other birds, notably gulls (Chapter 11). Food stealing by tundra plovers has been seen in the Grey Plover, and rarely in the Eurasian Golden Plover. At the Banc d'Arguin, Mauritania, Grey Plovers stole Giant Bloody Cockles (*Anadara senilis*) and Fiddler Crabs (*Uca tangieri*) from Eurasian Oystercatchers and Whimbrels (Zwarts *et al.* 1990a), and at Bolinas Lagoon, California, they took small fish (*Clevelandia los*) from Dunlins which themselves fed opportunistically on rich occurrences of these fishes (Warnock 1989). The Eurasian Golden Plovers took a few earthworms from conspecifics, but more usually had worms stolen from them by lapwings (rarely) and gulls (Chapter 11).

Fish, salamanders and even reptiles!

Fish are now and then recorded in the diet of all four species of tundra plovers. Dement'ev & Gladkov (1951) reported a small fish from a Grey Plover stomach in Turkmenia, while fish otoliths were found in stomach samples of Eurasian Golden Plovers from the coasts of Estonia (Kumari 1958). Witherby *et al.* (1940) reports small *Sicydium plumieri* in the diet of American Golden Plovers. In one stomach (out of 43) of Pacific Golden Plovers on autumn migration in the Lena Valley, Siberia, Labutin *et al.* (1988) found a fry of Burbot (*Lota lota*).

Other vertebrates are even rarer in the diet of tundra plovers. A Pacific Golden Plover held in captivity was offered a *Batrachoseps*, a thin worm-like salamander (Williams 1952). When the bird pecked at it, the salamander lost its tail, which the bird ate. In the Eastern Polynesia, Pacific Golden Plovers sometimes feed on Snake-eyed Skinks (*Ablephorus bountonii*; a small reptile exceptional in its habit of living in the marine littoral zone alongside crabs and snails). According to Clapp & Tilger (1967) and Holyoak & Thibault (1984) the species has been recorded in several Pacific Golden Plover stomachs, along with *Uca* crabs, snails, bivalves, worms and Crustacea.

SUMMARY

1. During the breeding season, tundra plovers feed largely on insects and berries, though if available earthworms are the preferred prey for Eurasian Golden Plovers. There appear to be some substantial differences between study sites, and the one-year or two-year emergence patterns of tipulids may bear on these.
2. In the non-breeding season, Grey Plovers feed largely at the coast and take a wide range of prey, tending towards smaller items in the north. Eurasian Golden Plovers feed largely on earthworms, and have been found to show a preference for the smaller (more profitable) worms. Less is known about the diet of Pacific Golden Plovers, and there is virtually no information on American Golden Plovers.

3. Chick–adult diet comparisons have been made for Eurasian Golden Plovers: there appear to be no marked differences. Juveniles take more surface items than adults. Females ingest rodent bones, evidently to assist eggshell formation.

4. Some examples of opportunistic feeding are given, including rare inter- and intra-specific food stealing (Grey Plover, Eurasian Golden Plover), scavenging (Grey Plover) and even egg thefts from seabirds (Pacific Golden Plover).

CHAPTER 13
Associations with others Birds

Curlew Sandpiper 'paging' Grey Plover

'*Plover-page, plover's-page*, dunlin & other birds said to follow golden plover.'

The Concise Oxford Dictionary of Current English, fifth edition (1964)

TUNDRA plovers associate with many species of birds in the course of their year. Most of these associates seem to exert little influence on the plovers, while others can have a significant, albeit short-lived, impact. This brief chapter explores the relationships between tundra plovers and other species. We have already dealt with responses to predators close to nests and chicks (Chapter 9), yet we touch again on predators below because predation risk influences the formation and nature of many of the associations.

COMPANIONS ON MIGRATION

In their non-breeding range, tundra plovers mingle with many shorebird species, especially on intertidal flats and beaches. Yet, during their migrational flights they seem to be more selective about their company. Observations of Grey Plovers departing for migraton (in the Netherlands, on Banc d'Arguin, and on the Pacific coast of North America) show that they are among those shorebirds which frequently migrate in mixed species flocks (Piersma *et al.* 1990b; Paulson 1993). They chose species of their own size as companions, such as Bar-tailed Godwits (particularly frequently), Red Knots, Short-billed Dowitchers and Common Greenshanks. Smaller species, such as sandpipers and other plovers (but also some of the larger shorebirds such as curlews and oystercatchers) are numerous on the flyways, yet only rarely accompany migrating Grey Plovers.

Presumably, structured flocks of birds of the same size, flight speed, and type of flight provide energetic advantages (Piersma *et al.* 1990b). Single species flocks therefore appear to be more common on migration. So, what causes Grey Plovers to associate actively or passively with other shorebirds on migration remains obscure.

'PROTECTIVE UMBRELLA' SPECIES

Several bird species manage to use aggressive chases to drive predators from their nesting territories. Less bold species may take advantage of this and nest under the 'protective umbrella' of these aggressive ones, thereby improving their nesting success at no apparent extra cost (e.g. Göransson *et al.* 1975; Dyrcz *et al.* 1981; Larsen & Moldsvor 1992; Larsen & Grundetjern 1997).

Of the tundra plovers, the golden plovers are the 'timid' species that tend not to defend their nests aggressively (although American and Pacific golden plovers may do so on occasions; Chapter 9). Grey Plovers, on the other hand, belong to the 'umbrella species', which may be exploited by others breeding on the tundra.

No study has compared the nest survival of golden plovers in relation to their proximity to nests of aggressive species. We do not know whether or not golden plovers deliberately nest within the neighbourhood of aggressive species, though a number of the more 'aggressive' species are present on many of their breeding grounds. At the Mallerstang limestone-blanket bog complex in Britain, Ratcliffe (1976) found Eurasian Golden Plovers co-existing with double their number of Northern Lapwings, and both seemed to draw on the same food supply. It is quite likely that these golden plovers may benefit from the aggressive predator chases of the lapwings, something which ought to be tested, though at Mallerstang numbers of lapwings and especially goldies have declined in the 1990s.

Eurasian Golden Plovers also nest within territories of Eurasian Curlew and Common Greenshank (also Ratcliffe 1976), and in the north frequently nest near Whimbrel (also Pulliainen & Saari 1993). Whilst curlews potentially offer a most protective 'umbrella' (cf. Göransson *et al.* 1975), greenshank associates probably provide early warning of danger, and can remonstrate loudly when humans, foxes and crows appear on the horizon, particularly during the chick rearing period. The highly aggressive Whimbrel was also breeding at Churchill, Manitoba, where territories covered most of those of the American Golden Plovers nesting in the area. It was possibly because of the presence of Whimbrels there that the latter did not engage in any aggressive chases of flying predators (Chapter 9).

A special relationship may exist with skuas, gulls and even raptors, all of which may act as umbrella species for tundra plovers on northern and arctic breeding grounds. In the Arctic, Peregrine Falcons and Rough-legged Buzzards frequently breed on level tundra, and they are highly effective in keeping predators away. However, they can themselves be predators on tundra plovers and their eggs and chicks. In northern Norway and at Yamal the Eurasian Golden Plover nests are not infrequently situated within the 'umbrella' of Long-tailed Skuas, and in north central Siberia nests of Pacific Golden Plovers have been found within this umbrella (Larsen & Grundetjern 1997). However, there are no data to suggest that they do so more often than at random, and that they gain or lose from this association. They may gain because skuas and raptors tend to breed on the tundra only in years of lemming 'peaks', when they prey mainly on the rodents. However, skuas and indeed raptors take chicks of tundra plovers (Maher 1974), and even Eurasian Curlews are known to eat eggs (Cramp & Simmons 1983). An interesting photo is shown in Piersma & Wiersma (1996, p. 401), of a Eurasian Golden Plover attacking a Eurasian Curlew on the ground.

Breeding Grey Plovers promptly chase away nest predators flying over their territories. At central Taimyr, Red Knots and Curlew Sandpipers with broods are strongly attracted to neighbouring Grey Plovers, evidently for protection (Soloviev & Tomkovich 1998). Yet, at Yamal IB saw a Curlew Sandpiper with chicks attacked by a Grey Plover, and then performing a broken wing display in front of it while approaching to within 10 m of the plover! On Victoria Island, Buff-breasted Sandpipers can breed close to nesting Grey Plovers (Paulson & Erckmann 1985), and may obtain benefits from this. Experiments in north Siberia with artificial nests demonstrated higher nest survival inside than outside the protective umbrella of nesting Grey Plovers (Larsen & Grundetjern 1997). Clearly there is ample scope for more work on the associations of nesting birds.

'PLOVER'S PAGE' BEHAVIOUR: VIGILANCE AND FEEDING

Shorebird feeding behaviour can be grouped into two main categories: (a) 'pause, run and strike', such as in many plovers (Chapters 2 and 12), and (b) 'continuous searching', which is often found among scolopacids. The latter involves much movement with the bill constantly probing the substrate for food. As the plover holds its head high during food searching it seems to be better able than the scolopacid to sustain a high level of vigilance (Barbosa 1995). So it is possible that scolopacids which feed with plovers can take advantage of the plovers' vigilance. This seems to be the case for scolopacids feeding with tundra plovers.

On their breeding grounds, feeding Dunlins have long been known to associate with Eurasian Golden Plovers. So remarkable is this phenomenon that in parts of England the Dunlin was referred to as the 'Plovers Page' (meriting an entry in the *The Concise Oxford Dictionary*), and in Iceland it is called 'Lóuþrall' (plover's slave; Ingram 1942; Oakes 1948). Single individuals or pairs of Dunlin follow individual Eurasian Golden Plovers only a metre or so away while feeding. When the golden plover takes flight, the Dunlin often follows, and when they land the Dunlin continues to page its companion. This can be a bizarre spectacle, with the Dunlin sometimes pursuing the golden plover high above the ground, often with the golden plover agitated by the presence of a ground predator.

At Hardangervidda, Dunlins showed a strong preference for associating with Eurasian Golden Plovers compared with alternative shorebirds present in the area (Eurasian Dotterel, Purple Sandpiper; Byrkjedal & Kålås 1983). Associations were seen throughout the breeding season, but most frequently during the pre-laying season (of both species). When with golden plovers the Dunlins flushed in response to humans at much greater distances (mean 81 m) than when alone or with conspecifics (mean 13 m), and they fed more continuously (looking up only 8 times min^{-1}, compared with over twice as much when not with plovers). Compared with when they were with golden plovers, Dunlins adopted a much more erect posture when looking up. The long flushing distances shown by Dunlins which associated with golden plovers, and their more attentive feeding, revealed that they capitalize on the vigilance and wariness of the plovers. They did not associate with the commonly occurring Eurasian Dotterel, a plover which is probably equally vigilant, yet far less wary than Eurasian Golden Plovers.

By sticking close to golden plovers the Dunlins probably spend more time feeding (which in turn is more efficient), while at the same time enduring a lower risk of their being surprised by a fox or a falcon. In a study in Scotland, Thompson & Thompson (1985) found a warning benefit not only for Dunlins paging Eurasian Golden Plovers, but also for the plovers themselves in mixed company with Dunlins. When they were with Dunlins, the plovers almost doubled the distance at which they flushed from an approaching human (possibly because they were feeding less effectively, and so more likely to detect an approaching predator). However, of the two species, the Dunlin gained most.

In these associations, Eurasian Golden Plovers may incur several costs. First, they may be more exposed to predation as the number of birds increased (1 plover versus plover with 1–2 Dunlins). Second, being the larger of the two, the plover may be selectively attacked by a predator. Third, because Dunlins are running about so close to the plovers, they may disturb the latter's prey (there was some evidence for a reduced intake rate in golden plovers with Dunlins at Hardangervidda, Byrkjedal & Kålås 1983). Fourth, the two species may be in direct competition over food (there was large food overlap found for the species at Hardangervidda). Eurasian Golden Plovers periodically try to chase away their Dunlin company, but this is to no avail as the Dunlin returns as soon as the goldie has turned its back on it (Byrkjedal & Kålås 1983; Yalden & Yalden 1988)! So, the golden plovers may suffer more disadvantages than benefits from the association (also Stinson 1988), and the Dunlin should perhaps be regarded more as a parasite!

Dunlins also associate with other tundra plovers. They sometimes paged Pacific Golden Plovers and Grey Plovers at Yamal, and a possible case of a Dunlin–Pacific Golden Plover association has been reported from St Lawrence Island (Sauer 1962). At Churchill, IB found no cases of Dunlins associating with American Golden Plovers (Dunlins were reasonably common). However, Short-billed Dowitchers there were repeatedly seen associating with American Golden Plovers on their breeding grounds (Byrkjedal 1987b).

Calidrine sandpipers other than Dunlin sometimes associate with tundra plovers. Curlew Sandpipers at Yamal paged Eurasian Golden Plovers (1 case) and Grey Plovers (6 cases). At Hardangervidda, Purple Sandpipers occasionally follow Eurasian Golden Plovers in the pre-laying period (Byrkjedal & Kålås 1983).

On their non-breeding grounds, flocks of Red Knots with one or more Grey Plovers among them have been observed to feed more 'unconcernedly' than when in conspecific flocks (Bent 1929). Feeding associations between Eurasian Golden Plovers and Northern Lapwings are dealt with in Chapter 11.

INTERSPECIFIC COMPETITION: IS THERE ANY?

On their breeding grounds each large territory of tundra plovers can often contain territories of several passerines and small waders. The relatively low taxonomic diversity of invertebrates on the tundra gives rise to high dietary overlap among the insectivorous birds breeding there. Thus, many other shorebirds and even passerines may compete with the tundra plovers for food. This is highly unlikely during most of the summer, however, because of the very high densities of insects available, notably during periods of mass emergence of adults (Chapter 12).

Nevertheless, Pacific and Eurasian golden plovers have been seen to leave their nests to chase nearby Lapland Buntings (also Sauer 1962), and Grey Plovers have done the same to Red Phalaropes and White-rumped Sandpipers (Mayfield 1973). It is of course possible that these chases had an anti-predator function, as birds moving towards the nest could increase the chances of a predator's attention being drawn to it.

At St. Lawrence Island, Pacific Golden Plovers vigorously attacked Ruddy Turnstones intruding on their breeding territories (Sauer 1962). In the Arctic, Ruddy Turnstones nest on the same general habitat as the tundra plovers, and they could be competitors for food as well as for space (territorial spacing could have an anti-predator function; Chapter 9). According to Sauer, the plovers initiated the aggression. The vigorous aggression displayed against turnstones appeared in one respect maladaptive, as turnstones would aggressively chase nest predators which could have benefited the plovers. However, a tendency for turnstones to take eggs of other birds probably explains the wariness of these tundra plovers (Breary & Hildén 1985; Morris & Wiggins 1986). There is even an observation of a Pacific Golden Plover performing nest protection behaviour in the presence of an Arctic Fox; the plover then neglected the fox and rounded on a Ruddy Turnstone that appeared on its territory (Sauer 1962)!

On the breeding grounds tundra plovers' most likely inter-specific competitors for both food and space are the tundra plovers themselves. We have already touched on this in Chapter 5. At Hardangervidda, the nesting and feeding habitats of Eurasian Dotterel and Eurasian Golden Plovers were compared (Byrkjedal 1989b). The species overlapped considerably in resource use, yet they showed no signs of resource partitioning even as snow-melt made new ground available. Aggression by golden plovers against dotterels could indicate some competitive interactions early in the season, when snow covered 75–95% of their feeding grounds. However, there was no correlation between their breeding numbers over six summers within a 6 km^2 study area. It would appear that competition between the two species is of little importance.

In the non-breeding season the nature of competitive interactions are somewhat different (Chapter 11), yet even then there is no evidence of widespread inter-specific competition involving any of the tundra plovers. Aggression between different species of tundra plovers feeding near each other has been seen on the non-breeding grounds, however, and usually the larger species wins (Chapter 5). Yet, according to Paulson (1993) American Golden Plovers associate freely with Grey Plovers feeding on mudflats on the Pacific coast of North America in winter. On the Zwartkops estuary in South Africa Grey Plovers and Whimbrels feed on the same prey, yet Whimbrels fed freely in Grey Plover territories (Turpie & Hockey 1996). In Paraguay, American Golden Plovers use habitats very similar to those used by some other shorebirds which spend the boreal winter there, notably Pectoral Sandpiper and the native Southern Lapwing (Hayes & Fox 1991).

Tundra plovers are subject to kleptoparasitism (gulls steal food from Eurasian Golden Plovers) and they sometimes act as kleptoparasites themselves (Grey Plovers may steal food from other shorebirds). This was dealt with in Chapters 11 and 12. For Grey Plovers there may be a link between their aggressive behaviour on their breeding grounds and kleptoparasitic behaviour in winter.

SUMMARY

1. Various types of associations between tundra plovers and other species are discussed. These largely fall under categories of associations on migration flights, the use of 'umbrella' species while breeding, and tolerance of 'paging' species.
2. On migration flights, tundra plovers tend to have large species of shorebirds as companions.
3. Tundra plovers regularly nest with, or close to, 'bold' shorebirds (which may provide early warning of danger and chase away predators), and sometimes nest close to breeding predators such as skuas, gulls and raptors. The Grey Plover may afford some protection to neighbouring nesting birds.
4. In 'plover's page' associations between Eurasian Golden Plovers and Dunlins, the latter appear to gain more. Similar paging associations are described.
5. There is little evidence for competition between tundra plovers and other species on their breeding or wintering grounds. Aggressive displays towards associates on territories are probably geared towards reducing the risks of adult, nest and chick predation.

CHAPTER 14

Conservation

Grey Plover, Dunlins and Bar-tailed Godwits

A century ago, the golden plover was probably the most abundant of the wind birds, closely followed by the Eskimo curlew . . .

Peter Matthiessen writing about the American Golden Plover compared with other shorebirds in *The Shorebirds of North America* (edited by Stout 1967).

THROUGHOUT the year individual tundra plovers encounter many obstacles to survival, principally in the form of predation risk. Conservation problems arise particularly when and where man upsets the balance between the birds and their environment: habitat loss, pollution and persecution of birds or nests are typical problems. This final chapter recaps on changes in the distribution and status of the tundra plovers (described in Chapter 6), especially those related to the activities of man, and offers some thought on solutions. The principal conservation issues (Table 16) are discussed in turn below.

LOSS OF NON-BREEDING GROUNDS

Coastal tidal flats

Throughout the world there have been major losses of coastal wetlands, and pressures on these areas continue. In Britain, many estuaries have lost between 25% and 90% of their original inter-tidal extent (e.g. Evans 1991; Davidson *et al.* 1991;

Finlayson & Moser 1991), and the figures are not so different for other parts of the world (e.g. Davidson & Pienkowski 1987; Bildstein *et al.* 1991; Sadayosi 1997). Land-claim is the principal on-going threat, though barrage construction and road construction, dock redevelopment and modification of sea defences pose additional local concerns. For the tundra plovers, especially Grey Plovers and Pacific Golden Plovers, this can result in the loss of feeding and roosting grounds (including staging posts important during migration flights).

Grey Plover populations have suffered local losses of their staging grounds in the western hemisphere and along the east Atlantic flyway (e.g. papers in Davidson & Pienkowski 1987; Bildstein *et al.* 1991). Lambeck *et al.* (1989), for example, studied changes in numbers of Grey Plovers and other shorebirds using the Roggenplaat tidal flats of the Oosterschelde Estuary (Netherlands Delta), where a substantial area of tidal flat was lost to land claim on an adjacent estuary (in 1971). They found no significant impact on Grey Plovers (though numbers of Eurasian Oystercatchers, Bar-tailed Godwits and Eurasian Curlews rose on the remaining flats). Townshend *et al.* (1984) suggested that Grey Plovers on the Tees increased in density (and more birds became territorial) following land-claim of some of the mudflats there. In Australia, it appears that numbers of Grey Plovers on the coast in recent years (1986–90) have declined in both summer and winter (Marchant & Higgins 1993), though the significance and causes of this are not clear. Furthermore, a study of trends in autumn migration numbers of shorebirds in the Atlantic provinces of Canada found a decline in Grey Plover numbers during 1974–77, which was arguably related to harsh weather on the breeding grounds (Morrison *et al.* 1994).

PLATE 56. *Industrial development in the Tees, North England. (Peter Evans)*

Nevertheless, it seems that overall the Grey Plover is not directly threatened by habitat loss in the non-breeding season. It is not included in the waterbird list of 46 species and 55 populations considered to be currently threatened in the western Palearctic (van Vessem, 1993).

The Pacific Golden Plover tends to feed on the coast, and often with the Grey Plover. In parts of coastal Australia and its islands it is the commonest shorebird. Numbers continue to fluctuate (e.g. Marchant & Higgins 1993), though some residential developments have destroyed feeding and roosting sites: Harris (1995) reports substantial declines (up to around 70%) at wintering sites between 1986 and 1995. Much of the non-breeding range of this species has been poorly studied, yet human populations and development continue to grow there. It would not surprise us if more studies pointed to local (and even widespread) declines. Many of the estuaries and soft sediment coasts along the Chinese, Taiwanese, Korean and Japanese shorelines provide important staging posts yet are subject to rapid rates of land-claim: few have any protected status (Lane & Parish 1991; Melville 1997; D.A. Stroud pers. comm.). This situation is especially serious as these countries lie along the East Asian–Australasian flyway. There are few known alternative sites along this flyway which can be used following coastal land claim, so the current chain of key stop-over sites is vulnerable to being broken. The rate of coastal habitat loss also appears to be high in the Philippines and Indonesia. However, the east–west distribution of their archipelagos across the flyway means that migrating shorebirds may be able to modify their flypaths in order to use alternative sites. But farther north, such alternatives are not available.

The East Asian–Australasian flyway appears to be the most vulnerable of the world's flyways (Lane & Parish 1991; Melville 1997). After all, the pressure of people on space there is considerable (56% of the world's population on 14% of its land area, growing by some 55 million people per annum; Scott & Poole 1989). The situation is particularly serious in Japan (where 33% of tidal flats were lost between 1945 and 1978, mainly to rice paddies, but also to port facilities, housing development and recent landfill for refuse; Sadayosi 1997) and South Korea (where the Government plans to claim 400 000 ha of inter-tidal flats including 155 estuaries on the west coast; Long *et al.* 1988; Lane & Parish 1991). In the future, pollution may well emerge as an important problem on the flyway, as a result of both nutrient enrichment and industrial discharges, though further studies are needed (Melville 1997). Around 15% of the flyway region is under partial or complete legal protection. However, about 50% of the wetlands identified as internationally significant are threatened with destruction or serious degradation (Scott & Poole 1989).

Grasslands

For Eurasian Golden Plovers, there have been major declines in the extent of 'old' pastures preferred in mid-winter. These grasslands have a thicker grass sward and more abundant earthworm numbers, and many have been used traditionally for centuries by wintering grassland plovers (e.g. Ratcliffe 1976; Fuller & Youngman 1979; Thompson 1983b,1984; Barnard & Thompson 1985). Nevertheless, flocks do vary in their use of some fields, and there may be much year-to-year variation in movements of flocks within winter ranges (Fuller 1988). In Chapter 6 we mentioned the decline of rough grassland extent in Great Britain (principally in England). Many of the old pastures are not now used for cattle grazing and have been ploughed for autumn-sown cereals (with applications of pesticides and inorganic nitrogen fertilizer).

On Chris Barnard and DBAT's study area in the English Midlands (Chapter 11), re-visited in March 1994 and intermittently in previous years, few old pastures persist from the early 1980s. Of the old pastures, 47% remained (*n*=82 fields visited), and of those which have been used by Eurasian Golden Plovers only 42% remained. Most had been converted to arable, and one had a large horse stable complex built on it. The golden plovers no longer over-winter in that area, and lapwings are seen only sporadically. This type of pasture conversion to arable is widespread in Britain (e.g. Fuller & Lloyd 1981), indeed this appears to be the case throughout much of pastoral Europe (Tucker & Evans 1997). This situation merits much closer examination, and we would like to see a systematic assessment of the extent and spatial changes in pastureland throughout Europe. We believe that this habitat is extremely vulnerable to rapid deterioration in Britain. In Ireland (where the majority of the golden plovers over-winter in the British Isles) there has been less of a reduction in the extent of old pastures because there is still a heavy dependency on cattle farming.

Such major losses of grassland habitats preferred by Eurasian Golden Plovers in winter (Chapter 11) have, in our view, had a critical impact on survival, particularly in years with cold winter weather. Kirby & Lack (1993) emphasize the sensitivity of golden plovers to cold winters, and infer from national counts that birds move to the English south coast, or even futher south, during harsh spells. A study of uniquely marked and radio-tracked birds in winter is needed. The type of study made by Goss-Custard (1996) of individual Eurasian Oystercatchers is overdue for the grassland plovers. Indeed, there are similarities between the oystercatcher's and plovers' use of mussel beds and old pastures, respectively (e.g. Goss-Custard & Sutherland 1997). It would be particularly useful to track the birds onto their breeding grounds in order to determine adult:juvenile ratios and individual differences in breeding success. Such work would give us a much clearer picture of the importance of winter habitat quality for the viability of the grassland plover population.

What has happened to Eurasian Golden Plovers that have quit the winter ranges with areas depleted of old pastures? Have they moved farther south, to the coast even, or died? There is, alas, a woeful lack of information founded on monitoring. As most of the British and Irish over-wintering birds originate from Iceland (Chapter 10) it would be invaluable to monitor birds on the coast of Iceland. At Kopavogur and Grafarvogur, SW Iceland, Eurasian Golden Plovers build up in large numbers during September–October on coastal pastures (Garðarsson & Nielsen 1989), where they complete their primary feather moult prior to migrating south. This would be an excellent area for monitoring changes in numbers of golden plovers. It is possible, for example, that numbers of adults recorded there will be lower in autumn years following severe winter years in Britain.

Janice van Vessem (1993) has included the west Siberian/Caspian population of Eurasian Golden Plovers in her list of 'threatened' waterbird species or populations in the western Palearctic. The British Isles/Danish/German population of Eurasian Golden Plovers is included in her list of 'vulnerable' species and populations (this contains a total of 54 wetland species and 65 populations) on account of their declining numbers in the western Palearctic.

The American Golden Plover also seems to have succumbed to habitat loss in some parts (Page & Gill 1994; Johnson & Connors 1996). For example, Wiersma (1996) mentions that at one small staging site in Texas numbers have declined by 34–69%, possibly reflecting degeneration of the Cheyenne Bottoms staging site in Kansas. In Indiana, where counts have been made during seven years (Erickson 1992), the count area was originally tallgrass prairie but is now intensely farmed. In spring, fields are ploughed, have a cover of winter wheat or retain maize or soybean stubble from the previous year. On average, around 80% of the American Golden Plovers were found on soybean stubble fields although these covered only around 40% (at least 25–30%) of the area. Erickson (1992) suggests the preference for soybean stubble related to a higher abundance of soil invertebrates in these (unlike maize, soybean fields are not routinely treated with insecticides).

On the cattle-grazed flooded pampas wintering grounds in Argentina and Uruguay, the American Golden Plover is vulnerable to agricultural development because arable farming may become more profitable (Blanco *et al.* 1993). On the coast there, some of the birds' habitats have already been claimed for housing and tourism. There is considerable scope for conservation-orientated surveys in this region.

Even the Grey Plovers may be susceptible to changes in pasture extent. Adjacent to the Humboldt Bay, Pacific coast of North America, they use pastures for 'extra-time' feeding. They are faithful to particular pastures (Colwell & Dodd 1997), which may be especially important candidates for protection.

DISTURBANCE ON THE NON-BREEDING GROUNDS

Disturbance ranges from bait digging, leisure boats, surfing, coastal walking, intensive farming activities through to hunting. We have already mentioned the massive decline in the American Golden Plover following the relentless slaughter of birds on passage in the 19th century (Chapter 6). Then, flights of 'millions' in New Orleans alone were reported, and almost 50 000 birds were killed in one day. On Nantucket Island, south-east of Boston in New England, Forbush (1912) made reference to flocks of American Golden Plovers and Eskimo Curlews which appeared in such waves as to 'almost darken the sun'. Along with the Pacific Golden Plover, the American Golden Plover is now protected throughout most of the western Hemisphere (Johnson & Connors 1996). However, in East Asia losses of Pacific Golden Plovers to commercial hunting may be high. In that region shorebirds and other waterbirds are hunted extensively for food (Parish & Howes 1990; Lane & Parish 1991).

The Grey Plover is still shot in some countries, though it is protected in the New World and in the western Palearctic. In 1911 the Migratory Bird Treaty Act established American Federal responsibility for the protection of migratory birds, and gave effect to treaties with Canada, Mexico, Japan and what is now Russia. From that year, shorebirds (with the exception of the Common Snipe and American Woodcock) were removed from the list of gamebirds.

The Eurasian Golden Plover is listed as a category 4 'Species of European Conservation Concern' (SPEC) by Tucker & Heath (1994). This category contains species whose populations are concentrated in Europe, but which have 'Favourable Conservation Status' there. However, the Eurasian Golden Plover can still be hunted in France (where up to 100 000 birds are taken annually), Belgium, Denmark, Greece, Ireland, Netherlands, Portugal, Austria, Norway and the UK. As is the case for a few other 'hunted' species, such as the Capercaillie (which currently has a Scotland-wide voluntary ban on hunting), it is listed under Annex 1 of the EC Birds Directive (79/409/EEC). This listing implies that habitat protection measures are of special importance in the conservation management of the species. The Birds Directive requires all European Union member states to protect a network of sites (Special Protection Areas, SPAs) with substantial breeeding numbers of Annex 1 species. In the UK, sites are considered for SPA classification if they have at least 1% of the national breeding population of each Annex 1 species.

We suggest that there should be a critical review of trends and numbers of the Eurasian Golden Plover in autumn and winter in north Spain, France, Belgium and the Netherlands. If numbers have declined there, as we believe to be the case, we suggest that the authorization of hunting should be reviewed. This is especially important if hunting is removing birds displaced south from Britain during cold weather spells, as is known to occur for some waterfowl (e.g. Ridgill & Fox 1990). Other than hunting, there is only limited evidence indicating impacts of other types of disturbance of tundra plovers outside the breeding season.

In the Dutch Wadden Sea, roosting Eurasian Golden Plovers seem to be relatively tolerant of disturbance from people (Smit & Visser 1993). On part of the Dee Estuary, Kirby *et al.* (1993) compared counts of roosting shorebirds in relation to disturbance events (mainly walkers and dogs, but also bird of prey attacks). They found a significant association between potential disturbance rate (voluntary wardens measured the occurrence of every walker, dog, bird of prey, etc.) and numbers of Grey Plovers (and six other shorebird species) observed on the beach. In most cases, Grey Plovers flew to another location or took-off and then returned within five minutes of being disturbed. On the Wash, where the largest wintering population of Grey Plovers in Britain is found (Chapter 10), over 4000 birds had been ringed at roost sites by 1993. Rehfisch *et al.* (1996) modelled the sorts of 'roost refuges' that would be needed on the Wash to limit disturbance. They suggested that these should be positioned 2, 4, and 7 km apart in order to put them within reach of 90%, 75% and 50%, respectively, of the Grey Plovers during their normal roost movements. Such refuges could be existing, protected roosting sites, or could even be created artificially.

LOSS AND DETERIORATION OF BREEDING GROUNDS

We have found evidence of only very local changes in tundra populations of the Grey Plover and the golden plovers (Chapter 6). Byrkjedal *et al.* (1997) review the current threats to tundra, mire and moorland birds and their habitats in Europe.

instance, Lapland has 13 watershed areas protected from potential power plant or other hydroelectric developments, the Norwegian Protection Plan for River Systems currently protects 111 river courses against hydroelectric exploitation, and in Alaska the Fish and Wildlife Conservation Act (1980, amended 1988) recognizes the importance of non-game migratory species and the need to plan for and manage them. This last Act also provides for financial assistance to states for the development of non-game conservation plans, and instructs all Federal agencies to conserve wildlife and their habitats.

According to CAFF (1994) and Byrkjedal *et al.* (1997) the principal threats to tundra habitats are: oil and gas exploration (especially around the Barents Sea coast); heavy grazing (reindeer in Russia, Norway and Finland; there are indications of local increases in caribou in North America); potential mining activities (for instance 130 000 km^2 were staked recently in a diamond rush in the Canadian Arctic); and the expansion of tourism (Finland and some other countries have strict regulations for visitors to their national parks and other protected areas). We have no evidence, however, of any of these activities having inimical impacts on the tundra plovers on tundra.

Moorland

We have already remarked on the declines in numbers of Eurasian Golden Plovers on moorland in Europe. At the turn of the 19th century Eurasian Golden Plovers were much more widespread in the western part of the North European Plain (Poland across to Belgium), Denmark, southern Norway and Sweden, and the British Isles (Chapter 6). Two factors seem to be implicated. First, there has been a conversion of moorland habitat to agricultural land involving ploughing and/or re-seeding with grasses, and heavy grazing by sheep (e.g. Thompson *et al.* 1995a,b). Second, there has been a deterioration in or loss of hill/moorland pastures important to pre-breeding and off-duty nesting birds (Chapter 6). It is possible, of course, that in the 19th century, and much earlier, populations of Eurasian Golden Plovers were bolstered as a result of the artificial conversion of woodland to moorland, and the 'keepering' for gamebirds which kept numbers of predators low. We should also recognize that other factors have contributed to the decline, notably afforestation (e.g. Thompson 1987; Thompson *et al.* 1988; Ratcliffe 1990; Avery & Leslie 1990; Parr 1992, 1993a) and possibly some very local factors such as recreation-related disturbance (though evidence for this is scant, Chapter 6).

Moorland is now recognized as an important habitat. Several moorland habitats are listed under the EC Habitats Directive (92/43/EEC). Under this Directive, European Union member states make recommendations on the classification of 'Special Areas for Conservation' (SACs) for sites to provide for the favourable conservation status of listed habitats in the EU. This could potentially protect important areas for tundra plovers in Great Britain, Ireland and Sweden in particular.

Each country also has its own legislation in place to protect important habitats such as moorland. In Britain, Sites of Special Scientific Interest (SSSIs) cover large expanses of moorland, and within these the Government's nature conservation agencies (English Nature, Countryside Council for Wales, Scottish Natural

PLATE 57. *Fenceline effect showing loss of heather moorland (right) to sheep grazing, near Kirkby Stephen, England. (DBAT)*

Heritage) are consulted on land-use changes. As a result of discussions with land owners and occupiers these conservation agencies may enter into 'Management Agreements' to prevent damage taking place. In the wider moorland environment, Environmentally Sensitive Areas (ESAs) cover substantial tracts of moorland and within these there are some incentives to improve the character of the moorland landscape. There are additional schemes, such as the Moorland Scheme in England and the the Scottish Countryside Premium Scheme in Scotland aimed partly at improving the condition of moorland (including provision of incentives to reduce densities of grazing sheep and improve other forms of management, such as heather burning). Furthermore, some of the National Parks in England and Wales provide some protection for moorland landscapes (Thompson 1990b). The European Union Common Agricultural Policy (EU CAP) is being reviewed and this may bring further reductions in pressures on moorland. Recently, *Agenda 2000* has been published by the European Commission. However, it would appear that the environmental interests are not well catered for in the new EC proposals (e.g. RSPB 1997).

We feel that the EC requires a strategic environmental assessment of moorland habitats in Europe, with a clear understanding of how past and current policies have shaped the present-day state of the land. This would build on the analysis of issues outlined by Byrkjedal *et al.* (1997). So far as Eurasian Golden Plovers are concerned there appear to be strong ties between some moorland areas and pastures (Chapters 6, 7 and 9). It would be helpful to have a scheme which draws together an expansion of heather moorland (including heather regeneration on rough grasslands) and improvements in the suitability of existing pasture fields. We are impressed with the CAFF programme for arctic regions of the world (mentioned above). Perhaps a network for moorland landscapes could be established to take forward a co-ordinated approach for a Europe-wide assessment and monitoring programme. This could foster closer collaboration on research, conservation and strategic land-use planning matters. After all, the Eurasian Golden Plover could be suffering because of winter habitat loss, hunting pressure and deterioration of breeding habitats, in combination or separately, in different parts of their range. At least an update of numbers of shorebirds breeding throughout Europe in the year 2000 is well in hand, which should provide a useful means of establishing some of the key population trends (Thorup *et al.* 1997).

We certainly need more research to identify the important habitat (and other) factors for the birds (e.g. O'Connell *et al.* 1996; Whittingham 1996a). Mark Whittingham, Andy Brown and Steve Percival's work has highlighted the importance of moorland being close to pastures (up to 4 km away), and for the moorland to have mosaics of grassy, heath, bog and flush habitats (Chapter 9). Similarly, Mark O'Connell, Chris Thomas, Ian Downie, Phil Whitfield and colleagues have stressed the importance of particular grasslands for the birds, and have identified some of the key prey types (Chapters 9 and 12). However, the evident suitability of eroded (possibly naturally) blanket bog/moorland heaths of north England and Lewis for golden plovers (e.g. Ratcliffe 1976; Brown 1993; Whitfield 1997a) is fascinating. Until we are clearer about the value of erosion surfaces for the birds we need to be cautious over any suggestion that Eurasian Golden Plovers are good indicators of subalpine or alpine (montane) heaths. These birds may benefit from features which do not suit other species, such as the Dunlin, Red Grouse or Eurasian Dotterel (e.g. Ratcliffe 1990; Thompson *et al.* 1996,1997).

GLOBAL WARMING

Some of the more recent predictions on global climate change point to 'warming' of between +1.5°C and +4.5°C by the end of the 21st century (IPCC 1996). Drastic reductions in CO_2 emissions will be needed to restrict the impacts of climate change on vegetation. Reductions are also being sought in emissions of Methane, Nitrous Oxides, CFCs and tropospheric ozone (e.g. Hossell 1994).

The predicted change in climate has major implications for agriculture, forestry, sea levels and natural ecosystem processes. Sea-levels may increase by 25–50 cm by the year 2050, with impacts greatest on areas with gently rising coastlines (e.g. Smit *et al.* 1987; IPCC 1996). This could be particularly serious for Grey Plovers, which show a preference for wet, fairly level tidal flat surfaces (Chapter 11).

Some coarse assessments of potential impacts of climate change on terrestrial habitats suggest that a +3°C rise will eliminate all tundra regions and reduce boreal forest cover by up to 96% in Europe (e.g. Nilsson & Pitt 1991); some workers anticipate such a rise by the year 2050 (Hossell 1994). Furthermore, a 3°C rise in temperature could reduce the extent of blanket bog by 25% and wipe out all arctic-alpine habitats (e.g. Bardgett *et al.* 1995; Hossell 1994). However, the area of heather-dominated moorland could increase during temperature rises of between +1°C and +3°C above present temperatures (Bardgett *et al.* 1995). These are ballpark estimates, and there is a growing scientific debate over the likely consequences of global warming and related pollution-induced events. One of the latest predictions from the International Panel on Climate Change (IPCC 1996) suggests that the massive Bering Glacier in Alaska may be melting at more that 0.5 km per year, well in excess of previous recorded rates. It still seems too early to determine the probable impacts of these changes on arctic tundra and moorland landscapes, though they may be catastrophic, particularly for the Grey Plover.

INTERNATIONAL CO-OPERATION

We have already mentioned the need for Europe-wide efforts to assess the impacts of hunting pressures on Eurasian Golden Plovers. It is reassuring to realize that positive steps are being taken at the governmental level on a number of migratory flyways to develop co-operation over international conservation. Such moves have the prospect of significantly strengthening existing national measures for conservation, as well as helping initiate further international actions.

The text of the *Agreement on the Conservation of African–Eurasian Migratory Waterbirds* (AEWA) (adopted under the Bonn Convention on migratory species) was finalized in 1995, and is close to being ratified by the necessary minimum number of Contracting Parties. It sets a broad framework of actions for the conservation of migratory waterbirds including the Eurasian Golden Plover and Grey Plover. As an inter-governmental treaty it will bind contracting parties to undertake a range of measures related to both site and species conservation (Boere & Lenten 1998).

The Asia–Pacific Migratory Waterbird Conservation Strategy: 1996–2000 (Anonymous 1996) is not a legal instrument in the way that the AEWA is, but sets a broad agenda for conservation actions within the East Asian–Australasian flyway. It identifies priorities for migratory waterbirds and their habitats, and is being implemented by a wide range of organizations under the general co-ordination of Wetlands International. The 'Brisbane Initiative' is establishing a network of listed sites along this flyway. This was formalized as a Recommendation of the Brisbane Conference of the Ramsar Convention in 1996. The proposal is to have a network of twinned protected areas ranging from Kamchatka in Russia to New Zealand. By November 1997 a total of 14 protected areas had been included in the network.

In the Americas, the success of the *Western Hemisphere Shorebird Reserve Network* (WHSRN) (established in 1985) is well known (e.g. Myers *et al.* 1987; Hunter *et al.* 1991; Watkins 1997). It has helped raise the profile of internationally important wetlands through 'twinning' mechanisms that do not, necessarily, rely on governmental endorsement (although this is usually forthcoming). The WHSRN is now supported by more than 100 conservation organizations of both governmental and non-governmental character throughout the western hemisphere. A total of 31 internationally important reserves are now protected through the network, offering protection to approximately 30 million shorebirds and over 1.6 million ha of wetlands. The inclusion of a site within the network can even be exploited to positive effect at the local level, and the contacts developed through site-twinning

mechanisms have fostered international sharing of site management and other expertise, data and knowledge.

It seems appropriate that we should end on a note of cautious optimism regarding the co-ordination of action to conserve habitats important for the tundra plovers. Clearly, global warming and threats in the Western Pacific Ocean region and in parts of Europe pose different sorts of significant challenges. For us it is beyond belief that the arctic tundra plains may persist widely for no more than another century. International co-operation will be vital for the future, not just in counting and monitoring the birds, but in order to secure some of the most enchanting sights and sounds of the far north.

SUMMARY

1. Four types of local or widespread threats are discussed: loss of non-breeding grounds; disturbance (including hunting) in the non-breeding season; loss and/or deterioration of the breeding grounds; and global warming and pollution.

2. Of the four species of tundra plovers only numbers of Eurasian Golden Plovers have declined in some regions on their non-breeding and breeding grounds.

3. The loss and deterioration of grasslands used in winter has possibly contributed to local declines in winter populations of Eurasian and American golden plovers. The Pacific Golden Plover may be vulnerable to on-going coastal developments in Australasia and to considerable habitat loss and hunting along the northern part of the East Asian–Australasian flyway.

4. Hunting of Eurasian Golden Plovers in autumn and winter in Europe still takes large numbers. A critical examination of numbers and trends of this species at its southern limits, where hunting may be having a significant impact, is recommended.

5. Some 5–10% of the arctic tundra breeding grounds of tundra plovers are presently protected. Moorland populations of Eurasian Golden Plovers have declined in Europe, evidently because of moorland conversion to agricultural land and possibly also deterioration and loss of hill pastures which are used by pre-breeding and off-duty nesting birds.

6. We stress the need for detailed work on population and behavioural processes in tundra plover populations on their breeding, staging and wintering grounds.

7. The worst scenarios of global warming point to local and even widespread losses of tundra; this could be particularly devastating for the Grey Plover.

8. There has been recent progress in the development of international co-operation on some conservation actions.

APPENDIX 1

Scientific names of birds and mammals mentioned in the book

Grey Plover attacking Artic Skua

English name	Scientific name
BIRDS	
Laysan Albatross	*Diomedea immutabilis*
Red-throated Diver	*Gavia stellata*
Golden Eagle	*Aquila chrysaetos*
Rough-legged Buzzard	*Buteo lagopus*
Merlin	*Falco columbarius*
Peregrine Falcon	*Falco peregrinus*

English name	Scientific name
BIRDS – *continued*	
Hen Harrier	*Circus cyaneus*
Eurasian Sparrowhawk	*Accipiter nisus*
Red Grouse	*Lagopus lagopus scoticus*
Rock Ptarmigan	*Lagopus mutus*
Eurasian Oystercatcher	*Haematopus ostralegus*
Pied Avocet	*Recurvirostra avosetta*
Stone Curlew	*Burhinus oedicnemus*
Northern Lapwing	*Vanellus vanellus*
Yellow-wattled Lapwing	*Vanellus malabaricus*
Brown-chested Lapwing	*Vanellus superciliosus*
White-tailed Lapwing	*Vanellus leucurus*
Pied Lapwing	*Vanellus cayanus*
Southern Lapwing	*Vanellus chilensis*
Red-kneed Dotterel	*Erythrogonys cinctus*
Grey Plover	*Pluvialis squatarola*
Eurasian Golden Plover	*Pluvialis apricaria*
Pacific Golden Plover	*Pluvialis fulva*
American Golden Plover	*Pluvialis dominica*
Red-breasted Plover	*Charadrius obscurus*
Common Ringer Plover	*Charadrius hiaticula*
Semipalmated Plover	*Charadrius semipalmatus*
Little Ringed Plover	*Charadrius dubius*
Wilson's Plover	*Charadrius wilsonia*
Kildeer	*Charadrius vociferus*
Piping Plover	*Charadrius melodus*
Kittlitz's Plover	*Charadrius pecuarius*
Three-banded Plover	*Charadrius tricollaris*
White-fronted Plover	*Charadrius marginatus*
Kentish Plover	*Charadrius alexandrinus*
Chestnut-banded Plover	*Charadrius pallidus*
Greater Sandplover	*Charadrius leschenaultii*
Caspian Plover	*Charadrius asiaticus*
Eurasian Dotterel	*Charadrius morinellus*
Black-fronted Dotterel	*Elseyornis melanops*
Inland Dotterel	*Peltohyas australis*
Wrybill	*Anarhynchus frontalis*
Diademed Plover	*Phegornis mitchelli*
Tawny-throated Dotterel	*Oreopholus ruficollis*
Magellanic Plover	*Pluvianellus socialis*
Pintail Snipe	*Gallinago stenura*
Common Snipe	*Gallinago gallinago*
Short-billed Dowitcher	*Limnodromus griseus*
American Woodcock	*Scolopax minor*
Black-tailed Godwit	*Limosa limosa*

English name	Scientific name
BIRDS – *continued*	
Hudsonian Godwit	*Limosa haemastica*
Bar-tailed Godwit	*Limosa lapponica*
Eskimo Curlew	*Numenius borealis*
Whimbrel	*Numenius phaeopus*
Bristle-thighed Curlew	*Numenius tahitiensis*
Eurasian Curlew	*Numenius arquata*
Spotted Redshank	*Tringa erythropus*
Common Redshank	*Tringa totanus*
Common Greenshank	*Tringa nebularia*
Common Sandpiper	*Actitis hypoleucos*
Ruddy Turnstone	*Arenaria interpres*
Great Knot	*Calidris tenuirostris*
Red Knot	*Calidris canutus*
Sanderling	*Calidris alba*
White-rumped Sandpiper	*Calidris fuscicollis*
Pectoral Sandpiper	*Calidris melanotos*
Semipalmated Sandpiper	*Calidris pusilla*
Little Stint	*Calidris minuta*
Baird's Sandpiper	*Calidris bairdii*
Curlew Sandpiper	*Calidris ferruginea*
Purple Sandpiper	*Calidris maritima*
Dunlin	*Calidris alpina*
Ruff	*Philomachus pugnax*
Buff-breasted Sandpiper	*Tryngites subruficollis*
Red Phalarope	*Phalaropus fulicarius*
Pomarine Skua	*Stercorarius pomarinus*
Arctic Skua	*Stercorarius parasiticus*
Long-tailed Skua	*Stercorarius longicaudus*
Common Gull	*Larus canus*
Herring Gull	*Larus argentatus*
Glaucous Gull	*Larus hyperboreus*
Black-headed Gull	*Larus ridibundus*
Bonaparte's Gull	*Larus philadelphia*
Kittiwake	*Rissa tridactyla*
Snowy Owl	*Nyctea scandiaca*
Northern Shrike	*Lanius excubitor*
Skylark	*Alauda arvensis*
Meadow Pipit	*Anthus pratensis*
Fieldfare	*Turdus pilaris*
Redwing	*Turdus iliacus*
White-crowned Sparrow	*Zonotrichia leucophrys*
American Tree Sparrow	*Spizella arborea*
Lapland Bunting	*Calcarius lapponicus*
Carrion Crow	*Corvus corone corone*

English name	Scientific name
BIRDS – *continued*	
Common Raven	*Corvus corax*
MAMMALS	
Norway Lemming	*Lemmus lemmus*
Red Fox	*Vulpes vulpes*
Arctic Fox	*Alopex lagopus*
Reindeer (Caribou)	*Rangifer tarandus*

Plumage variation in Eurasian Golden Plovers in Norway

Plumage distinctness shows up as geographical variation in the Eurasian Golden Plover. The variation ranges from almost no black and white frontal markings (not very different from non-breeding plumage) to a clearly marked frontal-lateral-ventral pattern in black and white. The following is a re-analysis of Byrkjedal (1978b) with some additional material included. Gradings of plumage distinctness were scored numerically according to Table A below. These were derived from separate scores for the various plumage parts (Fig. A). The scale of gradings was intended to be defined so that there should be equal distances between each step. The full range of plumage gradings is shown in Fig. B.

Separate scorings of the various plumage parts were done because the degree of distinctness of these does not show perfect co-variation. The scores for each plumage part are then summed to give an overall plumage distinctness score for each individual.

The data were collected in the field for territorial birds in the early part of the breeding season (well before onset of post-breeding moult). Data were collected

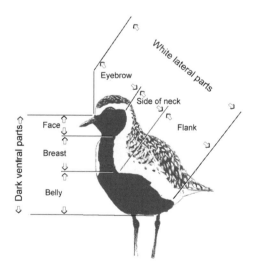

FIG. A.   *Demarcation of different plumage parts, showing white lateral parts and dark ventral parts (after Byrkjedal 1978b)*

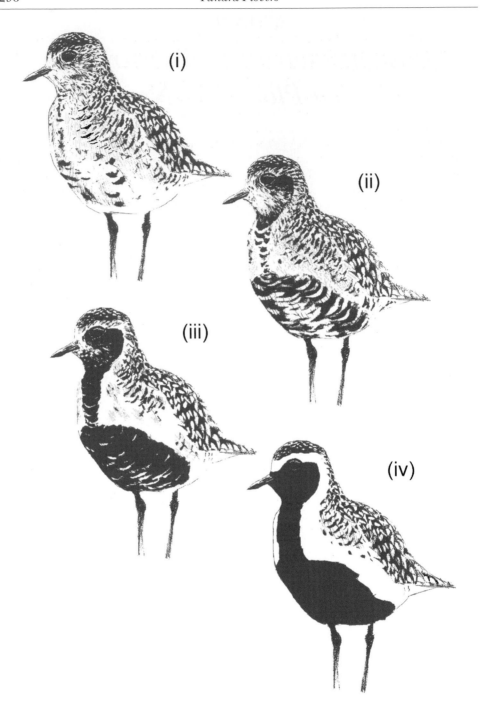

FIG. B.   *Overall plumage gradings, showing the full range of pale (i) to dark types (iv), cf. Table A (p. 298)*

with a reference illustration (similar to Fig. B) at hand, observing the birds through a telescope. Field observations were chosen instead of a study of museum skins, as the scoring depends on the feathers lying naturally, which is often not the case with skins. For further discussion of the method, see Byrkjedal (1978b).

Note that the scoring system used here is reversed in relation to that used by Byrkjedal (1978b), in order for it to follow the same direction as a scoring system used by Parr (1980) (scores increasing with plumage distinctness).

A simpler system for grading plumage distinctness has been used recently by Chris Thomas (pers. comm.). This system (shown in Fig. C) is similar to that of Parr (1980), but more detailed. While the system outlined above may be recommendable for studies of individual year-to-year variation, Thomas' scale may better serve the purpose in future recording of geographical variation.

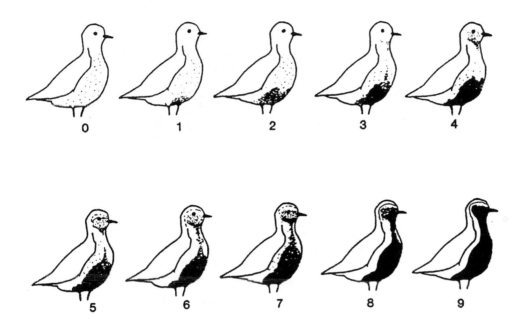

FIG. C.   *Plumage gradings used in Britain by Chris Thomas (unpublished)*

TABLE A. Definition of the plumage gradings. Demarcation of plumage parts is shown in Fig. A, and the overall plumage gradings are shown in Fig. B (referred to as B below).

Plumage parts	Description	Score
Ventral parts:		
Face	Dark facial markings barely visible, only as a grey-brown shadow towards the edge of the ear coverts. Resembles non-breeding plumage (B – (i))	0
	General impression: dirty, light brown. Feathers with brown-grey base and dark brown tips covering 2/3 of the face. Lores indistinctly marked. A few dark feathers may be present at the base of the upper mandible (B – (ii))	2
	General impression: dirty dark brown. A section, 1/3 of the facial area, extending from lores down ear coverts, having feathers with brown-grey bases and dark tips. Rest of face black/dark brown. Black feathers barely extending above the base of mandible (B – (iii))	4
	Black/dark brown; extending clearly above base of mandible (B – (iv))	6
Breast	Breast band absent, or indicated by a few scattered black or brown spots (B – (i))	0
	1/3 black (a few light feather margins may be present), 2/3 with distinct feather margins and spots (most often towards the lower part of the breast, where the black becomes discontinuous (B – (ii))	2
	2/3 black (a few narrow white feather margins may be present), 1/3 with distinct white feather margins and spots (most often the lower part of the breast) (B – (iii))	4
	Black; light feather margins absent (B – (iv))	6
Belly	Greyish belly, scattered dark spots (B – (i))	0
	Grey and white feathers prominent, outline of belly patch clearly evident. Midventrally a continuous dirty-white area with dark spots. Ventrolateral areas darker, but interrupted by broad white feather margins and spots (B – (ii))	2
	Black dominating, but a few light feather margins scattered over most of belly, concentrated midventrally into a spotted area (B – (iii))	4
	Black (B – (iv))	6
Lateral parts:		
Supercilium, side of neck, flanks		
	No white feathers (B – (i) and (ii))	0
	Equal amounts of white and pigmented feathers (B – (iii))	2
	Pure white, distinctly delimited (B – (iv))	4

APPENDIX 3

Descriptions of plumages of the tundra plovers

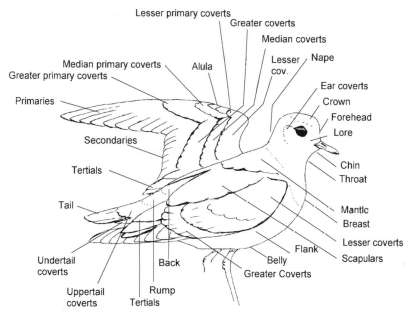

A   *Plumage topography of tundra plover adult.*

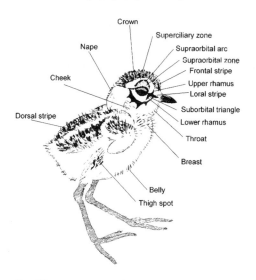

B   *Plumage topography of tundra plover chick.*

C. Juvenile, first non-breeding and adult non-breeding plumages of Grey Plover. Degree of feather renewal to the left (black = completely renewed, hatched = partially renewed, open = not renewed).

Juvenile plumage characterized by dark brownish-greyish dorsal feathers with small rounded edge spots at first pale yellow, later turning white–off-white. Breast and flanks with dark wedge at tip. Wing tip with minimal wear. First winter plumage shows a mixture of fresh winter plumage feathers and more or less worn juvenile feathers: paler dorsal winter feathers contrasting with darker juvenile feathers partly owing to wear of white edge spots of latter. Non-breeding plumage feathers differ from juvenile feathers by pale (off-white) edge fringes (notably at feather tips) rather than spots and by being paler (dorsally more greyish); furthermore, dorsal feathers show dark edge spots fading into greyer central parts of feathers (dark chevrons on tertials). Also, central tail feathers show different pattern from juveniles, notably outer part. Non-breeding adults show fresh primaries, while those of first winter plumage are worn; however, some adults suspend primary moult over the winter and those wintering in tropical and subtropic areas may still have worn wing-tips by mid-winter.

D.   Breeding plumage of Grey Plover. Dotted = active moult, other legends as in C.

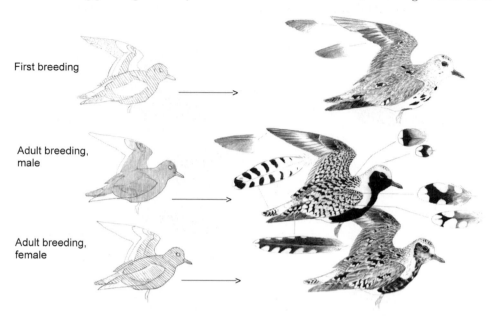

First breeding

Adult breeding,
male

Adult breeding,
female

Retained dorsal non-breeding plumage feathers are greyish-brown and pale feather spots and edges are largely abraded. New feathers are black with large, rounded white spots at the edge. The black of the belly extends up the flanks and merges with black axillaries. Vent, undertail coverts, and rump are white.

E. Juvenile, first non-breeding and adult non-breeding plumages of Eurasian Golden Plover. Legend as in C.

Blackish-brown dorsal feathers with numerous small rounded yellow edge spots characterize juveniles; breast feathers show dark brown wedge at tips, flank feathers brownish terminal band, both bordering yellowish part of feathers. Adult non-breeding plumage resembles juvenile, but feather tips with yellow fringes rather than spots and breast feathers are greyish-yellowish with white–off-white edge band. First non-breeding plumage shows a mixture of worn juvenile and fresh non-breeding plumage feathers. Wing-tips are more worn than those of adults. In adults secondaries show a mixture of new and old feathers, whereas all secondaries of first winter birds are equally worn. Central tail feathers have more complete yellowish-whitish transverse bands in adults than in juveniles.

F. Breeding plumage of Eurasian Golden Plover. Legend as in C.

Feathers less completely renewed in females and in birds on southwestern breeding grounds. In full plumage (northern males) face is blackish-brown, while breast and belly are black. Renewed dorsal feathers are black–blackish-brown with numerous small yellow spots along feather edges. Female northern and male southern birds are similar, though southern birds tend to show less dark around the base of the bill. In northern birds dark extends above upper mandible, even in females. In northern males and to some degree northern females, black feathers extend backwards including undertail coverts, whilst southern birds show white vent and undertail coverts. Central tail feathers show complete light (whitish) chevrons.

Eclipse plumage shows varying degree of yellowish breast feathers with dark tips, different from yellow/black feathers along the white breast band found in 'ordinary' breeding plumage. In eclipse plumage, breeding plumage feathers have started to abrade, and the birds look considerably less distinctive. Northern males acquire an appearance more like females.

G. Juvenile, first non-breeding and adult non-breeding plumages of Pacific Golden Plover. Legend as in C.

Juveniles have dark blackish-brown dorsal feathers with yellow, rounded edge spots. Yellowish colour from head to breast, extending and fading over flanks. Dark brownish-greyish wedge at breast feather tips and terminal band at flank feathers. Dorsal winter plumage feathers with terminal yellow bands (turning gradually paler) rather than rounded spots; rounded spots apparent along edges inwards from tip, interrupted by dark edge spots fading into lighter brownish–greyish central part of feathers (more complete chevrons on central tail feathers). Breast feathers (extending onto flanks) with greyish–brownish–yellowish centre, edged off-white. First winter birds show mixture of worn juvenile and fresh winter plumage feathers, and wing-tips are more worn than those of adults in winter plumage.

H. Breeding plumages of Pacific Golden Plover. Legend as in C.

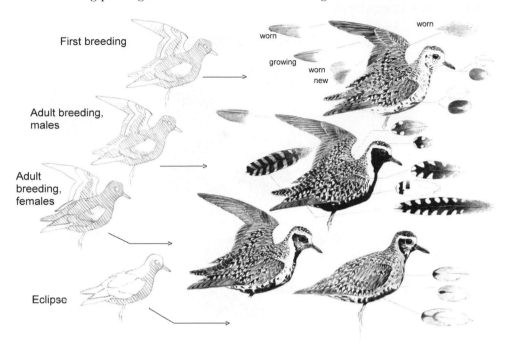

Females retain more winter (dorsally brownish-grey, pale edge spots and fringes abraded) feathers than males. Full plumage (males) shows jet black face-belly, and vent and undertail coverts show white spots; supercilium and sides of neck are made up by a broad, white band at flanks becoming boldly barred in black. Some males show dark grey flanks with bold black transverse bands. Dorsally the feathers are black with large yellow spots along feathered margins, a number of feathers showing white spots instead of yellow, notably at tip. Central tail feathers show white edge spots only along the margins, while the spots continue as greyish-brownish chevrons inwards towards the vane. At tip of tertials yellow spots border a greyish-brown (pale) spot at shaft, before the black part of the feather, a spot lacking (= black area) in American Golden Plover. As in Grey Plover, one-year old birds (on wintering ground) show little breeding plumage feathers, notably on face and underside, and their primaries are in active moult over the summer.

I. Juvenile, first non-breeding and adult non-breeding plumages of American Golden Plover. Legend as in C.

Juvenile dorsal feathers are blackish-brown with yellow edge spots fading off-white in late autumn. Note 'broken fringes' at tip rather than rounded spots, different from that of closely related Pacific Golden Plover. Also, spots on mantle feathers smaller than in Pacific Golden Plover. Yellowish colour of head stretches down breast and flanks, but paler than Pacific Golden Plover, turning off-white during autumn. Supercilium white/whitish compared to more yellow in Pacific Golden Plover. Yellowish-whitish central tail feather spots more triangular-elongated than in Pacific Golden Plover. Dorsal non-breeding plumage feathers greyer (paler) than in juvenile plumage and with yellow/off-white fringes rather than spots. Fringes broken by dark brown (blackish) spots fading into colour of central part of feathers (complete dark chevrons on central tail feathers and scapulars). Pale edge fringes and spots are smaller than in non-breeding plumage Pacific Golden Plover, perhaps most easily seen on tip of tertials. Non-breeding plumage breast feathers have greyish centres and pale (white/off-white) fringes. First non-breeding plumage shows a mixture of worn juvenile feathers and new non-breeding plumage feathers. Wing-tips are probably more worn than those of adult birds (but see Johnson 1985).

J.   Breeding plumages of American Golden Plover. Legend as in C.

Breding,
males

Breeding,
females

Females show less feather renewal than males, but more than in closely related Pacific Golden Plover. In full plumage (males) face to belly is jet black, extending to (and including) undertail coverts, and up the flanks. In females, flanks show white spots and transverse bars, and there may be numerous white spots among undertail coverts. Dorsally the feathers are black with yellow edge spots, differing from those of Pacific Golden Plovers by being: a) more spaced, b) smaller at feather tips, and (c) more sharply triangular. White edge spots, notably on feather tips occur as in Pacific Golden Plover. Central tail feathers resemble those of Pacific Golden Plovers, but greyish-brownish chevrons are darker. The white band along supercilium and sides of breast is broad, and terminates in a 'bulb' in front of the wings. The American Golden Plover is the darkest of all four tundra plovers.

The phylogeny of the tundra plovers

Godtfred A. Halvorsen*, Ingvar Byrkjedal &
D.B.A. Thompson

CHAPTER 5 summarized the phylogeny of the tundra plovers. This paper presents more details of our analysis, which is based exclusively on plumage characters. Tundra plovers were examined as skins and from photographs, as well as in the field. The species of the outgroup were examined as skins when possible, or from photographs or drawings and descriptions in the literature.

We found 19 characters varying in the ingroup, 12 characters (character 1–12) for the adults and juveniles, and seven characters (13–19) for the chicks. One adult (12) and one chick character (19) did not vary in the ingroup, and were assumed to be synapomorphies for the genus. Four of the characters were binary, and 15 were multistate characters. All characters were regarded as descriptive. Each character is described in Table A, and some are shown in Fig. A. The reader is directed to Forey *et al.*'s (1992) textbook for a full background explanation of the terms and methods employed below. We have provided a short glossary at the end.

CHOICE OF OUTGROUP

A cladistic re-analysis of Strauch's data (Mickewitch & Parenti (1980), Bjørklund (1994), and Chu (1995)) did not solve the relationship between the tundra plovers and the rest of the family Charadriidae (*sensu* Piersma & Wiersma, 1996). Neither did the original compatibility analyses of Strauch (1976, 1978). The DNA-DNA hybridization analysis of Sibley & Ahlquist (1990) placed the tundra plovers as the sistergroup to the rest of the Charadriidae, including the lapwings. However, Chu's (1995) analysis indicated that the lapwings were the sistergroup to the rest of the family Charadriidae with the exception of *Vanellus cayanus* (Latham). Based on this we excluded the lapwings from the outgroup.

In order to choose an outgroup we partly adopted the methodology outlined by Nixon & Carpenter (1993). We performed a preliminary analysis with a large outgroup, which included at least some of the variation inside the Charadriinae. This was done in order to test the putative monophyly of the tundra plovers. The species chosen were those in which data for chicks could be obtained. Species without good descriptions or illustrations of chicks were omitted. The following species were included: *Charadrius hiaticula* L., *C. semipalmatus* Bonaparte, *C. dubius* Scopoli, *C. wilsonia* Ord, *C. vociferus* L., *C. melodus* Ord, *C. leschenaultii* Lesson, *C.*

*Department of Zoology, University of Bergen, Allégaten 41, N-5007 Bergen, Norway

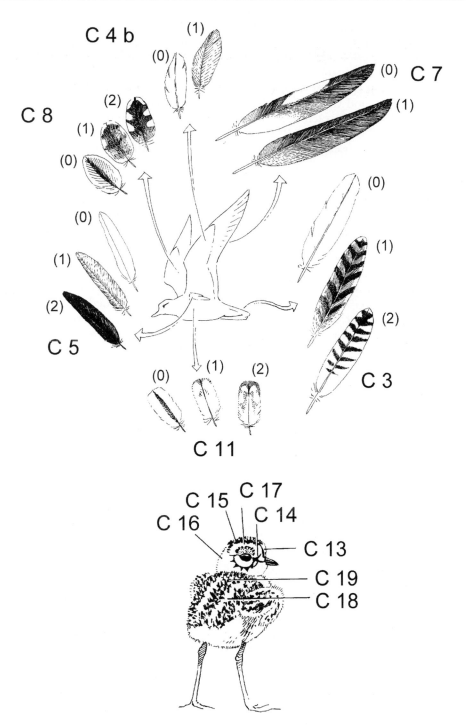

FIG A. *Plumage characters used to determine the phylogeny of the tundra plovers.*

asiticus Pallas, *C. alexandrinus* L., *C. pecuarius* Temminck, *C. pallidus* Strickland, *C. marginatus* Vieillot, *C. tricollaris* Vieillot, *and C. morinellus* L.

We also included seven characters (20–26) which varied in the outgroup, two binary and five multistate. We recognize that this amounted to too few characters for fully resolving the outgroup. However, we had to use the literature to identify these characters, and this restricted our choice. The codings are listed in the data matrix in Table B. Characters 4, 6 and 17 have two alternative codings (4a–4b, 6a–6b, and 17a–17b) in Table B. For the runs with the large outgroup, characters 4a, 6a and 17a were used. We will explain the use of the different codings later on.

ANALYSIS

The matrix was run with *Hennig86* (Farris 1988). The multistate characters 5, 6a, 16 and 17a were treated as unordered. This was done because we could not establish any reasonable hypothesis of transformation between the character states. For instance, characters 5 and 6a deal with differences in coloration. Character 5, the pigmentation of the axillaries in the adults, has three states – black, brownish-grey and white. None of these character states seems to be intermediate between the other two. Character 6a is even more complicated with five differently coloured states. Character 16, the pigmentation of the nape in the chicks, was also treated as unordered. This may actually consist of two characters, one comprising the extent of white feathers on the nape, and the other the intensity of pigmentation. Character 17a, the pigmentation of the superciliary area in the chicks, was also regarded as unordered when the large outgroup was included. A part of this transformation may be regarded as ordered, going from purely white, to white in the outer half only, to fully pigmented, or in the reverse direction. However, the state with spotted pigmentation, which was found in some of the species in the large outgroup, did not fit into the transformation, and this character was consequently treated as unordered. The rest of the multistate characters were regarded as having clear intermediate states between extremes, and were treated as ordered.

The analysis was run with the '**ie**' command in *Hennig86*. This algorithm finds all the shortest trees in a data matrix. The outcome was five equally parsimonious trees. The length of each tree was 92 steps, the consistency index (CI) was 0.57 and the retention index (RI) was 0.66. The ingroup was constant in all trees. What varied was the topology of the outgroup (more specifically, the position of the species *C. asiaticus* and *C. leschenaultii*). The rest of the outgroup remained constant in all trees. The strict consensus tree for these five trees is shown in Fig. B.

TUNDRA PLOVERS: A MONOPHYLETIC GROUP

One has to be very careful if trying to interpret the solution in the outgroup of this cladogram. Although the program also tries to solve the relationhips in the outgroup, we had far from enough characters to solve these. In addition, we did not include several other candidate species in the outgroup.

Our set of characters corroborates the hypothesis that the tundra plovers

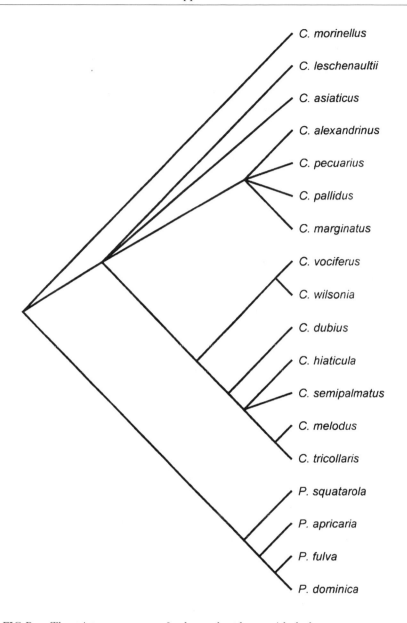

FIG B.   *The strict consensus tree for the tundra plovers with the large outgroup.*

comprise a monophyletic group. The Common Ringed Plover (*C. hiaticula*) does not appear to be the closest relative/sistergroup to the tundra plovers. The last point was also indicated in the compatibility analysis of osteological characters by Strauch (1976: p. 111).

We performed a new analysis of the tundra plovers with the Common Ringed Plover only as the outgroup. This was done in order to identify the synapomorphies

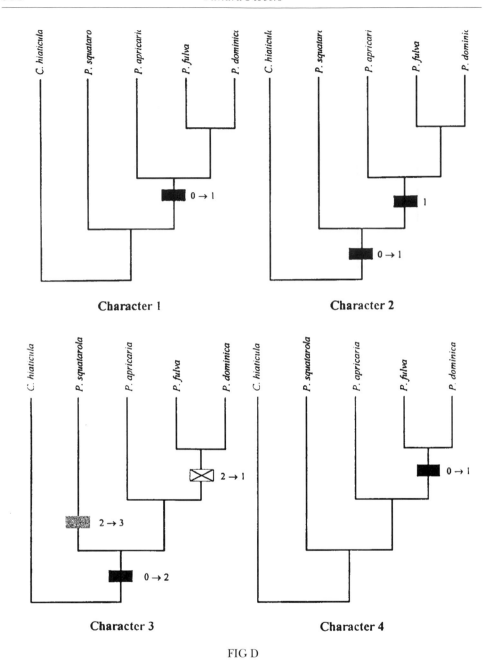

FIG D

Character 3

The ground colour of the middle rectrices is more difficult to optimize on the tree. No unambigous state can be found for the ancestor of both the tundra plovers and the golden plovers. The outgroup has character state 0 – the whole feather brown,

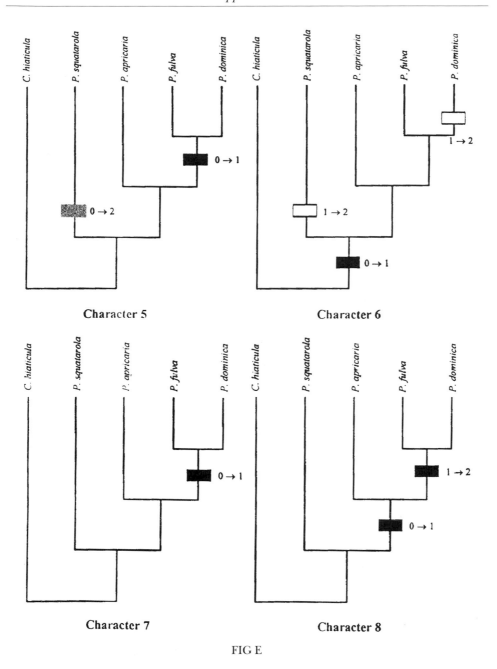

FIG E

and this state is only found in the outgroup of the large data matrix. The ancestor of the tundra plovers, however, may have had state 1 or 2, and the same applies for the ancestor of the golden plovers. When using the accelerated transformation criterion, the character changes from state 0 (the whole feather brown) to state 2

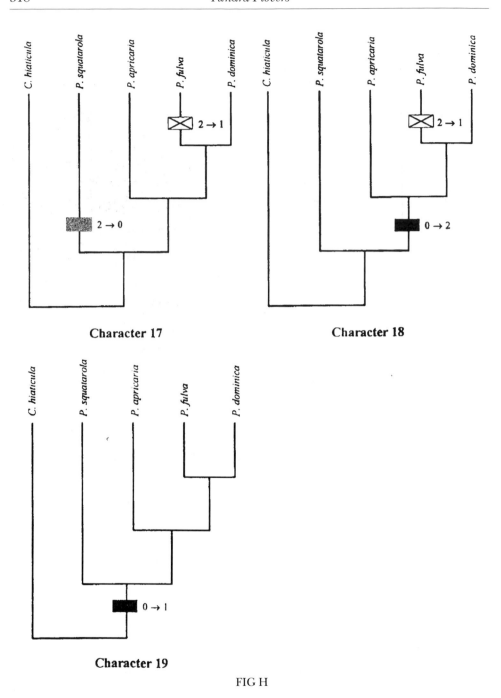

Character 17

Character 18

Character 19

FIG H

FIG D–H.   *The changes in characters 1–19 shown on the most parsimonious tree.
Filled rectangle = synapomorphy, shaded rectangle = autapomorphy, crossed rectangle =
secondary reduction, open rectangle = parallelism.*

us with the same topology, but the tree would be one step shorter. However, this would ignore the obvious ordered alternatives in the character from brown to extensively more white. In addition, the change in the character would be even more ambiguous. Treating the character as unordered would not enable us to set forward any hypothesis of character change, except that state 1 is a synapomorphy for the ancestor of the Pacific and the American golden plovers.

Character 4b

The pigmented underwing coverts are a synapomorphy for the Pacific and the American golden plovers. The character shows, however, outside parallelism. The pigmented coverts are also found in *C. asiaticus*, and an intermediate state is found in *C. tricollaris* (see the large data matrix, Table B).

Character 5

The pigmentation of the axillaries was treated as an unordered character. The black axillaries found in the Grey Plover are an autapomorphy for this species, explaining nothing about relationships in the tundra plovers. The brownish grey feathers are a synapomorphy for the Pacific and the American golden plovers. However, this character state has an outside parallelism in *C. asiaticus*.

Character 6b

The pigmentation of the flanks in the breeding plumage changes from state 0 (all feathers white) in the outgroup to state 1 (some feathers with black blotches) in the ancestor of the tundra plovers, and this character state is a synapomorphy for the genus. This character shows homoplasy. The change to black feathers in the Grey Plover and the American Golden Plover is actually an indication of a closer relationship between these two species. However, when evaluated together with the evidence from all the other characters, this change has to be explained as independently acquired in these two species, i.e. a parallelism.

Character 7

The absence of a white field on the innermost remiges is a synapomorphy for the Pacific and the American golden plovers. However, this character has an outside parallelism. It is also found in *C. tricollaris* and in *C. morinellus*.

Character 8

The character changes from white undertail coverts in the outgroup and the Grey Plover to white with black spots in the ancestor of the golden plovers, and this change is a synapomorphy for this group. The change from black spots to totally black is a synapomorphy for the Pacific and the American golden plovers.

Character 9

The presence of notched dorsal feather edges in the non-breeding plumage, both distinct and indistinct, is a synapomorphy for the tundra plovers. The change from indistinctly notched to distinctly notched is a synapomorphy for the golden plovers. The outgroup condition is fringed.

Character 10

The mere presence of golden feathers on the head in non-breeding plumage is a synapomorphy for the golden plovers. However, the three different states found in the three species do not contribute anything to the further resolution of the group.

Character 11

Dark terminal bands on the breast or flank feathers in the juvenile plumage is a synapomorphy for the tundra plovers. The character changes from state 0 (no bands) in the outgroup to state 1 (indistinct bands) in the ancestor of the tundra plovers. The change from indistinct to well developed bands (state 2) is a synapomorphy for the golden plovers.

Character 12

The continuous white bandings around the black face in the breeding plumage is a synapomorphy for the tundra plovers.

Character 13

Most of the species in the large outgroup lack the longitudinal frontal line in the chicks. However, an indistinct line (state 1) is present in *C. leschenaultii*, and a well developed line (state 2) is found in *C. morinellus*. Assuming that no line present (state 0) is the plesiomorphic state, this character changes from state 0 in the outgroup to state 1 or 2 in the ancestor of the golden plovers. This makes the presence of a frontal line a synapomorphy for the tundra plovers. However, as for all characters which display outside parallelism, it is not regarded as such strong evidence for monophyly as a character which is uniquely derived. This character may actually be a potential synapomorphy for the tundra plovers plus the two species above in an analysis of the whole subfamily Charadriinae, and not only a synapomorphy for the tundra plovers.

Again there are two equally parsimonious explanations for a further change in the character. First, state 2 may have developed in the ancestor of the golden plovers, a synapomorphy for this group, and then been secondarily reduced to the plesiomorphic condition in the Pacific Golden Plover. This secondary reduction then becomes an autapomorphy for the species. Second, the ancestor of the golden plovers may have had state 1, and state 2 was independently developed in the Eurasian and American golden plovers. There is one autapomorphy for each species.

Character 14

The mere presence of a transverse frontal line in the chicks is a synapomorphy for the golden plovers. As with the preceding character, we have two alternative explanations for the character change inside this group. We regard the well developed frontal line (state 2) as the plesiomorphic condition for the golden plovers, and the smaller line in the Pacific Golden Plover as secondary reduction. Alternatively, state 1 (the small line) may have been developed in the ancestor of the golden plovers, and state 2 developed twice in the Eurasian and American golden plovers.

Character 15

This character is difficult to interpret. As Table B shows, it has strong outside parallelism. All states in the ingroup are also present in the large outgroup. When only *C. hiaticula* is used as the outgroup, the analysis gives an ambiguous result for the ancestor of the tundra plovers. State 3 (distinct and continuous crown edge in the chicks) and state 2 (distinct, but discontinuous crown edge) are equally parsimonious. When this character is examined more closely in the large outgroup, state 2 appears as the plesiomorphic state in the basal polytomy as well as the state in the ancestor of the tundra plovers. Assuming that this is the case, the change to state 3 in *C. hiaticula* is an autapomorphy for this species. The total reduction of the crown edge in the Grey Plover (state 0) is an autapomorphy for this species also, and so is the change from state 2 to state 1 (present, but indistinct crown edge) in the Pacific Golden Plover. This means that the character is uninformative so far as the phylogeny of the tundra plovers is concerned.

Character 16

The plesiomorphic condition of this character is the white nape without any patterns of black. All of the outgroup species in the large matrix, plus the Grey Plover, have this state. The presence of dark pigment in the down of the nape is thus a synapomorphy for the golden plovers. However, the analysis does not give any clue as to what the character transformation may be inside the golden plovers. The character changes from state 3 to states 0, 1 and 2 which are autapomorphies for the Pacific, Eurasian and American golden plovers, respectively.

Character 17

The analysis shows that state 2, superciliary area in chicks with white down only, is the plesiomorphic state for this character. This was also found when the large matrix was run. The change from states 2 to 0 (area fully pigmented) in the Grey Plover is an autapomorphy for this species. This state is also found in one species, *C. tricollaris*, in the large outgroup. That is, it shows outside parallelism. The change from state 2 to state 1 (white feathers in outer half) is an autapomorphy for the Pacific Golden Plover. Owing to the ordering of the character, this is interpreted as a secondary reduction, partly back to the plesiomorphic condition. The character does not contribute to the solution of the relationships inside the tundra plovers.

Character 18

The absence of white dorsal stripes in the chicks (state 0) is regarded as plesiomorphic. The character changes to state 1 (faint stripes) or 2 (well developed stripes) in the ancestor of the golden plovers. Again two equally parsimonious explanations exist. One favours early change, i.e. that the character changes from states 0 to 2 in the ancestor with a secondary reduction to an intermediate state in the Pacific Golden Plover. Alternatively, the character may change from states 0 to 1 in the ancestor, and state 2 evolves twice in the Eurasian and American golden plover. Both states show outside parallelism, as both are present in other species in the large outgroup (Table B).

Character 19

The yellow dorsal colour of the chicks is a synapomorphy of the tundra plovers.

Summary

The cladistic analysis of the tundra plovers produced a cladogram which is shown in Fig. B. The monophyly of the tundra plovers was supported by eight synapomorphies, of which one (character 3) showed secondary reductions in the ingroup.

The golden plovers group was supported by 10 synapomorphies, of which three showed secondary reductions. Two of these characters with secondary reductions (character 13 and 18) also showed outside parallelism (i.e. the apomorphic character states were also found in some members of the large outgroup). The presence of secondary reductions and outside parallelisms weakens the character as evidence of monophyly.

The monophyly of the Pacific and the American golden plovers was supported by five characters, of which three (characters 4, 5 and 7) showed outside parallelism.

Glossary

(Parts of this glossary have been taken from Günter Bechly's (at Böblingen, Germany) glossary published on the Internet. It can be found on the homepage of the Willi Hennig Society – URL http://www.wims.edu/~mes/hennig/hennig.html

adaptation – change in an organism resulting from natural selection; a structure which is the result of such selection.
apomorphy (-ic) versus **plesiomorphy (-ic)**. A term used to characterize a character state, meaning '**derived**' (apomorphic) as opposed to '**primitive**' (plesiomorphic). The presence of feathers in birds is an apomorphic character state for birds compared with their closest living relatives, but a plesiomorphy or a plesiomorphic character within the birds' class. Shared derived (apomorphic) character states which are regarded as **homologous** are called **synapomorphies**. Shared plesiomorphic, homologous character states are called **symplesiomorphies**. Note that synapomorphies delineate natural or **monophyletic** groupings, while symplesiomorphies do not. These terms are used because they are neutral compared with the common human notions about primitive and derived conditions.

autapomorphy – an apomorphy or apomorphic character is unique for a single taxon, for instance a species. It is a relative term. If a group of species is analysed, each species ought to be characterized by its own autapomorphy in order to be recognized as a species. These characters, however, do not say anything about the relationships inside the group. If genera are analysed, the synapomorphies for each genus becomes an autapomorphy. An apomorphic character does not elucidate the relationships inside the group of genera under consideration.

character – heritable trait possessed by an organism (e.g. Fig. A), whose presence or absence is described by the 'state' present or absent.

cladogram – a diagram resulting from cladistic analysis, which depicts a hypothetical branching sequence of lineages leading to the taxa under consideration (i.e. four species of *Pluvialis*). The points of branching are called nodes.

clade – the monophyletic taxon. It includes the most recent common ancestor of all its members and all of its descendants. It is from the Greek word 'klados', branch or twig.

consistency index (CI) – an index that shows how well the characters fit a particular cladogram. The CI is the minium possible amount of character change on a given tree, divided by the actual amount of change. CI ranges from 0 to 1.0. In a datamatrix without any **homoplasy**, the CI will be 1.0.

convergence – similarities which have arisen independently in two or more organisms which are not closely related. Contrast with **homology**.

derived – a character state that is present in one or more subclades, but not all, of a **clade** under consideration. A derived character state is inferred to be a modified version of the **primitive condition** of that character, and to have arisen later in the evolution of the clade.

homology – two structures or behaviours are considered homologous when they are inherited from a common ancestor which possessed these. It can be very difficult to determine when the structure or behaviour has been modified through descent. Homologous characters may represent modifications of a single evolutionary novelty in a common ancestor of organisms. Homologies are therefore hypotheses about the singular evolutionary origin of particular similarities. Different aspects of this concept have been much debated in the literature!

homoplasy – a general term for all kinds of non-homology. All characters that have more than one step on a cladogram show homoplasy, and have to be explained.

ingroup – the group which has members which are hypothesized to be more closely related to each other (e.g. *Pluvialis*) than to any members in the **outgroup** (e.g. *Charadrius*). The ingroup is analysed with respect to its internal genealogical relationships.

monophyly – a group that consists of an ancestor and all of its descendants. Normally used for a group that includes the most recent common ancestor of all its members and all of its descendants. A monophyletic group is a **clade**.

outgroup – a group of species or a single species that is selected in order to help resolve the polarity of characters. It is used to identify the plesiomorphic and apomorphic character states in the **ingroup** (which reveals the internal relationships in the ingroup). It is hypothesized that the outgroup (e.g. *Charadrius*, or Common Ringed Plover) is less closely related to each of the taxa under consideration than they are to each other. A large literature is available on how to select the outgroup.

parallel development or parallelism – shared derived (apomorphic) characters, that are not the result of a single evolutionary origin but have evolved independently in closely related taxa.

parsimony – the principle of parsimony (also known as Occam's razor) requires that *ad hoc* assumptions should be minimized as far as possible in scientific explanations of natural phenomena. In other words, the explanation requiring the fewest assumptions is most likely to be correct! In phylogenetic systematics this means that of the vast number of theoretically possible cladograms one should choose the ones which minimize the number of hypotheses of non-homology (**homoplasy**) – the most parsimonious tree or trees.

phylogeny – the evolutionary relationships among organisms, showing the patterns of lineage branching by the true evolutionary history of the organisms being considered.

plesiomorphy (-ic) – see **apomorphy**.

polyphyletic – term applied to a group of organisms which does not include the most recent common ancestor of those organisms; the ancestor does not possess the character(s) shared by members of the group.

polytomy versus **dichotomy** – a node in a cladogram that has three or more branches as opposed to only two. It is not known whether or not this actually represents a species splitting into more than two sister-species, or the chosen characters fail to solve an actual dichotomy.

retention index (RI) – an index that shows the proportion of similarities on a tree interpreted as **synapomorphy**. The index ranges from 0 to 1.0.

sister group – the two **clades** resulting from the splitting of a single lineage.

synapomorphy – a character that is derived, and because it is shared by the taxa under consideration is used to infer common ancestry.

vicariance – speciation that occurs as a result of the separation and subsequent isolation of portions of an original population.

TABLE A   *Description of the characters used in the phylogeny analysis.*

Adult and juvenile characters:

Character 1
Presence of golden dorsal feather edges in breeding plumage. Binary character with present coded as (1) – absent (0).

Character 2
Transverse light bands on middle rectrices in breeding plumage. Multistate ordered character with three states, complete bands coded as (2) – uncomplete bands not reaching rachis (1) – absent (0).

Character 3
Extent of basic brown colour of middle rectrices in breeding plumage. Mustistate ordered character with three states, brown colour absent coded as (3) – brown colour present in a narrow band along the rachis (2) – brown extending almost to the fcather edges (1) – whole feather brown – (0).

TABLE A *Description of the characters used in the phylogeny analysis—continued*

Adult and juvenile characters—*continued*

Character 4a

Pigmentation of underwing coverts. Multistate ordered character with pigmented coded as (2) – partially pigmented (1) – unpigmented (0).

Character 4b

Pigmentation of underwing coverts. (The same character as above but recorded when only *C. hiaticula* was used as outgroup). Binary character with pigmented coded as (1) – unpigmented (0).

Character 5

Pigmentation of axillaries. Multistate unordered character with three states, black coded as (2) – brownish grey (1) – white (0).

Character 6a

Pigmentation of flanks in breeding plumage. Multistate unordered character with five states, feathers with chestnut colour coded as (4) – feathers pale buffish (yellow-brown) (3) – all feathers black (2) – some feathers with black blotches (1) – all feathers white (0).

Character 6b

Pigmentation of flanks in breeding plumage. Multistate ordered character with three states, all feathers black (2) – some feathers with black blotches (1) – all feathers white (0). The states 3 and 4 occurring in the large outgroup have been deleted, and the character is regarded as ordered.

Character 7

Outer vane on innermost remiges with or without white field. Binary character, without white field coded as (1) – with white field (0).

Character 8

Pigmentation of undertail coverts in breeding plumage. Multistate ordered character with three states, totally black coded as (2) – with black spots (1) – white (0).

Character 9

Dorsal feather edges on non-breeding plumage notched or fringed. Multistate ordered character with three states, distinctly notched coded as (2) – indistinctly notched (1) – fringed (0).

Character 10

Presence of golden feathers on head in non-breeding plumage. Multistate ordered character with four states, prominent coded as (3) – distinctive, but mixed with grey feathers (2) – traces of yellow (1) – absent (0).

Character 11

Breast/flank feathers in juvenile plumage. Multistate ordered character with three states, well developed dark terminal band coded as (2) – dark band present, but indistinct (1) – absent (0).

Character 12

Feathers behind ear coverts in breeding plumage. Binary character with white feathers present behind ear coverts, causing continuous white banding around black face coded as (1) – face differently patterned (0).

Chick characters:

Character 13

Longitudinal frontal line. Multistate ordered character with well developed line coded as (2) – indistinct (1) – absent (0).

TABLE A   *Description of the characters used in the phylogeny analysis—continued*

Chick characters—*continued*

Character 14
   Presence of transverse frontal line. Multistate ordered character with three states, present and well developed coded as (2) – present, but small (1) – absent (0).

Character 15
   Crown edge reduced or developed. Multistate ordered character with four states, distinct and continuous coded as (3) – distinct, but discontinuous (2) – present, but indistinct (1) – absent (0).

Character 16
   Nape pigmentation. Multistate unordered character with four states, nape white coded as (3) – pigment in a narrow band with white areas laterally (2) – pigment in a broad, median band with white areas laterally (1) – pigmented down scattered over the whole nape (0).

Character 17a
   Pigmentation of superciliary area. Multistate unordered with four states, purely white coded as (3) – white in outer half (2) – spotted (1) – fully pigmented (0).

Character 17b
   Pigmentation of superciliary area. Multistate ordered character with three states, purely white coded as (2) – white in outer half (1) – fully pigmented (0).

Character 18
   Presence of longitudinal, white dorsal stripes. Multistate ordered character with three states, well developed coded as (2) – faint (1) – absent (0).

Character 19
   Dorsal colour. Binary character, yellow coded as (1) – other colours (0).

Characters varying in the outgroup:

Character 20
   Bill colour of breeding plumage adults. Multistate character with three states, orange or yellow with black tip (2), black or blackish with some yellow at base of lower mandible (1), uniform black or blackish (0).

Character 21
   Bare coloured ring around the eyes. Binary character, present (1), absent (0).

Character 22
   Black frontal bar in breeding plumage. Multistate ordered character with three states, complete from eye to eye (2), not reaching eyes (1), absent (0).

Character 23
   Band from lores to ear-coverts in breeding plumage. Multistate ordered character with three states, complete (2), on ear-coverts only (1), absent (0).

Character 24
   White or whitish eyebrow band in breeding plumage. Multistate ordered character with three states, extending beyond ear-coverts (2), not beyond ear-coverts (1), absent (0).

Character 25
   White neck-ring in breeding plumage. Binary character, present (1), absent (0).

Character 26
   Chestnut on crown in breeding plumage. Binary character, chestnut present (1), chestnut absent (0).

TABLE B   *Data matrix used in the cladistic analysis.*

Taxa\Characters	Adult and juvenile characters														Chick characters								Characters varying in the outgroup						
	1	2	3	4a	4b	5	6a	6b	7	8	9	10	11	12	13	14	15	16	17a	17b	18	19	20	21	22	23	24	25	26
Binary or multistate ordered\unordered	b	o	o	o	b	u	u	o	b	o	o	o	o	b	o	o	o	u	u	o	o	b	o	b	o	o	o	o	b
P. dominica	1	2	1	2	1	1	2	2	1	2	2	1	2	1	2	2	2	2	3	2	2	1	0	0	0	0	1	0	0
P. fulva	1	2	1	2	1	1	1	1	1	2	2	2	2	1	1	1	1	0	2	1	1	1	0	0	0	0	1	0	0
P. apricaria	1	2	2	0	0	0	1	1	0	1	2	3	2	1	2	2	2	1	3	2	2	1	0	0	0	0	1	0	0
P. squatarola	0	1	3	0	0	2	2	2	0	0	1	0	1	1	1	0	0	3	0	0	0	1	0	0	0	0	1	0	0
C. hiaticula	0	0	0	0	0	0	0	0	0	0	0	0	0	0	0	0	3	3	3	2	0	0	2	0	0	2	1	0	0
C. semipalmatus	0	0	0	0	0	0	0	0	0	0	0	0	0	0	0	0	3	3	3		0	0	2	0	0	2	1	0	0
C. dubius	0	0	0	0	0	0	0	0	0	0	0	0	0	0	0	0	3	3	3		0	0	1	1	0	2	1	1	0
C. wilsonia	0	0	0	0	0	0	0	0	0	0	0	0	0	0	0	0	3	3	3		0	0	0	0	0	2	1	1	1
C. vociferus	0	0	0	0	0	0	0	0	0	0	0	0	0	0	0	0	3	3	3		0	0	0	1	2	2	1	2	0
C. melodus	0	0	0	0	0	0	0	0	0	0	0	0	0	0	0	0	3	3	3		1	0	2	0	2	0	1	2	0
C. leschenaultii	0	0	0	0	0	0	0	0	0	0	0	0	0	0	1	0	2	3	3		2	0	0	0	2	0	0	0	1
C. asiaticus	0	0	0	2	0	1	0	0	0	0	0	0	0	0	0	0	1	3	3		0	0	0	0	2	2	0	0	0
C. alexandrinus	0	0	0	0	0	0	0	0	0	0	0	0	0	0	0	0	1	3	1		2	0	0	0	0	1	1	0	1
C. pecuarius	0	0	0	0	0	0	3	0	0	0	0	0	0	0	0	0	1	3	1		0	0	0	0	2	1	2	2	0
C. pallidus	0	0	0	0	0	0	0	0	0	0	0	0	0	0	0	0	1	3	1		0	0	0	0	0	1	1	0	0
C. marginatus	0	0	0	0	0	0	0	0	0	0	0	0	0	0	0	0	2	3	1		0	0	0	0	0	1	1	0	0
C. tricollaris	0	0	0	1	0	0	0	0	1	1	0	0	0	0	0	0	3	3	0		0	0	2	1	0	1	2	0	0
C. morinellus	0	0	0	0	0	0	4		1	0	0	0	0	0	2	0	3	3	3		2	0	0	0	0	1	2	0	0

Breeding densities of tundra plovers in different parts of the world

Species	Geographic area	Zone*	Densities (pairs km⁻²)			N⁺	Sources
			Aver.	SD	Range		
Grey Plover	W Siberia; Yamal	A	1.7			1	1, 2
	W Siberia; Yamal	B	0.6	0.64	0.1–1.7	5	3
	Siberia; W Taimyr	A	2.8	1.52	0.2–5.0	9	4, 5
	Siberia; E Taimyr	I	0.6‡		0.57–0.64	2	46
	E Siberian Coast	A	1.3	1.48	0.3–3.0	3	6, 7, 8
	Chukchi Pen. Coast	B	1.1	1.62	0.1–3.0	3	6, 8
	Wrangel Island	A	4				6
	W Canadian Arctic	B			0.6–0.8		9
	E Canadian Arctic	A	1.6	2.82	0.3–8.0	7	10, 11
Eurasian Golden Plover							
	Great Britain (1970s)	C	3.2	3.33	0.7–16.4	65	12, 13, 14, 15, 16, 17
	Great Britain	C	1.7		0–7.0		47, 48
	(1980s and 1990s)	D	1.7		0–7.0		50
		D	2.0		0–7.0		49
	S Norway	C	3.2	0.76	2.7–4.1	3	2, 18
	Greenland	A	0.1			2	19
	Iceland	D	0.5	0.34	0.1–1.0	6	20
	Fennoscandia	D	3.6	2.53	0.7–8.8	19	2, 21, 22, 23, 24, 25, 26
	Fennoscandia	E	5.0	5.70	0.1–16.7	20	22, 23, 26, 27, 28, 29
	S Sweden	F	2.8	1.17	1.0–4.8	27	30, 31, 32, 33
	Finland	F	1.0			10	34
	E Baltic	F	3.9	4.75	0.6–14.5	8	35, 36, 37
	Öland	G	0.8				38
	W Siberia; Yamal	B	1.6	0.89	0.5–3.7	30	2, 3
Pacific Golden Plover							
	W Siberia; Yamal	B	0.7	0.62	0.1–2.1	8	3, 44
	W Siberia; Yamal	A	0.2			1	1, 2
	Siberia; W Taimyr	A	0.6			1	4
	Siberia; E Taimyr	I	0.6‡		0.5–0.64	2	46
	Chukchi Pen.	B	1.0	0.95	0.1–2.0	3	8
	Koryak Mtns.	E	3.9		1–6.7	2	45
American Golden Plover							
	N Alaska	B	1.4	1.34	0.4–3.3	4	39, 40
	Canadian Arctic	B	2.2		0.4–3.9	2	9, 41
	Canadian Arctic	A	3.5	1.32	2.7–5.0	3	10, 42
	Canadian Subarctic	H	6.1			1	43

* According to zone distributions in Fig. 5.3.
† Number of localities, study plots and/or years, as specified by the sources. Some sources gave only averages for several years for one study plot or location; these have been treated as N=1.
‡ Nest densities.
Zones: A = Lichen-moss tundra, B = Dwarf shrub tundra, C = Heather moor, D = Montane heath, E = Subalpine shrub and stunted forest zone, F = Boreal coniferous forest, G = 'Alvar' (dwarf shrub steppe zone), H = Transition forest tundra/dwarf shrub zone. I = Transition polar desert/lichen-moss tundra.
Sources: 1 V.K. Ryabitsev pers. comm., 2 I.B. pers. obs., 3 Danilov et al. (1984), 4 Tomkovich & Vronskij (1988a), 5 Tomkovich & Vronskij (1988b), 6 Flint & Kondratjew (1977), 7 Tomkovich (1988), 8 Kondrat'ev (1982), 9 Parmelee *et al.* (1967), 10 Drury (1961), 11 Hussell & Page (1976), 12 Ratcliffe (1976), 13 Parr (1980), 14 Langslow (1983), 15 Thomas *et al.* (1983), 16 Thomas & Hack (1984), 17 Nethersole-Thompson & Nethersole-Thompson (1986), 18 Byrkjedal (1977), 19 Meltofte (1985), 20 Wink (1973), 21 Granit (1939), 22 Merikallio (1958), 23 Bagge *et al.* (1963), 24 Alm *et al.* (1965), 25 Alm *et al.* (1966), 26 Moksnes (1973), 27 Dunker (1969), 28 Moksnes (1971), 29 Moksnes (1972), 30 Nilsson (1977), 31 Svensson (1978), 32 Kolmodin *et al.* (1987), 33 Alexandersson (1987), 34 Glutz von Blotzheim *et al.* (1975), 35 Kumari (1974) cited in 34, 36 Priednieks *et al.* (1989), 37 Irdet & Vilbaste (1974) cited in 30, 38 Steiniger (1959), 39 Maher (1959), 40 Sage (1974), 41 Sutton (1932), 42 Montgomerie *et al.* (1983), 43 Byrkjedal (1989a), 44 Uspenskij (1986), 45 Kistschinski (1980), 46 Underhill *et al.* (1993), 47 Brown (1993), 48 Whitfield (1997a), 49 Holt & Whitfield (1997a), 50 Shepherd & Whitfield (1995).

Nest site habitats of Grey Plovers, as percent of nests in various habitats

Habitat	Yamal, Siberia Arctic tundra 15 nests	Alaska E from Barrow, and Canada Arctic tundra 33 nests	W Alaska N to Barrow Subarctic tundra 36 nests
1. Lichen (D)	66.7	12.1	38.9
2. Dry sedge (D)	0	9.1	2.8
3. Dwarf shrub (D)	0	6.1	2.8
6. Shortgrown, leaved veget.(D)	0	12.1	0
7. Grass (D)	0	9.1	2.8
8. Moist sedge	20.0	30.3	2.8
10. Bare ground (D)	0	21.2	16.7[a]
13. Moss	13.3	0	33.3[b]
Dry habitats total, (i.e. total (D))	80.0	69.7	64.0[c]

[a]66.5% of which in sand dunes
[b]An unknown portion of 'Moss' is probably lichen
[c]If all 'Moss' here means lichen, 97.3% of the nests were on dry habitats
D, refers to dry habitats
Sources: IB; America: North American oological collections

Nest site habitats of Eurasian Golden Plovers as percent of nests in various habitats. Percent distribution of random points (RP) within defined study area given in parentheses

Habitat	Great Britain Several zones 192 nests	Jæren, SW Norway Heather moor 25 nests (168 RP)	Hardangervidda Low alpine heath 49 nests (570 RP)	Finnmarksvidda Open forest 21 nests (312 RP)	Yamal, Siberia Subarctic tundra 7 nests (44 RP)
1. Lichen (D)	3.6a	0 (0.6)	53.1 (20.5)**	42.9 (43.9)	14.3 (22.7)
2. Dry sedge (D)	3.1b	8.1c (17.3)	24.5d (19.6)	0 (0)	0 (2.3)
3. Dwarf shrub(D) (<0.2 m)	34.9e	64.0e (26.2)**	8.2f (7.7)	0 (0)	0 (0)
4. Lichen/*Betula nana* (D) g	0	0 (0)	2.0 (3.7)	42.9 (21.2)	85.7 (36.4)*
5. Dense *Betula nana/Salix herbacea*	0	0 (0)	0 (0)	0 (9.6)	0 (20.5)
6. Shortgrown, leaved veg.(D)	0	0 (0)	0 (20.4)i	0 (0)	0 (0)
7. Grass (D)	1.0	20.0j (35.1)	12.3j,k (17.4)	0 (0)	0 (0)
8. Moist sedge	31.3 l	4.0 c,l (16.0)	0 (10.9) l*	4.8 l (13.8)	0 (15.9)
9. Moist sedge/ shrub	13.0m	4.0n (4.8)	0 (0)	9.5 (11.5)	0 (0)
10. Mainly bare ground (D)	1.0o	0 (0)	0 (0)	0 (0)	0 (2.3)

Habitat	Great Britain Several zones 192 nests	Jæren, SW Norway Heather moor 25 nests (168 RP)	Hardangervidda Low alpine heath 49 nests (570 RP)	Finnmarksvidda Open forest 21 nests (312 RP)	Yamal, Siberia Subarctic tundra 7 nests (44 RP)
11. Dead bracken (D)	2.1	0 (0)	0 (0)	0 (0)	0 (0)
12. Other (D)	9.9p	0 (0)	0 (0)	0 (0)	0 (0)
Dry habitats, i.e., total (D)	55.6	92.1 (79.2)	100* (89.1)	85.8 (65.1)	100 (63.6)

a includes 'Montane heath', b 'Heather-Deer Sedge', c *Scirpus caespitosus*, d *Carex bigelowii* heath, e *Calluna vulgaris*, f *Vaccinium myrtillus* heath, g open patches of lichen-enclosed *Betula nana* shrub, h =>20–30 cm tall, i pure *Salix herbacea* stand, j pure *Nardus stricta* stand, k *Anthoxanthum*/herb mix., l *Eriophorum* (chiefly), m *Calluna/Eriophorum* mix., n *Eriophorum/Erica tetralix* mix., o old mine waste, p limestone turf. D, refers to dry habitats.

Chi-square tests for difference between nests and random points of selected habitats (DF=1) with Bonferoni-adjusted critical values: * $p<0.05$, [†] $p<0.001$

Sources: Great Britain, Ratcliffe (1976, based on nest cards); Jæren, Hardangervidda, and Yamal (IB 1972–74 and 1990, 1978–85, and 1989, respectively); Finnmarksvidda, T. Larsen, J. Moldsvor, IB (1987–90).

Nest site habitat of Pacific Golden Plovers, as percent of nests in various habitats. Percent distribution of random points (RP) within defined study area given in parentheses

Habitat	St. Lawrence Is., Alaska Subarctic tundra 7 nests	W Alaska mainland Subarctic tundra 18 nests	Yamal Siberia Subarctic tundra 7 nests (44 RP)
1. Lichen (D)	71.4	88.9[a]	71.4* (22.7)
2. Dry sedge (D)	0	0	0 (2.3)
4. Lichen/tall shrub (D)	0	0	28.6 (36.4)
5. Dense tall shrub	0	0	0 (20.5)
8. Moist sedge	0	0	0 (15.9)
10. Bare ground (D)	28.6	11.1	0 (2.3)
Dry habitats total, (i.e., total (D))	100	100	100** (63.7)

a incl 'Moss'

D, refers to dry habitats

Chi-square tests for difference between nests and random points of selected habitats (DF=1) with Bonferoni-adjusted critical values: * p<0.05, ** p<0.025

Sources: St. Lawrence Is.,: Sauer (1962), Mainland Alaska: North American oological collections; Yamal: IB (1989)

Nest habitat of American Golden Plovers, as percent of nests in various habitats. Percent distribution of random points (RP) within defined study area given in parentheses

Habitat	Churchill, Manitoba		Alaskan coast E from Barrow
	Subarctic tundra		Arctic tundra
	Sample A	Sample B	
	23 nests	21 nests (96 RP)	140 nests
1. Lichen (D)	66.7	71.4 * (33.3)	11.4
2. Dry sedge (D)	8.6	9.5 (27.1)	8.6
3. Dwarf shrub (<0.2 m) (D)	4.4	9.5a (3.1)	6.4b,c
4. Lichen/*Betula nana* or *B. glandulosa* (D)	0	0 (0)	3.6d
5. Tall dense shrub (>0.2 m) (D)	0	0 (13.5)e	0
6. Shortgrown, leaved (vegetation) (D)	0	9.5f (9.4)	19.3
7. Grass (D)	0	0 (0)	9.3
8. Moist sedge	6.7	0 (0)	20.0
9. Moist sedge/shrub mix	0	0 (0)	12.9
10. Bare ground (D)	13.3	0 (3.1)	3.6
13. Moss (Bryophyta)	0	0 (10.4)	5.0
Dry habitats (i.e., total (D))	93.3	100* (76.0)	62.2

a *Rhododendron lapponicum, Empetrum nigrum,* b *Cassiope,* c *Ledum,* d incl. 'Dry Riparian Willow', e *Salix* spp., *Betula glandulosa,* f *Dryas.* D, refers to dry habitats

Chi-square test for difference between nests and random points: * $p < 0.05$

Sources: Churchill, sample A: North American Nest Cards (several years, undefined study area); Churchill, sample B: IB defined area, details in Byrkjedal 1989a); Alaska: North American nest cards (several years, several sites pooled).

Breeding season alarm calls

Alarm calls were tape recorded at the observer's approach to nests and broods during ordinary nest checks and while recording antipredator behaviour. Most of the alarm calls of Grey Plover and Pacific Golden Plover were recorded by a Sony TC-55B cassette tape recorder fitted to a Sony F-27S cardioid microphone mounted in a parabolic reflector (Sony PBR 33). Some alarm calls were inadvertently recorded while dictating behaviour, using a Sony TCM-2 tape recorder with an internal microphone.

The recordings were done by IB; those of Grey Plover and Pacific Golden Plover at Yamal 1989, American Golden Plover at Churchill 1986, and Eurasian Golden Plover at Hardangervidda 1984.

The recorded material was listened to and at the same time watched as running sonagrams on a sonagraph screen (Uniscan II and Avisoft-Sonagraph Pro). Sonagram sections could be stopped or recalled to the screen as needed, and numerous printouts of sonagrams were made to compare calls for categorization. For each species, sonagrams and tables show the structures and relative occurrence, respectively, of the various sounds. The following species characteristics were found:

Grey Plover (Fig. A, Table A) Plaintive single-syllable whistles were most frequently used; composite whistles consisted of drawn-out, weakly frequency modulated, elements with abrupt frequency shifts (yodelling), one type almost identical to the song uttered in butterfly flight (see Chapter 8).

Eurasian Golden Plover (Fig. B, Table B) Plaintive single-syllable whistles, usually with moderate or no frequency modulations. Composite calls absent.

Pacific Golden Plover (Fig. C, Table C) Plaintive single-syllable whistles common, as well as 3-syllable calls with strongly frequency modulated elements.

American Golden Plover (Fig. D, Table D) Highly diversified. Plaintive single-syllable whistles frequently given, but composite calls more common, especially a yodelling 2-syllable whistle with negligible frequency modulation of each element. Many calls consisted of short, 'clicking' elements with strong frequency modulations, some of these resembling song uttered during butterfly flight (see Chapter 8).

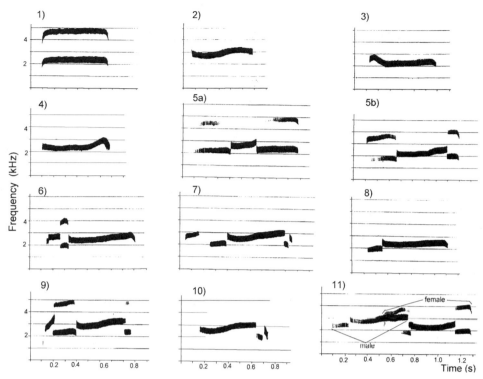

FIG. A. *Broad-band sonagrams of alarm calls of Grey Plovers near nests, Yamal 1986.*

From structural similarities possible homologies are outlined in Table E. The plaintive calls, frequently used by all four species, were simple and of rather similar structure. Also some of the composite calls resembled each other across the species. Notable similarities were Grey Plover sound No. 8 and American Golden Plover sound No. 4, also the latter's No. 3 compared to the commonly used No. 5 of Pacific Golden Plover. Moreover, Nos. 7 and 8 of Pacific Golden Plover bear similarities to the 3 first syllables of American golden plover call No. 18.

In American and Pacific golden plover and Grey Plover the sexes differed in their relative use of some of the calls, and in Grey Plover females had audibly deeper voice than males (Fig. A, sonagram 11) in spite of negligible body size differences between the sexes.

Data for American Golden Plover showed changes in the relative use of some of the alarm calls from the incubation period to post-hatching (Table D). Available recordings were insufficient for such analyses of the other species; however, Eurasian Golden Plover is more or less silent in the incubation period compared with what they are after hatching.

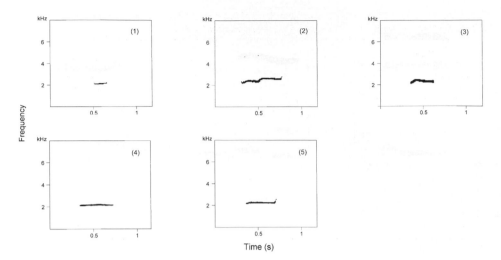

FIG. B.   *Broad-band sonagrams of alarm calls of Eurasian Golden Plovers near broods, Hardangervidda 1984.*

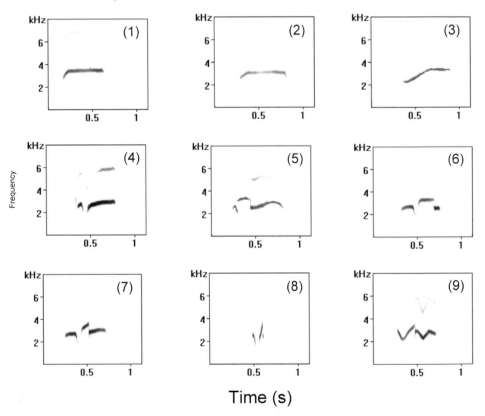

FIG. C.   *Broad-band sonagrams of alarm calls of Pacific Golden Plovers, Yamal 1989.*

TABLE A   *Use of various alarm calls by Grey Plovers when an observer approached their nests (data for a few parents with broods also included), Yamal 1989.*

Type of call (referring to sonagrams Fig. A)	Males Percent of calls (N=377)	Number of birds (N=19)	Females Percent of calls (N=111)	Number of birds (N=9)
1	59.4	14	51.4	6
2	1.9	2	0.9	1
3	1.1	3		
4	0.5	1	0.9	1
5	14.6	8	9.0	3
6	4.2	4	0.9	1
7	7.7	3	8.1	2
8	8.4	4	24.3*	4
9	0.3	1		
10	1.9	3	4.5	2

*Difference between males and females: $\chi_1^2 = 20.234$, $p < 0.001$

TABLE B   *Use of various alarm calls by Eurasian Golden Plovers when an observer approached their broods, Hardangervidda 1984.*

Type of call (referring to sonagrams Fig. B)	Percent of calls (N=280)	Number of birds or pairs (N=20)
1	5.0	8
2	5.0	8
3	52.9	18
4	35.7	16
5	1.4	2

TABLE C   *Use of various alarm calls by Pacific Golden Plovers when an observer approached their nests, Yamal 1989.*

Type of call (referring to sonagrams Fig. C)	Males Percent of calls (N=325)	Number of birds (N=8)	Females Percent of calls (N=109)	Number of birds (N=6)
1	17.5	5	65.1*	6
2	3.4	5	3.7	1
3	0.6	2		
4	15.7	5	13.8	3
5	7.4	2		
6	9.2	5		
7	45.5	7	17.4**	5
8	0.3	1		
9	0.3	1		

Differences between males and females: * $\chi_1^2 = 88.934$, $p < 0.001$; ** $\chi_1^2 = 27.240$, $p < 0.001$ (p< 0.002 after Bonferroni-adjustment)

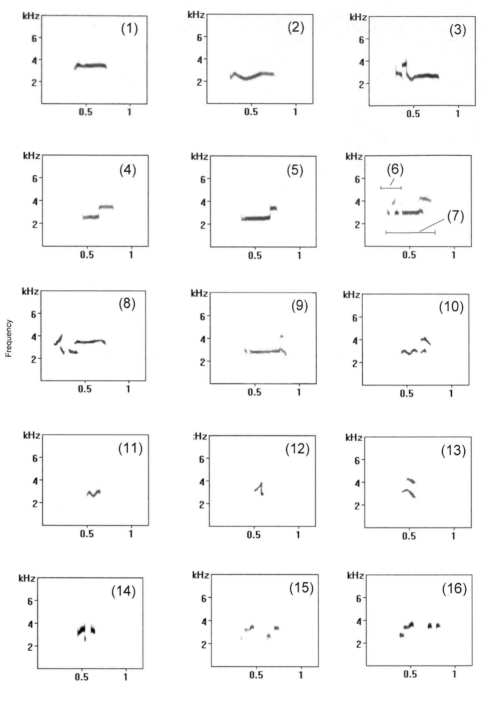

Time (s)

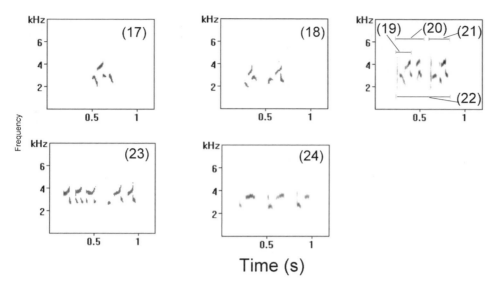

FIG. D.   *Broad-band sonagrams of alarm calls of American Golden Plovers near nests, Churchill 1986.*

TABLE D   *Use of various alarm calls by American Golden Plovers when an observer approached their nests and broods, Churchill 1986.*

Type of call (referring to sonagrams Fig. D)	Incubation period Males		Females		Post-hatching Males + females	
	Percent of calls (N=1140)	Number of birds (N=22)	Percent of calls (N=95)	Number of birds (N=7)	Percent of calls (N=450)	Number of pairs (N=9)
1	10.2	13	20.0	4	9.1	7
2	2.1	4	10.5	2	5.1	4
3	0.4	1			0.2	1
4	4.3	3			0.4	2
5	53.2	19	29.5	5	19.8	9
6	0.6	3			0.4	1
7	3.9	13	3.2	2	5.1	7
8	0.2	2				
9			3.2	1		
10	0.6	4				
11	1.4	7			23.8	5
12	0.8	5			1.8	3
13	0.1	1				
14	0.6	2				
15	1.9	7			0.7	2
16	0.9	4				
17	0.5	3	3.2	2	6.7	6
18	1.0	4	3.2	1	2.0	4
19	4.3	8			5.1	7
20	5.1	11			5.8	5
21	1.4	9	11.6	1		
22	4.4	8	15.8	2	11.1	5
23	0.1	1			1.8	3
24	0.1	1			0.4	1

TABLE E *Matrix of possible homologies of alarm calls, judged from structural similarities. The numerals correspond to the numbering of sonagrams for each species. Boldface denotes vocalizations used most or second most frequently by both species under comparison, parentheses less certain homologies.*

Grey Plover (Fig. A)	Eurasian Golden Plover (Fig. B)	Pacific Golden Plover (Fig. C)	American Golden Plover (Fig. D)
1	(1),**4**,(3)	**1**,(2)	**1**
2	(2)		(2)
3	(3)		2
4	(2),(5)	(3)	
5	(5),(6)	3	
8			4, (**5**)
10			(9)
Eurasian Golden Plover			
2		3	(12)
3		**1**	2
4		2	**1**
5			(5)
Pacific Golden Plover			
1			**1**
2			(2)
3			(4)
4			(8)
5			3
6			(3)
7			18*
8			18*
9			(11)

*Refers to first three elements of American Golden Plover sound 18; both sound 7 and 8 of Pacific Golden Plover resembles this fraction of sound 18.

Appendix 10

Geographical and temporal distribution of museum specimens used in the construction of Figs 10.1, 10.5, 10.6, 10.9, 10.10, 10.13, 10.14 and 10.17 (migration routes and phenologies of tundra plovers)

TABLE A   *Temporal distribution and sample sizes of museum specimens of tundra plovers used to construct migratory routes and schedules. Bold figures (based on N ≥ 5 specimens) were primarily those used as a basis for the isophenes.*

GREY PLOVER:

Area No.	Autumn (August–November)				Spring (February–May)			
	First date	Last date	Median date	Number of specimens	First date	Last date	Median date	Number of specimens
1	18.09	17.11	23.09	4			24.05	1
2			09.09	1				
3					22.02	11.04	16.03	4
4			23.11	1	01.05	18.05	**08.05**	5
5			09.10	1				
6	04.09	21.11	13.10	2	04.04	16.05	25.04	2
7	11.09	10.11	**05.10**	7	09.02	25.05	**16.05**	6
8	12.09	15.10	**27.09**	9	05.04	19.05	27.04	2
9			17.09	1				
10			27.11	1				
11	06.08	27.10	**14.10**	6	15.02	10.05	22.03	3
12	01.08	18.11	**04.09**	145	21.04	31.05	**19.05**	7
13	01.08	21.10	**14.09**	23				
14	28.08	09.10	**15.09**	14				
15			15.09	1				
16	17.10	21.11	30.10	2			01.05	1
17	18.08	03.11	22.10	4	17.02	18.02	18.02	4
18	26.09	23.10	15.10	4				
19	02.08	28.10	**17.08**	47				
20	18.09	06.10	06.10	3				
21	06.08	01.10	**01.10**	6				
22	24.09	15.10	**03.10**	17				
23	10.08	06.09	01.09	4				
24	11.09	23.10	**18.09**	5				
25			14.09	1				

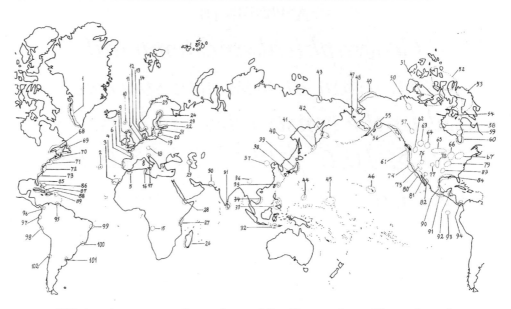

FIG. A.   *Areas corresponding to clusters of Grey Plover specimens. The numbers refer to 'Area No.' in Table A.*

TABLE A – *continued*

GREY PLOVER – *continued*

Area No.	Autumn (August–November)				Spring (February–May)			
	First date	Last date	Median date	Number of specimens	First date	Last date	Median date	Number of specimens
26	08.10	08.11	03.11	3			01.04	1
27	18.09	27.11	08.10	4	26.02	07.05	**11.04**	10
28			22.11	1			13.03	1
29					04.03	18.03	11.03	2
30					01.02	20.02	11.02	2
31			29.10	1				
32			13.11	1				
33					16.02	23.03	**16.03**	6
34	21.10	24.11	18.11	4	31.03	20.04	10.04	2
35					15.02	17.05	23.03	4
36	09.10	15.10	11.10	2				
37	08.08	08.10	**24.09**	17				
38	17.09	17.11	**01.10**	10			24.03	1
39	06.08	17.11	**11.10**	28	20.02	13.05	**06.05**	5
40			24.09	1				
41	04.09	02.11	04.10	2				
42	08.09	08.10	23.09	2				
43							30.05	1
44			27.08	1				
45			03.11	1				
46			31.10	1	23.02	13.03	13.03	3
47	03.08	16.09	**30.08**	6	01.05	27.05	**23.05**	10
48	01.08	02.08	02.08	2			11.05	1

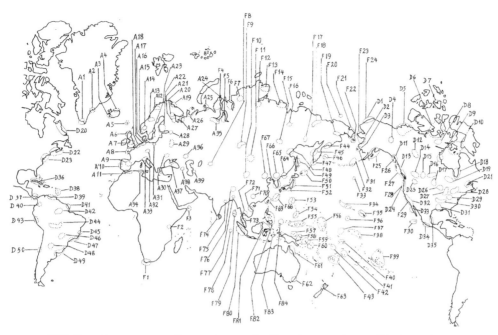

FIG. B. *Areas corresponding to clusters of golden plover specimens. The letters D, A, and F denote geographic areas for the American, Eurasian, and Pacific golden plovers, respectively. Other legends as in Fig. A.*

TABLE A – *continued*

GREY PLOVER – *continued*

Area No.	Autumn (August–November)				Spring (February–May)			
	First date	Last date	Median date	Number of specimens	First date	Last date	Median date	Number of specimens
49	03.08	04.09	**30.08**	16	27.05	29.05	28.05	2
50			05.09	1				
51	02.08	14.09	**26.08**	12				
52	02.08	01.09	**20.08**	26				
53	27.08	04.09	01.09	3				
54	25.08	28.09	**21.09**	9				
55					06.05	06.05	06.05	2
56	09.08	26.09	**19.09**	6	20.04	16.05	**02.05**	7
57							29.05	1
58	19.08	24.09	**17.09**	7				
59	12.08	16.09	16.09	3				
60	09.08	26.10	**16.09**	50				
61	05.08	27.11	**28.09**	26	05.02	31.05	**01.03**	40
62	01.09	05.10	**23.09**	23			24.05	1
63	07.08	30.10	**15.09**	46	15.05	29.05	**23.05**	18
64	19.08	29.09	**16.09**	14	19.05	27.05	**24.05**	16
65	10.08	07.11	**22.09**	31	20.05	31.05	**28.05**	20
66	13.08	29.10	**18.09**	49	18.05	29.05	**20.05**	9
67	09.08	25.11	**24.09**	157	26.04	31.05	**24.05**	46

EURASIAN GOLDEN PLOVER

Area No.	Autumn (August–November)				Spring (February–May)			
	First date	Last date	Median date	Number of specimens	First date	Last date	Median date	Number of specimens
A1	12.08	27.10	**21.09**	6	08.04	28.05	**07.05**	22
A2					04.05	27.05	**10.05**	5
A3	04.08	15.10	**26.09**	36	25.04	02.05	29.04	2
A4	02.08	04.10	**14.08**	8	24.04	25.05	**14.05**	19
A5	09.08	29.10	**04.09**	9	21.03	08.05	**29.04**	18
A6	24.08	29.09	29.09	4	26.04	19.05	09.05	3
A7	16.10	22.11	04.11	2	25.02	02.05	05.03	3
A8	24.09	18.10	**12.10**	9			15.03	1
A9			23.11	1				
A10	19.11	21.11	20.11	2			19.02	1
A11							11.02	1
A12	05.08	18.09	**23.08**	14	18.05	28.05	**24.05**	12
A13			17.08	1				
A14	01.08	19.09	**17.08**	28	11.05	15.05	**13.05**	30
A15	20.08	22.10	**11.09**	21	28.04	13.05	13.05	3
A16	02.08	30.11	**11.09**	135	03.02	27.05	**22.04**	30
A17	18.09	28.10	**30.09**	8				
A18			14.09	1				
A19	08.08	30.09	**26.08**	5	18.05	31.05	**28.05**	6
A20	17.09	24.09	23.09	3	28.05	31.05	30.05	2
A21			14.08	1	07.05	10.05	**08.05**	6
A22	03.08	29.09	**15.09**	23	27.04	29.05	**20.05**	21
A23	05.08	10.10	**18.09**	12	18.04	23.05	**10.05**	7
A24	04.08	06.08	04.08	3				
A25	19.08	10.10	14.09	2				
A26	08.08	02.09	**09.08**	7	10.05	12.05	11.05	2
A27	01.08	04.08	03.08	2				
A28			02.09	1				
A29	16.08	22.09	04.09	2			05.09	1
A30			30.10	1				
A31			22.09	1				
A32	25.09	18.11	**12.10**	12				
A33	27.08	17.11	**08.11**	5	20.02	07.04	26.03	3
A34			29.09	1			09.02	1
A35	01.08	12.08	**02.08**	5			30.05	1
A36							04.03	1
A37			06.11	1				
A38			19.08	1				
A39			22.11	1				
Total specimens				374				202

PACIFIC GOLDEN PLOVER:

| Area No. | Autumn (August–November) | | | | Spring (February–May) | | | |
	First date	Last date	Median date	Number of specimens	First date	Last date	Median date	Number of specimens
F1							03.03	1
F2	02.11	26.11	14.11	2				
F3							15.05	1
F4			12.09	1			31.05	1
F5			07.09	1				
F6	03.08	06.08	05.08	2				
F7	04.08	25.08	08.08	3				
F8			01.10	1				
F9	01.08	08.10	**02.09**	18	13.04	24.05	20.05	3
F10	23.08	19.09	**03.09**	7				
F11	13.08	25.10	**10.09**	12				
F12			26.09	1				
F13	26.08	08.09	06.09	4				
F14	21.08	01.09	21.08	3				
F15			30.08	1			31.05	1
F16	14.09	17.09	16.09	2				
F17							29.05	1
F18	01.08	15.09	**01.09**	9			27.05	1
F19	22.08	08.10	02.09	4	07.05	30.05	19.05	2
F20			07.09	1			28.05	1
F21	07.08	27.09	**24.09**	14				
F22	14.08	18.10	**14.09**	31			13.05	1
F23	03.08	13.10	**29.08**	17	07.05	09.08	08.05	2
F24	08.08	04.09	**27.08**	18	16.05	31.05	**27.05**	5
F25	03.09	01.10	01.10	4	11.05	19.05	**13.05**	5
F26					09.05	18.05	18.05	3
F27	10.08	02.11	**22.08**	5			30.04	1
F28	20.08	24.11	**10.10**	18	04.02	14.05	30.03	2
F29			21.11	1				
F30			22.08	1			21.05	1
F31	28.08	04.10	**15.09**	20				
F32	05.08	29.10	**31.08**	24	01.05	26.05	**20.05**	12
F33			21.10	1				
F34	07.09	13.11	**10.10**	14	12.02	30.05	**19.04**	20
F35	12.08	27.11	**21.10**	12	09.02	17.04	**15.03**	31
F36	22.08	19.11	**15.10**	17	03.02	30.04	**05.04**	18
F37	16.09	20.10	**16.10**	9	26.02	19.05	27.02	4
F38	17.09	28.11	**29.10**	23	16.03	27.05	**31.03**	7
F39	28.09	20.10	08.10	4	17.03	14.05	15.04	2
F40	18.09	08.11	**18.10**	20	09.02	25.05	**08.05**	6
F41	03.08	28.11	**26.08**	8	17.02	21.05	**14.03**	9
F42	19.08	19.11	**16.11**	13				
F43	23.09	28.11	28.11	3				
F44	02.08	11.10	**02.09**	9	24.05	24.05	24.05	2
F45	28.08	12.11	**28.09**	11				
F46	15.08	31.10	**01.10**	26	16.05	28.05	**25.05**	5
F47	20.08	23.10	**02.10**	6				
F48	01.09	16.10	**19.09**	8	21.05	27.05	22.05	3
F49	17.08	25.10	**29.09**	10	18.05	18.05	18.05	2

TABLE A – *continued*

PACIFIC GOLDEN PLOVER – *continued*

Area No.	Autumn (August–November)				Spring (February–May)			
	First date	Last date	Median date	Number of specimens	First date	Last date	Median date	Number of specimens
F50	13.08	23.10	**17.09**	11			30.05	1
F51	22.08	27.10	**11.10**	14	06.04	22.05	**16.04**	22
F52	23.08	11.10	**17.09**	7	15.04	06.05	29.04	3
F53					22.03	27.03	25.03	2
F54	31.08	02.11	**07.10**	20	15.02	21.04	**16.04**	7
F55					16.02	16.02	16.02	2
F56	15.08	11.11	**22.10**	16	02.03	29.05	**29.04**	9
F57	03.10	08.10	06.10	2			10.03	1
F58	17.08	23.10	**16.10**	6			12.04	1
F59	06.08	08.11	**28.10**	9				
F60	03.09	05.11	**23.10**	5				
F61			03.11	1			02.03	1
F62	24.11	24.11	24.11	2				
F63			06.11	1			30.05	1
F64	15.08	26.10	**18.09**	23	19.05	25.05	22.05	3
F65					13.05	23.05	18.05	3
F66	12.08	27.09	**17.09**	13				
F67	02.09	24.09	**12.09**	6				
F68	05.09	26.11	**20.09**	6	04.02	28.04	**17.02**	5
F69	13.08	20.10	**12.10**	27	23.03	30.04	**17.04**	26
F70			10.09	1				
F71							04.02	1
F72	11.09	26.11	**25.10**	18	08.02	09.05	**07.04**	27
F73			31.10	1	02.03	23.03	**21.03**	6
F74			11.09	1				
F75			02.08	1				
F76	15.09	02.11	**02.11**	9				
F77							25.04	1
F78			01.10	1				
F79	19.10	22.10	21.10	2			01.05	1
F80	13.08	11.11	**20.09**	7	23.02	22.03	**28.02**	5
F81	16.09	28.11	**08.10**	10	25.03	17.04	25.03	3
F82	12.09	25.11	**17.10**	18	02.02	13.04	**13.02**	9
F83			20.09	1			19.04	1
F84	16.08	20.09	**10.09**	12				
Total specimens				670				294

APPENDIX 11

Geographical distribution of references (below) used for the migration charts (Figs 10.1, 10.5, 10.6, 10.9, 10.10, 10.13, 10.14 and 10.17) and winter distribution maps (Figs 10.4, 10.8, 10.12, 10.16)

Ali & Ripley (1969), Allen (1939), Antas (1983), Ash (1980), Balanca (1984), Barter (1988), Belcher (1929), Belopol'skij *et al.* (1970), Bent (1929), Bergmann (1935), Bijlsma & Roder (1985), Blaszyk (1939), Blædel (1959–63), Booth *et al.*(1984), Branson & Minton (1976), Brazil (1991), Bregnballe *et al.* (1989), Brinkmann (1941), Buchanan (1988), Buden (1992), Byrd *et al.* (1974), Byrkjedal (1980c), Chapman (1923), Cogswell (1948), Collett (1921), Colwell *et al.* (1988), Cooke (1912), Cramp & Simmons (1983), Dabbene (1920), Degtyarev & Pozdnyakov (1980), Delacour (1947), Dement'ev & Gladkov (1951), Dierschke & Dierschke (1990), Dijk *et al.* (1984, 1990), Dinsmore *et al.* (1984), Dolgushin (1962), Dominguez (1990), Dott (1985), Edelstam (1972), Edwards & Parish (1988), Eerden & Keij (1979), Erickson (1992), Evans *et al.* (1984), Feare & High (1977), Ferns (1977), Fjeldså & Krabbe (1990), Fuller & Lloyd (1981), Gabór (1985), Gabrielson & Jewett (1970), Garðarsson & Nielsen (1989), Gifford (1913), Gill & Handel (1990), Gill & Jorgenson (1979), Girard (1989), Glenister (1955, 1971), Glushchenko (1988), Glutz von Blotzheim (1963), Glutz von Blotzheim *et al.* (1975), Godfrey (1986), Gordeev (1980), Gore & Pyong-Oh (1971), Green *et al.* (1994), Grimes (1974), Gromme (1974), Gudmundsson & Garðarsson (1993), Harvey (1990), Haviland (1915), Haviland (1916), Hayes & Fox (1991), Hayes *et al.* (1990), Hazevoet (1992), Henry (1955), Henshaw (1910), Hicklin (1987), Hirschfeld (1994), Hogg *et al.* (1984), Holyoak & Thibault (1984), Hubbard (1978), Imhof (1976), Janssen (1987), Jehl & Smith (1970), Johnson *et al.* (1981b), Johnson (1985), Johnston & McFarlane (1967), Jukema & Hulscher (1988), Jukema (1989), Karpovich & Kochanov (1967), Kenyon (1961), Kinsky & Yaldwyn (1981), Kistshcinski *et al.* (1983), Kokhanov & Skokova (1967), Korzukov (1991), Kozlova (1961), Kretchmar *et al.* (1991), Kube *et al.* (1994), Kube & Struwe (1994), Labutin *et al.* (1988), Lack (1986), Lambeck *et al.* (1989), Landing (1991 and pers. comm.), Lane (1987), Larionov *et al.* (1991), LeCroy & Peckover (1983), Lord Medway & Wells (1976), Lust (1984), Maestri (1931), Mainardi (1987), Makatsch (1950), Manson-Bahr (1953), Marchant & Higgins (1993), Marsh & Wilkinson (1991),

FIG. A.   *Distribution of localities covered by the references.*

Martinez-Vilalta (1985), Mason (1969), Mayr (1945), McClure (1974), McKenzie (1967), Meinertzhagen (1954), Meininger (1989), Meltofte *et al.* (1972), Meltofte *et al.* (1994), Meltofte (1987, 1993), Merikallio (1958), Morrison & Ross (1989), Morrison (1984), Mumford & Keller (1984), Munro (1960), Myers & Myers (1979), Nankinov (1989), Nørrevang (1959), Ntiamoa-Baidu & Grieve (1987), OAG Münster (1988), Oberholser (1938), Page *et al.* (1979), Parish *et al.* (1987), Parr (1980), Paulson (1993), Paulson & Lee (1992), Peklo & Ochapovskij (1973), Perco (1984), Peters & Burleigh (1951), Pfeifer (1988), Pienkowski *et al.* (1985), Piersma *et al.* (1987, 1990a,b), Pulliainen & Saari (1993), Rachilin (1973), Robbins (1991), Roos (1975), Root (1988), Rowan (1923), Rufino (1984), Rufino & Araujo (1987), Salomonsen (1967a), Sampath & Krishnamurthy (1990), Sauer (1962), Sauer (1963a,b), Schick *et al.* (1984), Schneider & Mallory (1982), Sealy *et al.* (1971), Shadle & Wagnitz (1991), Shkatulova (1980), Slater (1901), Smart *et al.* (1983), Smirenskij *et al.* (1980), Smit & Wolff (1981), Smit (1986), Smith & Stiles (1979), Smith (1957), Smythies (1953), Smythies (1960), Snow (1971), Sordahl (1981b), Speek (1978), Stahlbaum (1965), Stone (1937, 1965), Stotz *et al.* (1992), Stout (1967), Straka (1991, 1992), Summers *et al.* (1987), Thomas (1987), Todd (1940), Tolchin *et al.* (1973), Tolchin & Pyzh'yanov (1980), Tomkovich & Sorokin (1983), Tubbs (1991), Tye & Tye (1987), Tye (1987), Ulfstrand *et al.* (1974), Urban *et al.* (1986), Urner & Storer (1949), van Marle & Voous (1988), Vaurie (1972), Velasco & Alberto (1993), Vengerov (1973b), Verheugt *et al.* (1990), Viksnc & Mikhel'son (1985), Voous (1983), Voronov & Voronov (1980), Williams & Williams (1988), Wishart *et al.* (1981), Witherby *et al.* (1940), Wolff & Smit (1990), Wymenga *et al.* (1990), Yeatman-Berthelot & Jarry (1991), Zubakin *et al.* (1988), Zwarts *et al.* (1991).

APPENDIX 12

Number of Grey Plovers counted or estimated in various parts of their wintering range

Area	Number of birds	References
SOUTH AMERICA		
Colombia: Caribbean coast	1241	Morrison & Ross (1989)
Venezuela	403	Morrison & Ross (1989)
Trinidad	173	Morrison & Ross (1989)
Guyana	598	Morrison & Ross (1989)
Suriname	3940	Morrison & Ross (1989)
French Guyana	640	Morrison & Ross (1989)
Brazil: North Coast	16 777	Morrison & Ross (1989)
Brazil: East Coast	247	Morrison & Ross (1989)
Uruguay	365	Morrison & Ross (1989)
Argentina	10	Morrison & Ross (1989)
Chile: Tierra del Fuego	0	Morrison & Ross (1989)
Chile: Pacific Coast	28	Morrison & Ross (1989)
Peru	1344	Morrison & Ross (1989)
Ecuador	1082	Morrison & Ross (1989)
Colombia: Pacific Coast	419	Morrison & Ross (1989)
WESTERN EUROPE		
Britain & Ireland	20 000	Lack (1986)
Britain & Ireland	40 500	Tubbs (1991)
German Wadden Sea	1300	Prokosch (1984)
Dutch Wadden Sea	2500	Wolff & Smit (1984)
Dutch Delta	6200	Leewis et al. (1984)
Danish-German-Dutch Wadden Sea	3100–20 800[1]	Meltofte et al. (1994)
France[2]	17 000	Yeatman-Berthelot & Jarry (1991)
Iberian Peninsula	9700	Dominguez (1990)
Spain, excl. Mediterranean coast	5400	Velasco & Alberto (1993)
MEDITERRANEAN COASTS		
Spain	600–1020	Martinez-Vilalta (1985)
Spain	700	Velasco & Alberto (1993)
France	250	Smit (1986)
Gulf of Venice	1750	Smit (1986)
Greece	350	Smit (1986)
Turkey	70	Smit (1986)
Cyprus	10	Smit (1986)
Egypt: Nile Delta	500–1000	Smit (1986)
Tunisia	20 500	Smit (1986)
Algeria	40	Smit (1986)

Area	Number of birds	References
AFRICA, ATLANTIC COASTS		
Canary Islands	300	Velasco & Alberto (1993)
Morocco	6000	Glutz von Blotzheim *et al.* (1975), Kersten & Smit (1984)
Mauritania	14 200–24 000	Engelmoer *et al.* (1984)
Senegal	1000–1500	Meininger (1989)
Guinea Bissau:		
Arquipélago dos Bijagós	39 100	Asbirk *et al.* (1994)
Sierra Leone	5800	Tye & Tye (1987)
Ghana	1700	Ntiamoa-Baidu & Grieve (1987)
Gabon	6700–7500	Dijk *et al.* (1993)
Namibia: Skeleton Coast	5500	Summers *et al.* (1987)
Namibia: Southern Coast	200	Summers *et al.* (1987)
South Africa	5000	Summers *et al.* (1987)
AFRICA, INDIAN OCEAN COASTS		
South Africa	2770	Summers *et al.* (1987)
Tanzania	17 000–21 000	Bregnballe *et al.* (1989)
Kenya, coast	4500	Summers *et al.* (1987)
Kenya, inland	20	Summers *et al.* (1987)
MIDDLE EAST		
Egypt: Red Sea Coast	400–600	Summers *et al.* (1987)
Sudan: Red Sea Coast	1000	Summers *et al.* (1987)
Egypt: Nile Valley	100–200	Summers *et al.* (1987)
Arab Peninsula: Persian Gulf	>7500	Zwarts *et al.* (1991), Smart *et al.* (1983)
Arab Peninsula: Oman; Barr al Hikman	2600	Green *et al.* (1994)
Iran: Persian Gulf	550–1200	Summers *et al.* (1987)
Iran: Gulf of Oman	200–500	Summers *et al.* (1987)
Iran: Caspian Coast	260–415	Summers *et al.* (1987)
SE ASIA		
Thailand	171	Bijlsma & Roder (1985)
AUSTRALIA		
Western Australia	3370	Lane (1987)
Northern Territory	110	Lane (1987)
Queensland	1650	Lane (1987)
New South Wales	20	Lane (1987)
Victoria	670	Lane (1987)
South Australia	2530	Lane (1987)

1) Low numbers in severe winters
2) Including Mediterranean part of France

APPENDIX 13

Winter populations of Eurasian Golden Plovers in parts of their range

Area	Number of birds	References
Britain and Ireland	695 000	Fuller (1986)
Ireland	200 000	Cramp & Simmons (1983)
Denmark (November)	64 000	Eerden & Keij (1979)
Niedersachsen (November)	46 000	Eerden & Keij (1979)
Netherlands (November)	405 000	Eerden & Keij (1979)
Danish-German-Dutch Wadden Sea	50–29 000*	Meltofte *et al.* (1994)
France: Département Vienne	1000–20 000	Yeatman-Berthelot & Jarry (1991)
Morocco: Rhab–Merja-Zerga	15 000–20 000	Blondel & Blondel (1964)
Spain: Ebro Delta	150–1250	Martinez-Vilalta (1985)
Italy: Livorno Province	38	Mainardi (1987)
Egypt: Nile Valley	100–1000	Summers *et al.* (1987)
Iran: Inner Persian Gulf	200–500	Summers *et al.* (1987)
Iran: Caspian Sea	500–850	Summers *et al.* (1987)

* High numbers in mild winters

Number of American Golden Plovers counted in winter on aerial surveys along the coast of South America, 1982–86 (from Morrison & Ross 1989)

Region	Number of birds	Percent
North Coast:		
Colombia-French Guiana	0	
Brazil, north of Amazon	47	1.2
Brazil, northeast coast from Amazon	82	2.0
East Coast:		
Brazil, Salvador coast	0	
Brazil, Rio	0	
Brazil, Sao Paulo	0	
Brazil, Rio Grande do Sul	629	15.5
Uruguay	3167	78.1
Argentina, Buenos Aires	85	2.1
Argentina, Rio Colorado	30	0.7
Valdes Peninsula-Tierra del Fuego	0	
Pacific Coast:		
Chile, Chiloe-Valparaiso	0	
Chile, La Serena	14	0.3
Chile, Antofagasta	0	
Chile, Arica	1	0.02
Peru-Colombia	0	
TOTAL COUNTED	4055	

References

Grey Plover scolding a Snowy Owl

Species of *Pluvialis* dealt with specifically are indicated in square brackets at the end of the relevant references: A = American Golden Plover, E – Eurasian Golden Plover, G = Grey Plover, P = Pacific Golden Plover, A/P = American *and/or* Pacific golden plover.

AHLÉN, I. & TJERNBERG, M. 1992. *Artfakta; Sveriges hotade och sällsynta ryggradsdjur 1992*. Databanken för hotade arter, Uppsala. [E]

AHTI, T. 1961. Taxonomic study on reindeer lichens (*Cladonia*, subgenus *Cladina*). *Ann. Bot., Soc. Zool. Bot. fenn. "Vanamo"*, 32: 1–157.

ALATALO, R.V., GOTTLANDER, K. & LUNDBERG, A. 1987. Extra-pair copulations and mate guarding in the polyterritorial Pied Flycatcher *Ficedula hypoleuca*. *Behaviour*, 101: 139–155.

ALERSTAM, T., HJORT, C., HÖGSTEDT, G., JÖNSSON, P.E., KARLSSON, J. & LARSSON, B. 1986. Spring migration of birds across the Greenland inland ice. *Medd. Grønland, Biosci.* 21: 1–38.

ALERSTAM, T. & JÖNSSON, P.E. 1986. Distribution and migration of arctic shorebirds: the importance of stop-over places during spring migration. *Wader Study Group Bull.* 47: 9.

ALEXANDERSSON, H. 1987. Ljungpiparens *Pluvialis apricaria* förekomst och täthet på kalmossar i sydvästra Sverige: Betydelse av mossarnas storlek och inbördes avstånd. *Acta Reg. Soc. Litt. Gothoburgensis, Zoologica*, 14: 9–19. [E]

ALI, S. & RIPLEY, S.D. 1969. *Handbook of the birds of India and Pakistan together with those of Nepal, Sikkim, Buthan and Ceylon*. Oxford Univ. Press, Bombay. [E,G,P]

ALLEN, A.A. 1939. *The golden plover and other birds*. Comstock, Ithaca. [A]

ALM, B., ENEMAR, A., MYHRBERG, H. & SVENSSON, S. 1965. The density of birds in two study areas of the alpine region on southern Lapland in 1964. *Acta Univ. Lund*, 2(4): 1–14. [E]

ALM, B., MYHRBERG, H., NYHOLM, E. & SVENSSON, S. 1966. Densities of birds in alpine heaths. *Vår Fågelvärld*, 25: 193–201. [E]

ALSTRÖM, P. 1990. Calls of American and Pacific Golden Plovers. *Brit. Birds*, 83: 70– 73. [A,P]

AMERICAN ORNITHOLOGISTS' UNION. 1993. Thirty-ninth supplement to the American Ornithologists' Union's check-list of North American birds. *Auk*, 110: 675–682. [A,P]

ANDERSEN, G. & BORNS JR, H. W. 1995. *The Ice Age World. An introduction to Quaternary history and research with emphasis on North America and Northern Europe during the last 2.5 million years.* Scandinavian University Press, Oslo.

ANDERSSON, M. 1994. *Sexual selection.* Princeton Univ. Pr., Princeton.

ANDERSSON, M., WICKLUND, C.G. & RUNDGREN, H. 1980. Parental defence of offspring: a model and an example. *Anim. Behav.* 28: 536–542.

ANDREEVA, T.R. (АНДРЕЕВА, Т.Р.) 1989. Pischevye svyazi kulikov plakornykh tundr yuzhnogo Yamala. Pp. 129–152 *in* Chernov, Yu. I. (ed.). *Ptitsy v soobschestvakh tundrovoj zony.* Nauka, Moscow. [E]

ANDRLE, R.F. 1966. North American migrants in the Sierra de Tuxtla of southern Veracruz, México. *Condor,* 68: 177–184. [A]

ANON. 1994. *The UK Biodiversity Action Plan.* HMSO, London.

ANON. 1996. *Asia–Pacific migratory waterbird conservation strategy: 1996–2000.* Wetlands International–Asia Pacific, Kuala Lumpur, Publ. No. 117, and International Waterfowl and Wetlands Research Bureau–Japan Committee, Tokyo. [G,P]

ANTAS, P. DE T.Z. 1983. Migration of nearctic shorebirds (Charadriidae and Scolopacidae) in Brasil – flyways and and their different seasonal use. *Wader Study Group Bull.* 39: 52–56. [A,G]

ARCHER, G. & GODMAN, E.M. 1937. *The birds of British Somaliland and the Gulf of Aden.* Gurney & Jackson, London. [E,G,P]

ÅRHEIM, P. 1979. Några problem kring fågelögats fysiologi. *Vår Fågelvärld,* 38: 73–82. [E,G]

ARMITAGE, P., CRANSTON, P.S. & PINDER, L.C.V. 1995. *The Chironomidae: The biology and ecology of non-biting midges.* Chapman & Hall, London.

ARMSTRONG, E.A. 1965. Distraction display and the human predator. *Ibis,* 98: 641–654.

ASBIRK, S., SALVIG, J.C., RASMUSSEN, P.A.F. & KJELDSEN, J.P. 1994. Et vadehav i Vestafrika. *Dansk Orn. Foren. Tidsskr.* 88: 6–8. [G]

ASH, J.S. 1980. The Lesser Golden Plover *Pluvialis dominica* in northeast Africa and the southern Red Sea. *Scopus,* 4: 64–66. [P]

AVERY, M.I. 1989. Effects on upland afforestation on some birds of the adjacent moorlands. *J. Appl. Ecol.* 26: 957–966. [E]

AVERY, M.I. & HAINES-YOUNG, R.H. 1990. Population estimates for the Dunlin (*Calidris alpina*) derived from remotely-sensed imagery of the Flow Country in northern Scotland. *Nature,* 344: 860–862.

AVERY, M.I. & LESLIE, D.C. 1990. *Birds and forestry.* Poyser, Calton. [E]

BAGGE, P., LEHTOVUORI, M. & LIUNDQVIST, O. 1963. Havaintoja Inarin ja Enonteköin Lapin linnustotsa kesällä 1961. *Ornis Fennica,* 40: 21–31. [E]

BAHR, H.E.S. 1895. Aves regionis Stavangriensis. *Stavanger Museum Aarsberetning,* 6: 29–152. [E,G]

BAILEY, A.M. 1926. A report on the birds of northwestern Alaska and regions adjacent to Bering Strait. Part 3. *Condor,* 28: 84–86. [A,G,P]

BAINES, D. 1988. The effects of improvements of the upland, marginal grasslands on the distribution and density of breeding wading birds (Charadriiformes) in northern England. *Biol. Conserv.* 45: 221–236. [E]

BAKER, M.C. 1973. Stochastic properties of the foraging behavior of six species of migratory shorebirds. *Behaviour,* 45: 242–270.

BAKER, M.C. 1974. Foraging behavior of Black-bellied Plovers (*Pluvialis squatarola*). *Ecology,* 55: 162–167. [G]

BAKER, M.C. 1977. Shorebird food habits in the eastern Canadian Arctic. *Condor,* 79: 56–62. [A]

BALANCA, G. 1984. Migrations et hivernage du Vanneau huppé (*Vanellus vanellus*) et du Pluvier doré (*Pluvialis apricaria*) dans le sud de la Brie: déterminism météorologique, selection de l'habitat et activites. *L'Oiseau et Rev. Fr. Oiseaux,* 54: 333–349. [E]

BARASH, D.P. 1975. Evolutionary aspects of parental behavior: distraction behaviour of the Alpine Accentor. *Wilson Bull.* 87: 367–373.

BARBOSA, A. 1995. Foraging strategies and their influence on scanning and flocking behaviour of waders. *J. Avian Biol.* 26: 182–186. [G]

BARDGETT, R.D., MURSDEN, J.H., HOWARD, D.C. & HESSELL, J.E. 1995. The extent and condition of heather in moorland, and the potential impact of climate change. Pp. 43–50 *in* Thompson, D.B.A., Usher, M.B. & Hester, A.J. (eds.). *Heaths and moorland: cultural landscapes.* Huso, Edinburgh.

BARNARD, C.J. & THOMPSON, D.B.A. 1985. *Gulls and plovers: the ecology and behaviour of mixed-species feeding groups.* Croom Helm. London. [E]

BARNARD, C.J., THOMPSON, D.B.A. & STEPHENS, H. 1982. Time budgets, feeding efficiency, and flock dynamics in mixed-species flocks of Lapwings, Golden Plovers, and gulls. *Behaviour,* 80: 44–69. [E]

BARTER, M.A. 1988. Biometrics and moult of Lesser Golden Plovers *Pluvialis dominica fulva* in Victoria. *Stilt,* 13: 15–19. [P]

BATESON, P. (ed.) 1983. *Mate choice.* Cambridge Univ. Press, Cambridge.

BAUER, S. & THIELCKE, G. 1982. Gefahrdete Brutvogelarten in der BDR und im Land Berlin. *Vogelwarte,* 31: 183–391. [E]

BAXTER, E.V. & RINTOUL, L.J. 1953. *The Birds of Scotland.* Oliver & Boyd, Edinburgh. [E,G]

BEINTEMA, A.J., THISSEN, J.B., TERSEN, D. & VISSER, G.H. 1991. Feeding ecology of Charadriiform chicks in agricultural grassland. *Ardea,* 76: 31–34.

BELCHER, C. & SMOOKER, G.D. 1935. Birds of the colony of Trinidad and Tobago. Part II. *Ibis,* 77: 279–297. [A]

BELCHER, W.J. 1929. Fragmentary notes on bird life in the Fijis. *Condor,* 31: 19–20. [P]

BELOPOL'SKIJ, L.O., BIANKI, V.V. & KOCHANOV, V.D. (БЕЛОПОЛЬСКИЙ, Л.О., БИАНКИ, В.В., КОХАНОВ, В.Д.) 1970. Materialy po ekologii kulikov (Limicolae) Belogo Morya. *Trudy Kandalakschskogo gos. zapovednika,* 8: 3–84. [E,G]

BENGTSON, S.-A. & BLOCH, D. 1983. Island bird population densities in relation to island use and habitat quality on the Faroe Islands. *Oikos,* 41: 507–522. [E]

BENGTSON, S.-A., NILSSON, A., NORDSTRÖM, S. & RUNDGREN, S. 1976. Effect of bird predation on lumbricid populations. *Oikos,* 27: 9–12. [E]

BENGTSON, S.-A., NORDSTRÖM, R. & RUNDGREN, S. 1979. Selective predation by lumbricids by Golden Plovers *Pluvialis apricaria. Oikos,* 31: 164–168. [E]

BENGTSON, S.-A. & PERSSON, J. 1965. Ljungpipare (*Charadrius apricarius*) och grönbena (*Tringa glareola*) i N.E. Skåne 1965. *Medd. Skånes Ornitologiska Förening,*4: 57–65. [E]

BENNETT, K.D. 1997. *Evolution and ecology: The pace of life.* Cambridge Univ. Press, Cambridge.

BENT, A.C. 1929. *Life histories of North American shorebirds. Part 2.* Dover, New York. [A,E,G,P]

BERG, B. 1917. *Min vän fjällpiparen.* Norstedt, Stockholm.

BERGMANN, S. 1935. *Zur Kenntnis nordostasiatischer Vögel.* Bonniers, Stockholm. [G,P]

BEZZEL, E. 1985. *Kompendium der Vögel Mitteleuropas: Nonpasseriformes-Nichtsingvögel.* Aula, Wiesbaden. [A,E,G,P]

BIJLSMA, R.G. & RODER, F.E. DE. 1985. A ground survey of waders along the coast of Thailand, November and December 1984. *Wader Study Group Bull.* 43: 21–22. [G,P]

BILDSTEIN, K.L., BANCROFT, G.T., DUGAN, P.J., GORDON, D.H., ERWIN, R.M., NOL, E., PAYNE, L.X. & SENNER, S.E. 1991. Approaches to the conservation of coastal wetlands in the Western Hemisphere. *Wilson Bull.* 103: 218–254.

BIRKHEAD, T.R. 1987. Sperm competition in birds. *Trends Ecol. Evol.* 2: 268–272.

BIRKHEAD, T.R. 1991. *The Magpies: The ecology and behaviour of Black-billed and Yellow-billed Magpies.* Poyser, London.

BIRKHEAD, T.R., ATKIN, L. & MØLLER, A.P. 1987. Copulation behaviour in birds. *Behaviour,* 101: 101–138. [G]

BIRKHEAD, T.R., & MØLLER, A.P. 1992. *Sperm competition in birds.* Cambridge Univ. Press, Cambridge.

BJØRKLUND. M. 1994. Phylogenetic relationships among charadriiformes: Reanalysis of previous data. *Auk*, 114: 825–833.

BLANCO, D.R., BANCHS, R., CALAVARI, P. & OSTERHELD, M. 1993. Winter sites for the Eskimo Curlew *Numenius borealis*, and other Nearctic shorebirds in Argentina and Uruguay. *Wetland for the Arrentas*. Report to the US Fish & Wildl. Serv. [A]

BLISS, L.C. 1977. *Truelove Lowland, Devon Island, Canada: a high arctic ecosystem.* Univ. Alberta Press, Edmonton. [A,G]

BLÆDEL, N. 1959–63. *Nordens fugle i farver. Vol. 4.* Munksgaard, Copenhagen. [E,G]

BLASZYK, P. 1939. Zum Herbstzug des Goldregenpfeifers (*Charadrius apricarius*) und Mornellregenpfeifer (*Charadrius morinellus*) in der östlichen Kurmark und der nördlichen Kreisen der Grenzmark. *Orn. Monatsschr.* 47: 71–73. [E]

BLOCH, D. 1981. Fugletælling på Færøerne sommeren 1981 - foreløbig rapport. *Dansk Orn. Foren. Tidsskr.* 75: 1–6. [E]

BLONDEL, J. & BLONDEL, C. 1964. Remarques sur l'hivernage des limicoles et autres oiseaux au Maroc. *Alauda*, 32: 250–279. [E,G]

BOCK, W.J. 1958. A generic review of the plovers (Charadriinae, Aves). *Bull. Mus. Comp. Zool.* 118: 25–97. [E,G,A/P]

BOERE, G.C. & LENTEN, B. 1998. A model for international waterfowl management agreements: the Greenland White-fronted Goose *Anser albifrons flavifrons*. *International Wader Studies* 10: in press.

BOERTMANN, D. 1994. An annotated checklist to the birds of Greenland. *Medd. Grønland, Biosci.* 38. [A,E,G,P]

BOND, J. 1974. *Birds of the West Indies.* Collins, London. [A,G]

BOOBYER, G. 1992. *Population trends of the Golden Plover* Pluvialis apricaria *in Britain.* Joint Nature Conservation Committee, Peterborough, UK. [E]

BOOTH, C., CUTHBERT, M. & REYNOLDS, P. 1984. *The birds of Orkney.* Orkney Press, Stromness. [E,G]

BRANDT, H. 1943. *Alaska bird trails.* Bird Res. Foundation, Cleveland. [G,P]

BRANSON, N.J.B.A. & MINTON, C.D.T. 1976. Moult, measurements and migration of the Grey Plover. *Bird Study*, 23: 257–266. [G]

BRAZIL, M. 1991. *The birds of Japan.* Helm, London. [G,P]

BREARY, D.M. & HILDÉN, O. 1985. Nesting and egg-predation by Turnstones *Arenaria interpres* in larid colonies. *Ornis Scand.* 16: 283–292.

BREGNBALLE, T., PETERSEN, I.K., HALBERG, K., THORUP, O. & HANSEN, L. 1989. Wader surveys on the coast of Tanzania. *Wader Study Group Bull.* 57: 28–29. [G]

BREHM, C.L. 1831. *Handbuch der Naturgeschichte der Vögel Deutschlands.* [E, diagnosis of *altifrons*, p. 542]

BRENNINKMEJER, A., KLAASSEN, M. & STIENEN, E.W.M. 1997. Sandwich Terns *Sterna sandvicensis* feeding on shell fractions. *Ibis*, 139: 397–400.

BRINKMANN, M. 1962. Die letzten Goldregenpfeifer im deutschen Raum. *Rat f. Vogelschutz, deutsche Sect., Ber.* 2: 29–41. [E]

BRINKMANN, W. 1941. Vom Zug- und Brutleben des Goldregenpfeifers. *Orn. Monatsber.* 49: 12–15. [E]

BRINKMANN, W. 1961. Zur Wiederentdeckung des Goldregenpfeifers. *Orn. Mitt. Stuttgart*, 13: 108–110. [E]

BRISSON, M.J. 1760. *Ornithologie, ou methode contenant la division des oiseaux. Vol. 1 and 2.* [*Pluvialis*: diagnosis of genus, vol. 1 p. 46, vol. 2 p. 42]

BRITISH ORNITHOLOGISTS' UNION. 1924. Fourth report of the committee on the nomenclature and records of occurrence of rare birds in the British Islands and certain necessary changes in the nomenclature of the B.O.U. list of British birds. *Ibis*, 66: 152–158. [E]

BRITISH ORNITHOLOGISTS' UNION. 1932. Eighth report of the committee on the nomenclature and records of the occurrences of rare birds in the British Islands, and certain necessary changes in the nomenclature of the B.O.U. list of British birds. *Ibis*, 74: 94–100. [E]

BRITISH ORNITHOLOGISTS' UNION. 1933. Ninth report of the committee on the nomenclature and records of the occurrences of rare birds in the British Isles. *Ibis*, 75: 343–351. [E]

BROOKS, W.S. 1967. Organisms consumed by various migrating shorebirds. *Auk*, 84: 128–130. [A]

BROWN, A., BIRKS, H.J.B. & THOMPSON, D.B.A. 1993. A new biogeographical classification of the Scottish uplands. II. Vegetation-environment relationships. *J. Ecol.* 81: 231–250.

BROWN, A.F. 1993. The status of Golden Plover *Pluvialis apricaria* in the south Pennines. *Bird Study*, 40: 196–202. [E]

BROWN, A.F. & BAINBRIDGE, I.P. 1995. Grouse moors and upland breeding birds. Pp 51–66 *in* Thompson, D.B.A., Hester, A.J., & Usher, M.B. (eds.). *Heaths and moorland: cultural landscapes.* HMSO, Edinburgh. [E]

BROWN, A.F. & SHEPHERD, K.B. 1993. A method for censusing upland breeding waders. *Bird Study*, 40: 189–195. [E]

BROWN, A.F. & STILLMAN, R.A. 1993. Bird-habitat associations in the eastern Highlands of Scotland. *J. Appl. Ecol.*, 30: 31–42. [E]

BRUNDIN, I.Z. 1988. Phylogenetic Biogeography. Pp. 343–369 *in* Myers, A.A. & Giller, P.S. (eds.). *Analytical Biogeography.* Chapman & Hall, London.

BRUNTON, D.H. 1988 a. Sexual differences in reproductive effort: time-activity budgets of monogamous Killdeer, *Charadrius vociferus*. *Anim. Behav.* 36: 705–717.

BRUNTON, D. 1988 b. Energy expenditure in reproductive effort of male and female Killdeer (*Charadrius vociferus*). *Auk*,105: 553–564.

BRUNTON, D.H. 1990. The effects of nesting stage, sex, and type of predator on parental defense by Killdeer (*Charadrius vociferous* [sic]): testing models of avian parental defense. *Behav. Ecol. Sociobiol.* 26: 181–190.

BUCHANAN, J.B. 1988. The abundance and migration of shorebirds at two Puget Sound estuaries. *Western Birds*, 19: 69–78. [A,G]

BUCHER, E.H. & NORES, M. 1988. Present status of birds in steppes and savannas of northern and central Argentina. Pp. 71–79 *in* Goriup, P.D. (ed.). *Ecology and conservation of grassland birds.* ICBP Technical Publ. No. 7. [A]

BUCKLAND, S.T. In press. *Sampling methods for estimating species populations on designated sites.* Research Review Report, Scottish Natural Heritage, Battleby.

BUCKLAND, S.T., ANDERSON, D.R., BURNHAM, K.P. & LAAKE, J.L. 1993. *Distance sampling: estimating abundance of biological populations.* Chapman & Hall, London.

BUDEN, D.W. 1992. The birds of Long Island, Bahamas. *Wilson Bull.* 104: 220–243. [A,G]

BURGER, J. & GOCHFELD, M. 1984. Seasonal variation in size and function of the nasal salt gland of the Franklin's Gull (*Larus pipixcan*). *Comp. Biochem. Physiol.* 77A: 103–110.

BURKE, T. & THOMPSON, D.B.A. Unpublished. *Breeding and social systems of birds of the Western Palaearctic.* [E,G]

BURTON, N.H.K., EVANS, P.R. & ROBINSON, M.A. 1966. Effects on shorebird numbers of disturbance, the loss of our roost site and its replacement by an artificial island at Hartlepool, Cleveland. *Biol. Conserv.* 77: 193–201. [G]

BURTON, P.J. 1974. *Feeding and the feeding apparatus in waders: a study of anatomy and adaptations in the Charadrii.* Brit. Mus. (Nat. Hist.), London. [A/P,E,G]

BYRD, G.V., GIBSON, D.D. & JOHNSON, D.L. 1974. The birds of Adak Island, Alaska. *Condor*, 76: 288–300. [A]

BYRKJEDAL, I. 1974. Heiloen, *Pluvialis apricaria*, som hekkefugl i Rogaland. *Sterna*, 13: 1–14. [E]

BYRKJEDAL, I. 1975. Smågnagerbein som kalsiumkilde ved eggproduksjon hos heilo. *Sterna*, 16: 211–216. [E]

BYRKJEDAL, I. 1977. Tetthet av hekkende fugler i lyngheibiotop på Høg-Jæren. *Sterna,* 16: 211–216. [E]

BYRKJEDAL, I. 1978 a. Altitudinal differences in breeding schedules of Golden Plovers *Pluvialis apricaria* (L.) in South Norway. *Sterna,* 17: 1–20. [E]

BYRKJEDAL, I. 1978 b. Variation and secondary intergradation in SW-Norwegian Golden Plover *Pluvialis apricaria* populations. *Ornis Scand.* 9:101–110. [E]

BYRKJEDAL, I. 1978 c. Autumn diet of Golden Plovers *Pluvialis apricaria* on farmland and a coastal heather moor in South Norway. *Cinclus,* 1: 22–28. [E]

BYRKJEDAL, I. 1980 a. Summer food of the golden plover *Pluvialis apricaria* at Hardangervidda, South Norway. *Holarctic Ecol.* 3: 40–49. [E]

BYRKJEDAL, I. 1980 b. Nest predation in relation to snow-cover – a possible factor influencing the start of breeding in shorebirds. *Ornis Scand.* 11: 249–252. [E]

BYRKJEDAL, I. 1980 c. Høsttrekkets forløp hos en del vadere på Jæren. *Fauna norv. Ser. C, Cinclus,* 3: 60–64. [E,G]

BYRKJEDAL, I. 1985 a. Time-activity budget for breeding Greater Golden-Plovers in Norwegian mountains. *Wilson Bull.* 97: 486–501. [E]

BYRKJEDAL, I. 1985 b. Time budget and parental labour division in breeding Black-tailed Godwits *Limosa l. limosa. Fauna norv. Ser. C, Cinclus,* 8: 24–34.

BYRKJEDAL, I. 1987 a. Antipredator behavior and breeding success in Greater Golden-Plover and Eurasian Dotterel. *Condor,* 89: 40–47. [E]

BYRKJEDAL, I. 1987 b. Short-billed Dowitchers associate closely with Lesser Golden-Plovers. *Wilson Bull.* 99: 494–495. [A]

BYRKJEDAL, I. 1989 a. Nest habitat and nesting success of Lesser Golden-Plovers. *Wilson Bull.* 101: 93–96. [A]

BYRKJEDAL, I. 1989 b. Habitat use and resource overlap by breeding Golden Plovers and Dotterels (*Pluvialis apricaria, Charadrius morinellus*). *J. Orn.* 130: 197–206. [E]

BYRKJEDAL, I. 1989 c. Time constraints and vigilance: breeding season diet of the Dotterel (*Charadrius morinellus*). *J. Orn.* 130: 293–302.

BYRKJEDAL, I. 1989 d. Nest defense behavior of Lesser Golden-Plovers. *Wilson Bull.* 101: 579–590. [A]

BYRKJEDAL, I. 1991. The role of drive conflicts as a mechanism for nest-protection behaviour in the shorebird *Pluvialis dominica. Ethology,* 87: 149–159. [A]

BYRKJEDAL, I. & BERNHOFT-OSA, A. 1982. Trends in the numbers of migrating shorebirds at Revtangen Bird Observatory, SW Norway in the 21-year period 1947–67. *Fauna norv. Ser. C, Cinclus,* 5: 53–58. [G]

BYRKJEDAL, I., CAMPBELL, L., GALUSHIN, V., KÅLÅS, J.A., MISCHENKO, A., MOROZOV, V., SAARI, L., STRANN, K-B., TATARINKOVA, I.P., THOMPSON, D.B.A. & STRAZDS, M. 1997. Tundra-mires and moorland. Pp. 159–186 *in* Tucker, G.M. & Evans, M.I. (eds.). *Habitats for Birds in Europe: a Conservation Strategy for the Wider Environment.* BirdLife International (BirdLife Conservation Series 6), Cambridge, UK. [G,E]

BYRKJEDAL, I. & KÅLÅS, J.A. 1983. Plover's Page turns into Plover's Parasite: a look at the Dunlin/Golden Plover association. *Ornis Fennica,* 60: 10–15. [E]

BYRKJEDAL, I. & KÅLÅS, J.A. 1985. Seasonal variation in egg size in Golden Plover *Pluvialis apricaria* and Dotterel *Charadrius morinellus* populations. *Ornis Scand.* 16: 108–112. [E]

CAFF (Conservation of arctic flora and fauna). 1994. *The state of protected areas in the circumpolar arctic 1994.* CAFF Habitat Conservation Report No. 1. Directorate for Nature Management, Trondheim, Norway.

CAMPBELL, J.W. 1935. Shore birds and mollusks. *Brit. Birds,* 29: 183. [E]

CAMPBELL, J.W. 1936. On the food of some British birds. *Brit. Birds,* 30: 209–218. [E]

CAMPBELL, J.W. 1946. Notes on the food of some British birds. *Brit. Birds,* 39: 371– 373. [E]

CAREY, C. 1988. Avian reproduction in cold climates. *Acta XIX Congr. Intern. Ornithol.,* (Ottawa): 2708–2715.

CASTRO, G. & MYERS, J.P. 1989. Flight range estimates for shorebirds. *Auk*, 106: 474–476. [G]

CATLEY, G.P., HUME, R.A., & THE RARITIES COMMITTEE. 1994. A golden plover: but which one? *Brit. Birds*, 87: 16–23. [P,A].

CHANDLER, R.J. 1989. *North Atlantic shorebirds*. Macmillan, London. [A,E,G,P]

CHAPMAN, A. 1924. *The borders and beyond*. Edward Arnold, London.

CHAPMAN, F.M. 1923 (1966). *Handbook of birds of eastern North America*. Dover, New York. [A,G]

CHERNOV, YU.I. 1985. *The living tundra*. Cambridge Univ. Press, Cambridge. [E,G,P]

CHU, P.C. 1994. Historical examination of delayed plumage maturation in the shorebirds (Aves: Charadriiformes). *Evolution*, 48: 327–350.

CHU, P.C., 1995. Phylogenetic reanalysis of Strauch's osteological data set for the Charadriiformes. *Condor*, 97: 174–196.

CLAPP, B.B. & TILGER, G. 1967. Predation on Snake-eyed Skink (*Ablephorus bountonii*) by two Pacific shore birds. *Herpetologica*, 23: 76. [P]

CLUTTON-BROCK, T. & GODFRAY, C. 1991. Parental investment. Pp. 234–262 *in* Krebs, J.R. & Davies, N.B. (eds.). *Behaviour ecology: an evolutionary approach*. (3rd edition.) Blackwell, Oxford.

COGSWELL, H.L. 1948. Summer observations of birds of Okinawa, Ryukyu Islands. *Condor*, 50: 16–25. [G,P]

COLLETT, R. 1894. Mindre meddelelser vedrørende Norges fuglefauna i aarene 1881–1892. *Nyt Mag. Naturvidensk*. 35: 1–387. [E,G]

COLLETT, R. 1921. *Norges fugle, vol. 2*. Aschehoug, Kristiania. [E,G]

COLWELL, M.A. & DODD, S.L. 1997. Environmental and habitats correlates of pasture use by nonbreeding shorebirds. *Condor*, 99: 337–344. [G].

COLWELL, M.A., FELLOWS, S.D., & ORING, L.W. 1988. Chronology of shorebird migration at Last Mountain Lake National Wildlife Area, Saskatchewan, Canada. *Wader Study Group Bull*. 52: 18–22. [A,G]

CONNORS, P.G. 1983. Taxonomy, distribution, and evolution of golden plovers (*Pluvialis dominica* and *Pluvialis fulva*). *Auk*, 100: 607–620. [A,P]

CONNORS, P.G., MCCAFFERY, B.J. & MARON, J.L. 1993. Speciation in golden plovers, *Pluvialis dominica* and *P. fulva*: evidence from the breeding grounds. *Auk*, 110: 9–20. [A,P]

CONOVER, B. 1945. The breeding golden plover of Alaska. *Auk*, 62: 568–574. [A,P]

COOKE, W.W. 1912. Distribution and migration of North American shorebirds. *US Dep. Agric. Biol. Surv. Bull*. 35. [A,G,P]

COTT, H.B. 1940. *Adaptive coloration in animals*. Methuen, London.

COULSON, J.C. 1988. The structural importance of invertebrate communities on peatlands and moorlands, and effects of environmental and management changes. Pp. 365–380 *in* Usher, M.B. & Thompson, D.B.A. (eds.). *Ecological change in the uplands*. Blackwell, Oxford.

COULSON, J.C., FIELDING, C.A. & GOODYEAR, S.A. 1992. The management of moorland areas to enhance their nature conservation interests. *Joint Nature Conservation Committee Report No. 134*. Joint Nature Conservation Committee, Peterborough.

COULSON, J.C., BAVER, L.J., BUTTERFIELD, J.E.L., DOWNIE, I.S., CRANNA, L. & SMITH, C. 1995. The invertebrate fauna of the northern Scottish Flows in comparison with other peatland communities. Pp. 74–94 *in* Thompson, D.B.A., Hester, A.J. & Usher, M.B. (eds.). *Heaths and moorland: cultural landscapes*. HMSO, Edinburgh.

COX, C.B. & MOORE, P.D. 1993. *Biogeography: an ecological and evolutionary approach*. Blackwell Scientific Publications, Oxford.

CRAMP, S. & SIMMONS, K.E.L. (eds.). 1983. *The birds of the western Palearctic, vol. 3*. Oxford Univ. Press, Oxford. [A,E,G,P]

CRANSWICK, P.A., KIRBY, J.S. & WATERS, R.J. 1996. *Wildfowl and wader counts 1995–96*. BTO, RSPB, INCC, Wildfowl and Wetlands Trust, Gloucester. [E,G]

CRESSWELL, W. 1994. Flocking is an effective anti-predation strategy in Redshank (*Tringa totanus*). *Anim. Behav.* 47: 433–442.

CURTIS, D.J. & THOMPSON, D.B.A. 1985. Spacing and foraging behaviour of Black-headed Gulls (*Larus ridibundus*) in an estuary. *Ornis Scand.* 15: 245–252.

CUSTER, T.W. & PITELKA, F.A. 1975. Correction factors for digestion rates for prey taken by Snow Buntings *Plectrophenax nivalis*. *Condor*, 77: 210–212.

CUVIER, G. 1817. *Le régne animale: les oiseaux*. *Vol. 1*. [*Squatarola*, diagnosis of genus, p. 467]

DABBENE, R. 1920. Notas sobre los chorlos de Norte America que invernan en la Republica Argentina. *Hornero*, 11: 99–128. [A]

DANILOV, N.N., RYZHANOVSKIJ, V.N. & RYABITSEV, V.K. (ДАНИЛОВ, Н.Н., РЫЖАНОВСИЙ, В.Н., РЯБЦЕВ, В.К) 1984. *Ptitsy Yamala*. Nauka, Moscow. [E,G,P]

DAVIDSON, N.C., LAFFOLEY, D. D'A, DOODY, J.P., WAY, L.P., GORDON, J., KEY. R., DRAKE, C.M., PIENKOWSKI, M.W., MITCHELL, R. & DUFF, K.L. 1991. *Nature conservation of estuaries in Great Britain*. Nature Conservancy Council, Peterborough. [E,G]

DAVIDSON, N.C. & PIENKOWSKI, M.W. 1987. The conservation of international flyway populations of waders. *Wader Study Group Bull.* 49. [A,E,G,P]

DAVIES, N.B. & HOUSTON, A.I. 1984. Territory economics. Pp. 148–169 *in* Krebs, J.R. & Davies, N.B. (eds.). *Behavioural ecology: an evolutionary approach*. Second edition. Blackwell Sci. Publ., Oxford.

DAVIES, N.B. & LUNDBERG, A. 1985. The influence of food on time budgets and timing of breeding of the Dunnock *Prunella modularis*. *Ibis*, 127: 100–110.

DEGTYAREV, A.G. & POZDNYAKOV, V.I. (ДЕГТЯРЕВ, А.Г., ПОЗДНЯКОВ, В.И.) 1980. Materialy po vesennemu proletu kulikov v bassejne sredej Leny. Pp. 99–101 *in* Flint, V.E. (ed.). *Novoe v izuchenii biologii i rasprostranenii kulikov*. Nauka, Moscow. [G,P]

DELACOUR, J. 1947. *Birds of Malalaysia*. Macmillan, New York. [G,P]

DEMENT'EV, G.P. & GLADKOV, N.A. 1951. *Birds of the Soviet Union*. IPST (1969), Jerusalem. [A,E,G,P]

DERRICKSON, K.C. & WARKENTIN, I.G. 1991. The role of egg-capping in the evolution of eggshell removal. *Condor*, 93: 757–759.

DIERSCHKE, V. & DIERSCHKE, J. 1990. Das Rastvorkommen der Limikolen (Aves: Charadrii) an den Schlammteichen der Zuckerfabrik Nörten-Hardenberg (Süd-Niedersachsen). *Göttinger Naturkundl. Schriften*, 2: 73–110. [E,G]

DIJK, A.J. VAN, DIJK, K. VAN, DIJKSEN, L.J., SPANJE, T.M. VAN, & WYMENGA, E. 1984. Waders of the Gulf of Gabes, Tunisia, January to March 1984. *Wader Study Group Bull.* 41: 16–18. [E,G]

DIJK, A.-J. VAN, DIJKSTRA, B., GELDER, W. VAN, HAGEMEIJER, W., MARTEIJN, E., RODER, F. DE, SCHEPERS, F. & CHRISTY, P. 1993. Coastal waterbirds in Gabon winter 1992. *WIWO-report No. 41*. [G,P]

DIJK, A.J. VAN, RODER, F.E. DE, MARTEIJN, E.C.L. & SPIEKMAN, H. 1990. Summering waders on the Banc d'Arguin, Mauritania: a census in June 1988. *Ardea*, 78: 145–156. [G]

DIJKSTRA, C., VUURSTEEN, L., DAAN, S. & MASMAN, D. 1982. Clutch size and laying date in the Kestrel *Falco tinnunculus*: effect of supplementary food. *Ibis*, 124: 210–213.

DINSMORE, J.J., KENT, T.H., KOENIG, D., PETERSEN, P.C. & ROOSA, D.M. 1984. *Iowa birds*. Iowa State Univ. Press, Ameo. [A,G]

DOLGUSHIN, I.A. (ДОЛГУШИН, И.А.) 1962. *Ptitsy Kazakhstana*. *Vol. 2*. Akad. Nauk Kazakhskoy SSR, Alma Ata. [E,G,P]

DOLMAN, P.M. & SUTHERLAND, W.J. 1995. The response of bird populations to habitat loss. *Ibis*, 137 suppl., 38–46.

DOLMAN, P.M. & SUTHERLAND, W.J. 1997. Spatial patterns of depletion imposed by foraging vertebrates: theory, review and meta-analysis. *J. Anim. Ecol.* 66: 481–494.

DOMINGUEZ, J. 1990. Distribution of estuarine waders wintering in the Iberian Peninsula in 1978–1989. *Wader Study Group Bull.* 59: 25–28. [E,G]

DOMM, S. & RECHER, H.F. 1973. The birds of One Tree Island with notes on their yearly cycle and feeding ecology. *Sunbird,* 4: 63–86. [G,P]

DOTT, H.E.M. 1985. North American migrants in Bolivia. *Condor,* 87: 343–345. [A]

DOWNIE, I.S., COULSON, J.C., O'CONNELL, M.J., EVANS, P.R., THOMAS, C.J. & WHITFIELD, D.P. 1996. Functional ecology of peatland animals in the Flow Country of northern Scotland: II. Invertebrate distribution and availability. Research and Advisory Services Directorate Report. Scottish Natural Heritage, Edinburgh. [E].

DRURY, W.H. 1961. The breeding biology of shorebirds on Bylot Island, Northwest Territories, Canada. *Auk,* 98: 176–219. [A,G]

DUGAN, P.J. 1981. The importance of nocturnal foraging in shore birds: a consequence of increased invertebrate prey activity. Pp. 251–260 *in* Jones, N.V. & Wolff, W.J. (eds.). *Feeding and survival strategies of estuarine organisms.* Plenum, New York. [G]

DUGAN, P.J. 1982. Seasonal changes in patch use by a territorial Grey Plover: weather-dependent adjustments in foraging behaviour. *J. Anim. Ecol.* 51: 849–858. [G]

DUGAN, P.J., EVANS, P.R, GOODYER, L.R. & DAVIDSON, N.C. 1981. Winter fat reserves in shorebirds: disturbance of regulated levels by severe weather conditions. *Ibis,* 123: 356–363. [E,G]

DUNKER, H. 1969. Bestandsendringer hos heilo, *Pluvialis apricaria,* 1963–67. *Fauna (Oslo),* 22: 201–206. [E]

DUNKERLEY, D.L, DECKKER, P. DE, KERSHAW, A.P. & STOKES, T. 1993. *Quaternary environments.* Edward Arnold, London.

DURELL, S.E.A. LE V. DIT & KELLY, C.P. 1990. Diets of Dunlin *Calidris alpina* and Grey Plover *Pluvialis squatarola* on the Wash as determined by dropping analysis. *Bird Study,* 37: 44–47. [G]

DYBBRO, T. 1976. *De danske ynglefugles udbredelse.* Dansk Orn. Foren., Copenhagen. [E]

DYBBRO, T. 1981. En oversikt over de danske vadefuglebestande. *Proc. Second Nordic Congr. Ornithol.* 1979: 109–110. [E]

DYRCZ, A., WITKOWSKI, J. & OKULEWICZ, J. 1981. Nesting of 'timid' waders in the vicinity of 'bold' ones as an antipredator adaptation. *Ibis,* 123: 542–545.

EDELSTAM, C. 1972. The visible migration of birds at Ottenby, Sweden. *Vår Fågelvärld, Suppl. 7.* [E,G]

EDWARDS, C.A. & LOFTY, J.R. 1993. *Biology of earthworms.* Chapman & Hall, London.

EDWARDS, P.J. 1982. Plumage variation, territoriality and breeding displays of the Golden Plover *Pluvialis apricaria* in southwest Scotland. *Ibis,* 124: 88–96. [E]

EDWARDS, P.J. & PARISH, D. 1988. The distribution of migratory waders in south-west Sarawak. *Wader Study Group Bull.* 54: 36–40. [G,P]

EENSHUISTRA, O. 1973. *Goudplevier en wilstervangst.* Fryske Akademy, Leeuwarden. [E,G,P]

EERDEN, M. VAN & KEIJ, P. 1979. Counting of Golden Plovers *Pluvialis apricaria* on passage: some results of two country-wide surveys in the Netherlands. *Wader Study Group Bull.* 27: 25–27. [E]

EMLEN, S.T. & ORING, L.W. 1977. Ecology, sexual selection and evolution of mating systems. *Science,* 197: 215–223.

ENÉMAR, A. 1959. On the determination of the size and composition of a passerine population during the breeding season. A methodological study. *Vår Fågelvärld,* suppl. 2: 1–114.

ENGELMOER, M., PIERSMA, T., ALTENBURG, W. & MES, R. 1984. The Banc d'Arguin (Mauritania). Pp. 293–309 *in* Evans, P.R., Goss-Custard, J.G. & Hale, W.G. (eds.). *Coastal waders and wildfowl in winter.* Cambridge Univ. Press, Cambridge. [G]

ENS, B.J., PIERSMA, T. & TINBERGEN, J.M. 1994. Towards predictive models of bird migration schedules: theoretical and empirical bottlenecks. *Netherlands Institute for Sea Research (NIOZ) – Rapport No. 5.* NIOZ Texel.

ENS, B.J., PIERSMA, T., WOLFF, W.J. & ZWARTS, L. 1990. Homeward bound: problems waders face when migrating from the Banc d'Arguin, Mauritania, to their northern breeding grounds in spring. *Ardea,* 78: 1–16.

ERCKMANN, W.J. 1983. The evolution of polyandry in shorebirds: an evaluation of hypotheses. Pp. 113–168 *in* Wasser, S.K. (ed.). *Social behavior of female vertebrates.* Academic Press, London.

ERICKSON, H.T. 1992. Spring migration of Lesser Golden-Plovers in Benton County, Indiana. *Indiana Audubon Quarterly,* 70: 87–91. [A]

ERIKSTAD, K.E. & SPIDSØ, T.K. 1982. The influence of weather on food intake, insect prey selection and feeding behaviour in Willow Grouse chicks in northern Norway. *Ornis Scand.* 13: 176–182.

EVANS, P.R. 1991. Introductory remarks: habitat loss – effects on shorebird populations. *Acta XX Congr. Int. Ornithol. (New Zealand)*: 2149–2198. [G]

EVANS, P.R., DAVIDSON, N.C., PIERSMA, T. & PIENKOWSKI, M.W. 1991. Implications of habitat loss at migration staging posts for shorebird populations. *Acta XX Int. Ornithol. Congr. (New Zealand)*: 2228–2235. [E]

EVANS, P.R., GOSS-CUSTARD, J.D. & HALE, W.G. (eds.). 1984. *Coastal waders and wildfowl in winter.* Cambridge Univ. Press, Cambridge. [E,G]

EVANS, P.R., HERDSON, D.M., KNIGHTS, P.J. & PIENKOWSKI, M.W. 1979. Short-term effects of reclamation of part of Seal Sands, Teesmouth, on wintering waders and Shelduck. I. Shorebird diets, invertebrate densities, and the impact of predation on the invertebrates. *Oecologia,* 41: 183–206. [G]

EVANS, P.R. & PIENKOWSKI, M.W. 1984. Population dynamics of shorebirds. Pp. 83–123 *in* Burger, J. & Olla, B.L. (eds.). *Behavior of marine animals, vol. 5, shorebirds: breeding behavior and populations.* Plenum, New York. [G]

EVANS, P.R. & TOWNSHEND, D.J. 1988. Site faithfulness of waders away from the breeding grounds: how individual migration patterns are established. *Acta XIX International Ornithological Congress (Ottawa, Canada)* 1: 594–603. [G]

EWALD, P.W. & ROHWER, S. 1982. Effects of supplementary feeding on timing of breeding, clutch-size and polygyny in Red-winged Blackbirds *Agelaius phoeniceus. J. Anim. Ecol.* 51: 429–450.

EXO, K.-M. & WAHLS, S. 1996. Origin and movements of Grey Plovers *Pluvialis squatarola* ringed in Germany. *Wader Study Group Bull.* 81: 42–45. [G].

FABRICIUS, O. & HALD MORTENSEN, P. 1969. Hjejlen (*Pluvialis apricaria*) som ynglefugl i Danmark 1963–1966, med bemærkninger om artens raceforhold, udbredelse og antal. *Dansk Orn. Foren. Tidsskr.* 63: 137–160. [E]

FALLA, R.A., SIBSON, R.B. & TURBOTT, E.G. 1970. *A field guide to the birds of New Zealand.* Collins, London. [G,P]

FALLET, M. 1962. Über Bodenvögel und ihre terricolen Beutetiere. Technik der Nahrungssuche-Populationsdynamik. *Zool. Anz.* 168: 187–212. [E]

FARRIS, J.S., 1988. *Hennig86. Ver. 1.5.* Port Jefferson Station, New York.

FEARE, C.J. & HIGH, J. 1977. Migrant shorebirds in the Seychelles. *Ibis,* 119: 323–338. [G,P]

FERNS, P.N. 1977. *Wading birds of the Severn Estuary.* NCC, Cardiff. [E,G]

FERNS, P.N., THOMAS, C.J. & HACK, P.C. 1983. Why are waders like Topsy? *Wader Study Group Bull.* 39: 41. [E].

FINLAYSON, C.M. & MOSER, M.E. 1991. *Wetlands. Facts on file.* IWRB, Slimbridge. [E,G]

FJELDSÅ, J. 1977. *Guide to the young of European precocial birds.* Skarv Nature Publications, Tisvilde. [E, G]

FJELDSÅ, J. & KRABBE, N. 1990. *Birds of the High Andes.* Zoological Museum, Copenhagen. [A,G]

FLINT, V.E. 1976. Characteristics of wader populations in North Asia. *Proc. Int. Conf. Conservat. Wetlands and Waterfowl, Heiligenhafen, Federal Republic of Germany, 2–6 Dec. 1974*: 289. [G,P]

FLINT, V.E., BOEME, R.L., KOSTIN, YU.V. & KUZNETSOV, A.A. (ФЛИНТ, В.Е., БЁМЕ, Р.Л., КОСТИН, Ю.В., КУЗНЕЦОВ, А.А..). 1968. *Ptitsy SSSR.* Mysl', Moscow. [E,G,P]

FLINT, V.E. & KONDRATJEW, A.J. 1977. Materialien zur Biologie der Kiebitzregenpfeifers (*Pluvialis squatarola* L.). *Beitr. Vogelkunde*, 23: 265–277. [G]

FORBUSH, E.H. 1912. *Game birds, wildfowl, and shorebirds*. Massachusetts Board of Agriculture, Boston. [A]

FOREY, P.L., HUMPHRIES, C.J., KITCHING, I.J., SCOTLAND, R.W., SIEBERT, D.J. & WILLIAMS, D.M. 1992. *Cladistics. A practical course in systematics. The Systematics Association publication no. 10*. Clarendon Press, Oxford.

FRENZEL, B., PÉSCI, M. & VELICHKO, A.A. 1992. Atlas of paleoclimates and paleoenvironments of the northern hemisphere; late Pleistocene-Holocene. Gustav Fischer Verlag, Stuttgart.

FRIEDMAN, H. 1934. The instinctive emotional life of birds. *Psychoanal. Rev.* 21. 1–57.

FRIMER, O. 1993. Breeding and summering North American waders on Quamassoq, Disko, West Greenland. *Dansk Orn. Foren. Tidsskr.* 87: 255–257. [G]

FRIMER, O. & NIELSEN, S.M. 1990. Bird observations in Aqajarua-Sullorsuaq, Disko, West Greenland, 1989. *Dansk Orn. Foren. Tidsskr.* 84: 151–158. [A,G]

FULLER, R.J. 1986. Golden Plover. Pp. 184–185 *in* Lack P. (ed.). *The Atlas of Wintering Birds in Britain and Ireland*. Poyser, Calton. [E]

FULLER, R.J. 1988. Wintering golden plovers in central Buckinghamshire: numbers and distribution. *Buckingham Bird Report 1988*: 4–8. [E]

FULLER, R.J. 1996. Relationships between grazing and birds with particular reference to sheep in the British Uplands. *BTO Research Report No. 164*. British Trust for Ornithology, Thetford, UK. [E]

FULLER, R.J. 1997. Sheep and upland birds. *British Trust for Ornithology News*, 210/211: 14–15. [E]

FULLER, R.J. & LLOYD, D. 1981. The distribution and habitats of wintering Golden Plovers in Britain, 1977–1978. *Bird Study*, 28: 169–185. [E]

FULLER, R.J. & YOUNGMAN, R.E. 1979. The utilization of farmland by Golden Plovers wintering in southern England. *Bird Study*, 26: 37–46. [E]

GÁBOR, K. 1985. Az aranylile (*Pluvialis apricaria* L.) a Hortobágyon (1975–1984). *Aquila*, 92: 97–103. [E,G]

GABRIELSON, I.N. & JEWETT, S.G. 1970. *Birds of the Pacific northwest with special reference to Oregon*. Dover, New York. [A,G]

GABRIELSON, I.N. & LINCOLN, F.C. 1959. *The birds of Alaska*. Telegraph Press, Harrisburg. [A,G,P]

GALBRAITH, C.A., GRICE, P.V., MUDGE, G.P., PARR, S. & PIENKOWSKI, M.W. 1994. The role of the statutory bodies in ornithological conservation within the UK. *Ibis* suppl. 137: 224–231.

GALBRAITH, H. 1988 a. Effects of egg size and composition on the size, quality and survival of Lapwing *Vanellus vanellus* chicks. *J. Zool. Lond.* 214: 383–398.

GALBRAITH, H. 1988 b. Effects of agriculture on the breeding ecology of Lapwings *Vanellus vanellus*. *J. Appl. Ecol.* 25: 487–503.

GALBRAITH, H. 1988 c. Adaptation and constraint in the growth pattern of Lapwing *Vanellus vanellus* chicks. *J. Zool., Lond.* 215: 537–548.

GALBRAITH, H. 1989. The diet of Lapwing (*Vanellus vanellus*) chicks on Scottish farmland. *Ibis*, 131: 80–84.

GALBRAITH, H., DUNCAN, K., MURRAY, S., SMITH, R., WHITFIELD, D.P. & THOMPSON, D.B.A. 1993. Diet and habitat use of the Dotterel (*Charadrius morinellus*) in Scotland. *Ibis*, 135: 148–155.

GANTLETT, S. & MILLINGTON, R. 1992. The Pacific Golden Plover at Cley, Norfolk. *Birding World*, 4: 438–439. [A,P]

GARÐARSSON, A. & NIELSEN, Ó.K. 1989. [Seasonal variation in numbers of birds on tidal mudflats in SW Iceland. Part I. Shorebirds.] *Natturufræðingurinn* 59: 59–84. [E]

GAUTHREAUX, S.A.J. 1982. The ecology and evolution of avian migration systems.

Pp. 93–167 *in* Farner, D.S., King, J.R., Parkes, K. C. (eds.). *Avian Biology Vol. 6.* Academic Press, New York. [E]

GAVRIN, V.F. (ГАВРИН, В.Ф.) 1973. O vesennem prolete kulikov v okrestnostyakh oz. Kurgal'dzhin. Pp. 92–93 *in* Flint, V.E. (ed.). *Fauna i ekologiya kulikov. Vol. 2.* Nauka, Moscow. [G]

GEIGER, R. 1961. *Das Klima der bodennahen Luftgeschicht.* Vieweg, Braunschweig.

GERSTENBERG, R.H. 1979. Habitat utilization by wintering and migrating shorebirds on Humboldt Bay, California. *Stud. Avian Biol.* 2: 33–40. [G]

GIBBONS, D.W., AVERY, M.I. & BROWN, A.F. 1996. Population trends in breeding birds in the UK since 1800. *Brit. Birds,* 89: 291–304. [E]

GIBBONS, D.W., REID, J.B. & CHAPMAN, R.A. 1993. *The new atlas of breeding birds in Britain and Ireland: 1988–1991.* Poyser, London. [E]

GIFFORD, E.W. 1913. Expedition of the California Academy of Sciences to the Galapagos Islands, 1905–1906. Vol. 8. *Proc. California Acad. Sci. Ser. 4, Vol. 2, Part 1*: 1–132. [G]

GILL, R.E. JR. & HANDEL, C.M. 1990. The importance of subarctic intertidal habitats to shorebirds: a study of the central Yukon-Kuskokwim Delta; Alaska. *Condor,* 92: 709–725. [G]

GILL, R.E. JR., BUTLER, R.W., TOMKOVICH, P.S., MUNDKUR, T. & HANDEL, C.N. 1995. Conservation of North American shorebirds. *Wader Study Group Bull.* 77: 82–91. [A]

GILL, R.E. JR. & JORGENSON, P.D. 1979. A preliminary assessment of timing and migration of shorebirds along the northcentral Alaskan Peninsula. *Stud. Avian Biol.* 2: 113–123. [A]

GILLINGS, S. & FULLER, R.J. 1996. Winter ecology of Lapwing and Golden Plover: a review. Unpublished report, British Trust for Ornithology, Thetford. [E]

GILYAZOV, A.S. 1998. Long-term changes in wader populations at the Lapland Nature Reserve and its surroundings 1887–1991. *International Wader Studies,* 10: In press. [E]

GIMINGHAM, C.H. 1975. *An introduction to heathland ecology.* Oliver & Boyd, Edinburgh.

GIRARD, O. 1989. Phénologie des stationnement de limicoles dans le Marais d'Olonne (Vendée). *Gibier Faune Sauvage,* 6: 321–360. [G]

GJERSHAUG, J.O., THINGSTAD, P.G., ELDØY, S. & BYRKJELAND, S. 1994. *Norsk fugleatlas.* Norsk ornitologisk forening, Klæbu. [E]

GLENISTER, A.G. 1955 (1971). *The birds of the Malay Peninsula, Singapore, and Penang.* Oxford Univ. Press, London. [G,P]

GLUSHCHENKO, YU.N. (ГЛУЩЕНКО, Ю.Н.) 1988. Materialy k poznanin migratsij kulikov na poberezh'e Zaliva Petra Velikogo. Pp. 31–37 *in* Flint, V.E. & Tomkovich, P.S. (eds.). *Kuliki SSSR: rasprostrnaenie, biologiya i okhrana.* Nauka, Moscow. [G,P]

GLUTZ VON BLOTZHEIM, U.N. 1963. Der Limikolenzug durch die Schweiz. *Orn. Beob.* 60: 81–106. [E,G]

GLUTZ VON BLOTZHEIM, U.N., BAUER, K.M. & BEZZEL, E. (eds.) 1975. *Handbuch der Vögel Mitteleuropas. Vol. 6.* Akad. Verlagsges., Wiesbaden. [A,E,G,P]

GLUTZ VON BLOTZHEIM, U.N., BAUER, K.M. & BEZZEL, E. (eds.) 1977. *Handbuch der Vögel Mitteleuropas. Vol. 7.* Akad. Verlagsges., Wiesbaden.

GMELIN, J.F. 1788–89. *Systema naturae. 13th ed. Vol. 1(2).* Beer, Lipsiae. [P, species diagnosis, p. 687]

GOCHFELD, M. 1984. Antipredator behavior: aggressive and distraction displays of shorebirds. Pp. 289–375 *in* Burger, J. & Olla, B.L. (eds.). *Behavior of marine animals, vol. 5, shorebirds: breeding behavior and populations.* Plenum, New York. [A,E,G,P]

GODFREY, W.E. 1979, 1986. *The birds of Canada.* Bryant Press, Toronto. [A,E,G,P]

GOLLEY, M. & STODDART, A. 1991. Identification of American and Pacific Golden Plovers. *Birding World,* 4: 195–204. [A,(E),P]

GOLLOP, J.B., BARRY, T.W. & IVERSEN, E.H. 1986. *Eskimo Curlew: a vanishing species?* Saskatchewan Nat. Hist. Soc., Regina. [A]

GÖRANSSON, G., KARLSSON, J., NILSSON, S.G. & ULFSTAND, S. 1975. Predation on birds' nests in relation to antipredator aggression and nest density: an experimental study. *Oikos*, 26:117–120.

GORDEEV, YU.I. (ГОРДЕЕВ, Ю.И.) 1980. Vesenniy prilet kulikov v okrestnost g. Khanty-Mansiyska. Pp. 98–99 *in* Flint, V.E. (ed.). *Novoe v izuchenii biologii i rasprostranenii kulikov.* Nauka, Moscow. [G]

GORE, M.E. & PYONG-OH, W. 1971. *The birds of Korea.* Royal Asiatic Soc., Seoul. [G,P]

GOSS-CUSTARD, J.D. 1969. The winter feeding ecology of the Redshank *Tringa totanus. Ibis*, 111: 338–356.

GOSS-CUSTARD, J.D. (ed.) 1996. *The Oystercatcher: From individuals to populations.* Oxford Univ. Press, Oxford.

GOSS-CUSTARD, J.D., JONES, R.E. & NEWBERRY, P.E. 1977. The ecology of the Wash, I. Distribution and diet of wading birds (Charadrii). *J. Appl. Ecol.* 14: 681–700. [G]

GOSS-CUSTARD, J.D. & SUTHERLAND, W.J. 1997. Individual behaviour, populations and conservation. Pp. 373–395 *in* Krebs, J.R. & Davies, N.B. (eds.). *Behavioural Ecology. 3rd edition.* Blackwell Science, Oxford.

GOSS-CUSTARD, J.D. & VERBOVEN, N. 1993. Disturbance of feeding shorebirds on the Exe Estuary. *Wader Study Group Bull.* 68: 59–66. [G]

GRANIT, O. 1939. Versuch zur quantitativen Untersuchungen der Vogelfauna einer Fjeldgegend in Nordfinnland. *Ornis Fennica*, 15: 53–65. [E]

GRANT, C. 1945. Drone bees selected by birds. *Condor*, 47: 261–263. [G]

GRAUL, W.D. 1973. Possible functions of head and breast markings in Charadriidae. *Wilson Bull.* 85: 60–70. [A,E,P]

GREEN, G.H., GREENWOOD, J.J.D. & LLOYD, C.S. 1977. The influence of snow conditions on the date of breeding of wading birds in north-east Greenland. *J. Zool., Lond.* 183: 311–328.

GREEN, M., MCGRADY, M., NEWTON, S. & UTTLEY, J. 1994. Counts of shorebirds at Barr al Hikman and Ghubbat al Hashish, Oman, winter 1989–90. *Wader Study Group Bull.* 72: 39–43. [G,P]

GREGORY, R.D. 1987. Comparative winter feeding ecology of Lapwings *Vanellus vanellus* and Golden Plovers *Pluvialis apricaria* on cereals and grasslands in the lower Derwent valley, North Yorkshire. *Bird Study*, 43: 244–250. [E]

GREGORY, R. & BASHFORD, R. 1996. Breeding bird survey: 1994–1995 index report. *BTO News*, 206: 5–8. [E]

GRIMES, L.G. 1974. Radar tracks of palearctic waders departing from the coast of Ghana in spring. *Ibis*, 116: 165–171.

GROMME, O.J. 1974. *Birds of Wisconsin.* University of Wisconsin Press, Madison. [A,G]

GROPPALI, R. 1992. Sull 'alimentazione di sette specie di Charadriiformes in Italia. *Riv. ital. Orn.* 63: 35–40. [E]

GUDMUNDSSON, G.A. & GARÐARSSON, A. 1993. Numbers, geographic distribution and habitat utilization of waders (Charadrii) in spring on the shores of Iceland. *Ecography*,16: 82–93. [E]

HAFTORN, S. 1971. *Norges fugler.* Universitetsforlaget, Oslo. [A,E,G,P]

HAGAR, J.A. 1966. Nesting of the Hudsonian Godwit at Churchill, Manitoba. *Living Bird*, 5: 5–43. [A]

HAGEN, Y. 1952. *Rovfuglene og viltpleien.* Gyldendal, Oslo.

HAGEN, Y. 1969. Norske undersøkelser over avkomsproduksjonen hos rovfugler og ugler sett i relasjon til smågnagerbestandens vekslinger. *Fauna (Oslo)*, 22: 73–126.

HALE, W.G. 1980. *Waders.* Collins, London. [A,E,G,P]

HANCOCK, M. & AVERY, M. 1998. Changes in breeding bird population in north east Sutherland and Caithness between 1988 and 1995. *Scottish Birds* 19: 195–205. [E]

HANSEN, P.S. 1986. Første forekomst af sibirsk tundrahjejle *Pluvialis dominica fulva* i Danmark, med bemærkninger om feltkendetegn. *Dansk Orn. Foren. Tidsskr.* 80: 1–4. [P]

HANSON, H.C., QUENEAU, P. & SCOTT, P. 1956. *The geography, birds, and mammals of the Perry River Region.* Arctic Institute of North America. [A,G]

HARDING, N., GREEN, R.E. & SUMMERS, R.W. 1993. *The effects of future changes in land use on upland birds in Britain.* Royal Society for the Protection of Birds, Edinburgh. [E]

HARRIS, K. 1995. Population monitoring counts: summer 1995. *Stilt,* 27: 27–29. [P]

HARRIS, M.P. 1969. Effect of laying dates on chick production in Oystercatchers and Herring Gulls. *British Birds,* 62: 72–75.

HARRISON, C. 1982. *An atlas of the birds of the Western Palaearctic.* Collins, London. [E,G]

HARRISON, J.R. & IRVING, K. 1954. Effect of lowered incubation temperature on the growth and differentiation of the chick embryo. *Biol. Bull.* 106: 1–48.

HARSHMAN, J. 1994. Reweaving the tapestry: What can we learn from Sibley and Ahlquist (1990)? *Auk,* 111: 377–388.

HARVEY, W.G. 1990. *Birds of Bangladesh.* University Press, Dhaka. [G,P]

HAVERSCHMIDT, M.F. 1943. De goudplevierenvangst in Nederland. *Ardea,* 32: 35–74. [E]

HAVILAND, M.D. 1915. Notes on the breeding habits of the Asiatic Golden Plover. *Brit. Birds,* 9: 82–89. [P]

HAVILAND, M.D. 1916. Notes on the Grey Plover on the Yenisei. *Brit. Birds,* 9: 162–166. [G]

HAWORTH, P.F. & THOMPSON, D.B.A. 1990. Factors associated with the breeding distribution of upland birds in the south Pennines, England. *J. Appl. Ecol.* 27: 562–577. [E].

HAYES, F.E. & FOX, J.A. 1991. Seasonality, habitat use, and flock sizes of shorebirds at the Bahia de Asunción, Paraguay. *Wilson Bull.* 103: 637–649. [A]

HAYES, F.E., GOODMAN. S.M., FOX, J.A., TAMAYO, T.G. & LÓPEZ, N.E. 1990. North American migrants in Paraguay. *Condor,* 92: 947–960. [A]

HAYMAN, P., MARCHANT, J. & PRATER, T. 1986. *Shorebirds: an identification guide to the waders of the world.* Croom Helm, London. [A,E,G,P]

HAZEVOET, C.J. 1992. Migrant and resident waders in the Cape Verde Islands. *Wader Study Group Bull.* 64: 46–50. [A,G]

HEDGES, S.B., PARKER, P.H., SIBLEY, C.G. & KUMAR, S. 1996. Continental breakup and the ordinal diversification of birds and mammals. *Nature,* 381 (16 May 1996): 226–229.

HENRIKSEN, K. 1985. Den postnuptiale fældning af svingfjerene hos hjejle *Pluvialis apricaria. Dansk Orn. Foren. Tidsskr.* 79: 141–150. [E]

HENRY, G.M. 1955. *A guide to the birds of Ceylon.* Oxford Univ. Press, London. [G,P]

HENSHAW, H.W. 1910. Migration of the Pacific Golden Plover to and from the Hawaiian islands. *Auk,* 27: 245–262. [P]

HESP, L.S. & BARNARD, C.J. 1989. Gulls and plovers: age-related differences in kleptoparasitism among Black-headed Gulls (*Larus ridibundus*). *Behav. Ecol. Sociobiol.* 24: 297–304.

HESPENHEIDE, H.A. 1975. Selective predation by two swifts and a swallow in Central America. *Ibis,* 117: 82–99.

HICKLIN, P.W. 1987. The migration of shorebirds in the Bay of Fundy. *Wilson Bull.* 99: 540–570. [A,G]

HICKLIN, P.W. & SMITH, P.C. 1979. The diet of five species of migrant shorebirds in the Bay of Fundy. *Proc. N.S. Inst. Sci.* 29: 483–488. [G]

HILL, D., HOCKIN, D., PRICE, D., TUCKER, G., MORRIS, R. & TREWEEK, J. 1997. Bird disturbance: improving the quality and utility of disturbance research. *J. Appl. Ecol.* 34: 275–288.

HILDÉN, O. & HYYTIÄ, K. 1981. Finlands häckande vadare–populationstendenser och nuvarande utbredning. *Proc. Second Nordic Congr. Ornithol.* 1979: 9–18. [E]

HINDE, R.A. 1966. *Animal behavior: a synthesis of ethology and comparative psychology.* McGraw-Hill, New York.

HIRSCHFELD, E. 1994. Migration patterns of some regularly occurring waders in Bahrain 1990–1992. *Wader Study Group Bull.* 73: 36–49. [G,P]

HÖFMANN, H. & HOERSCHELMANN, H. 1969. Nahrungsuntersuchungen bei Limikolen dursch Mageneinhatsanalysen. *Corax*, 3: 1–22. [E,G]

HOGG, P., DARE, P.J. & RINTOUL, J.V. 1984. Palearctic migrants in the central Sudan. *Ibis*, 126: 307–331. [E,G]

HÖGSTEDT, G. 1974. Length of the pre-laying period in the Lapwing *Vanellus vanellus* L. in relation to its food resources. *Ornis Scand.* 5: 1–4.

HÖHN, E.O. 1957. Observations on display and other forms of behavior of certain arctic birds. *Auk*, 74: 203–214. [A,G]

HÖHN, E.O. 1958. Observations on certain arctic birds. *Arctic*, 11: 93–100. [A]

HÖHN, E.O. 1959. Birds of the mouth of the Anderson River and Liverpool Bay, Northwest Territories. *Can. Field-Nat.* 73: 93–114. [A,G]

HOLLAND, P. 1992. Recent recoveries of waders. *Wader Study Group Bull.* 64: 63–64. [G]

HOLLOWAY, S. 1995. *The historical atlas of breeding birds in Britain and Ireland.* Poyser, London. [E]

HOLMES, R.T. 1966 a. Breeding ecology and annual cycle adaptations of the Red-backed Sandpiper (*Calidris alpina*) in northern Alaska. *Condor*, 68: 3–46.

HOLMES, R.T. 1966 b. Molt cycle of the Red-backed Sandpiper (*Calidris alpina*) in western North America. *Auk*, 83: 517–533.

HOLMES, R.T. 1972. Ecological factors influencing the breeding season schedule of Western Sandpipers. *Amer. Midl. Nat.* 87: 472–491.

HOLMES, R.T. & BLACK, C.P. 1973. Ecological distribution of birds in the Kolomak River – Askinuk Mountain region, Yukon–Kuskokwim Delta, Alaska. *Condor*, 75: 150–163. [A]

HOLMES, R.T. & PITELKA, F.A. 1968. Food overlap among co-existing sandpipers on northern Alaskan tundra. *Systematic Zoology*, 17: 305–318.

HOLMES, W.N. & PHILLIPS, J.G. 1985. The avian salt gland. *Biol. Rev.* 60: 213–256.

HOLT, S. & WHITFIELD, D.P. 1996. Montane ecology project site report series. *Research and Advisory Services Directorate Reports (confidential)*. Scottish Natural Heritage, Edinburgh. [E].

HOLYOAK, D.T. 1980. *Guide to Cook Islands birds*. Cook Islands Library and Museum Society inc., New Zealand. [G,P]

HOLYOAK, D.T. & THIBAULT, J.-C. 1984. *Contribution a l'etude des oiseaux de Polynesie Orientale*. NH Mus., Paris. [G,P]

HORSFIELD, D. & THOMPSON, D.B.A. 1997. *The uplands: guidance on terminology regarding altitudinal zonation and related terms.* Information and Advisory Note, Scottish Natural Heritage, Battleby.

HOSSELL, J. 1994. *The implications of global climate change for biodiversity.* Royal Society for the Protection of Birds, Sandy.

HOWEY, P., BOARD, R.G., DAVIS, D.H. & KEAR, J. 1984. The microclimate of the nests of waterfowl. *Ibis*, 126: 16–32.

HUBBARD, J.P. 1978. Revised check-list of the birds of New Mexico. *New Mexico Orn. Soc. Publ.* No. 6. [A,G]

HUDSON, P.J. 1992. *Grouse in space and time.* The Game Conservancy Trust, Fordingbridge.

HUDSON, P.J. 1995. Ecological trends and grouse management in upland Britain. Pp. 282–293 *in* Thompson, D.B.A., Hester, A.J. & Usher, M.B. (eds.). *Heaths and Moorland: Cultural Landscapes.* HMSO, Edinburgh.

HUDSON, R., TUCKER, G.M. & FULLER, R.J. 1994. Lapwing *Vanellus vanellus* populations in relation to agricultural changes: A review. Pp. 1–33 *in* Tucker, G.M., Davies, S.M. & Fuller, R.J. (eds.). *The ecology and conservation of Lapwings* Vanellus vanellus. Joint Nature Conservation Committee, Peterborough.

HUMPHRIES, C.J. & PARENTI, L.R. 1986. *Cladistic Biogeography. Oxford monographs on biogeography no. 2.* Clarendon Press, Oxford.

HUNTER, L., CANEVARI, P., MYERS, J.P. & PAINE, L.X. 1991. Shorebird and wetland conservation in the Western Hemisphere. ICBP Technical Publication No. 12: 279–290.

HUSSAIN, S.A. 1987. Conservation of wader habitats in India. *Wader Study Group Bull.* 49, suppl.: 128–131. [G,P]

HUSSELL, D.J.T. & HOLROYD, G.L. 1974. Birds of the Truelove Lowlands and adjacent areas of northeastern Devon Island. *Can. Field-Nat.* 88: 197–212. [G]

HUSSELL, D.J.T. & PAGE, G.W. 1976. Observations on the breeding biology of Black-bellied Plovers on Devon Island, N.W.T., Canada. *Wilson Bull.* 88: 632–653. [G]

HUTCHINSON, C.D. 1989. *Birds in Ireland.* Poyser, Calton. [E,G]

HUTCHINSON, G.E. 1959. Homage to Santa Rosalia, or why are there so many kinds of animals? *Amer. Natur.* 93: 145–159.

HYYTIÄ, K., KELLOMÄKI, E. & KOISTINEN, J. 1983. *Suomen lintuatlas.* SLY:n Lintutieto Oy, Helsinki. [E]

IL'IČEV, V.D. & FLINT, V.G. 1985. *Handbuch der Vögel der Sovjetunion. Vol. 1.* Ziemsen, Wittenberg Lutherstadt.

IMHOF, T.A. 1950. Additional bird records for Panamá. *Auk*, 67: 255–257. [A]

IMHOF, T.A. 1976. Alabama birds. University of Alabama Press. [A,G]

INGRAM, C. 1942. Field-notes on the birds of Iceland. *Ibis*, 84: 485–498. [E]

IPCC (INTERGOVERNMENTAL PANEL ON CLIMATE CHANGE). 1996. *Climate change 1996.* The Supplementary Report to the IPCC. Cambridge Univ. Press, Cambridge.

JANSSEN, R.B. 1987. *Birds of Minnesota.* University of Minnesota Press, Minneapolis. [A,G]

JÄRVINEN, O. & VÄISÄNEN, R.A. 1975. Estimating relative densities of breeding birds by the line transect method. *Oikos*, 26: 316–322.

JÄRVINEN, O. & VÄISÄNEN, R.V. 1977. Long-term changes of the North European land bird fauna. *Oikos*, 29: 225–228.

JÄRVINEN, O. & VÄISÄNEN, R.A. 1983. Confidence limits for estimates of population density in line transects. *Ornis Scand.* 14: 129–134.

JEHL, J.R. JR. 1968. Patterns of hatching success in subarctic birds. *Ecology*, 52: 169–173. [A]

JEHL, J.R. JR. & SMITH, B.A. 1970. *Birds of the Churchill Region, Manitoba.* Manitoba Mus. Man & Nature, Winnipeg. [A,G]

JIANWAI, C. & KELVIN, C. 1987. The conservation status of wetlands in China and their future prospects. *Proc. Workshop Internatl. Conf. Wetlands and Development, Kuala Lumpur, 9–13 Oct. 1995*: 117–126. [P]

JOHANSEN, H. 1958. Revision und Entstehung der arktischen Vogelfauna II. *Acta Arctica*, 9(2): 1–132. [A,E,G,P]

JOHANSEN, H. 1960. Die Vogelfauna Westsibiriens. *J. Orn.* 101: 472–491. [E,G,P]

JOHNSGARD, P.A. 1981. *The plovers, sandpipers, and snipes of the world.* Univ. Nebraska Press, Lincoln. [A,E,G,P]

JOHNSON, D.E. 1941. Golden Plover in central Indiana. *Auk*, 58: 255–256. [A]

JOHNSON, O.W. 1973. Reproductive condition and other features of shorebirds resident at Eniwetok Atoll during the boreal summer. *Condor*, 75: 336–343. [P]

JOHNSON, O.W. 1977. Plumage and molt in shorebirds summering at Enewetak Atoll. *Auk*, 94: 222–230. [P]

JOHNSON, O.W. 1979. Biology of shorebirds summering on Enewetak Atoll. *Stud. Avian Biol.* 2: 193–205. [P]

JOHNSON, O.W. 1985. Timing of molt in first-year Golden Plovers and some evolutionary implications. *Wilson Bull.* 97: 237–239. [P]

JOHNSON, O.W 1993. The Pacific Golden Plover (*Pluvialis fulva*): discovery of the species and other historical notes. *Auk*, 110: 136–141. [P]

JOHNSON, O.W. & CONNORS, P.G. 1996. American Golden Plover *Pluvialis dominica*; Pacific Golden Plover *Pluvialis fulva*. Pp. 1–40 *in* Poole, A. & Gill, F. (eds.). *The Birds of North America, No. 201–202*. Acad. Natural Sci., Philadelphia, and American Ornithologists' Union, Washington, DC. [P,A].

JOHNSON, O.W., CONNORS, P.G., BRUNER, P.L. & MARON, J.L. 1993. Breeding ground fidelity and mate retention in the Pacific Golden Plover. *Wilson Bull.* 105: 60–67. [P]

JOHNSON, O.W. & JOHNSON, P.M. 1983. Plumage-molt-age relationships in "over-summering" and migrating Lesser Golden-Plovers. *Condor,* 85: 406–419. [P]

JOHNSON, O.W., JOHNSON. P. & BRUNER, P. 1981 a. Wintering behavior and site faithfulness of American Golden Plovers *Pluvialis dominica fulva* in Hawaii. *Wader Study Group Bull.* 31: 44. [P]

JOHNSON, O.W., JOHNSON, P.M. & BRUNER, P.L. 1981 b. Wintering behavior and site-faithfulness of golden plovers on Oahu. *Elepaio,* 41: 123–130. [P]

JOHNSON, O.W., JOHNSON, P. , BRUNER, P.L., BRUNER, A.E., KIENHOLZ, R.J. & BRUSSEAU, P.A. 1997. Male-biased breeding ground fidelity and longevity in American Golden Plovers. *Wilson Bull.* 109: 348–351. [A]

JOHNSON, O.W., MORTON, M.L., BRUNER, P.L. & JOHNSON, P.M. 1989. Fat cyclicity, predicted migratory flight ranges, and features of wintering behavior in Pacific Golden-Plovers. *Condor,* 91: 156–177. [P]

JOHNSON, O.W. & NAKAMURA, R.M. 1981. The use of roofs by American Golden Plovers *Pluvialis dominica fulva* wintering on Oahu, Hawaiian Islands. *Wader Study Group Bull.* 31: 45–46. [P]

JOHNSON, O.W., WARNOCK, N., BISHOP, M.A., BENNETT, A.J., JOHNSON, P.M. & KIENHOLZ, R.J. 1997. Migration by ratio-tagged Pacific Golden-Plovers from Hawaii to Alaska, and their subsequent survival. *Auk,* 114: 521–524. [P]

JOHNSON, S.R. & HERTER, D.R. 1989. *The birds of the Beaufort Sea*. BP Exploration (Alaska) Inc., Anchorage. [A,G,(P)]

JOHNSTON, D.W. & MCFARLANE, R.W. 1967. Migration and bioenergetics of flight in the Pacific Golden Plover. *Condor,* 69: 156–168. [P]

JÖNSSON, P.E. & ALERSTAM, T. 1990. The adaptive significance of parental role division and sexual size dimorphism in breeding shorebirds. *Biol. J. Linn. Soc.* 41: 301–314.

JUKEMA, J. 1982. Rui en biometrie van de Goudplevier *Pluvialis apricaria*. *Limosa,* 55: 79–84. [E]

JUKEMA, J. 1986. De vorjaarsrui bij Goudplevieren *Pluvialis apricaria* in Friesland. *Limosa,* 59: 111–113. [E]

JUKEMA, J. 1987 a. De Goudplevier als jagdvogel. *De Nederlandse Jager,* 92: 554–556. [E]

JUKEMA, J. 1987 b. Was de Kleine Goudplevier (*Pluvialis fulva*) eens en talrijke doortrekker in Friesland? *Vanellus,* 40: 85–98. [P]

JUKEMA, J. 1987 c. Were Lesser Golden Plovers *Pluvialis fulva* regular winter visitors to Friesland, The Netherlands, in the first half of the 20th century? *Wader Study Group Bull.* 51: 56–58. [P]

JUKEMA, J. 1989. Veerenkleedmerkmalen van nordlijke en zuidlijke Goudplevieren *Pluvialis apricaria* op doortrek in Nederland. *Limosa,* 62: 147–152. [E]

JUKEMA, J. & HULSCHER, J.B. 1988. Terugmeldingskans van geringde Goudplevieren *Pluvialis apricaria* in relatie tot de strengheid van de winter. *Limosa,* 61: 85–90. [E]

JUKEMA, J. & PIERSMA, T. 1987. Special moult of breast and belly feathers during breeding in Golden Plovers *Pluvialis apricaria*. *Ornis Scand.* 18: 157–162. [E]

KÅLÅS, J.A. & BYRKJEDAL, I. 1981. Vadefuglenes hekkestatus i Norge med Svalbard. *Proc. Second Nordic Congr. Ornithol. 1979*: 57–74. [E]

KÅLÅS, J.A. & BYRKJEDAL, I. 1984. Line transects of waders in an alpine area: a methodological study. *Ann. Zool. Fennici,* 21: 399–402. [E]

KÅLÅS, J.A. & LØFALDLI, L. 1987. Clutch size in the Dotterel *Charadrius morinellus*: an adaptation to parental incubation behaviour? *Ornis Scand.* 18: 316–319.

MURTON, R.K. & WESTWOOD, N.J. 1974. Some effects of agricultural change on the English avifauna. *Brit. Birds*, 67: 41–69. [E]

MUSACCHIA, X.J. 1953. A study of the lipids in arctic migratory birds. *Condor*, 55: 305–312. [A, (P?)]

MYERS, J.P. 1981. A test of three hypotheses for latitudinal segregation of the sexes in wintering birds. *Can. J. Zool.* 59: 1527–1534.

MYERS, J.P. 1983. Space, time and pattern of individual associations in a group-living species: Sanderlings have no friends. *Behav. Ecol. Sociobiol.* 12: 129–134.

MYERS, J.P. 1984. Spacing behavior of non-breeding shorebirds. Pp. 271–321 *in* Burger, J. & Olla, B.L. (eds.). *Shorebirds: migration and foraging behavior*. Plenum, New York. [A,G]

MYERS, J.P., CONNORS, P.G. & PITELKA, F.A. 1979. Territoriality in non-breeding shorebirds. *Stud. Avian Biol.* 2: 231–246. [A,G]

MYERS, J.P., CONNORS, P.G. & PITELKA, F.A. 1981. Optimal territory size and the Sanderling: compromises in a variable environment. Pp. 135–158 *in* Kamil, A.C. & Sargent, T.D. (eds.). *Foraging behavior: ecological, ethological and psychological approaches*. Garland STPM Press, New York.

MYERS, J.P. & MCCAFFERY, B.J. 1984. Paracas revisited: do shorebirds compete on their wintering grounds? *Auk*, 101: 197–199. [A,G]

MYERS, J.P., MCLAIN, P.D., MORRISON, R.I.G., ANTAS, P.Z., CANEVARI, P., HARRINGTON, B.A., LOVEJOY, T.E., PULIDO, V., SALLABERRY, M. & SENNER, S.E. 1987. The Western Hemisphere shorebird reserve network. *Wader Study Group Bull.* 49: 122–124.

MYERS, J.P. & MYERS, L.P. 1979. Shorebirds of coastal Buenos Aires Province, Argentina. *Ibis*, 121: 186–200. [A,G]

MYHRE, K. & STEEN, J.B. 1979. Body temperature and aspects of behavioural temperature regulation in some neonate subarctic and arctic birds. *Ornis Scand.* 10: 1–9. [E]

MYKLEBOST, H. & STRØMME, S. 1963. *Norge, land og folk. Vol. 1.* Cappelen, Oslo.

NANKINOV, D. 1989. The status of waders in Bulgaria. *Wader Study Group Bull.* 56: 16–25. [E,G]

NERC (NATURAL ENVIRONMENT RESEARCH COUNCIL). 1997. *Climate change: scientific certainties and uncertainties.* Natural Environment Research Council, Swindon.

NETHERSOLE-THOMPSON, D. 1957. Ecological notes on Golden Plovers in the Cairngorms. *Scottish Naturalist*, 69: 119–120. [E]

NETHERSOLE-THOMPSON, D. 1973. *The Dotterel.* Collins, London.

NETHERSOLE-THOMPSON, C. & NETHERSOLE-THOMPSON, D. 1939. *Some observations on the sexual-life and breeding-biology of the Southern Golden Plovers* (Charadrius a. apricarius) *as observed in Inverness-shire.* Unpublished, hand-written manuscript by D. Nethersole-Thompson. Original held by M. Nethersole-Thompson; sole copies with IB and DBAT. [E]

NETHERSOLE-THOMPSON, C. & NETHERSOLE-THOMPSON, D. 1942. Egg-shell disposal by birds. *Brit. Birds*, 35: 162–169, 190–200, 214–223, 241–250. [E]

NETHERSOLE-THOMPSON, C. & NETHERSOLE-THOMPSON, D. 1943. Nest site selection by birds. *Brit. Birds*, 37: 70–74, 88–94, 108–113. [E]

NETHERSOLE-THOMPSON, D. & NETHERSOLE-THOMPSON, C. 1961. The breeding behaviour of the British Golden Plover. Pp. 206–214 *in* Bannerman, D.A. (ed.) *The birds of the British Isles, vol. 10.* Oliver & Boyd, Edinburgh. [E]

NETHERSOLE-THOMPSON, D. & NETHERSOLE-THOMPSON, M. 1979. *Greenshanks.* Poyser, Berkhamsted.

NETHERSOLE-THOMPSON, D. & NETHERSOLE-THOMPSON, M. 1986. *Waders, their breeding, haunts and watchers.* Poyser, Calton. [E]

NETHERSOLE-THOMPSON, D. & WATSON, A. 1981. *The Cairngorms. Their natural history and scenery.* Melven Press, Perth. [E]

NETTLESHIP, D.N. 1973. Breeding ecology of Turnstones at Hazen Camp, Ellesmere Island in N.W.T. *Ibis*, 115: 202–217.

NEWTON, I. 1977. Timing and success of breeding in tundra-nesting geese. Pp. 113–126 *in* Stonehouse, B. & Perrins, C. (eds.) *Evolutionary ecology*. MacMillan, London.

NEWTON, I. 1986. *The Sparrowhawk*. Poyser, Calton. [E,G]

NEWTON, I. 1995. Presidential address. The contribution of some recent research on birds to the ecological understanding. *J. Anim. Ecol.* 64: 675–696.

NIKOLAEV, V. I. 1998. The importance of the peatlands of the Upper Volga Area as habitats for waders. *International Wader Studies* 10: In press. [E].

NILSSON, S. & PITT, S. 1991. Mountain world in danger. Earthscan, London.

NILSSON, S.G. 1977. Häckfågelfaunan på högmossar i sydvästra Småland. *Fauna Flora*, 72: 227–233. [E]

NIXON, K.C. 1993. *CLADOS. Ver. 1.2 (beta version)*. Cornell University, Ithaca.

NIXON, K.C. & CARPENTER, J.M. 1993. On outgroups. *Cladistics*, 9: 413–426.

NOL, E. 1986. Incubation period and foraging technique in shorebirds. *Amer. Natur.* 128: 115–119. [A?]

NORLIN, Å. 1965. Zur Nahrungswahl von Limicolen in Schweden (Beobachtungsstation Ledskär). *Vogelwarte* 23: 97–101. [G]

NØRREVANG, A. 1959. The migration patterns of some waders in Europe, based on the ringing results. *Vidensk. Medd. Dansk Naturhistorisk Forening*, 121: 181–222. [E,G]

NTIAMOA-BAIDU, Y. & GRIEVE, A. 1987. Palearctic waders in coastal Ghana in 1985/86. *Wader Study Group Bull.* 49: 76–78. [G]

OAG MÜNSTER 1988. Zielsetzungen und erste Ergebnisse der Internationalen Limikolenzählungen: Wegzug von Limicolen durch das Binnenland. *Vogelwelt*, 109: 3–25. [G]

OAKES, C. 1948. "Plover's Page" behaviour of Dunlin. *Brit. Birds*, 41: 226–228. [E]

OBERHOLSER, H.C. 1938. *The bird life of Louisiana*. Dept. Conserv., New Orleans. [A,G]

O'CONNELL, M.J., THOMAS, C.J., TWISS, S.D., DOWNIE, I.S., EVANS, P.R. & WHITFIELD, D.P. 1996. Functional ecology of peatland animals in the Flow Country of northern Scotland. I. Habitat requirements of breeding waders (Charadrii). Research and Advisory Services Directorate Report. Scottish Natural Heritage Edinburgh. [E]

OLSEN, K.M. 1992. *Danmarks fugle – en oversikt*. Dansk Ornitologisk Forening, Copenhagen. [E]

ONNO, S. 1966 Faunistical and ecological researches. Pp. 10–20 *in* Kumari, E. (ed.). *Ornithological researches in Estonia*. Tallin. [E]

ORING, L.W. 1967. Egg laying of a golden plover *Pluvialis apricaria*. *Ibis*, 109: 434. [E]

ORING, L.W. 1982. Avian mating systems. Pp. 1–92 *in* Farner, D.S., King, J. & Parker, K.C. (eds.). *Avian Biology, Vol. 6*. Academic Press, New York.

ORING, L.W. & LANK, D.B. 1984. Breeding area fidelity, natal philopatry, and the social systems of sandpipers. Pp. 125–147 *in* Burger, J. & Olla, B.L. (eds.). *Behavior of marine animals, vol. 5, shorebirds: breeding behavior and populations*. Plenum, New York.

ORING, L.W., REED, J.M. & ALBERICO, J.A.R. 1996. Mate acquisition tactics in polyandrous Spotted Sandpiper (*Actitis macularia*): the role of age and experience. *Behav. Ecol.* 5: 9–16.

OWENS, I.P.F. 1981. Sexual selection in the sex-role reversed Eurasian Dotterel (*Charadrius morinellus*). Unpublished PhD thesis, University of Leicester, UK.

OWENS, I.P.F., DIXON, A., BURKE, T. & THOMPSON, D.B.A. 1995. Strategic paternity assurance in the sex-role reversed Eurasian Dotterel (*Charadrius morinellus*): behavioural and genetic evidence. *Behav. Ecol.* 6: 14–21.

OWENS, I.P.F. & THOMPSON, D.B.A. 1995. Sex differences, sex ratios and sex roles. *Proc. Royal Soc. London, B.* 258: 93–99.

PAGE, G.W. & GILL, R.E.G. JR. 1994. Shorebirds in western North America: late 1800s to late 1900s. *Studies in Arctic Biology*, 15: 147–160. [A,G,P]

PAGE, G.W., STENZEL, L.E. & WOLFE, C.M. 1979. Aspects of the occurrence of shorebirds on a Central Californian estuary. *Stud. Avian Biol.* 2: 15–32. [A,G]

PALLAS, P.S. 1776. *Reise durch verschidene Provinzen des russischen Reiches, 1768 und 1769sten Jahre. Vol 3.* St. Petersburg. [G, ssp. diagnosis, p. 699]

PARISH, D. & HOWES, J.R. 1990. Waterbird hunting and management in SE Asia. Pp. 128–131 *in* Matthews, G.V.T. (ed.). *Managing waterfowl populations.* International Waterfowl and Wetlands Research Bureau, Slimbridge, UK.

PARISH, D., LANE, B., SAGAR, P. & TOMKOVICH, P. 1987. Wader migration systems in East Asia and Australasia. *Wader Study Group Bull.* 49: 4–14. [G,P.]

PARISH, D.M.B. 1996. Behavioural ecology of the Lapwing *Vanellus vanellus* L. in upper Teesdale. PhD Thesis, University of Durham, UK.

PARKER, G.R. & ROSS, R.K. 1973. Notes on the birds of Southampton Island, Northwest Territories. *Arctic*, 26: 123–129. [A,G]

PARMELEE, D.F., STEPHENS, H.A. & SCHMIDT, R.H. 1967. The birds of southeastern Victoria Island and adjacent small islands. *Natl. Mus. Can. Bull.* 222: 1–229. [A,G]

PARR, R. 1979. Sequential breeding by Golden Plovers. *Brit. Birds,* 72: 499–503. [E]

PARR, R. 1980. Population study of Golden Plover *Pluvialis apricaria*, using marked birds. *Ornis Scand.* 11: 179–189. [E]

PARR, R. 1992. The decline to extinction of a population of Golden Plover in NE Scotland. *Ornis Scand.* 23: 152–158. [E]

PARR, R. 1993 a. *Moorland birds and their predators in relation to forestry in the uplands.* PhD thesis, University of Aberdeen, UK. [E]

PARR, R. 1993 b. Nest predation and numbers of Golden Plover and other moorland waders. *Bird Study,* 40: 223–231. [E]

PATTIE, D.L. 1990. A 16-year record of summer birds on Truelove Lowland, Devon Island, Northwest Territories, Canada. *Arctic,* 43: 275–283. [A,G]

PAULSON, D.R. 1993. *Shorebirds of the Pacific Northwest.* Univ. of Washington Press, Seattle. [A,G,P]

PAULSON, D.R. 1995. Black-bellied Plover (*Pluvialis squatarola*). Pp. 1–28 *in* Poole, A. & Gill, F. (eds.). *The Birds of North America, No. 186.* Acad. Natural Sciences, Philadelphia and American Ornithologists' Union, Washington, DC. [G].

PAULSON, D.R. & ERCKMANN, W.J. 1985. Buff-breasted Sandpipers nesting in association with Black-bellied Plovers. *Condor,* 87: 429–430. [G]

PAULSON, D.R. & LEE, D.S. 1992. Wintering of lesser golden-plovers in eastern North America. *Journ. Field Ornithol.* 63: 121–128. [A, (P)]

PAYNE, R.B. & HOWE, H.F. 1976. Cleptoparasitism by gulls of migrating shorebirds. *Wilson Bull.* 88: 349–351. [G]

PEARCE-HIGGINS, J.W. & YALDEN, D.W. (unpublished). *Plumage variation in populations of Golden Plover,* Pluvialis apricaria. [E]

PEARSALL, W.H. 1971. *Mountains and moorlands.* Collins, London.

PECK, G.K. 1972. Birds of the Cape Henrietta Maria Region, Ontario. *Can. Field-Nat.* 86: 333–347. [A]

PECK, G.K. & JAMES, R.D. 1983. *Breeding birds of Ontario; nidology and distribution, vol. 1: Nonpasserines.* Royal Ont. Mus., Toronto. [A]

PEKLO, A.M. & OCHAPOVSKIJ, V.S. (ПЕКЛО. А.М.. ОЧАПОВСИЙ, В.С.). 1973. Zolotistaya rzhanka v Krasnodarskom krae. Pp. 69 *in* Flint, V.E. (ed.). *Fauna i ekologiya kulikov. Vol. 2.* Nauka, Moscow. [E]

PERCO, F. 1984. Estimates of wader numbers during midwinter in northern Adriatic coastal wetlands. *Wader Study Group Bull.* 40: 49–50. [G]

PERRINS, C.M. 1970. The timing of birds' breeding seasons. *Ibis,* 112: 242–255.

PERRINS, C.M. 1979. *British tits.* Collins, London.

PERRINS, C. 1987. *Collins New Generation Guide to the Birds of Britain and Europe.* Collins, London. [E,G]

PETERS, H.S. & BURLEIGH, T.D. 1949. New avian records from Newfoundland. *Auk,* 66: 172–176. [A]

PETERS, H.S. & BURLEIGH, T.D. 1951. *The birds of Newfoundland.* Houghton Mifflin, Boston. [A,G]

PFEIFER, R. 1988. Aussergewöhnlich starke Heimzugsammlung des Goldregenpfeifers *Pluvialis apricaria* bei Bayeruth. *Anz. orn. Ges. Bayern,* 27: 291–292. [E]

PHILLIPS, J. & WATSON, A. 1995. Key requirements for management of heather moorland: now and for the future. Pp. 344–361 *in* Thompson, D.B.A., Hester, A.J. & Usher, M.B. (eds.). *Heaths and moorland: cultural landscapes.* HMSO, Edinburgh.

PHILLIPS, R.E. 1980. Behaviour and systematics of New Zealand plovers. *Emu,* 80: 177–197.

PICOZZI, N. 1975. Crow predation on marked nests. *J. Wildl. Manage.* 39: 151–155.

PIENKOWSKI, M.W. 1978/79. Differences in habitat requirements and distribution patterns of plovers and sandpipers as investigated by studies of feeding behaviour. *Verh. orn. Ges. Bayern,* 23: 105–124. [G]

PIENKOWSKI, M.W. 1981. How foraging plovers cope with environmental effects on invertebrate behaviour and availability. Pp. 179–192 *in* Jones, N.V. & Wolff, W.J. (eds.). *Feeding and survival strategies of estuarine organisms.* Plenum, New York. [G]

PIENKOWSKI, M.W. 1982. Diet and energy intake of Grey and Ringed plovers, *Pluvialis squatarola* and *Charadrius hiaticula,* in the non-breeding season. *J. Zool. Lond.* 197: 511–549. [G]

PIENKOWSKI, M.W. 1983. The effects of environmental conditions on feeding rates and prey-selection of shore plovers. *Ornis Scand.* 14: 227–238. [G]

PIENKOWSKI, M.W. 1984. Breeding biology and population dynamics of Ringed Plovers *Charadrius hiaticula* in Britain and Greenland: nest-predation as a possible factor limiting distribution and timing of breeding. *J. Zool. Lond.* 202: 53–114.

PIENKOWSKI, M.W., EVANS, P.R. & TOWNSHEND, D.J. 1985. Leap-frog and other migration patterns of waders: a critique of the Alerstam and Högstedt hypothesis, and some alternatives. *Ornis Scand.* 16: 61–70. [E,G]

PIENKOWSKI, M.W., FERNS, P.N., DAVIDSON, N.C. & WORRALL, D.H. 1984. Balancing the budget: measuring the energy intake and requirements of shorebirds in the field. Pp. 29–56 *in* Evans, P.R., Goss-Custard, J.D. & Hale, W.G. (eds.). *Coastal waders and wildfowl in winter.* Cambridge Univ. Press, Cambridge. [G]

PIERSMA, T. 1982. Foraging of Grey Plover. Pp. 150–153 *in* Altenburg, W., Engelmoer, M., Mes, R. & Piersma, T. (eds.). *Wintering waders on the Banc d'Arguin, Mauritania.* Stichting Vethot steun aan Waddenonderzoek, Leiden. [G]

PIERSMA, T. 1985. Abundance of waders in the Nakdong Estuary, South Korea, in September 1984. *Wader Study Group Bull.* 44: 21–26. [G,P]

PIERSMA, T. (ed.) 1986. Breeding waders in Europe: a review of population size estimates and a bibliography of information sources. *Wader Study Group Bull. 48, Suppl.* [E]

PIERSMA, T. 1987. Hop, skip or jump? Constraints on migration of Arctic waders by feeding, fattening and flight speed. *Limosa,* 60: 185–191.

PIERSMA , T., BEINTEMA, A.J., DAVIDSON, N.C., OAG MÜNSTER & PIENKOWSKI, M.W. 1987. Wader migration systems in the East Atlantic. *Wader Study Group Bull.* 49: 35–56. [E,G]

PIERSMA, T., GILS, J. VAN & WIERSMA, P. 1996. Family Scolopacidae (sandpipers, snipes and phalaropes). Pp. 444–533 *in* del Hoyo, J. Elliott, A. & Sargatal, J. (eds.). *Handbook of the Birds of the World. Vol. 3: Hoatzin to auks.* Lynx Edicions, Barcelona.

PIERSMA, T., KLAASEN, M., BRUGGEMANN, J.H., BLOMERT, A.-M., GUEYE, A., NTIAMOA-BAIDU, Y. & BREDERODE, N.E. VAN. 1990a. Seasonal timing of the spring departure of waders from the Banc d'Arguin, Mauritania. *Ardea,* 78: 123–134. [G]

PIERSMA, T. & NTIAMOA-BAIDU, Y. 1995. *Ecology and the management of coastal wetlands in Ghana.* NIOZ-Report 1995–96. Texel. [G]

PIERSMA, T. & WIERSMA, P. 1996. Family Charadriidae (plovers). Pp. 384–442 *in* del Hoyo, J., Elliott, A. & Sargatal, J. (eds.). *Handbook of the Birds of the World. Vol. 3: Hoatzin to auks.* Lynx Edicions, Barcelona. [A,E,G,P]

PIERSMA, T., WIERSMA, P. & GILS, J. VAN. 1997. The many unknowns about plovers and sandpipers of the world. Introduction to a wealth of research opportunities highly relevant for shorebird conservation. *Wader Study Group Bull.* 82: 22–33. [A,E,G,P]

PIERSMA, T., ZWARTS, L. & BRUGGEMANN, J.H. 1990b. Behavioural aspects of the departure of waders before long-distance flights: flocking, vocalizations, flight paths and diurnal timing. *Ardea,* 78: 157–184. [G]

PITELKA, F.A., HOLMES, R.T. & MACLEAN, S.F. JR. 1974. Ecology and evolution of social organization in arctic sandpipers. *Amer. Zool.* 14: 185–204.

POOT, M., RASMUSSEN, L.M., ROOMEN, M. VAN, RÖSNER, H.-U. & SÜDBECK, P. 1996. Migratory waterbirds in the Wadden Sea 1993/94. *Wadden Sea Ecosystem* 5. [E,G]

PORTENKO, L.A. 1972. *Birds of the Chukchi Peninsula and Wrangel Island.* Amerind Pbl. Co., New Dehli (1981). [A,G,P]

PORSILD, A.E. 1943. Birds of the Mackenzie Delta. *Can. Field-Nat.* 57: 19–35. [A,G]

POULSEN, G.J. & AEBISCHER, N.J. 1995. Quantitative comparison of two methods of assessing diet of nestling Skylarks (*Alauda arvensis*). *Auk,* 112: 1070–1072.

POYNTING, F. 1895–96. *Eggs of British birds, Limicoles.* R.H. Porter, London. [G,E].

PRATER, A.J. 1981 a. *Estuary birds of Britain and Ireland.* Poyser, Calton. [E,G]

PRATER, A.J. 1981 b. A review of the patterns of primary moult in palearctic waders (Charadrii). Pp. 393–409 *in* Cooper, J. (Ed.). *Proc. Symp. Birds of the Sea and Shore, 1979.* Cape Town. [E,G]

PREBLE, E.A. 1923. A biological survey of the Pribilof Islands, Alaska. *North American Fauna* No. 46. [P]

PRESTON, F.W. 1949. The Pacific flyway of the Golden Plover. *Auk,* 66: 87–88. [P]

PRICE, T., KIRKPATRICK, M. & ARNOLD, S.J. 1988. Directional selection and the evolution of breeding dates in birds. *Science,* 240: 798–799.

PRIEDNIEKS, J., STRAZDS, M., STRAZDS, A. & PETRINS, A. 1989. *Latvian breeding bird atlas 1980–1984.* Zinatne, Riga. [E]

PROKOSCH, P. 1984. The German Wadden Sea. Pp. 224–237 *in* Evans, P.R., Goss-Custard, J.D. & Hale, W.G. (eds.). *Coastal waders and wildfowl in winter.* Cambridge University Press, Cambridge. [G]

PULLIAINEN, E. & SAARI, L. 1993. Breeding biology of the Golden Plover *Pluvialis apricaria* in eastern Finnish Lapland. *Ornis Fennica,* 70: 40–43. [E]

PYM, A. 1982. Identification of Lesser Golden Plovers and status in Britain and Ireland. *Brit. Birds,* 75: 112–124. [A,E,G,P]

RACHILIN, V.K. (РАХИЛИН, В.К.). 1973. Oprolete kulikov v tsentral'nom Sikhote-Aline. Pp. 98–103 *in* Flint, V.E. (ed.). *Fauna i ekologiya kulikov. Vol. 2.* Nauka, Moscow. [G,P]

RAMSAR RESOLUTION, VI 4, 1996. Adoption of population estimates for operation of the specific criteria based on waterfowl. Sixth Meeting of the Conference of the Contracting Parties, Brisbane, Australia 19–27 March 1996. (Ramsar Conference Proceedings, VI 4/12 Resolutions.

RASMUSSEN, L.M. 1994. Landsdækkende optælling af hjejler *Pluvialis apricaria* i Danmark, oktober 1993. *Dansk Orn. Foren. Tidsskr.* 88: 161–169. [E]

RATCLIFFE, D.A. 1976. Observations on the breeding of the Golden Plover in Great Britain. *Bird Study,* 23: 63–116. [E]

RATCLIFFE, D.A. 1990. *Bird life of mountain and upland.* Cambridge Univ. Press, Cambridge. [E]

RATCLIFFE, D.A. 1997. *The Raven.* Poyser, London.

RATCLIFFE, D.A. & THOMPSON, D.B.A. 1988. The British uplands: their ecological character and international significance. Pp. 9–36 *in* Usher, M.B. & Thompson,

D.B.A. (eds.). *Ecological change in the Uplands.* Blackwell Scientific Publications, Oxford. [E]

RAY, P.H. 1885. *Report of the international polar expedition to Point Barrow, Alaska.* US Signal Office, Arctic Publications, Washington DC, USA. [G]

RECHER, H.F. 1966. Some aspects of the ecology of migrant shorebirds. *Ecology,* 47: 393–407. [G]

REHFISCH, M.M., CLARK, N.A., LANGSTONE, R.H.W. & GREENWOOD, J.J.D. 1996. A guide to the provision of refuges for waders: an analysis of 30 years of ringing data from the Wash, England. *J. Appl. Ecol.* 33: 673–687. [G]

REID, E., MORTIMER, G.N., LINDSAY, R.A. & THOMPSON, D.B.A. 1994. Blanket bogs in Great Britain: an assessment of large-scale pattern and distribution using remote sensing and GIS. Pp. 229–246 *in* Edwards, P.J., May, R. & Webb, N.R. (eds.). *Large Scale Ecology and Conservation Biology.* Blackwell, Oxford.

RENAUD, W.E., JOHNSON, S.R. & HOLLINGDALE, D. 1979. Breeding birds of Arctic Bay, Baffin Island, NWT, with notes on the biogeographic significance of the avifauna. *Arctic,* 32: 122–134. [A,G]

RENAUD, W.E., JOHNSTON, W.G. & FINLEY, K.J. 1981. The avifauna of the Pond Inlet region, NWT. *American Birds,* 35: 119–129. [A,G]

REYNOLDS, J.D., COLWELL, M.A. & COOKE, F. 1986. Sexual selection and spring arrival times of Red-necked and Wilson's Phalaropes. *Behav. Ecol. & Sociobiol.* 18: 303–310.

RIDGILL, S.C. & FOX, A.D. 1990. Cold weather movements of waterfowl in western Europe. *IWRB Special Publication No. 13,* Slimbridge, UK.

RIPLEY, S.D. 1982. *A synopsis of the birds of India and Pakistan together with those of Nepal, Buthan, Bangladesh, and Sri Lanka.* Second edition. Bombay Natural History Society, Bombay. [E,G,P]

RITTINGHAUS, H. 1969. Ein Beitrag zur Ökologie und zur Verhalten des Goldregenpfeifers, *Pluvialis apricarius,* zu Beginn der Brutzeit. *Vogelwarte,* 25: 57–65. [E]

ROBBINS, S.D. 1991. *Wisconsin birdlife: population and distribution past and present.* Univ. Wisconsin, Madison. [A,G]

ROBERTS, N. 1989. *The holocene: an environmental history.* Cambridge Univ. Press, Cambridge.

ROHWEDER, D. 1996. Nocturnal habitat use and foraging behaviour of Pacific Golden Plover (*Pluvialis fulva*) in northern NSW. *Southern Hemisphere Ornithologists' Congress, Royal Australian Ornithologist Union, October 5–6, 1996:* 56. [P].

ROHWEDER, D.A. & BAVERSTOCK, P.R. 1996. Preliminary investigation of nocturnal habitat use by migratory waders (Order Charadriformes) in Northern New South Wales. *Wildlife Research,* 23:169–184. [P].

ROJAS DE AZUAJE, L.M., TAI, S. & MCNEIL, R. 1993. Comparison of rod/cone ratio in three species of shorebirds having different nocturnal strategies. *Auk,* 110: 141–145. [G]

ROOS, G. 1975. De arktiska vadarnas flyttning över Falsterbo sommaren 1974 enligt tre olika registreringsmetoder. *Anser,* 14: 79–92. [G]

ROOT, T. 1988. *Atlas of wintering North American birds.* Univ. Chicago Press, Chicago. [A,G]

ROSE, P.M. & SCOTT, D.A. (comp.) 1994. Waterfowl population estimates. *International waterfowl and wetlands research bureau publication No. 29.* IWWRB, Slimbridge, UK. [G,E,P,A]

ROSE, P.M. & STROUD, D.A. 1994. Estimating international waterfowl populations. Current activity and future directions. *Wader Study Group Bulletin,* 73: 19–26.

ROSELAAR, C.S. 1990. Identification and occurrence of American and Pacific Golden Plover in the Netherlands. *Dutch Birding,* 12: 70–71. [A,P]

ROTTENBORN, S.C. 1996. The use of coastal agricultural fields in Virgina as foraging habitat by shorebirds. *Wilson Bull.* 108: 783–796. [G,A].

ROWAN, W. 1923. Migrations of the Golden Plover and Black-bellied Plovers in Alberta. *Condor,* 25: 21–23. [A,G]

RSPB 1997. *Agenda 2000. July 1997. RSPB briefing on the European Commission's Agenda 2000 proposals.* Royal Soc. Protection Birds, Sandy.

RUDDIMAN, W.F. & KUTZBACH, J.E. 1990. Late Cenozoic plateau uplift and climate change. *Transactions of the Royal Society of Edinburgh: Earth Sciences* 81: 301–314.

RUFINO, R. 1984. Autumn and winter numbers of waders in the Tejo Estuary, Portugal. *Wader Study Group Bull.* 42: 43–44. [G]

RUFINO, R. & ARAUJO, A. 1987. Seasonal variation in wader numbers and distribution at the Ria de Faro. *Wader Study Group Bull.* 51: 48–53. [G]

RYABITSEV, V.K. 1987. Repeat clutches and bicyclicity in Yamal birds. *Ekologiya* 18(2): 63–122. [E]

RYABITSEV, V.K. & ALEKSEEVA, N.S. 1998. Nesting density dynamics and site fidelity of waders on the middle and northern Yamal. *International Wader Studies* 10: In press. [G,E,P].

SADAYOSI, T. 1997. Habitat loss and alteration in Japan – a history of large-scale destruction. Pp. 35–43 *in* Straw, P. (ed.). *Shorebird conservation in the Asia–Pacific region.* Australian Water Study Group Conference, 1996, Brisbane, Australia.

SAGE, B. 1974. Ecological distribution of birds in the Atigun and Sagavaniriktok river valleys, Arctic Canada. *Can. Field-Natur.* 88: 281–291. [A]

SAGE, B.L. 1975. Recent observations in the Wrangell Mountains, Alaska. *Condor,* 77: 206–207. [A]

SAGE, B. 1986. *The Arctic and its wildlife.* Croom Helm, London. [G,P]

SALOMONSEN, F. 1955. The evolutionary significance of bird migration. *Danm. Biol. Medd.* 22: 1–62.

SALOMONSEN, F. 1967 a. *Fugletrækket og dets gåder.* Munksgaard, Copenhagen. [A,E,G,P]

SALOMONSEN, F. 1967 b. *Fuglene på Grønland.* Rhodos, Copenhagen. [A,E,G]

SAMPATH, K. & KRISHNAMURTHY, K. 1990. Shorebirds (Charadriiformes) of the Pichavaram mangrove, Tamil Nadu, India. *Wader Study Group Bull.* 58: 24–27. [G,P]

SAUER, E.G.F. 1962. Ethology and ecology of Golden Plovers on St. Lawrence Island, Bering Sea. *Psychol. Forschung,* 26: 399–470. [P]

SAUER, E.G.F. 1963 a. Migration habits of Golden Plovers. *Proc. XIII Int. Orn. Congr. Ithaca:* 454–467. [P]

SAUER, E.G.F. 1963 b. Golden Plover migration, its evolution and orientation. *XVI Int. Congr. Zool.* Washington. [P]

SAVILE, D.B.O. 1951. Bird observations at Chesterfield Inlet, Keewatin, in 1950. *Can. Field-Nat.* 65: 145–157. [A,G]

SCHARRINGA, C.J.G. 1976. Broedvogel van de Goudplevier, *Pluvialis apricaria apricaria,* in Brabant. *Limosa,* 49: 109–110. [E]

SCHICK, C.T., JOHNSON, T.M., KUNDE, C.M. & MYERS, J.P. 1984. Aerial censuses of Sanderlings and estimates for other shorebirds on the Baja California Peninsula, Mexico, 1983–1984. *Wader Study Group Bull.* 41: 14–15. [G]

SCHMIDT-NIELSEN, K., JØRGENSEN, C.B. & OSAKI, H. 1958. Extrarenal salt excretion in birds. *Amer. J. Physiol.* 193: 101–107.

SCHMITHÜSEN, J. 1976. *Atlas zur Biogeographie.* Bibliogr. Institut AG, Zürich.

SCHNEIDER, D. & MALLORY, E.P. 1982. Spring migration of shorebirds in Panama. *Condor,* 84: 344–345. [G]

SCHNEIDER, D.C. 1985. Predation on the urchin *Echinometra lucunter* (Linnaeus) by migratory shorebirds on a tropical reef flat. *J. Exp. Mar. Biol. Ecol.* 92: 19–27. [G]

SCHNEIDER, D.C. & HARRINGTON, B.A. 1981. Timing of shorebird migration in relation to prey depletion. *Auk,* 98: 801–811. [G]

SCOTT, D.A. & POOLE, C.M. 1989. *A status overview of Asian wetlands.* Report to Asian Wetland Bureau, Kuala Lumpur. [G,P]

SEALY, S.G., FAY, F.H., BÉDARD, J. & UDVARDY, M.D.F. 1971. New records and zoogeographical notes on the birds of St. Lawrence Island, Bering Sea. *Condor,* 73: 322–336. [G,P]

SEEBOHM, H. 1888. *The geographical distribution of the family Charadriidae, or the plovers, sandpipers, snipes, and their allies.* Sotheran, London. [A,E,G,P]

SEEBOHM, H. 1901. *The birds of Siberia.* Alan Sutton, Dursley (1976). [E,G,P]

SEEBOHM, H. & HARVIE BROWN, J.A. 1876. Notes on the birds of the lower Petchora. *Ibis,* 18: 105–126. [E,G]

SHADLE, J. & WAGNITZ, R. 1991. Black-bellied Plover in Buffalo County. *Nebraska Bird Rev.* 59: 38. [G]

SHARROCK, J.T.R. (comp.) 1976. *The atlas of breeding birds in Britain and Ireland.* Poyser, Calton. [E]

SHEPHERD, K.B. & WHITFIELD, D.P. 1995. *A survey of montane breeding birds in the Cairngorms, Scotland in 1995.* Research and Advisory Services Directorate Report. Scottish Natural Heritage, Edinburgh. (E).

SHKATULOVA, A.P. (ШКАТУЛОВА, А.П.). 1980. Chislennost' kulikov v period vesennikh migratsij v okrestnost Ulan-Ude. Pp. 124–127 *in* Flint, V.E. (ed.). *Novoe v izuchenii biologii i rasprostranenii kulikov.* Nauka, Moscow. [P]

SIBLEY, C.G. 1951. Notes on the birds of New Georgia, Central Solomon Islands. *Condor,* 53: 81–92. [P]

SIBLEY, C.G. & AHLQUIST, J.E. 1990. *Phylogeny and classification of birds: a study in molecular evolution.* Yale Univ. Press., New Haven.

SIMMONS, K.E.L. 1952. The nature of the predator-reactions of breeding birds. *Behaviour,* 4: 161–171.

SIMMONS, K.E.L. 1955. The nature of the predator-reactions of waders towards humans; with special reference to the role of the aggressive-, escape- and brooding drives. *Behaviour,* 8: 130–173. [E]

SJÖRS, H. 1956. *Nordisk växtgeografi.* Bonniers, Stockholm.

SKARTVEIT, A., RYDÉN, B.E. & KARENLAMPI, L. 1975. Climate and hydrology of some Fennoscandian tundra ecosystems. Pp. 41–53 *in* Wielgolaski, F.E. (ed.). *Fennoscandian tundra ecosystems, part 1.* Springer, New York.

SLATER, H.H. 1901. *Manual of the birds of Iceland.* D. Douglas, Edinburgh. [E,G]

SMART, I., MILES, G.A. & WEST, M. 1983. Waders and waterbirds on Dubai Creek. *Wader Study Group Bull.* 37: 29–30. [G]

SMIRENSKIJ, S.M., SMIRENSKAYA, E.M. & MISHCHENKO, A.L. (СМИРЕНСКИЙ, С.М., СМИРЕНСКАЯ, Е.М., МИЩЕНКО, А.Л.). 1980. O prolete kulikov v srednem Priamur'e. Pp. 120–121 *in* Flint, V.E. (ed.). *Novoe v izuchenii biologii i rasprostranenii kulikov.* Nauka, Moscow. [G,P]

SMIT, C.J. 1986. Wintering and migrating waders in the Mediterranean. *Wader Study Group Bull.* 46: 13–15. [G]

SMIT, C.J., LAMBECK, R.H.D. & WOLFF, W.S. 1987. Threat to coastal wintering and staging areas of waders. *Wader Study Group Bull.* 49: 105–113.

SMIT, C.J. & PIERSMA, T. 1989. Numbers, midwinter distribution and migration of wader populations using the East Atlantic flyway. Pp. 24–64 *in* Boyd, H. & Pirot, J.-Y. (eds.). *Flyways and reserve networks for water birds.* IWRB Special Publication No. 9, Slimbridge, UK.

SMIT, C.J. & VISSER, J.M. 1993. Effects of disturbance on shorebirds: a summary of existing knowledge from the Dutch Wadden Sea and Delta area. *Wader Study Group Bull.* 68: 6–19. [E,G]

SMIT, C.J. & WOLFF, W.J. 1981. *Birds of the Wadden Sea.* Balkema, Rotterdam. [E,G].

SMITH, A.G., SMITH, G.D. & FUNNELL, B.M. 1992. *Atlas of mesozoic and cenozoic coastlines.* Cambridge Univ. Press, Cambridge.

SMITH, R.W.J. 1957. "Northern" Golden Plovers in Midlothian during spring. *Scottish Naturalist,* 69: 84–88. [E]

SMITH, S.M. & STILES, G.F. 1979. Banding studies of migrant shorebirds in northwestern Coasta Rica. *Stud. Avian Biol.* 2: 41–47. [A,G]

SMYTHIES, B.E. 1953. *The birds of Burma.* Oliver & Boyd, Edinburgh. [G,P]

SMYTHIES, B.E. 1960. *The birds of Borneo.* Oliver & Boyd, Edinburgh. [G,P]

SNOW, D.W. 1967. A guide to moult in British birds. *BTO Field Guide No. 11.*

SNOW, D.W. 1971. *The status of birds in Britain and Ireland.* Blackwell, Oxford. [A,E,G,P]

SOLOVIEV, M.Y. & TOMKOVICH, P.S. 1998. The phenomenon of brood aggregations and their structure in waders in northern Taimyr. *International Wader Studies* 10: In press. [G]

SONERUD, G.A. 1988. To distract display or not: grouse hens and foxes. *Oikos,* 51: 233–237.

SORDAHL, T.A. 1981 a. Predator mobbing in the shorebirds of North America. *Wader Study Group Bull.* 31: 41–44. [A,G]

SORDÁHL, T.A. 1981 b. Phenology and stratus of the shorebirds in northern Utah. *Western Birds,* 12: 173–180. [A,G]

SORDAHL, T.A. 1990. The risks of avian mobbing and distraction behavior: an anecdotal review. *Wilson Bull.* 102: 349–352.

SØRENSEN, U.G. 1995. Truede og sjældne danske ynglefugle 1976–1991. Status i relation til den generelle landskabsudvikling. *Dansk Orn. Foren. Tidsskr.* 89: 1–48. [E]

SPAANS, A.L. 1979. Wader studies in Suriname, South America. *Wader Study Group Bull.* 25: 32–37. [G]

SPEEK, B.J. 1978. Trekwegen van in Nederland geringde vogels (Goudplevier, *Pluvialis apricaria*). *Vogeljaar,* 26: 15–17. [E]

STAALAND, H. 1967. Anatomical and physiological adaptations of the nasal glands in charadriiform birds. *Comp. Biochem. Physiol.* 23: 933–944. [E]

STAHLBAUM, G. 1965. Frühjarsbeobachtungen des Goldregenpfeifers (*Pluvialis apricaria*) bei Neuruppin. *Beitr. Vogelkd.* 11: 113–114. [E]

STEINIGER, F. 1959. *Die grossen Regenpfeifer.* Die neue Brehm-Bücherei, Ziemsen, Wittenberg. [A,E,G,P]

STENSETH, N.C., ØSTBYE, E., HAGEN, A., LIEN, L. & MYSTERUD, I. 1979. Application of a model for territorial behaviour and density fluctuations in alpine passerines. *Oikos,* 32: 309–319.

STINSON, C.H. 1977. The spatial distribution of wintering Black-bellied Plovers. *Wilson Bull.* 89: 470–471. [G]

STINSON, C.H. 1980. Flocking and predator avoidance: models of flocking and observations on the spatial distribution of foraging wintering shorebirds. *Oikos,* 34: 35–43. [G]

STINSON, C.H. 1988. Does mixed species flocking increase vigilance or skittishness? *Ibis,* 130: 303–304. [E]

STISCHOV, M.S. (СТИШОВ, М.С.). 1989. Ekologo-geograficheskaya klassifikatsiya i prostranstvenno-tipologicheskaya struktura ptich'ego naseleiya Ostrova Vrangelya. Pp. 187–212 *in* Chernov, Yu.I. (ed.). *Ptitsy v soobschestvakh tundrovoj zony.* Nauka, Moscow. [E,G]

STISCHOV, M.S., PRIDATKO, V.I. & BARANYUK, V.V. (СТИШОВ, М.С., ПРИДАТКО, В.И., БАРАНЮК, В.В.). 1991. *Ptitsy Ostrova Vrangelya.* Nauka, Novosibirsk. [A,G,P]

STONE, B.H., SEARS, J., CRANSWICK, P.A., GREGORY, R.D., GIBBONS, D.W., REHFISCH, M.M., AEBISCHER, M.J. & REID, J.B. 1997. Population estimates of birds in Britain and in the United Kingdom. *Brit. Birds,* 90: 1–22. [G,E].

STONE, W. 1937 (1965). *Bird studies at Old Cape May: an ornithology of coastal New Jersey. Vol. 1.* Dover, New York. [A,G]

STORER, R.W. 1951. The seasonal occurrence of shorebirds on Bay Farm Island, Alameda County, California. *Condor,* 53: 186–193. [G,A/P]

STOTZ, D.F., BIERREGAARD, R.O., COHN-HAFT, M., PETERMANN, P., SMITH, J., WHITTAKER, A. & WILSON, S.V. 1992. The status of North American migrants in central Amazonian Brazil. *Condor,* 94: 608–621. [A,G]

STOUT, G.D. (ed.) 1967. *The shorebirds of North America.* Viking Press, New York. [A,E,G,P]

STRAKA, U. 1991. Zum Vorkommen des Goldregenpfeifers, *Pluvialis apricaria* L., in Ackergebieten Ostösterreichs. *Egretta,* 34: 97–103. [E]

STRAKA, U. 1992. Der Frühjahrszug des Kiebits (*Vanellus vanellus*) in einem Ackergebiet im südlichen Weinviertel (NÖ) in den Jahren 1991 und 1992. *Vogelkdl. Nachrichten aus Ostösterreich* 3(3): 1–3. [E]

STRAUCH, J.G. JR. 1976. *The cladistic relationships of the Charadriiformes.* PhD thesis, University of Michigan, 213 pp.

STRAUCH, J.R. JR. 1978. The Phylogeny of the Charadriiformes (Aves): a new estimate using the method of character compatibility analysis. *Trans. Zool. Soc. Lond.* 34: 263–345.

STRESEMANN, E. & STRESEMANN, V. 1966. Der Mauser der Vögel. *J. Orn. 107; Sonderheft.* 445 pp. [A,E,G,P]

STROUD, D.A. & REED, T.M. 1986. The effect of plantation proximity on moorland breeding waders. *Wader Study Group Bull.* 46: 25–28. [E]

STROUD, D.A., REED, T.M. & HARDING, N.J. 1990. Do moorland breeding waders avoid plantation edges? *Bird Study,* 37: 177–186. [E]

STROUD, D.A., REED, T.M., PIENKOWSKI, M.W. & LINDSAY, R.A. 1987. *Birds, bogs and forestry: the peatlands of Caithness and Sutherland.* Nature Conservancy Council, Peterborough. [E]

SUMMERS, R.W., UNDERHILL, L.G., PEARSON, D.J. & SCOTT, D.A. 1987. Wader migration systems in southern and eastern Africa and western Asia. *Wader Study Group Bull.* 49: 15–34. [E,G,P]

SUTHERLAND, W.J. 1996. *From individual behaviour to population ecology.* Oxford Univ. Press, Oxford.

SUTHERLAND, W.J. & GOSS-CUSTARD, J.D. 1991. Predicting the consequence of habitat loss on shorebird populations. *Acta XX Congressus Internationalis Ornithologici (New Zealand):* 2199–2207.

SUTTON, G.M. 1932. The exploration of Southampton Island, part 2, zoology, sect. 2, the birds of Southampton Island. *Mem. Carnegie Mus.* 12: 1–275. [A,G]

SUTTON, G.M. & PARMELEE, D.F. 1956. On certain charadriiform birds of Baffin Island. *Wilson Bull.* 68: 210–223. [A,G]

SVENSSON, S. 1978. Förenklad revirkarteringsmetod för inventering av fåglar på myrar och mossar. *Vår Fågelvärld,* 37: 9–18. [E]

SVERIGES ORNITOLOGISKA FÖRENING. 1962. *Förteckning övers Sveriges fåglar.* Svensk Natur, Stockholm. [G,E,P]

SWARTH, H.S. 1934. Birds of Nunivak Island, Alaska. *Pacific Coast Avifauna No. 22.* [P]

TALLIS, J.H. 1991. *Plant community history: long-term changes in plant distribution and diversity.* Chapman & Hall, London.

TAPPER, S.C. 1992. *Game heritage: An ecological review from shooting and gamekeeping records.* Game Conservancy, Fordingbridge. [E,G]

THAYER, J.E. & BANGS, O. 1914. Notes on the birds and mammals of the arctic coast of Siberia. Birds. *Proc. New Engl. Zool. Club,* 5: 1–48. [G, ssp. diagnosis]

THIBAULT, M. & MCNEIL, R. 1994. Day/night variation in habitat use by Wilson's Plovers in northeastern Venezuela. *Wilson Bull.* 106: 299–310.

THOM, V.M. 1986. *Birds in Scotland.* Poyser, Calton. [G,E]

THOMAS, B.T. 1987. Spring shorebird migration through central Venezuela. *Wilson Bull.* 99: 571–578.

THOMAS, C.J. 1986. *Distribution and plumage variability of Golden Plovers at Mallerstang.* Unpublished Report. Nature Conservancy Council, Edinburgh. [E]

THOMAS, C.J. & HACK, P.C. 1984. *Breeding biology of Dunlins and Golden Plovers in Central Wales in 1983.* Report to Royal Society for the Protection of Birds, Cardiff. [E]

THOMAS, C.J., HACK, P.C. & FERNS, P.N. 1983. *Breeding biology of Dunlins and Golden*

Plovers in Central Wales in 1982. Report to Royal Society for the Protection of Birds, Cardiff. [E]

THOMAS, C.J., THOMPSON, D.B.A. & GALBRAITH, H. 1989. Physiognomic variation in Dotterel (*Charadrius morinellus*) clutches. *Ornis Scand.* 20: 145–150.

THOMPSON, C.F. 1967. Notes on the birds of the northeast cape of St. Lawrence Island and of the Punuk Islands, Alaska. *Condor,* 69: 411–419. [P]

THOMPSON, D.B.A. 1983 a. Prey assessment by plovers (Charadriidae): net rate of energy intake and vulnerability to kleptoparasites. *Anim. Behav.* 31: 1226–1236. (E).

THOMPSON, D.B.A. 1983 b. Winter gold. *Birds,* 9: 32–33. [E]

THOMPSON, D.B.A. 1984. *Foraging economics in flocks of Lapwings* (Vanellus vanellus), *Golden Plovers* (Pluvialis apricaria) *and Black-headed Gulls* (Larus ridibundus). PhD Thesis, University of Nottingham, UK. [E]

THOMPSON, D.B.A. 1986. The economics of kleptoparasitism: optimal foraging, host and prey selection by gulls. *Anim. Behav.* 34: 1189–1205. [E]

THOMPSON, D.B.A. 1987. Battle of the bog. *New Scientist,* 1542: 41–44.

THOMPSON, D.B.A. 1990 a. Golden Plovers. *Discover Scotland,* 65(4): 1244–1245. [E]

THOMPSON, D.B.A. 1990 b. Wilder areas of the National Parks: the importance for wildlife and objectives for nature conservation. Pp. 6–21 *in* Newsome, S. (ed.). *The Management of the Wilder Areas of the National Parks.* Countryside Commission, Cheltenham.

THOMPSON, D.B.A. & BARNARD, C.J. 1983. Anti-predator responses in mixed species associations of Lapwings, Golden Plovers and Black-headed Gulls. *Anim. Behav.* 31: 585–593. [E]

THOMPSON, D.B.A. & BARNARD, C.J. 1984. Prey selection by plovers: optimal foraging in mixed species groups. *Anim. Behav.* 32: 554–563. [E]

THOMPSON, D.B.A. & BOOBYER, G. 1993. Golden Plover. Pp. 164–165 *in* Gibbons, D.W., Reid, J.B. & Chapman, R.B. (eds.). *The New Atlas of Breeding Birds in Britain and Ireland, 1988–1991.* Poyser, London. (E)

THOMPSON, D.B.A. & BROWN, A. 1992. Biodiversity in montane Britain: habitat variation, vegetation diversity and some objectives for conservation. *Biodiversity and Conservation,* 1: 179–209.

THOMPSON, D.B.A., CURTIS, D.J. & SMYTH, J.C. 1986. Patterns of association between birds and invertebrates in the Clyde Estuary. *Proceedings of the Royal Society of Edinburgh, Series B* 90: 185–202.

THOMPSON, D.B.A., GILLINGS, S., GALBRAITH, C.A., REDPATH, S.M. & DREWITT, J. 1997. The contribution of game management to biodiversity: a review of the importance of grouse moors for upland birds. Pp. 198–212 *in* Fleming, L.V., Newton, A.C., Vickery, J.A. & Usher, M.B. (eds.). *Biodiversity of Scotland* . The Stationery Office, Edinburgh. [E]

THOMPSON, D.B.A., HESTER, A.J. & USHER, M.B. (eds.) 1995 a. *Heaths and Moorland: cultural landscapes.* HMSO, Edinburgh and London.

THOMPSON, D.B.A., HORSFIELD, D., GORDON, J.E. & BROWN, A. 1994. The environmental importance of the Cairngorms massif. Pp. 15–24 *in* Watson, A. & Conroy, J. (eds.). *The Cairngorms: planning ahead.* Kincardine and Deeside District Council, Stonehaven.

THOMPSON, D.B.A. & LENDREM, D.W. 1985. Gulls and plovers: host vigilance, kleptoparasite success and a model of kleptoparasite detection. *Anim. Behav.* 33: 1318–1324. [E].

THOMPSON, D.B.A., MACDONALD, A.J. & HUDSON, P.J. 1995 c. Upland moors and heaths. Pp. 292–326 *in* Sutherland, W.J. & Hill, D.A. (eds.). *Managing Habitats for Conservation.* Cambridge Univ. Press, Cambridge.

THOMPSON, D.B.A., MACDONALD, A.J., MARSDEN, J.H. & GALBRAITH, C.A. 1995b. Upland heather moorland in Great Britain: a review of international importance, vegetation change, and some objectives for nature conservation. *Biol. Conserv.* 71: 163–178. [E]

THOMPSON, D.B.A. & MILES, J. 1995. Heaths and moorland: some conclusions and questions regarding environmental change. Pp. 362–387 *in* Thompson, D.B.A., Hester, A.J. & Usher, M.B. (eds.). *Heaths and moorland: cultural landscapes.* HMSO, London and Edinburgh. [E]

THOMPSON, D.B.A., STROUD, D.A. & PIENKOWSKI, M.W. 1988. Effects of afforestation on upland birds: consequences for population ecology. Pp. 237–259 *in* Usher, M.B. & Thompson, D.B.A. (eds.). *Ecological change in the uplands.* Blackwell Scientific Publications, Oxford. [E]

THOMPSON, D.B.A. & THOMPSON, M.L.P. 1985. Early warning and mixed species association: the 'plover's page' revisited. *Ibis*, 127: 559–562. [E]

THOMPSON, D.B.A., THOMPSON, P.S. & NETHERSOLE-THOMPSON, D. 1986. Timing of breeding and breeding performance in a population of Greenshanks (*Tringa nebularia*). *J. Anim. Ecol.* 55: 181–199.

THOMPSON, D.B.A., THOMPSON, P.S. & NETHERSOLE-THOMPSON, D. 1988. Dispersal and philopatry in breeding Redshank (*Tringa totanus*) and Greenshank (*T. nebularia*). *Proc. International Ornithol. Congr. (Ottawa)*, 19: 168–181.

THOMPSON, D.B.A., WATSON, A., RAE, S. & BOOBYER, G. 1996. Recent changes in breeding bird populations in the Cairngorms. *Bot. J. Scotland*, 48: 99–110. [E]

THOMPSON, D.B.A. & WHITFIELD, D.P. 1993. Research on mountain birds and their habitats. *Scottish Birds*, 17: 1–8.

THOMPSON, P.S., BAINES, D., COULSON, J.D. & LONGRIGG, G. 1994. Age at first breeding, philopatry and breeding site fidelity in the Lapwing *Vanellus vanellus*. *Ibis*, 136: 474–484.

THOMPSON, P.S. & THOMPSON, D.B.A. 1991. Greenshanks (*Tringa nebularia*) and long-term studies of breeding waders. *Ibis*, 133, Suppl.1: 99–122.

THORUP, O., O'BRIEN, M. & BACCETT, N. 1997. Breeding waders in Europe 2000. *Wader Study Group Bull.* 82: 10–11.

TINBERGEN, N. 1952. 'Derived' activities; their causation, biological significance, origin, and emancipation during evolution. *Quart. Rev. Biol.* 27: 1–31.

TINBERGEN, N., BROEKHUYSEN, G.J., FEEKES, F., HOUGHTON, J.C.W., KRUUK, H. & SZULC, E. 1963. Egg shell removal by the Black-headed Gull *Larus ridibundus* L.; a behaviour component of camouflage. *Behaviour*, 19: 74–117.

TODD, W.E.C. 1940. *Birds of western Pennsylvania.* Univ. Pittsburgh Press, Pittsburgh. [Λ,G]

TODD, W.E.C. 1963. *The birds of the Labrador Peninsula and adjacent areas.* Univ. Toronto Press, Toronto. [A,G]

TOLCHIN, V.A., BEZBORODOV, V.I. & VAJNSHTEJN, B.G. (ТОЛЧИН, В.А., БЕЗБОРОДОВ, В.И., ВАЙНШТЕЙН, В.Г.). 1973. Nabludeniya za proletom kulikov na Bratskom Vodokhranilishche. Pp. 105–108 *in* Flint, V.E. (ed.). *Fauna i ekologiya kulikov. Vol. 2.* Nauka, Moscow. [G,P]

TOLCHIN, V.A. & PYZH'YANOV, S.V. (ТОЛЧИН, В.А., ПБІЖ'ЯНОВ, С.В.). 1980. K osennemu proletu kulikov na Minusinskoj Kotlosiny. Pp. 123–124 *in* Flint, V.E. (ed.). *Novoe v izuchenii biologii i rasprostranenii kulikov.* Nauka, Moscow. [P]

TOMKOVICH, P.S. (ТОМКОВИЧ, П.С.). 1988. Ptitsy yuzhnogo poberezh'ya guby Buor-Khaya (Severnaya Yakutia). Pp. 3–37 *in* Rossolimo, O.L. (ed.) *Ptitsy osvaivaemykh territorij.* Moscow Univ. Press. Moscow. [G,P]

TOMKOVICH, P.S. 1992. Breeding-range and population changes of waders in the former Soviet Union. *Brit. Birds*, 85: 344–365. [E]

TOMKOVICH, P.S. & SOLOV'EV, M.YU. (ТОМКОВИЧ, П.С., СОЛОВЬЕВ, М.Ю.).1988. Novye nakhodki kulikov na Chukotke. *Zool. Zhurn.* 67: 1756–1757. [A]

TOMKOVICH, P.S. & SOLOVIEV, M. YU. 1994. Site fidelity in high arctic breeding waders. *Ostrich*, 65: 174–180. [G]

TOMKOVICH, P.S. & SOROKIN, A.G. (ТОМКОВИЧ, П.С., СОРОКИН, А.Г.). 1983. Fauna ptits vostochnoj Chukotki. *Sbornik trudov Zoologicheskogo muzeya MGU* 21: 77–159. [G,P]

TOMKOVICH, P.S. & VRONSKIJ, N.V. (ТОМКОВИЧ, П.С., ВРОНСКИЙ, Н.В.). 1988 a. Fauna i naselenie ptits arkticheskikh tundr berega Kharitona Lapteva (Severo-zapadnyj Tajmyr). Pp. 5–47 *in* Rogacheva, E.V. (ed.) *Materialy po faune Srednej Sibiri i prilezhashchikh rajonov Mongolii.* Nauka, Moscow. [G,P]

TOMKOVICH, P.S. & VRONSKIJ, N.V. (ТОМКОВИЧ, П.С., ВРОНСКИЙ, Н.В.). 1988 b. Fauna ptits okrestnostej Diksona. Pp. 39–77 *in* Rossolimo, L.O. (ed.). *Ptitsy osvaivaemykh territorij.* Moscow Univ. Press, Moscow. [E,G,P]

TOWNSHEND, D.J. 1985. Decision for a lifetime: establishment of spatial defence and movement patterns by juvenile Grey Plovers (*Pluvialis squatarola*). *J. Anim. Ecol.* 54: 267–274. [G]

TOWNSHEND, D.J. 1986. Grey Plover. Pp. 186–187 in Lack, P. (ed.). *The atlas of wintering birds in Britain and Ireland.* Poyser, Calton. [G]

TOWNSHEND, D.J., DUGAN, P.J. & PIENKOWSKI, M.W. 1984. The unsociable plover – use of intertidal areas by Grey Plovers. Pp. 140–159 *in* Evans, P.R., Goss-Custard, J.D. & Hale, W.G. (eds.). *Coastal waders and wildfowl in winter.* Cambridge Univ. Press, Cambridge. [G]

TUBBS, C. 1991. The population history of Grey Plovers *Pluvialis squatarola* in the Solent, southern England. *Wader Study Group Bull.* 61: 15–21. [G]

TUBBS, C.R. 1996 a. Estuary birds – before the counting began. *British Wildlife,* 7 (4): 226–235. [G]

TUBBS, C.R. 1996 b. Shooting waterfowl. *British Trust for Ornithology News,* 203: 19. [G]

TUCK, L.M. 1968. Recent Newfoundland bird records. *Auk,* 85: 304–311. [E]

TUCKER, B.W. 1949. A note on racial variation in Golden Plovers. *Brit. Birds,* 42: 383–384. [E]

TUCKER, G.M., DAVIES, S.M. & FULLER, R.J. (eds.) 1994. *The ecology and conservation of the Lapwing* (Vanellus vanellus). UK Nature Conservation No. 9. Joint Nature Conservation Comittee, Peterborough, UK.

TUCKER, G.M. & EVANS, M.I. (eds.) 1997. *Habitats for birds in Europe: a conservation strategy for the wider environment.* BirdLife International Series No. 6, Cambridge, UK. [E,G]

TUCKER, G.M. & HEATH, M.F. (eds.). 1994. *Birds in Europe: their conservation status.* BirdLife Conservation Series No.3, Cambridge, UK. [E,G]

TURPIE, J.K. 1995. Non-breeding territoriality: causes and consequences of seasonal and individual variation in Grey Plover *Pluvialis squatarola* behaviour. *J. Anim. Ecol.* 64: 429–438. [G]

TURPIE, J.K. & HOCKEY, P.A.R. 1993. Comparative diurnal and nocturnal foraging behaviour and energy intake of premigratory Grey Plovers *Pluvialis squatarola* and Whimbrels *Numenius phaeopus* in South Africa. *Ibis,* 135: 156–165. [G]

TURPIE, J.K. & HOCKEY, P.A.R. 1996. Foraging ecology and seasonal energy budgets of estuarine Grey Plovers *Pluvialis squatarola* and Whimbrels *Numenius phaeopus* at the southern tip of Africa. *Ardea,* 84: 57–73. [G]

TURPIE, J.K. & HOCKEY, P.A.R. 1997. Adaptive variation in the foraging behaviour of Grey Plover *Pluvialis squatarola* and Whimbrel *Numenius phaeopus. Ibis,* 139: 289–298. [G].

TYE, A. 1987. Identifying the major wintering grounds of palearctic waders along the Atlantic coast of Africa from marine charts. *Wader Study Group Bull.* 49: 20–27.

TYE, A. & TYE, H. 1987. The importance of Sierra Leone for wintering waders. *Wader Study Group Bull.* 49: 71–75. [G]

ULFSTRAND, S., ROOS, G., ALERSTAM, T. & ÖSTERDAHL, L. 1974. Visible bird migration at Falsterbo, Sweden. *Vår Fågelvärld, Suppl. 8.* [E,G]

UNDERHILL, L.G., PRYS-JONES, R.P., SYROECHKOVSKIJ, E.E. JR., GROEN, N.M., KARPOV, V., LAPPO, H.G., ROOMEN, M.W.J. VAN, RYBKIN, A., SCHEKKERMAN, H., SPIEKMAN, H. & SUMMERS, R.W. 1993. Breeding of waders (Charadrii) and Brent Geese *Branta bernicla bernicla* at Pronchishcheva Lake, northeastern Taimyr, Russia, in a peak and a decreasing lemming year. *Ibis,* 135: 277–292. [G,P]

UNDERHILL, L.G. & SUMMERS, R.W. 1993. Relative masses of primary feathers in waders. *Wader Study Group Bull.* 71: 29–31. [G]

UNEP 1997. *Global environmental outlook.* Oxford Univ. Press, Oxford.

URBAN, E.K., FRY, C.H. & KEITH, S. 1986. *The birds of Africa. Vol. 2.* Acad. Press, London. [E,G,P]

URNER, C.A. & STORER, R.W. 1949. The distribution and abundance of shorebirds on the north and central New Jersey coast. *Auk,* 66: 177–194. [A,G]

USHER, M.B. & THOMPSON, D.B.A. (eds.) 1988. *Ecological Change in the Uplands.* Blackwell Scientific Publications, Oxford.

USHER, M.B. & THOMPSON, D.B.A. 1993. Variation in the upland heathlands of Great Britain: conservation importance. *Biol. Conserv.* 66: 69–81. [E]

USPENSKIJ, S.M. 1986. *Life in high latitudes: a study of bird life.* Balkema, Rotterdam. [E,G,P]

VAURIE, C. 1964. Systematic notes on palearctic birds. No. 53. Charadriidae: the genera *Charadrius* and *Pluvialis. Amer. Mus. Novit.* 2177: 1–22. [A,E,G,P]

VAURIE, C. 1972. *Tibet and its birds.* Witherby, London. [G,P]

VAUGHAN, R. 1992. *In search of Arctic Birds.* Poyser, London. [A,E,G,P]

VAUGHAN, R. 1980. *Plovers.* Terence Dalton, Suffolk. [A/P,E,G]

VELASCO, T. & ALBERTO, L.J. 1993. Numbers, main localities and distribution maps of waders wintering in Spain. *Wader Study Group Bull.* 70: 33–41. [E,G]

VENGEROV, M.P. (ВЕНГЕРОВ, М.П.). 1973 a. Kuliki zapodnoj i yugozapodnoj Turkmenii. Pp. 23–25 *in* Flint, V.E. (ed.). *Fauna i ekologiya kulikov. Vol. 2.* Nauka, Moscow. [E,G]

VENGEROV, M.P. (ВЕНГЕРОВ, М.П.).1973 b. Migratsii kulikov v poyme niznej Obi. Pp. 94–95 *in* Flint, V.E. (ed.). *Fauna i ekologiya kulikov. Vol. 2.* Nauka, Moscow. [E]

VEPRINTSEV, B.V. 1982. *Birds of the Soviet Union: a sound guide. Divers. Waders: plovers and lapwings.* LP record, C90 18023 001, Melodiya, Moscow. [E,G,P]

VERHEUGT, W.J.M., DANIELSEN, F., SKOV, H., PURWOKO, A., KADARISMAN, R. & SUWARMAN, U. 1990. Seasonal variations in the wader populations of the Banyuasin Delta, South Sumatra, Indonesia. *Wader Study Group Bull.* 58: 28–35. [G,P]

VESSEM, J. VAN. 1993. *Priorities for the selection of water bird species in need of international conservation planning in the western Palearctic.* JNCC Report 172. Joint Nature Conservation Committee, Peterborough. [E,G]

VIKSNE, YA.A. & MIKHEL'SON, KH.A. (ВИКСНЕ, Я.А., МИХЕЛЬСОН, Х.А.). 1985. *Migratsii ptits Vostochnoj Evropy i severnoj Azii.* Nauka, Moscow. [E]

VILCHEK, G.E. & BYKOVA, O.YU. 1992. The origin of regional ecological problems within the northern Tyumen Oblast, Russia. *Arct. Alpine Res.* 24: 99–107.

VINK, J.A.J., VAUGHAN, R. & LOK, C.M. 1988. Birds at Cambridge Bay, Victoria Island, Northwest Territories, Canada, in 1986. *Circumpolar Journal,* 3: 13–26. [A,G]

VISSER, G.H. & RICKLEFS, R.E. 1993. Temperature regulation in neonates of shorebirds. *Auk,* 110: 445–457. [A]

VOOUS, K.H. 1973. List of recent Holarctic bird species. Non-passerines. *Ibis,* 115: 612–638 [A,E,G,P]

VOOUS, K.H. 1983. *Birds of the Nederlands Antilles.* De Walburg Pers, Utrecht. [A,G]

VORONOV, V.G. & VORONOV, G.A. (ВОРОНОВ, В.Г., ВОРОНОВ, Г.А.). 1980. Prolet kulikov na Sachaline i Kuril'skikh Ostrovakh. Pp. 91–93 *in* Flint, V.E. (ed.). *Novoe v izuchenii biologii i rasprostranenii kulikov.* Nauka, Moscow. [G]

WALKINSHAW, L.H. 1948. Nestings of some shorebirds in western Alaska. *Condor,* 5: 220–223. [G,P]

WALTER, H. 1902. Ornithologische Beobachtungen an der westlichen Taimyrhalbinsel von September 1900 bis August 1901. *Ezhegodnik Zool. muz. Akad. nauk,* 7: 305–334. [G]

WALTER, H., HARNICKELL, E. & MUELLER-DOMBOIS, D. 1975–78. *Climate-diagram maps of the individual continents and the ecological climatic regions of the Earth.* Springer, Berlin.

WATERS, R.J. & CRANSWICK, P.A. 1993. *The wetland bird survey 1992–93: wildfowl and wader counts.* BTO/WWT/RSPB/JNCC, Slimbridge. [G,E]

WATKINS, D. 1997. East Asian–Australasian shorebird reserve network. Pp. 132–137 *In* Straw, P. (ed.). *Shorebird conservation in the Asia–Pacific region.* Australasian Wader Study Group Conference, 1996, Brisbane, Australia.

WARNOCK, N. 1989. Piracy by Ring-billed Gulls on Dunlin. *Wilson Bull.* 101: 96–97. [G]

WETMORE, A. 1960. *A classification of the birds of the world.* Smithsonian Misc. Coll. 139: 1–37.

WHITFIELD, D.P. 1990. Individual feeding specializations of wintering Turnstone *Arenaria interpres. J. Anim. Ecol.* 59: 193–211.

WHITFIELD, D.P. 1997a. Waders (Charadrii) on Scotland's Blanket Bogs: recent changes in breeding birds. Pp. 103–111 *in* Parkyn, L., Stoneman, R.E. & Ingram, H.A.P. (ed.). *Peatlands, Proceedings of the 1995 Peatlands Convention.* CAB International, Wallingford, UK. [E]

WHITFIELD, D.P. 1997b. Habitat requirements of breeding waders on blanket bogs in northern Scotland. *Information and Advisory Note.* Scottish Natural Heritage, Battleby. [E].

WHITFIELD, D.P. & TOMKOVICH, P.S. 1996. Mating system and timing of breeding in Holarctic waders. *Biol. J. Linn. Soc.* 57: 277–290. [A,E,G,P]

WHITTINGHAM, M.J. 1996 a. *Habitat requirements of breeding Golden Plover* Pluvialis apricaria. PhD thesis, University of Sunderland, UK. [E]

WHITTINGHAM, M.J. 1996 b. The use of radio telemetry to measure the feeding behavior of breeding European Golden-Plovers. *J. Field Ornithol.* 67: 463–470. [E]

WIERSMA, P. 1996. Family Charadriidae (plovers): species accounts. Pp. 411–442 *in* del Hoyo, J., Elliott, A. & Sargatal, J. (eds.). *Handbook of the Birds of the World, vol. 3 (Hoatzin to auks).* Lynx Edicions, Barcelona, Spain. [A,E,G,P].

WILLIAMS, L. 1952. Feeding behavior of Golden Plover in captivity. *Condor,* 54: 169–170. [P]

WILLIAMS, T.C. & WILLIAMS, J.M. 1988. Radar and visual observations of autumnal (southward) shorebird migration on Guam. *Auk,* 105: 460–466. [P]

WILLIAMSON, K. 1948. Field-notes on nidification and distraction-display in the Golden Plover. *Ibis,* 90: 90–98. [E]

WINK, M. 1973. Siedlungsdichtenuntersuchungen in Heidebiotopen und Lavafeldern Nord-Islands. *Vogelwelt,* 94: 41–50. [E]

WISHART, R.A., CALDWELL, P.J. & SEALY, S.G. 1981. Feeding and social behaviour of some migrant shorebirds in southern Manitoba. *Can. Field-Natur.* 95: 183–185. [A,G]

WITHERBY, H.F., JOURDAIN, F.C.R., TICHURST, N.F. & TUCKER, B.W. 1940. *The handbook of British Birds. Vol. 4.* London. [A,E,G,P]

WOLFF, W.J. & SMIT, C.J. 1984. The Dutch Waddensea. Pp. 238–252 *in* Evans, P.R., Goss-Custard, J.D. & Hale, W.G. (eds.). *Coastal waders and wildfowl in winter.* Cambridge Univ. Press, Cambridge. [G]

WOLFF, W.J. & SMIT, C.J. 1990. The Banc d'Arguin, Mauritania, as an environment for coastal birds. *Ardea,* 78: 17–38. [G]

WOOD, A.G. 1986. Diurnal and nocturnal territoriality in the Grey Plover at Teesmouth, as revealed by radio telemetry. *J. Field Ornithol.* 57: 213–221. [G]

WYMENGA, E., ENGELMOER, M., SMIT, C.J. & SPANJE, T.M. VAN. 1990. Geographic breeding origin and migration of waders wintering in West Africa. *Ardea,* 78: 83–112. [G]

WYNNE-EDWARDS, V.C. 1957. The so-called 'Northern Golden Plover'. *Scottish Natur.* 69: 89–93. [E]

YALDEN, D.W. 1974. The status of Golden Plover (*Pluvialis apricaria*) and Dunlin (*Calidris alpina*) in the Peak District. *Naturalist,* 930: 81–91. [E]

YALDEN, D.W. 1986. The status of Golden Plovers in the Peak Park, England, in relation to access and recreational disturbance. *Wader Study Group Bull.* 46: 34–35. [E]

YALDEN, D.W. 1991. Radio-tracking of golden plover *Pluvialis apricaria* chicks. *Wader Study Group Bulletin*, 63: 41–44. [E]

YALDEN, D.W. & PEARCE-HIGGINS, J.W. 1997. Density-dependence and winter weather as factors affecting the size of a population of Golden Plovers *Pluvialis apricaria*. *Bird Study*, 44: 1–18. [E]

YALDEN, D.W. & YALDEN, P.E. 1989. *Golden Plovers and recreational disturbance.* Report No. 64. Nature Conservancy Council, Edinburgh. [E]

YALDEN, D.W. & YALDEN, P.E. 1991. Efficiency of censusing Golden Plovers. *Wader Study Group Bull.* 62: 32–36. [E]

YALDEN, P.E. & YALDEN, D.W. 1988. Plover's Page or Plovers Parasite? Aggressive behaviour of Golden Plover toward Dunlin. *Ornis Fennica*, 65: 169–171. [E]

YALDEN, P.E. & YALDEN, D.W. 1990. Recreational disturbance of breeding Golden Plovers *Pluvialis apricarius*. *Biol. Conserv.* 51: 243–262. [E]

YEATMAN-BERTHELOT, D. & JARRY, G. 1991. *Atlas des Oiseaux de France en hiver.* Soc. Ornithol. Franc., Paris. [E,G]

ZACH, R. & FALLS, J.B. 1978. Prey selection by captive ovenbirds (Aves: Parulidae). *J. Anim. Ecol.* 47: 929–943.

ZAR, J.H. 1984. *Biostatistical analysis.* Prentice-Hall, Englewood Cliffs, New Jersey.

ZUBAKIN, V.A., MOROZOV, V.V., KHARITONOV, S.P., LEONOVICH, V.V. & MISHCHENKO, A.L. (ЗУБАКИН, В.А., МОРОЗОВ, В.В., ХАРИТОНОВ, С.П., ЛЕОНОВИЧ, В.В., МИЩЕНКО, А.Л.). 1988. Ornitofauna Vinogradskoj pojmy (Moskovskaya oblast'). *Sbornik trudov Zoologicheskogo Muzeya MGU*, 26: 126–167. [E]

ZWARTS, L. 1985. The winter exploitation of Fiddler Crabs (*Uca tangeri*) by waders in Guinea Bissau. *Ardea*, 73: 3–12. [G]

ZWARTS, L., BLOMERT, A.-M., ENS, B.J., HUPKES, R. & SPANJE, T.M. VAN. 1990 a. Why do waders reach high feeding densities on the intertidal flats of the Banc d'Arguin, Mauritania? *Ardea*, 78: 39–52. [G]

ZWARTS, L., BLOMERT, A.-M. & HUPKES, R. 1990 b. Increase of feeding time in waders preparing for spring migration from the Banc d'Arguin, Mauritania. *Ardea*, 78: 237–256. [G]

ZWARTS, L., FELEMBAN, H. & PRICE, A.R.G. 1991. Wader counts along the Saudi Arabian coast suggest the gulf harbours millions of waders. *Wader Study Group Bull.* 63: 25–32. [G]

Tables

TABLE 1 *Body size measurements of male and female tundra plovers, based on museum specimens. Data sources given in text*

Measurement, species and sex		Average mm	SD	N	t	P
WING LENGTH						
Grey Plover	Males	198.8	6.305	164	0.65	NS
	Females	199.4	6.741	86		
Eurasian Golden P.	Males	185.4	4.806	279	1.63	NS
	Females	186.2	4.890	158		
Pacific Golden P.	Males	164.1	5.057	114	0.13	NS
	Females	164.2	4.611	79		
American Golden P.	Males	178.8	4.176	166	2.00	0.047
	Females	179.8	4.691	116		
BILL LENGTH						
Grey Plover	Males	29.3	1.656	164	0.64	NS
	Females	29.0	1.506	85		
Eurasian Golden P.	Males	21.5	1.017	277	0.12	NS
	Females	21.5	1.101	157		
Pacific Golden P.	Males	23.1	1.121	111	1.93	NS
	Females	22.7	1.184	78		
American Golden P.	Males	22.6	1.087	164	0.19	NS
	Females	22.5	1.056	115		
TARSUS LENGTH						
Grey Plover	Males	47.3	2.286	162	1.56	NS
	Females	46.8	2.164	87		
Eurasian Golden P.	Males	39.7	1.283	281	3.18	0.002
	Females	39.3	1.373	158		
Pacific Golden P.	Males	43.9	1.722	114	0.73	NS
	Females	43.7	1.724	78		
American Golden P.	Males	43.5	1.823	161	0.98	NS
	Females	43.3	1.950	112		

SD = standard deviation, N = sample size, t = t-statistic, p = probability, NS = non significant

TABLE 2 *Body size measurements of tundra plover chicks at hatching, given as mean ($\bar{x}$) and standard deviation (SD)*

Species	Geogr. origin	Bill (culmen) (mm)	Tarsus (mm)	Tarsus/ culmen ratio	Body mass (g)	Hallux (mm)	Source
GREY PLOVER							
x	America	12.3	32.2	2.62	22.3	2.5	1,2,4
SD		0.684	0.390	0.124	1.791		
N		6	6	6	3	2	
x	Siberia	8.3	35.3	4.26	23.5		5
SD		0.570	0.643	0.312	0.637		
N		7	7	7	7		
EURASIAN GOLDEN PLOVER							
x	Fennoscandia	12.5	33.8	2.71	21.9		3,4,5
SD		0.625	1.327	0.144	0.992		
N		33	33	33	13		
AMERICAN GOLDEN PLOVER							
x	America	11.9	30.0	2.46	19.0		4,5
SD		0.912	0.586	0.184	0.846		
N		9	9	9	7		
PACIFIC GOLDEN PLOVER							
x	Siberia	11.2	33.6	3.04	17.9		4
SD		0.662	1.065	0.163	0.396		
N		6	6	6	4		

7 specimens of Eurasian Golden Plover indicated 8% longer tarsi in fresh compared with dried (skinned) specimens. 8% has been added to tarsus length of skinned specimens used (2 Grey Plovers, 4 Eurasian Golden Plovers and 5 Pacific Golden Plovers).

Sources: 1 Parmelee *et al.* (1967), 2 Hussell & Page (1976), 3 Pulliainen & Saari (1993), 4 museum specimens, 5 field measurements (IB).

TABLE 3 *Comparison of tundra plover chicks: characteristics showing interspecific variation (see also Frontispiece and Appendix 3B)*

Character	Species Grey Plover	Eurasian Golden Plover	American Golden Plover	Pacific Golden Plover
Suborbital arc	Less bold	Bold	Very bold	Less bold
Subloral triangle	Yellow	Yellow	Yellow	Pale yellow
Loral stripe rhami	No	Bold	Bold	Faint
Supraloral, frontal, area	Yellow	Whitish	White	Pale yellow/ yellow
Supraorbital arc	Discontinuous	Continuous frontal half	Continuous frontal half	Discontinuous
Superciliary zone	Yellow	White	White	Pale yellow
Crown, black spots	Less bold, evenly distributed	Bold evenly distributed	Very bold, black edge to crown discernible	Less bold, black edge to crown discernible
Nape	Purely white	Whitish, dark grey spots, some-times more concentrated medially	White, dark grey spots may form narrow, discontinuous medial band	Faint yellowish, dark grey spots, frequently more concentrated medially
Cheeks	Whitish/ pale yellow, grey spots	Whitish/ pale yellow, grey spots	White, a few yellow & grey spots	Pale yellow/ greyish white
Longitudinal dorsal stripes	Absent, black dorsal spots evenly distributed	Whitish	Whitish	Pale yellow
Black dorsal mottling	Bold	Bold	Very bold	Less bold
Thigh spot: black spots	Bold, black ca 50%	Bold, black ca 50%	Very bold black >50%	Less bold, black <50%
Breast	Whitish/ yellowish	Whitish/ yellowish	Whitish	Whitish/pale greyish/ yellowish

All four species have white suborbital zone, discontinuous longitudinal midfrontal stripe, yellow supraorbital zone, white throat, and whitish belly.

TABLE 4   *Field marks of tundra plovers*

Character	Grey Plover	Eurasian Golden Plover	American Golden Plover	Pacific Golden Plover
STRUCTURE				
Build	Bulky	Plump body	Slender body	Somewhat plump body, slender neck
Bill	Heavy, back-ward projection behind eye	Rel. small, backw. projection to rear end of eye	Rel. small, backw. projection to rear end of eye	Rel. long, backw. projection well behind eye
Tarsus	Rel. long	Rel. short	Rel. long	Rel. long
Bare tibia	≅half bill	<half bill	=half-whole bill length	≥bill length
Wing-tip	Pointed (1 primary), projects past tail	Pointed (1 primary), projects marginally past tail	Pointed (1 primary), projects well past tail	Less pointed (2 primaries), projects past tail
Primary projection (vs. tertials)	Medium, 4(5) primaries visible	Medium, 4 primaries visible	Long,(4)5(6) primaries visible	Short, (2)3(4) primaries visible
Tip of longest tertial	To inner third of tail	To ca mid-tail	To inner fourth of tail	To outer third of tail, or beyond
Toe projection behind tail in flight	None	None	None–very little	Prominent, most of toes visible
COLOURS				
All plumages:				
Axillaries	Black	White	Smoke grey	Smoke grey
Under wing coverts	White	White	Dusky grey	Dusky grey
White wing bars	Strong bars	Narrow bar, most white on primaries	Almost none	Almost none
Rump & upper tail coverts	White/whitish	Dark	Dark	Dark
Fully developed breeding plumages (males):				
White superciliary stripe	Very broad, merging into cap	Medium broad	Broad	Medium broad
White forehead 'bridge'	Very broad	Broad	Very broad	Broad
Face	Black	Dark brown	Black	Black
Flanks	Black	White, varyingly spotted black, brown, yellow	Black	White, varyingly spotted (barred) black, yellow

TABLE 4 – *continued*

Character	Grey Plover	Eurasian Golden Plover	American Golden Plover	Pacific Golden Plover
COLOURS – *continued*				
Vent & under tail coverts	White	White, varying amount of black	Black	Black, varying amount of white
Dorsal spangles	Black with large white spots	Black/dark brown with small yellow spots	Black with varying-sized yellow & white spots	Black/dark brown with equal-sized small–larger yellow & white spots
Juvenile plumages				
Yellow	Pale yellow of fresh plumage turning white	Prominent yellow, staying through to moult	Paler yellow fading whitish	Prominent yellow, staying through to moult
Supercilium	Whitish	Yellowish	Prominent, white	Yellowish
Crown's contrast with paler nape & face	Much	Moderate	Very much	Moderate
Vocalizations				
Alarm call (Appendix 9)	tiuì	tui	tùli	tjuìtt
Song (Fig. 8.5)	tuliuuu	pu-pi-uu	tulick	ptiuuliii
Trill (Fig. 8.8, Appendix 8)	pi-rrrwt- pu-plui- puli-pui	pu-pi- pyuiu- pyuiu- pyuiu	witt-wi- wyu-witt- witt (some variation)	t'wi-witt- wiy-wyu-witt- wju (some variation)

TABLE 5 *Correlations between plumage score and environmental factors in Eurasian Golden Plovers, southern Norway*

Region and sex Variables	Spearman R$_s$	Kendall τ	Kendall partial corr., τ, controlling for variable (a)	(b)	(c)
Southern Norway:					
MALES (N=154)					
(a) Habitat contrasts	0.60***	0.476***		0.426***	0.429***
(b) Altitude	0.36***	0.266***	0.130*		
(c) Date of last frost night	0.33***	0.238***	0.065*		
FEMALES (N=127)					
(a) Habitat contrasts	0.61***	0.480***		0.466***	
(b) Date of last frost night	0.19*	0.141*	0.055		
(c) Altitude	0.13	0.090			
Southwestern Coast (Jæren & Karmøy):					
MALES (N=87)					
(a) Altitude	0.27**	0.195**		0.150*	
(b) Habitat contrasts	0.23*	0.194*	0.148*		
(c) Distance to farmland	0.19	0.132			
(d) Date of last frost night	0.10	0.079			
FEMALES (N=77)					
(a) Habitat contrasts	0.21	0.170			
(b) Date of last frost night	0.05	0.040			
(c) Distance to farmland	−0.01	−0.015			
(d) Altitude	0.02	0.002			

* P<0.05, ** P<0.01, *** P<0.001

TABLE 6 *Pair-wise size ratios for different species, for body mass and bill length*

Species pairs	Size ratios for Body mass	Bill length
Grey Plover vs. Eurasian Golden Plover	1.28	1.28
Grey Plover vs. Pacific Golden Plover	1.92	1.25
Grey Plover vs. American Golden Plover	1.53	1.30
Eurasian vs. Pacific Golden Plover	1.50	1.03
Eurasian vs. American Golden Plover	1.20	1.01
American vs. Pacific Golden Plover	1.25	1.04

Data from Johnsgard (1981), Connors (1983)

TABLE 7 *Recorded inter-specific aggression between tundra plovers*

(The largest species won all 24 encounters on the non-breeding grounds, but the smallest species won 15 out of 17 contests on the breeding grounds.)

Season	Locality	Species:		Number of cases	Sources
		Winner	Loser		
Non-br.	SW Norway	Grey P	Eurasian GP	6	1
Non-br.	S Manitoba	Grey P	American GP	18	2,3
Breeding	Melville Pen., NWT	American GP*	Grey P	7	4
Breeding	Yukon Delta, Ak	Grey P*	'Lesser' GP**	?	5
Breeding	Yamal, Siberia	Eurasian GP*	Pacific GP	2	1
Breeding	Yamal, Siberia	Pacific GP*	Eurasian GP	4	1
Breeding	Bylot Is., NWT	American GP*	Grey P	4	6

Grey P, Grey Plover; GP, golden plovers.
* Winner on own territory.
** Unspecified Pacific/American Golden Plover, from Connors (1983) most likely Pacific.
Sources: 1 IB, 2 Wishart *et al.* (1981), 3 Michael (1934), 4 Montgomerie *et al.* (1983), 5 McCaffery & Peltola (1986), 6 Drury (1961)

TABLE 8   *Estimated present-day sizes of breeding populations (thousand pairs)*

Country/ geographic area	Grey Plover	Eurasian Golden Plover	Pacific Golden Plover	American Golden Plover	Sources
Greenland	(+)	+	–	(+)	1,2,3
Svalbard	–	(+)	–	–	4
Iceland	–	300	–	–	5
Faroes	–	0.3–1.0	–	–	6,7,8
Great Britain	–	23.0	–	–	9
Republic of Ireland	–	0.4	–	–	8,9
Belgium	–	(+)	–	–	5
Netherlands	–	(+)	–	–	10
Germany	–	0.025–0.03	–	–	8
Denmark	–	+	–	–	11
Norway	–	100–200	–	–	4,8
Sweden	–	50–75	–	–	8,12
Finland	–	50–80	–	–	8,13
Estonia	–	1	–	–	14
Lithuania	–	0.06–0.15	–	–	8,15
Latvia	–	0.3–0.4	–	–	16
Russia	1030–2189	584–1409	1042–2367	(+?)	17,18
Canada	352–841	–	–	737–1772	17
Alaska	73–166	–	107–241	305–710	17
Total world	1455–3196	1109–1930	1149–2608	1042–2482	

+ = < 10 pairs; in brackets = do not breed annually

Sources: 1 Korte *et al.* (1981), 2 Frimer (1993), 3 Boertmann (1994), 4 Kålås & Byrkjedal (1981), 5 Piersma (1986), 6 Bergston & Bloch (1983), 7 Bloch (1981), 8 Tucker & Health (1994), 9 Thompson & Boobyer (1993), 10 Scharringa (1976), 11 Dybbro (1981), 12 Ahlén & Tjernberg (1992), 13 Koskimies (1989), 14 Onno (1966), 15 Glutz von Blotzheim *et al.* (1975), 16 Priedrieks *et al.* (1989), 17 our estimates, 18 Tomkovich & Solov'ev (1988).

We made our estimates for arctic and subarctic areas by assuming the breeding density per km² of all four species to be between 1 and 2 pairs in the 'core areas' (Fig.6.1) and between 0.1 and 0.5 pairs in the 'marginal areas'. (A summary of breeding densities is given in Appendix 5.)

TABLE 9   *Egg dimensions of tundra plovers (means ± standard deviations)*

Species	Egg length (mm)	Egg breadth (mm)	Egg volume (ml)	Egg volume: female mass ratio	Number of eggs (clutches)
Grey Plover	51.9 ± 1.357	35.8 ± 0.500	30.5 ± 1.451	0.161	48 (13)
Eurasian Golden Plover	51.5 ± 1.562	35.7 ± 0.874	30.2 ± 1.446	0.172	337 (94)
Pacific Golden Plover	46.9 ± 1.676	32.5 ± 0.845	23.1 ± 1.442	0.185	36 (9)
American Golden Plover	48.3 ± 1.718	32.8 ± 0.770	24.2 ± 1.474	0.164	88 (23)

Volumes (V) were calculated from the regression $V = 0.000443(\text{Length} \times \text{Breadth}^2) + 1.092$ obtained from measured volumes (water-filling) of 30 Eurasian Golden Plover eggs in museum collections. The egg samples of Grey Plovers and Pacific Golden Plovers were from Yamal, of American Golden Plovers from Churchill, and of Eurasian Golden Plovers from Jæren, Hardangervidda, Finnmark and Yamal.

TABLE 10 *Characteristics of song flights, based on field observations by I.B. The song flights were observed from beginning to end, except in American Golden Plovers. The figures give percent of number of flights observed.*

Characteristics	Grey Plover[1] 7 flights 7 birds	Eurasian[2] Golden Plover 42 flights 27 birds	Pacific[1] Golden Plover 18 flights 6 birds	American[3] Golden Plover 13 flights 5 birds
Fluttering ascent	100	100	100	100
Butterfly Flight				
Shallow wingbeats[4]	100	76.2	11.1	100
Deep wingbeats[5]		7.1	88.9	
Wings in V above back		16.7		
Fluttering Flight		83.3	33.3	+
Descent				
Dive, wings near closed	85.7	40.5	21.4	
Dive, wings V above back		21.4	7.1	
Fluttering dive	14.3	38.1	7.1	
Continued butterfly flight			64.3	
Before landing				
Skimming low	100	11.9	7.1	+
Stall			100	
After landing				
Wings high		38.1	88.9	+

1) Yamal (1989)
2) Yamal (1989) and Jæren (1989–91)
3) Churchill (1986). + = positively seen
4) Downstroke not notably below horizontal
5) Downstroke clearly below horizontal

TABLE 11 *Behaviour used in communication between the sexes during the pre-laying period. The figures refer to the sources reporting the behaviour.*

Behaviour	Grey Plover	Eurasian Golden Plover	Pacific Golden Plover	American Golden Plover
Torpedo run	1,2,3	4,5,6,7	4	9
Forward-tilted walk		4,6,8	4	
Bill to bill		4		
Standing w. tail raised, bill down	2	4(a)	8,9(a)	9(a)
Rapid wing-flicking		6,7		
Standing with tail down	1(b)			
Male exposing side to female			8	
Male standing w. erect back feathers			8	
Pursuit flights		5,6,7		

Sources: 1 Flint & Kondratjew (1977), 2 Parmelee *et al.* (1967), 3 Drury (1961), 4 I. Byrkjedal (pers. obs.), 5 Nethersole-Thompson & Nethersole-Thompson (1961), 6 Edwards (1982), 7 Cramp & Simmons (1983), 8 Sauer (1962), 9 Connors *et al.* (1933)
Contexts: (a) by male during female's inspection of nest scrape, (b) after torpedo run

TABLE 12   *Anti-predator behaviour of tundra plovers during the incubation period, reported in the literature*

Predator type & behaviour	Grey Plover	Eurasian Golden Plover	Pacific Golden Plover	American Golden Plover
Ground-living predators[1]				
Departing and staying cryptic	1, 2	3, 4, 5, 6, 7	8a	
Explosive departure		3, 4, 5, 7, 9, 10		
Scolding & circling		5, 6	8, 13, 14	1, 11, 12
Persistent distraction	1, 2, 12, 15, 16, 18	5, 9, 10	8a, 13, 20	1, 12, 19
Aerial attack	2a, 18		8a	
Avian predators				
Departing and staying cryptic			8b	
Squatting silently	18f	5, 21	8bdefi	
Aerial attack	1ef, 2cef, 18e, 22, 23, 24, 26j	5gh	26j, 27f	1eg, 23, 24f, 25b

Humans if not otherwise stated; other predators: a Arctic Fox, b Glaucous Gull, c Herring Gull, d Kittiwake, e Artic Skua, f Long-tailed Skua, g birds of prey, h crows, i Common Raven, j birds and mammals unspecified

Sources: 1 Drury (1961), 2 Flint & Kondratjew (1977), 3 Steiniger (1959), 4 Ratcliffe (1976), 5 Cramp & Simmons (1983), 6 Nethersole-Thompson & Nethersole-Thompson (1986), 7 Yalden & Yalden (1990), 8 Sauer (1962), 9 Williamson (1948), 10 Nethersole-Thompson & Nethersole-Thompson (1961), 11 Sutton & Parmelee (1956), 12 Parmelee *et al.* (1967), 13 Walkinshaw (1948), 14 Portenko (1972), 15 Seebohm & Harvie Brown (1876), 16 Sutton (1932), 17 Mayfield (1973), 18 Hussell & Page (1976), 19 Höhn (1958), 20 Haviland (1915), 21 Glutz von Blotzheim *et al.* (1975), 22 Brandt (1943), 23 Sordahl (1981a), 24 McCaffery (1982), 25 Macpherson & Manning (1959), 26 Kondrat'ev (1982), 27 T. Larsen pers. comm. (Taimyr)

TABLE 13   *Frequencies of responses by attending tundra plovers to overflying predators*

Species, predators, and response distances (m)	Behaviour Crouching	Leaving nest & standing	Approaching predator, no attack	Attacking
DURING INCUBATION				
Grey Plover (7 nests)				
Rough-legged Buzzard (300)				2
Snowy Owl				1
Arctic Skua (200)				3
Long-tailed Skua (170)				2
Herring Gull (100)				1
Eurasian Golden Plover (3 nests)				
Common Raven (100–150)	11			
Peregrine Falcon (200)				1
Pacific Golden Plover (4 nests)				
Snowy Owl (100)	1			
Long-tailed Skua (100)	3			
Herring Gull (100)	1			
American Golden Plover (4 nests)				
Hen Harrier (50–100)		5		
Arctic Skua (100–150)	6			
Herring Gull (25–60)	4			
Northern Shrike (50–70)	3			
AFTER HATCHING				
Eurasian Golden Plover (3 broods)				
Common Raven (100–150)	3			
American Golden Plover (2 broods)				
Arctic Skua (100)			1	
Herring Gull (50)	1			
Common Raven (50–100)	4		1	
TOTALS				
Grey Plover				9
Eurasian Golden Plover	14			1
Pacific Golden Plover	5			
American Golden Plover	18	5	2	

Sources: IB, at Churchill (American Golden Plover), Jæren and Hardangervidda (Eurasian Golden Plover), and Yamal (Grey Plover, Pacific Golden Plover)

TABLE 14   *The percentage of kleptoparasitic attacks by Black-headed Gulls that are successful against grassland plovers*

| Location | % successful gull attacks (% of all attacks) | | Source |
	Northern Lapwings	Eurasian Golden Plovers	
Lancashire	70 (64)	37 (36)	DBAT
Aberdeenshire	76 (?)	41 (?)	McLennan (1979)
Sweden	72 (?)	39 (?)	Källander (1977)
Midlands (1980–84)	72 (66)	38 (34)	Thompson (1986)
Midlands (1986–88)	39 (a)	–	Hesp & Barnard (1989)
	53 (b)	–	Hesp & Barnard (1989)

All sample sizes for >50 observations. ?, no data available. (a), immature gulls, (b), adult gulls, – denotes no Eurasian Golden Plovers in these flocks

TABLE 15 Comparison[1] of the breeding season food of Eurasian Golden Plover by sex and age at Hardangervidda: (A) Proportions (by number of items) of surface- and soil (incl. carcase)-living invertebrates, and berries, (B) estimated dry mass and number of prey items, (C) niche widths, and (D) number of stomachs with bone fragments of small rodents. For (A)–(C) data sources used by Byrkjedal (1978c [Jæren],1980a [Hardangervidda]) were reanalysed, while (D) is from Byrkjedal (1975).

Food aspect	Breeding grounds (Hardangervidda)								Migration (Jæren)	
	May[2]		June[3]		July[4]		August[5]		August–October	
	Males (22)	Females (8)	Males (4)	Females (3)	Males (22)	Females (8)	Adults[6] (18)	Juveniles[7] (16)	Adults (17)	Juveniles (17)
(A)										
median % surface prey	18.6	17.8	76.0	82.6	73.5 **	51.8	12.6 **	24.9	45.6	36.7
quartiles: lower	11.8	11.5	48.2		54.2	13.8	8.5	14.9	17.1	23.2
upper	36.0	29.8	85.6		90.2	64.9	21.8	64.0	61.2	66.7
median % subsurface prey	43.4	45.4	24.0	15.2	18.2 **	46.4	19.7	25.2	29.7	39.0
quartiles: lower	29.0	29.8	14.4		6.2	35.1	8.4	9.1	7.0	17.1
upper	55.6	60.4	51.8		44.7	86.2	31.6	41.5	43.5	65.7
median % berries	32.4	30.3	0	2.2	0	0	68.4(*)	44.1	0	0
quartiles: lower	10.7	21.4	0		0	0	54.9	0.4	0	0
upper	53.2	51.8	0		0	0	75.5	67.2	0	0
(B)										
average mg dry mass	992.5	* 1514.1	464.8	646.0	596.2 **	1248.9	2095.3 ***	997.6	113.2	165.6
SD	588.8	630.8	170.3	404.7	300.7	783.0	976.4	108.7	115.1	123.2
average n prey items	54.0	76.1	28.3	41.3	34.0 *	80.6	87.9 **	55.6	11.5	9.9
SD	33.3	25.7	10.5	20.4	23.3	80.9	19.9	35.9	10.7	6.0
average niche width[8]	3.64	3.33	3.58	3.43	3.77	3.89	2.15 **	3.67	3.69	4.84
SD	1.18	1.29	1.10	1.45	1.54	1.80	0.13	1.94	2.14	1.89
average adjusted niche w.[9]	0.37	0.28	0.45	0.32	0.48	0.53	0.14 **	0.30	0.72	0.71
SD	0.19	0.10	0.15	0.18	0.21	0.31	0.05	0.21	0.24	0.24
C										
% stomachs with bones	0	*** 62.5	0	33.3	0	0	0	0	0	0

[1] Means were compared statistically by t-tests and medians of percentages by t-tests on arcsine transformed proportions (Freeman-Tukey version, Zar 1984). Proportions of stomachs with bones of small rodents were tested by Fisher's exact tests. Significance levels: (*) $p=0.051$, * $p<0.05$, ** $p<0.01$, *** $p<0.001$; [2] Pre-laying; [3] Incubation; [4] Early post-hatching; [5] Around fledging time for the young; [6] 16 males, 2 unsexed birds; [7] 4 were nearly fledged, the others could fly; [8] $B=\Sigma(p_i^2)^{-1}$ (Levins, from Hespenheide 1975), averaged for each bird category from niche widths calculated for individual birds; [9] To obtain niche widths that were independent of number of prey items, which differed between individual birds, adjusted niche widths were calculated as $(B-1)/(n-1)$ (Hespenheide 1975).

TABLE 16   *Range of threats experienced by tundra plovers*

Species	Loss of non-breeding habitats	Disturbance (including hunting) on non-breeding habitats	Loss/deterioration of breeding habitats	Global warming
Grey Plover	L	(L)	–	W?
Eurasian Golden Plover	W	L	L	L?
Pacific Golden Plover	W?	L?	–	W?
American Golden Plover	W?	(L?)	–	W?

Distinctions are made between widespread, W, and local, L, threats. (L) denotes relatively minor threats: – no particular threat; ?, uncertainty about the extent or impact of threat.

Index